176: naming PF
why? significance?
poder?

...pots & pans

178: Suarez comparison

Right-Wing Women in Chile

ch.7: lioness comparison

"The Epic of the Empty Pots" - Teresa Lorca

food lines
woman to woman
phone trees
newspapers
radio

187 - example of US
lack of aid $$

RIGHT-WING WOMEN IN CHILE

Feminine Power and the Struggle Against Allende

1964–1973

Margaret Power

The Pennsylvania State University Press | University Park, Pennsylvania

Library of Congress Cataloging-in-Publication Data

Power, Margaret, 1953–
Right-wing women in Chile : feminine power and the struggle
against Allende, 1964–1973 / Margaret Power.
p.   cm.
Includes bibliographical references and index.
ISBN 0-271-02174-8 (cloth : alk. paper)
ISBN 0-271-02195-0 (pbk. : alk. paper)
1. Women in politics—Chile—History—20th century.
2. Conservatism—Chile—History—20th century.   3. Opposition (Political
science)—Chile—History—20th century.   I. Title.

HQ1236.5.C5 P69 2002
306'.2'0820983—dc21   2001056039

I dedicate this book to my mother,
Margaret Flora MacDonald Power,
and to my sisters,
Kathleen Kuffel and *Melinda Power.*

Contents

Figures, Tables, and Maps

Abbreviations

CODE	Confederación de la Democracia *(Democratic Confederation)*
PF	Poder Femenino *(Feminine Power)*
ENU	Escuela Nacional Unificada *(National Unified Education)*
FRAP	Frente de Acción Popular *(Popular Action Front)*
JAPS	Juntas de Abastecimiento y Control de Precios *(Price and Supply Committees)*
MAPU	Movimiento de Acción Popular Unitario *(Movement of Unified Popular Action)*
MEMCh	Movimiento pro Emancipación de la Mujer Chilena *(Movement for the Emancipation of Chilean Women)*
MIR	Movimiento de Izquierda Revolucionaria *(Movement of the Revolutionary Left)*
PC	Partido Comunista *(Communist Party)*
PDC	Partido Demócrata Cristiana *(Christian Democratic Party)*
PN	Partido Nacional *(National Party)*
PS	Partido Socialista *(Socialist Party)*
RN	Renovación Nacional *(National Renewal)*
SOL	Solidaridad, Orden y Libertad *(Solidarity, Order, and Liberty)*
TFP	Tradición, Familia y Propiedad *(Tradition, Family, and Property)*
UDI	Unión Demócrata Independiente *(Independent Democratic Union)*
UP	Unidad Popular *(Popular Unity)*

Map 1 Locator map of Chile

Preface

WHEN I ENTERED graduate school in 1991, I did not plan to study right-wing women in Chile. Rather, I wanted to analyze how seventeen years of military dictatorship and neoliberalism had affected the Chilean working class. But as I explored the discipline of Women's Studies, I changed my scholarly focus: I chose to study the women who opposed the Allende government and called for the military coup. My decision was based, in part, on the fact that I simply could not understand them. What motivated them? Why did they reject the Popular Unity government (1970–73) and its call for socialism and embrace the brutal military dictatorship instead? Why did they fight for the imposition of a repressive and patriarchal regime that sternly and forcefully opposed women's liberation?

Unlike many scholars, who examine people they admire, I studied people whose beliefs profoundly differed from my own. It was very difficult for me to interview women who lauded the military regime that killed, tortured, exiled, and impoverished people I know and love as well as hundreds of thousands of other Chileans. In order to talk to these women about their ideas and activities, I had to suspend many of my thoughts and emotions and concentrate on the information I hoped to obtain from them. The people with whom I spoke were gracious, hospitable, and enthusiastic about sharing their ideas and rarely asked me my opinions. As a result, I never had to be dishonest with them or conceal my beliefs.

I hope that this book will contribute to the ongoing discussion of why the Chilean right, sectors of the Christian Democratic Party, the Chilean armed forces, and the U.S. government were able to defeat the Popular Unity government. This study highlights the important role that rightist women played in undermining that government. In so doing, it illustrates why it is so critical for the left to defend the liberation of women staunchly and to struggle for a progressive understanding and practice of gender politics.

Scholarly Analyses of Gender, Women's History, and Latin America

My study has benefited from the efforts of other researchers working in related areas. Feminist scholar Joan Scott's theoretical work on women's history and gender, for instance, has paved the way for a new generation of researchers. Scott defines gender as "a constitutive element of social relationships based on perceived differences between the sexes, and . . . a primary way of signifying relationships of power." She argues that historians need to incorporate gender into their theoretical framework, because "when historians look for the ways in which the concept of gender legitimizes and constructs social relationships, they develop insight into the reciprocal nature of gender and society and into the particular and contextually specific ways in which politics constructs gender and gender constructs politics."[1]

Temma Kaplan's study of women in Barcelona in the early twentieth century and her exploration of what she calls "female consciousness" provide important insights into the political activity of working-class women—and are particularly applicable to my study. Kaplan argues that "female consciousness centers upon the rights of gender, on social concerns, on survival. Those with female consciousness accept the gender system of their society; indeed, such consciousness emerges from the division of labor by sex, which assigns women the responsibility of preserving life." Her article examines how female consciousness can lead women into politically progressive action, but points out that women's "attempts to act according to notions held by their class and in their historical period about what women do sometimes lead them to a reactionary stance, as in the French Vendée and in Salvador Allende's Chile."[2] Kaplan has also suggested that "female consciousness more often serves the interests of conservative forces than of progressive movements."[3]

Much of the recent literature on women and the right challenges the traditional perspective that ignored or minimized the importance of rightist women and the centrality of gender ideology to these movements. Highlighting the extent to which rightist movements around the world have used maternalism to mobilize women in support of conservative projects, such works illustrate how right-wing women and men appeal to women—as mothers—to oppose political forces that offer a vision of more progressive social relations.

Sandra McGee Deutsch's pioneering studies on the right in Argentina, Brazil, and Chile convincingly establish that women were active participants in these movements and made critical contributions to building and

---

1 Joan Wallach Scott, "Gender: A Useful Category of Historical Analysis," in *Gender and the Politics of History* (New York: Columbia University Press, 1988), 46.

2 Temma Kaplan, "Female Consciousness and Collective Action: The Case of Barcelona, 1910–1918," *Signs* (Spring 1982): 545–46, 565.

3 Temma Kaplan, personal communication, 24 August 1998.

sustaining them. Her work also demonstrates how rightist movements both support distinct gender roles for men and women and are able to develop a more flexible (or opportunist!) interpretation of them as the situation warrants. The Chilean Movimiento Nacionalista Socialista (Movement of National Socialism, or Nacis) is a case in point. In the early 1930s, the Nacis consigned women to the home, because their "physique and delicate sedentary nature oriented the women toward motherhood and homemaking." In 1935, one year after Chilean women obtained the right to vote in municipal elections, the Nacis decided to admit women to the party. This shift did not reflect the Nacis' abandonment of essentialist notions about gender, however. The Nacis wanted women to add "the feminine touch" to their social action programs—and to vote for them.[4]

Several scholars have written specifically about women during the Allende period. In 1974, María de los Angeles Crummett interviewed women who had been active members of the anti-Allende women's organizations Poder Femenino (Feminine Power) and SOL (Solidaridad, Orden y Libertad [Solidarity, Order, and Liberty]). She finds that "middle- and upper-class housewives comprised the bulk" of Poder Femenino, but that the organization "made a concerted effort to expand its rank and file." These women believed that "an imaginary community of interests unites housewives of all social classes" and, as a result, they "sought to transform frustrated emotions into unified organizational energies in the service of the opposition."[5]

Michèle Mattelart discusses the bourgeoisie's use of Chilean cultural traditions to mobilize women against the Allende government. She writes that the bourgeoisie exploited the belief that women were not political and encouraged them to take to the streets by defining their activity as "devoid of political content." Women's demonstrations were interpreted—and advocated—as "the spontaneous reaction of the most apolitical sector of public opinion."[6] By emphasizing the importance of women and culture to the development of politics, Mattelart broadens the discussion of what transpired in Chile beyond the traditional focus on political parties.

4 Sandra McGee Deutsch, *Counterrevolution in Argentina, 1900–1932: The Argentine Patriotic League* (Lincoln: The University of Nebraska Press, 1986); *Las Derechas: The Extreme Right in Argentina, Brazil, and Chile, 1890–1939* (Stanford: Stanford University Press, 1999), 171–73.

5 María de los Angeles Crummett, "El Poder Femenino: The Mobilization of Women Against Socialism in Chile," *Latin American Perspectives* 4, no. 15 (Fall 1977): 108.

6 Michèle Mattelart, "Chile: The Feminine Side of the Coup, or When Bourgeois Women Take to the Streets," NACLA's *Latin America and Empire Report* 9, no. 6 (September 1975): 19. Mattelart was a French sociologist who lived in Chile during the 1960s and early 1970s.

Camilla Townsend examines the relationship between the Popular Unity (Unidad Popular, UP) government and women. She points out that although the UP government set up some programs to help women, the left failed to take women's experiences and points of view into serious consideration. This, she argues, was due to the fact that in large part men dominated the Chilean left. As Townsend points out, "socialism in Chile was largely born in the all-male world of the nitrate fields and its language of liberty was in many ways intimately connected with machismo."[7]

This book builds upon the insightful work of all these scholars. It argues that the study of women and the right is critical to understanding modern Chilean history.

Sources and Methodology

In writing this book, I relied on newspapers, journals, magazines, electoral data, Chilean and U.S. government documents, and interviews with Chilean women and men representing a range of political opinions.

Practically all Chilean newspapers—and most journals and magazines—reflected the perspective of the political tendency from which they received editorial and financial support. Some of the political parties owned newspapers outright. For example, *El Siglo* was the paper of the Communist Party of Chile and consistently echoed its political views. After Allende became president, the National Party created *La Tribuna* with the express purpose of agitating against the Popular Unity government. Newspapers that purported to be independent, such as *El Mercurio*, reflected the ideas of the right, shaped political attitudes, and suggested political strategies that the opposition should adopt.[8] This lack of objectivity does not negate the media's value as a resource: it provides insight into how the various political parties and female activists projected their ideas.[9]

In Chile, men and women vote separately, so I could use electoral results to determine how each gender voted. The results illustrate that both class and gender influenced voting patterns. They disprove the idea that class alone determined working-class women's votes, because many

7 Camilla Townsend, "Refusing to Travel *La Via Chilena:* Working-Class Women in Allende's Chile," *Journal of Women's History* 4, no. 3 (Winter 1993): 54. Also see Georgina Waylen, "Rethinking Women's Political Participation and Protest: Chile 1970–1990," *Political Studies* 40, no. 2 (1992): 307–8.

8 Fred Landis, "Psychological Warfare and Media Operations in Chile, 1970–1973" (Ph.D. diss., University of Illinois, 1975).

9 For a discussion of the historian's use of newspapers, see Jerry W. Knudson, "Late to the Feast: Newspapers as Historical Sources," *Perspectives* (October 1993).

more women in poor and working-class neighborhoods voted for conservative candidates than their male counterparts did. Indeed, voting patterns in Chile show a marked gender gap: women in Chile tend to vote for the more conservative candidate, while men vote for the more progressive one (the opposite of what occurs in the United States).

In order to detail my findings, I paid particular attention to voting patterns in Santiago—the focus of the anti-Allende women's movement and much of Chilean political life. I selected certain Santiago neighborhoods that typified either poor/working-class areas, middle-class ones, or upper-class ones (see Map 2), and I tabulated the voting results in each. The results are listed in tables throughout the text.

Chilean and U.S. government documents proved to be a rich source of material for this study. Documents from the Chilean Congress were essential to my discussions of the Scare Campaigns of 1964 and 1970 and the March of the Empty Pots and Pans of December 1971. The congressional texts, many of which record lively debates between hostile deputies and senators, provide a wealth of detail and a window onto the thinking of political leaders.

The 1975 Church Committee report on U.S. covert action in Chile, issued by the U.S. Senate, details the U.S. government's attempts to prevent Allende from winning the 1964 and 1970 elections and its efforts to sabotage the Popular Unity government after Allende's 1970 victory.[10] The report establishes that Washington had supported right-wing women in Chile and their work against Allende since the early 1960s. This aspect of the U.S. government's covert actions in Chile—one that has not previously been explored—reveals that forces within the CIA, and perhaps the State Department, were conscious of the importance of women in Chilean politics and astute enough to design programs geared toward influencing their political viewpoints and actions.

Beginning in 1998, various U.S. government agencies (including the CIA and the State Department) released thousands of pages of documents on Chile. To date, these documents have revealed some important new information about the nature and extent of U.S. government efforts to undermine the Allende government; by and large, however, they do not

10 U.S. Senate, Select Committee to Study Governmental Operations with Respect to Intelligence Activities, *Covert Action*, Hearings before the Select Committee to Study Governmental Operations with Respect to Intelligence Activities, 94th Cong., 1st sess., 4–5 December 1975; U.S. Senate, Select Committee to Study Governmental Operations with Respect to Intelligence Activities, *Covert Action in Chile, 1963–1973: Staff Report of the Select Committee to Study Governmental Operations with Respect to Intelligence Activities*, 94th Cong., 1st sess., 18 December 1975 (Washington, D.C.: Government Printing Office).

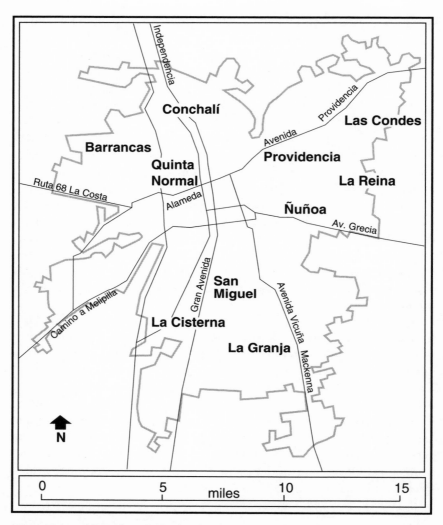

Map 2 Selected Santiago neighborhoods

discuss or even mention women. The CIA has repeatedly denied my Freedom of Information Act (FOIA) requests for information on the relationship between the U.S. government and right-wing women in Chile. However, I continue to search for these links.

In recent years, oral history has gained popularity among feminist historians, who have turned to interviews as one method to "recover the voices of suppressed groups."[11] Although some scholars may question the use of interviews, arguing that their essentially subjective nature weakens their reliability as data, others view this subjectivity as a strength. Luisa Passerini's discussion of the issue of subjectivity in her study of the Turin working class's memory of fascism is relevant here. Passerini affirms that "the oral sources presented . . . emphasize the subjective character of their interpretation. The subjective dimension does not allow a direct reconstruction of the past, but it links past and present in a combination which is laden with symbolic significance."[12]

Like the works of other feminist historians, this study uses interviews to bring to light the historical memories of its subjects.[13] However, I depart from the path taken by many feminist scholars in that I study women who opposed socialism, worked to install a military dictatorship, and rejected feminism. Kathleen Blee, who writes on women in the Indiana Ku Klux Klan in the 1920s and in contemporary right-wing movements, discusses the specific issues that confront scholars who study "ordinary people whose political agendas they find unsavory, dangerous or deliberately deceptive." Blee found that "accounts by those who have participated in campaigns for racial and religious supremacy, for example, often are laced with deceptive information, disingenuous denials of culpability, and dubious assertions about their political motivation." However, she continues, "with careful scrutiny and critical interpretation, even these interviews can yield surprisingly informative and complex historical information."[14]

11 Sherna Berger Gluck and Daphne Patai, eds., *Women's Words: The Feminist Practice of Oral History* (New York: Routledge, 1991), 9.

12 Luisa Passerini, *Fascism in Popular Memory: The Cultural Experience of the Turin Working Class* (Cambridge: Cambridge University Press, 1987).

13 For a discussion of methods used by feminists in carrying out oral history, see Susan Geiger, "What's So Feminist About Doing Women's Oral History?" *Journal of Women's History* 2, no. 1 (Spring 1990). Two French historians believe that doing oral history helps to empower women: to "give them [women] back their memory is to give them back their past." See Sylvie Vandecasteele-Schweitzer and Daniele Voldman, "The Oral Sources for Women's History," in *Writing Women's History*, ed. Michelle Perrot (Oxford: Blackwell, 1984), 43.

14 Kathleen Blee, "Evidence, Empathy, and Ethics: Lessons from Oral Histories of the Klan," *Journal of American History* (September 1993): 415–16. It is important to point out that few (if any) informants are completely candid. Most structure their responses to convey the impression

Blee's experiences and thoughts mirror my own. There were many issues that the women I interviewed did not reveal. For example, they concealed the exact nature of the relationship between PF (Poder Femenino, the anti-Allende women's organization), the opposition parties, and the U.S. government; the source of the group's funding; and personal conflicts that arose within their families or among themselves as a result of their political involvement. But there were many other important matters that they *did* discuss. The interviews disclose how significant ideas about gender were in these women's lives and their political organizing. Over and over again, the women who opposed Allende explained their political activity as an extension of their role as mothers. For example, María Correa Morandé, who had been a congressional deputy, an ambassador to Mexico, and a leader of the National Party, attributed her activism primarily to her maternal instincts.

What greatly surprised me was the willingness, even enthusiasm, with which these women and men accepted my requests to interview them. Many were very conscious of the fact that the U.S. government and broad sectors of the North American public believe that the military regime was guilty of terrible human rights abuses. My informants rejected that assumption and welcomed the opportunity to recount their version of events. They believed that up until the 1990s, the USSR and "communists" controlled the international media and were responsible for this "false image" of the military government. Therefore, they saw an interview with a North American researcher as a way (however limited) to expose what they believed to be the abuses committed by the Allende government and to correct what they considered to be the distorted impression that so many North Americans had of the military government. Many of the women I spoke with remembered their years of activism as a period of intense emotion, involvement, excitement, and above all, success. They relished the occasion to relive that period and to highlight the critical role they played in bringing down the Popular Unity government.

Although each woman recalled particular circumstances and unique experiences, common threads ran through their different accounts. My informants equated the Allende years with shortages, lines, chaos, violence, and disorder; they associated the military rule with order, discipline,

---

they wish to give—consciously or unconsciously. What may be distinctive in the cases of the Klan women Blee interviewed and the right-wing women I questioned is that these women supported organizations directly tied to the abuse of other human beings. As a result, they had powerful reasons to deny those links and to present a more humane, acceptable version of their past experiences.

authority, and control. The frequent repetition of these themes was not merely the result of having lived through the same historical period. It also stemmed from the fact that the women with whom I spoke had spent seventeen years of their lives in a country controlled by the Chilean military—and that the military's command of the media allowed it to impress such images in people's minds.

Although many of the women I interviewed had memories that were, in part, the product of the military-run media, their memories were neither carbon copies of each other nor false. Each woman fashioned her own individual recollection, even if it was influenced by the more general model developed by the dictatorship. At the same time, memory tends to be the product of both conscious and unconscious decisions on the part of the individual to remember the past in light of the present. Moreover, because they supported the dictatorship, these women emphasized the problems of the Allende years in order to justify military rule.

Acknowledgments

Many people have helped me with this book. I would like to begin by thanking my friend, Mary Kay Vaughan, for her insights, enthusiasm, and encouragement, and for her understanding of how important gender is to the making of history. She was an ideal dissertation adviser, and I feel very fortunate to have worked with her. Bruce Calder has also been a good friend. I especially appreciate his extensive knowledge of Chilean and church history, his attention to detail, and his exhortations that I write clearly. Sandra McGee Deutsch, my friend and colleague, has pioneered the study of the right and gender in the Southern Cone. She has generously shared her knowledge and insights with me. Marion Miller has an encyclopedic knowledge of social history—particularly European history—for which I am very grateful. Her observations on the development and impact of fascism in Europe broadened my comprehension of how the right operates in other regions of the world. Margaret Strobel has been an ongoing inspiration to me. Her knowledge of women's history is vast, as is her ability to encourage me even when I feel unsure or overwhelmed. Leo Schelbert welcomed me to graduate school and has helped me cheerfully and extensively throughout the years.

My research in Chile would not have been possible without the help of many people. I warmly thank Irene Pilquinao, Mariano Olivares, and Antonio and Isabel Olivares Pilquinao, who welcomed me into their family and provided me with critical insights into Chilean politics and ideas about gender. I am also grateful for the help and friendship of Lydia

Casas, Corinna Posado, and Patricio Mason, who assisted me with interviews, translations, and my political understanding of the period. (The
translations in the text are mine, unless otherwise noted.) I thank the staff
of the Biblioteca del Congreso Nacional, particularly Carmen Ponce, and
the staff of the Biblioteca Nacional de Chile, especially those who worked
in the Sala de Fundadores.

Many people shared their ideas with me, read and commented on
drafts of the chapters, and encouraged my work. I want them all to know
how essential their insights and support were to me. I would particularly
like to thank María de los Angeles Crummett, who very generously lent
me her notes from the interviews she had conducted with right-wing
women in 1974; Leigh and Sam Bailey, who gave me excellent stylistic
and editorial advice; Carlos Banda, who transcribed many of the interviews; John Bartlett, for his help in resolving computer problems and for
being such a good friend; Jennifer Cohen, for her critical readings of several drafts of my chapters; Riet Delsing, for sharing her understanding of
gender and politics in Chile with me; Elisa Fernández, for her constant
encouragement and for sharing her understandings of the Chilean military and gender with me; Teresa Fernández, for her helpful suggestions
and ongoing support; Lessie Jo Frazier, for her enthusiasm, her challenging questions about my work, and her help in setting up the interviews in
Iquique; Elizabeth Hutchinson, who offered both encouragement and
suggestions; Susan McNish, for her warm friendship; Patricio Navia, who
encouraged my work, read the manuscript, challenged some of my ideas,
and set up interviews for me; Cristián Pérez, for the countless ways he has
supported me; Corinne A. Pernet, for her friendship and important comments on earlier drafts; Aurora Posado, for her friendship, our talks on
Chilean politics and gender, and her help in setting up interviews; Karin
Rosemblatt, for our discussions on Chilean politics and history and on
being an academic; Ivonne Szasz, for her insights on the Popular Unity;
Joan Supplee, for her comments on earlier drafts; and Luis Torres, for our
discussions about Chilean politics and his support of my work. I was also
extremely fortunate to be able to share much of my work, research, ideas,
and ups and downs with Lisa Baldez. Since part of our research over-
lapped, we conducted interviews together, discussed our findings, and
shared our work. Since then, our e-mail exchanges, meetings, and phone
conversations have been extraordinarily helpful to me, both emotionally
and intellectually. I would like to express my gratitude to Mara Dodge,
who encouraged me to go to graduate school and, throughout the years,
has critiqued much of my work and remains someone with whom I can

share so much. Ana María Kapelusz, too, has been a wonderful friend and colleague. Her willingness to read and critique my work, discuss ideas with me, and talk about our mutual concerns has sustained me. Thanks to Ray Brode as well for his careful, precise work on the maps used in this book.

I would also like to thank four people who read drafts of this book and who shared their invaluable knowledge. I first met Temma Kaplan in Chile while I was doing dissertation research. Since then, she has helped me formulate some of my ideas and clarify others; her overall encouragement and support and her generosity toward me and toward so many others serve as a model of how feminist historians can work together. Camilla Townsend reviewed this manuscript and offered key advice. I particularly appreciate her suggestion that I provide additional historical background to make the book more accessible to the general reader and her challenging questions about the Mothers' Centers and the relationship between the elite and working-class women who composed the anti-Allende women's movement. Steve Volk also read and commented on a previous draft of this manuscript. His knowledge of Chilean history and the politics of the Popular Unity period were particularly helpful. I am glad that both he and Peter Winn pushed me to examine rightist men's responses to the unprecedented role played by women in the anti-Allende movement. In addition, Peter Winn reviewed this manuscript, generously offering suggestions. He encouraged me to contextualize the right-wing women's movement and to clarify the connections between this movement and the parties. Thank you again for your remarks, all of which have greatly improved this book.

My research and writing received grant assistance from the Organization of American States (OAS), the Woodrow Wilson National Dissertation Writing Fellowships in Women's Studies, the University of Illinois, the Harry Frank Guggenheim Foundation, and the Mellon Fellowship from the Illinois Institute of Technology (IIT). I would particularly like to thank John Root at IIT for his support and encouragement, as well as Paul Barrett and Tom Misa.

Sandy Thatcher has been a wonderful editor. I appreciate his precise and encouraging comments, his prompt replies to my questions, and his overall enthusiasm and willingness to help. I am very happy to have become friends with members of his family, including Robin Thatcher. I have also been very lucky to work with Laura Reed-Morrisson at The Pennsylvania State University Press. Her editorial suggestions and attention to detail have made this a better book.

I would also like to thank Issam El Naqa for his love and friendship. On countless occasions, he has helped me with my work, making it more enjoyable. I appreciate his optimism and encouragement.

Finally, I am very grateful to my family. They supported and encouraged me every step of the way. My mother, a right-wing woman in her own right, always believed in me, even when she did not quite understand why I would write about women with whom I did not agree politically. Her faith in me, her unstinting love, and her unfailing optimism have been a source of comfort. Thank you, Mom. Equally important has been the unwavering support of my twin sister, Melinda. Not only did she read every draft of every chapter, but she often read them immediately, putting aside her own work. And, regardless of what state they were in, she always found something positive to say about them. I do not think I could have written this without you.

Introduction

MANY WOMEN'S SHARPEST memory of the Unidad Popular (UP, Popular Unity) years, from 1970 to 1973, is that of standing in lines to buy food for their families.¹ They made this very clear to me on 16 January 2000— close to three decades later—when I went to La Florida, a lower-middle-class district in Santiago, to gauge how women felt about the presidential elections being held that day. The majority of women in La Florida supported Ricardo Lagos, the candidate of the governing Concertación² and a member of the Partido Socialista (Socialist Party). A sizable minority voted for Joaquín Lavín, a member of the Unión Demócrata Independiente (UDI, Independent Democratic Union) and of the conservative Catholic organization Opus Dei.³ I asked the women who voted for Lavín what they thought about Lagos. All of them, without exception, said that they would never vote for Lagos because he was a socialist and would resurrect the UP government. Those years meant two things to them: shortages and disorder. Conversely, the women who voted for Lagos said that a vote for Lavín signified a vote for General Augusto Pinochet, the dictator who ruled Chile from 1973 to 1990. For these women, Pinochet and Lavín represented a lack of democracy and the abuse of human rights. Their responses revealed very clearly how strongly people's memories or images of the past influence their present attitudes and shape their current actions.⁴

1 The Popular Unity (UP) government was a coalition of leftist parties that included the Socialist, Communist, Radical, and Social Democratic parties as well as MAPU (Movimiento de Acción Popular Unitario [Movement of Unified Popular Action]). Its candidate, Salvador Allende, was elected in the September 1970 presidential elections. The armed forces overthrew the UP on 11 September 1973 and held dictatorial power until 1990.

2 The Concertación is a center-left coalition of parties that formed in 1989 to oppose the Pinochet dictatorship. It won the 1990 presidential elections (the first elections since 1973) and the two subsequent presidential elections as well. Lagos won the 2000 presidential election with 51.31 percent of the vote. He obtained only 197,000 more votes than Joaquín Lavín did. Lavín received 48.68 percent of the vote, and 102,000 more women voted for him than for Lagos.

3 Opus Dei is a very conservative Catholic movement that began in Spain in 1928. "Its purpose is to train cadres of Catholic professionals and technocrats to infiltrate secular institutions and influence them from a traditional Catholic perspective. It is geared to upper-middle-class educated Catholics, is authoritarian and male-dominated, highly secretive, and a staunch defender of corporatist values." See Brian H. Smith, *The Church and Politics in Chile: Challenges to Modern Catholicism* (Princeton: Princeton University Press, 1982), 141.

4 The inverse is also true; people's beliefs also affect how they view the past. I use both "memories" and "images" here, because some of the women I spoke with were old enough to remember both

1

Although General Pinochet's dictatorial regime ended in 1990, his shadow still fell over politics in Chile during the 2000 presidential elections. For many years and for many people, the impact of his rule on Chile—both on those who suffered from it and those who profited from it—lay unexamined, dimmed by the government's reluctance to prosecute those responsible for the abuse of human rights and by the right's perpetual exaltation of his government. The October 1998 arrest of Pinochet in London on charges of murder, terrorism, and torture transformed politics in Chile. Family members of those murdered by the military have brought charges against the armed forces for their crimes. More than two hundred separate suits have been filed against Pinochet himself. The public discussion of the crimes committed by the military has served to vindicate the tireless work of the human rights community, which for years has been ignored by the Concertación and despised by the right. Far from destabilizing Chile, this more open exploration of the past has helped many Chileans come to terms with their own history. For the first time, a few military officers have come forward to testify about crimes perpetrated by the armed forces.[5] By and large, the civilian right has not acknowledged its responsibility for the human rights abuses carried out by the regime it brought to power and supported; in February 2001, however, María Pía Guzmán, a deputy with Renovación Nacional, broke the right's silence and admitted that she knew about the abuse of human rights during the Pinochet years but did nothing, because "it was easier to keep your eyes shut."[6]

This study examines the women who opposed the UP government and called on the Chilean armed forces to overthrow it. Although no period in Chilean history has been studied more than the years of the UP government, this is the first book-length examination of the women who contributed to the demise of democracy in Chile and the installation of the seventeen-year-long military dictatorship headed by General Augusto Pinochet. I attribute the lack of interest in these women to the mistaken belief that the principal actors during these years were men—as well as to many scholars' reluctance to study people with whom they fundamentally disagree and whose views they find distasteful. Further, my study challenges the notion that the unified working class solidly backed Allende

---

the Pinochet dictatorship and the UP government, while others were in their early twenties and had not even been alive when Allende was president.

5 For an excellent description of the unraveling of Pinochet's support and influence in Chile, see Marc Cooper, "Chile and the End of Pinochet," *The Nation*, 26 February 2001.

6 *Santiago Times*, 1 March 2001.

and that elite men, the military, and the United States were principally responsible for his overthrow (an idea that perhaps other researchers have been reluctant to explore). Instead, I show that women were important actors in the drive to remove Allende and that a large number of working-class women opposed the Popular Unity government.

I hope that this study will dispel the idea that men were the primary political actors during the UP years. The book should convincingly illustrate why it is, in fact, essential to incorporate the study of rightist women—and the right in general—into the scholarly agenda. In the literature on Latin America, the prevailing focus on leftist or progressive forces obscures the significant role that rightist sectors have played in the history of the region. It also offers an incomplete and distorted picture of the different elements that compose society. Furthermore, a clearer understanding of the beliefs, appeal, and impact of rightist women can elucidate the nature of the corresponding tendencies of their leftist and centrist counterparts.

This book makes six central and interrelated arguments. First, far from being marginal to the political process, the women who opposed Allende were critical actors whose activities helped shape the destiny of the UP government. They were central to the construction of a movement that undermined the UP government, encouraged the armed forces to overthrow Allende, and offered support and legitimacy to the military dictatorship that took power in September 1973. Second (and contrary to what is commonly assumed about this movement), poor and working-class women, not just middle- and upper-class ones, participated. Third, although elite women started the movement, they shared ideas about gender and politics with many poor and working-class women, which greatly facilitated their efforts to build a cross-class anti-Allende women's movement. Fourth, although the opposition political parties—the rightist National Party (Partido Nacional, PN) and the centrist Christian Democratic Party (Partido Demócrata Cristiana, PDC)—and the U.S. government backed these women, the efforts, skills, determination, and insights of the anti-Allende women made their movement a success. Fifth, the Chilean left concentrated on organizing male workers. The inadequate attention it paid to women, including working-class women, favored the efforts of both the PDC and the right to consolidate women's support for them and their political agenda. Sixth, the U.S. government promoted the organization of right-wing women. Blending its knowledge of gender relations in Chile with previous efforts to oppose progressive or leftist governments (all "communists," in its eyes), the U.S. government used ideas about gender and the threat of communism to sow fear of Allende among Chilean women.

I use a gender-based analysis to examine the anti-Allende women's movement. I illustrate how ideas about gender, even when unacknowledged (as they more typically were), symbolized and exacerbated the conflicts then raging in Chilean society. To ignore the impact of gender on the development of politics in Chile, as most studies of the Popular Unity period have done, is to disregard not only the language used by both sides to describe themselves and their opponents, but much of the substance of the conflict as well.

The Study of Right-Wing Women

Most contemporary research on women highlights their importance as historical actors. This is an important corrective to previous studies that either ignored women or defined them as passive spectators to the decisions and actions taken by men. Studies today underscore how women have affected and assumed control over society and their own lives. Scholars who examine rightist women are no exception to this trend.

The last two decades have witnessed the proliferation of important works on women and the right.[7] As a body, these texts illustrate that far from being dupes manipulated by right-wing men and parties, large numbers of women willingly embraced right-wing ideas and enthusiastically joined rightist organizations. These studies convincingly demonstrate the significant contributions that conservative women have made to the efforts of rightist forces to obtain and maintain power and to spread their messages of hate and their politics of exclusion. This work effectively dispels the idea that women are naturally more inclined than men to seek social justice and work for peace. Women have endorsed fascist regimes, brutal military dictatorships, and racist movements. Their support has enabled these rightist regimes to achieve power and implement repressive policies—and women have lent that support in the name of patriotism and motherhood, concepts that lend themselves to a variety of interpretations

---

7 Some of the more important examples of this literature are Paola Bacchetta, *Gendered Nationalisms: The RSS, the Samiti, and Their Different Projects for a Hindu Nation* (New Delhi: Kali for Women, 2001); Kathleen M. Blee, *Women of the Klan: Racism and Gender in the 1920s* (Berkeley and Los Angeles: University of California Press, 1991); Beatrix Campbell, *The Iron Ladies: Why Do Women Vote Tory?* (London: Virago, 1987); Victoria de Grazia, *How Fascism Ruled Women: Italy, 1922–1945* (Berkeley and Los Angeles: University of California Press, 1992); Martin Durham, *Women and Fascism* (London: Routledge, 1998); Andrea Dworkin, *Right-Wing Women* (New York: Wideview/Perigee, 1983); Victoria González and Karen Kampwirth, eds., *Radical Women in Latin America: Left and Right* (University Park: The Pennsylvania State University Press, 2001); Rebecca E. Klatch, *Women of the New Right* (Philadelphia: Temple University Press, 1987); Claudia Koonz, *Mothers in the Fatherland: Women, the Family, and Nazi Politics* (New York: St. Martin's, 1987).

and uses.[8] As Claudia Koonz points out in *Mothers in the Fatherland*, her study of women in Nazi Germany, "women made possible a murderous state in the name of concerns they defined as motherly."[9]

My exploration of the anti-Allende women's movement in Chile confirms the importance of the prevailing emphasis on women's agency (the recognition of the ability to choose and the exercising of that choice). But it also leads me to raise three questions about rightist women's roles as political actors. First, what impact did class have on Chilean women's lives and agency? Second, to what end did these women exert agency? Third, how did their political involvement affect these women?

Class influenced many aspects of Chilean women's lives, including the resources available to them; the education they received; the social, political, and economic power they had; and their sense of who they were and what they could expect from life. It also affected how women understood the causes and purposes of their political activity. These differences became very clear to me when I examined the relationship between shortages and the anti-Allende women's movement. Since shortages were the single most important factor that convinced many women that the UP government did not benefit them, they offer a prism through which to analyze how agency and class played out during the early 1970s in Chile.

The scarcity of food and other essential products provoked or exacerbated many women's anti-UP feelings, because it went to the heart of their identities. For most Chileans, being a woman was synonymous with being a mother. Motherhood represented not only what women did, but also who they were. Their inability to feed their children due to scant supplies of food meant that their children were hungry and that they were not good mothers—a feeling they could not endure. Their worry and anger motivated them to act.

From 1972 until the military coup in September 1973, it became more and more difficult for many women to find the goods they needed to sustain their families. Many products were in short supply—from toilet paper, toothpaste, and diapers to flour, meat, and cooking and heating

8 In addition to the works cited above, the following studies focus specifically on the right and motherhood: Renate Bridenthal, Atina Grossman, and Marion Kaplan, eds., *When Biology Became Destiny* (New York: Monthly Review, 1984); Glen Jeansonne, *Women of the Far Right: The Mother's Movement and World War II* (Chicago: University of Chicago Press, 1997); Alexis Jetter, Annelise Orleck, and Diana Taylor, eds., *The Politics of Motherhood: Activist Voices from Left to Right* (Hanover: University Press of New England, 1997); Julie Peteet, "Icons and Militants: Mothering in the Danger Zone," *Signs* 23, no. 11 (1997); Leila J. Rupp, "Mothers of the *Volk*: The Image of Women in Nazi Ideology," *Signs* 2, no. 21 (1977).

9 Koonz, *Mothers in the Fatherland*, 5.

oil. The burden was not shared equally by all women; it fell most heavily on the shoulders of middle-class and poor women. Elite women had money to purchase goods on the black market (and could afford to hoard them as well). Moreover, they could send their maids to wait in lines for food and supplies and obtain goods from their rural estates. Middle-class women lacked the resources elite women enjoyed and often were unable to acquire goods. Since many of them opposed the UP government, they refused to join the government-sponsored Juntas de Abastecimiento y Control de Precios (JAPs, Price and Supply Committees), thereby declining the opportunity to procure at least some of the products they wanted.[10] Poor and working-class women, even those who belonged to the JAPs, had to stand in long lines and, frequently, go without.

The opposition, which included the centrist Christian Democratic Party and the rightist National Party, helped create Chile's economic crisis and reaped the most benefit from it.[11] It convinced a large number of Chilean women that the economic program of the UP government made their efforts as mothers and wives more difficult. Anti-Allende women argued that instead of improving women's lives, the government harmed them. They used the rage and frustration the shortages produced to mobilize women against the government.

Four elements weakened the UP government's ability to counter effectively the charges leveled at it by the opposition. First, the UP did not operate from a position of superior political power; it did not even have the benefit of a level playing field. The opposition controlled most of the media, industries, financial institutions, and commerce of Chile. In addition, the right enjoyed significant influence within the military, controlled the judiciary, and, along with the Christian Democrats, maintained a majority within Congress. The opposition also benefited from a close working relationship with the U.S. government, which gave it access to funds and intelligence and enhanced its ability to sabotage the UP government financially.

Second, the left failed to emphasize the organization of women to the extent that the right and the Christian Democrats did.[12] Instead, the left focused much of its energy on male workers and peasants, who provided the

10 The UP government set up the JAPs to mitigate the shortages that many poor and working-class Chileans experienced. Staffed primarily by working-class women, they opposed hoarding and the black market and attempted to ensure an equitable distribution of goods in the poor neighborhoods.

11 For discussions of the economic crisis, see Chapters 1 and 5.

12 As part of its efforts to gain support among women (and to counter the opposition's attempts to organize them), the UP created the Frente Patriótica de Mujeres (Patriotic Women's Front) in October 1972. Among other things, the Frente collected penicillin for children and worked with the Mothers' Centers. See *Puro Chile*, 21 October 1972.

most reliable base of support and for whose benefit its political program was designed. Many of the UP men who headed the parties and held government positions had been schooled in the masculine world of party and trade union politics and the Marxist tradition that emphasized the working class. As a result, these men lacked both the practical experience and the ideological tools they needed to develop a successful strategy to organize poor and working-class women, most of whom were housewives. Party leaders realized that their inability to win the support of working-class women cost them dearly in the elections. However, instead of asking women directly why they voted against the UP, Allende, for example, accused UP men of not being manly enough to have convinced the women in their lives that they should vote for the UP. In a speech that primarily served to affirm men's role as the central political actors, Allende proclaimed, "We lost the election. Why? Because you did not talk to your *compañeras*. . . . Every man has a wife, a mother, a *compañera*. What kind of man are you? You can't be much of a man if you can't convince the woman who is next to you [to vote for the UP]. Put the pants on once and for all, or let them loose, but do it like a man!"[13]

Third, members of the UP parties believed that their plans to create a more just, democratic, and equitable society would improve the lives of the working class, men and women alike. As a result, they did not initially develop programs that dealt with the specific realities and problems poor and working-class women faced. In contrast to the presidential platforms of rightist Jorge Alessandri and Christian Democrat Radomiro Tomic, Allende's 1970 electoral program had no special section on women.[14] Carmen Gloria Aguayo, an important UP activist, recalls that "all our policies regarding women were integrated with the general struggle for a better life. We believed that the struggle for women was part of the struggle for a better society."[15] This failure to analyze women's distinct realities and to develop programs that would improve them undermined the UP's ability to counter charges that it was responsible for the shortages and other problems that plagued women during its rule.

Fourth, the opposition fought, usually successfully, to block any UP programs or legislation that would help women. For example, the government

---

13 Gerardo Sánchez Díaz, *Archivo Salvador Allende: Los trabajadores y el gobierno popular* (Puebla: Universidad Nacional Autónoma de México, 1986), 162.

14 Michael Francis and Patricia A. Kyle, "Chile: The Power of Women at the Polls," in *Integrating the Neglected Majority: Government Response to Demands for New Sex-Roles*, ed. Patricia A. Kyle (Brunswick, Ohio: King's Court Communications, [1976]), 108–10.

15 Carmen Gloria Aguayo, interview by author, tape recording, Santiago, 7 June 1994.

attempted to establish people's tribunals in the poor neighborhoods that would have tried men who beat their wives, neglected their children, or were publicly drunk. The opposition, which held the majority of the votes in Congress, refused to pass the legislation needed to set the tribunals up and forced the UP to withdraw the bill.[16] As part of its political program, the UP proposed the formation of the Ministry of the Family, whose mission included obtaining legal equality for women, incorporating women into the workforce, and improving the health and living conditions of children. For three years, the opposition debated the proposed Ministry and did not allow the proposal to get out of Congress. The September 1973 coup ended both the discussion and the proposal.[17]

The Chilean left was not monolithic on the issue of gender any more than it was on many other political questions. Certainly, the dominant image of women that the left projected was of the working-class or peasant woman who struggled to sustain her family and worked in unison with her *compañero*. But alternative visions also emerged. For example, *Ramona*, the Communist Party's magazine for young people, included articles about sexuality, featured women working, and highlighted the accomplishments of female activists. *Punto Final*, the journal of the Movimiento de Izquierda Revolucionaria (MIR, Movement of the Revolutionary Left), published several articles that discussed women's liberation and the need to increase women's political involvement.[18] Many younger female leftists, inspired both by the dynamic political struggle in which they were engaged and the growing international demand for women's liberation, also questioned male supremacy and women's oppression within the left. However, theirs were not the dominant voices. Instead, the traditional leaders of the left, who were mainly men, defined the male worker and peasant as the protagonists of the revolution.

It was not until September 1972, nearly two years after it came to power, that the UP created the Office of the National Secretariat of

---

16 NACLA, *NACLA's Latin America and Empire Report* 5, no. 1 (March 1971): 11.

17 *La Nación*, 1 September 1972, and Teresa Valdés and Marisa Weinstein, *Mujeres que sueñan: Las organizaciones de pobladoras en Chile, 1973–1989* (Santiago: FLACSO, 1993), 65–66.

18 For examples of these articles, see *Ramona*, 4 February 1972, 4 April 1972, 9 May 1972, and 22 August 1972. *Ramona* also featured a monthly forum entitled "Mi compañero y yo," in which women discussed life with their male partners. For articles in *Punto Final*, see Vania Bambirra, "Liberación de la mujer y lucha de clase," *Punto Final*, no. 151, 15 February 1972, and Danda Prado, "Mujer y política," *Punto Final* no. 176, 30 January 1973. MIR supported the Popular Unity government but rejected participation in the electoral process. Also see various articles from *Chile Hoy* on female workers and women's political involvement, especially from 30 June 1972, 6 October 1972, and 19 April 1973.

Women.[19] According to Paloma Rodríguez,[20] a leader of this institution, Allende created the Secretariat because female activists in the UP parties organized for it and because he felt a genuine concern for the health and well-being of women. The UP women who administered the office established several pilot programs to benefit women directly. One program offered cooked meals to female factory workers at the end of their shifts to alleviate some of the burdens of the double day.[21] Another helped several poor communities set up communal laundries. The government required factories to open day-care centers at the workplace. However, according to Rodríguez, the Secretariat "lacked money and didn't have real power or weight."[22] Consequently, these programs reached only a small number of working-class women, and the shortages in basic necessities, the long lines, and the high prices charged on the black market overshadowed them.

The UP failed, then, to emphasize women's concerns to the extent that both the National Party and the Christian Democrats did. But in addition, no feminist movement existed in Chile at that time to challenge the prevailing gender politics and offer women an alternative vision of their role in society. Although a few individual women defined themselves as feminists (notably the renowned author, Isabel Allende), most women rejected feminism.[23] Much of the left denounced feminism as a bourgeois movement that attempted to divide the working class and encouraged poor, working-class, and peasant women to erroneously view men—not the bourgeoisie—as their enemy. No political force in Chile called for the liberation of women.[24] Both the right and the center rejected feminism as an attack on the family, which they defined as the critical unit of society. Ignoring the fact that feminist movements had emerged in Chile during the early part of the twentieth century, all the political forces agreed that the women's liberation movement was a North American phenomenon, one that had little to do with Chilean reality.[25]

19 *El Mercurio*, 5 September 1972.

20 Paloma Rodríguez [pseud.], interview by author, tape recording, Santiago, 7 June 1994. During the UP years, Rodríguez was a member of MAPU.

21 *Chile Hoy*, 27 October 1972.

22 Rodríguez, interview.

23 Isabel Allende, *Paula* (New York: Harper Collins, 1994), 138–40.

24 Camilla Townsend discusses the (male) Chilean left's policies and attitudes toward women historically and during the Popular Unity years. See Townsend, "Refusing to Travel *La Vía Chilena*."

25 For a helpful discussion of the early feminist movements in Chile and the rest of Latin America, see Asunción Lavrin, *Women, Feminism, and Social Change in Argentina, Chile, and Uruguay, 1890–1940* (Lincoln: University of Nebraska Press, 1995), and Francesca Miller, *Latin American Women and the Search for Social Justice* (Hanover: University Press of New England, 1991).

Women's agency is influenced by and embedded in social relations and networks of power. Scholars' efforts to highlight the "weapons of the weak" should not blind us to the importance and effectiveness of the weapons of the strong.[26] The Chilean elite used its powerful arsenal of resources to sabotage the economy, create shortages, and then convince many people, including poor and working-class women, that the UP government was responsible for the scarcity they confronted. The attempts undertaken by the UP government to disprove these accusations and to overcome the dearth of goods foundered on the cold shoals of reality: despite all its efforts, the shortages persisted and worsened.

Although non-elite women joined with elite ones to oppose the Allende government, neither their experiences nor their goals were the same. The upper-class women fought to maintain their privileged position and high standard of living. To achieve their goals, they exploited the scarcity of goods to mobilize women from other classes into joining them. The working- and middle-class women who opposed the Allende government did so, in part, to end the nightmare of long waits in lines and the anxiety and despair of not finding the goods they needed. Most were unaware that the Chilean upper class and the United States had fomented the economic crisis in order to undermine the Allende government; they did not realize that their efforts to remove Allende served the interests of the upper class. Some of the middle- and working-class women I interviewed who had marched against the UP government understood this only in retrospect.[27] These women now believe that if they had understood the roles that the elite and the U.S. government played in creating shortages during the Allende years, then they might very well have directed their protests against the right—not against the UP government.

However, the poor, working-class, and middle-class women who united against the UP government were not merely puppets of powerful forces beyond their control. The women who opposed Allende did so willingly. They acted rationally, according to what they perceived to be in their own and their families' best interest. These women were significant social

26 See James C. Scott, *Weapons of the Weak: Everyday Forms of Peasant Resistance* (New Haven: Yale University Press, 1985). For a provocative discussion of the relationship between subalterns and agency, see Alan Knight, "Subalterns, Signifiers, and Statistics: Perspectives on Latin American Historiography" (paper presented at the Latin American Studies Association meeting, Miami, Fla., March 2000).

27 Most of the women who did so were supporters of the centrist Christian Democratic Party. Along with their party, they had opposed the Pinochet dictatorship in the 1980s. At the time I interviewed them, their party was allied with the Socialist Party in the governing coalition (the Concertación).

actors who made choices that affected their lives and those of others around them. However, we cannot ignore the fact that just as material resources shape the range of options available to women, unequal power relations affect women's agency. Any assessment of women's activism must consider the power wielded by the poor, the working class, and the elite, and must take into account the latter's ability to influence the former.

In addition to exploring how class influences agency, this study examines the consequences of right-wing women's agency. Agency is not neutral; it is highly politically charged. When we speak of women's political involvement, we must examine the ends to which women engage in political action. For what purpose do women empower themselves? Just as feminist activity can secure more rights for women, rightist women's work tends to result in a loss of rights for women and a more repressive society. The women who acted against Allende worked to end Chile's most democratic government. They voted and marched against a government that sought to create a society in which everyone had enough to eat, a decent place to live, the opportunity to be fully educated, access to health care, and dignity. In its place, they supported a military regime that ruled Chile dictatorially for seventeen years.

The anti-Allende women embraced an essentialized vision of gender.[28] They believed that men and women were naturally different and should remain so. For them, women were mothers whose duty was to feed, clothe, and take care of their families. The shortages prevented them from adequately fulfilling their maternal responsibilities. Their inability to be good mothers—rather than their rights as citizens, demands for their own liberation, or concerns for social justice—spurred them to action. Their activism propagated a very conservative view of what it means to be a woman or a man (and of social relations in general), a view that the military fully supported and attempted to impose on Chilean society after the coup.

The anti-Allende women used this shared identity of women as mothers and housewives to build their movement. It allowed them to unite with women across class lines and offered them an ideological rationale for their actions. They converted their lack of political experience and party membership into one of their major assets—the ability to portray themselves as *abnegada* (self-sacrificing) mothers who acted solely in defense of their children and the nation, the family writ large. They exploited the image of the selfless mother and expressed their belief in their moral superiority

28 So did the Popular Unity. Like the opposition, the UP believed that women were naturally and fundamentally mothers, wives, and *duenas de casa* (housewives).

11

both to justify their unprecedented political activity and to empower themselves.[29] Thus they accepted (indeed, embraced) their roles as mothers and housewives. They used their power to undermine the Allende government, not to transform ideas and practices of gender.

My study also led me to ask how their political involvement affected these women. Unlike women who organize in order to promote their rights as women, the anti-Allende women did not struggle to change their subordinate position within society, but rather to maintain it. As mothers, they believed that the Allende government prevented them from fulfilling their natural role.[30] Their stated goal was not to expand their power in the public sphere, which they considered the domain of men, but to allow them to continue their duties in the domestic realm.

Nevertheless, the question remains: How did their activity, their taste of power in the public sphere, affect them? The answer, unfortunately, is ambiguous. From my interviews, it is clear that most rightist women felt extremely proud of the part they had played in bringing down the Allende government. Some of the centrist Christian Democratic women regretted their role, while others felt that the policies implemented by the UP justified their work against it. Many rightist women stated that they felt they did not receive the recognition they deserved and that the world had a false impression of the military dictatorship. They were more than willing to be interviewed so that they could tell their story. Only one rightist woman was willing to criticize the Pinochet dictatorship and the right's role in bringing him to power.[31]

Once the coup took place, the military regime suspended all political activity—a fact that complicates the discussion of how women's involvement

29 For an early discussion of women and *marianismo*—"the cult of female spiritual superiority"—and why women accept it, see Evelyn P. Stevens, "Marianismo: The Other Face of Machismo," in *Female and Male in Latin America*, ed. Ann Pescatello (Pittsburgh: University of Pittsburgh Press, 1973), 90–100.

30 For a comparative discussion of anti-Allende and anti-Pinochet women, see Lisa Baldez, *Why Women Protest: Women's Movements in Chile* (New York: Cambridge University Press, 2002). On the movements of mothers who struggled against the military, see Jo Fisher, *Mothers of the Disappeared* (London: Zed, 1989); Marysa Navarro, "The Personal Is Political: Las Madres de Plaza de Mayo," in *Power and Popular Protest: Latin American Social Movements*, ed. Susan Eckstein (Berkeley and Los Angeles: University of California Press, 1989); and Jennifer Schirmer, "The Seeking of Truth and the Gendering of Consciousness: The Co-Madres of El Salvador and the CONAVIGUA Widows of Guatemala," in *VIVA: Women and Popular Protest in Latin America*, ed. Sarah A. Radcliffe and Sallie Westwood (London: Routledge, 1993).

31 The sole woman who did criticize the dictatorship was from the upper class; she was a member of the National Party and active in the anti-Allende women's movement. She believes that the right has not yet recognized its responsibility for bringing the military to power and ending

in public political activity affected them. Most could not continue to act as leaders or activists and had to abandon the roles they had developed as part of their work against the UP government. Many women expressed relief, not anger, at the regime's decision to terminate political activity as it had been practiced in Chile. Only a few women expressed regret that the military's seizure of power brought their activity to an abrupt end. Most understood that the overthrow of the UP government meant they could return to their homes and families and resume their roles as wives and mothers, living those roles as they had prior to Allende's presidential victory.

None of the women was willing to share with me how her political activity influenced her personal relationships. In response to my questions, most of the women simply stated that their work against the UP had not disturbed their relationships with their husbands or their children.

Overview of the Book

The following two chapters provide a survey of twentieth-century Chilean history. Chapter 1 examines significant trends in Chile's social and political history and focuses on the Popular Unity years. In order to contextualize the right and women during the Popular Unity years, Chapter 2 explores the relationship between women and the right until the 1960s. It discusses why the right enjoyed particular success with women. In order to illustrate how ideas about gender affected women, the chapter also analyzes women's relationship to work.

Chapter 3 offers an account of Acción Mujeres de Chile (Women's Action of Chile) and the 1964 Scare Campaign. The Scare Campaign attempted to organize women against Allende by telling them that his victory signified the destruction of their families. The 1960s saw heightened political mobilization and increased support for the left; in response to what they perceived to be the growing threat posed by the left, elite Chilean women mobilized, and in 1963, they formed the anticommunist women's group Acción Mujeres de Chile. To prevent Allende's election in 1964, the right, the Christian Democratic Party, and the U.S. government supported Christian Democratic candidate Eduardo Frei and jointly sponsored the Scare Campaign.

---

democracy in Chile. She was also critical of the extensive human rights abuses the dictatorship carried out. However, she refused to make public her concerns and insisted that I shut off my tape recorder when she voiced her opinions of the military regime and of Augusto Pinochet and Lucía Hiriart de Pinochet.

Women's support for Eduardo Frei facilitated his victory. Recognizing the importance of women's political backing, the Frei administration launched a national campaign to organize previously unorganized women. To do so, his government established Mothers' Centers throughout many of the poor neighborhoods of Chile. The Mothers' Centers—and their impact on women's political development—are the subject of Chapter 4.

Rightist women mobilized again in 1970 to prevent Allende's presidential victory. His electoral triumph dismayed and confused the National and Christian Democratic parties, which were unable to mount a strong offensive against him for much of the following year. In December 1971, women from the National and Christian Democratic parties (along with independents) organized the March of the Empty Pots and Pans. Chapter 5 discusses rightist women's work against Allende during the presidential campaign and focuses on the significance of this march.

Chapters 6 and 7 analyze the anti-Allende women's movement, focusing on Poder Femenino, the opposition women's group. The origins, ideology, activities, and importance of Poder Femenino are explored in Chapter 6. In order to illustrate Poder Femenino's efforts to build a cross-class alliance, Chapter 7 examines the group's relationship with working-class women.

Because the opposition was unable to obtain the number of votes it needed to impeach Allende in the March 1973 parliamentary elections, it decided that he had to be overthrown. Opposition women worked hard to build a climate favorable to a coup and to encourage the armed forces to intervene. Their work to accomplish these goals is the subject of Chapter 8.

Finally, the Conclusion summarizes the book's findings and addresses how the female activists against Allende viewed their political work and the impact it had on their lives. A brief epilogue follows: it examines right-wing women's response to the arrest of Pinochet in London, England, in October 1998 and the 2000 presidential elections.

1

Economic, Political, and
Social Change in Chile

1938–1973

THE SINGLE MOST important event that gave birth to the right-wing women's movement in Chile was the presidential victory of longtime Partido Socialista (PS, Socialist Party) leader Salvador Allende on 4 September 1970.[1] Allende's electoral victory surprised many in Chile, including members of his own coalition, Popular Unity. His triumph reflected not only the failure of the Christian Democrats under President Eduardo Frei (1964–70) to deliver on their reformist promises, but also the national progression to the left that intensified in the late 1960s and early 1970s. In order to explain Allende's victory and contextualize the emergence of the anti-Allende women's movement, this chapter begins by analyzing some of the key transformations that took place in Chile from the late 1930s to the 1970s. It then discusses why Allende was elected in 1970, what Popular Unity did once it assumed power, how the opposition organized against the leftist government, and what the U.S. government's relationship to Chile was.

The 1930s to the 1960s: Urbanization, Industrialization, and the Democratization of Chilean Politics

From the late 1930s onward, Chile underwent significant economic and demographic changes that altered political relationships in the nation. Chile ceased to be a predominantly rural, agriculture-based economy and

---

1 Allende obtained 36.3 percent of the vote, rightist candidate Jorge Alessandri received 34.9 percent, and Christian Democrat Radomiro Tomic came in third with 27.8 percent. República de Chile, Servicio Electoral (Santiago: n.d.).

2 The Popular Unity coalition formed in 1969 and included the Socialist and Communist parties, which were the largest and most influential parties within the coalition, as well as the Radical and Social Democratic parties and MAPU (Movimiento de Acción Popular Unitario, Movement for Unitary Popular Action). See note 34 for more information on MAPU.

became an urban and industrialized one. From 1938 to 1952, the Popular Front coalition—consisting, at various times, of the Radical, Socialist, and Communist parties—governed Chile.[3] The centrist Radical Party dominated the coalition and provided the three presidents elected during these years. The economic program implemented by the Popular Front governments fostered industrialization and encouraged urbanization in Chile.

The Popular Front sponsored industrialization in order to develop Chile's productive capacity, decrease its dependence on foreign imports and investment, expand the internal market, and improve the standard of living for the working and middle classes.[4] By World War II, industry, not mining or agriculture, ruled the Chilean economy.[5] The government-backed industrialization projects offered rural workers, northern nitrate miners, and the urban poor new employment possibilities in cities such as Antofagasta, Santiago, Valparaíso, and Concepción and accelerated the development of an urban working class. In response to the government's initiatives, hundreds of thousands of peasants abandoned the countryside and their miserable standard of living to seek better working conditions, higher salaries, and more freedom in the cities. The urban population rapidly expanded, and "by 1960 more than half of Chileans lived in cities of at least 20,000 people or more."[6] All Chilean cities, including provincial ones such as Talca and Temuco in the south, experienced growth during these decades; the population increase in Santiago, however, far surpassed that of all other cities. From 1920 to the early 1960s, the number of people living in Santiago quadrupled from 500,000 to 2,000,000. During the 1960s alone, the population of Santiago grew by 800,000.[7]

One notable feature of the century-long rural-to-urban migration is that more women than men left the countryside to move to the cities. In 1970, Chile's population reached 8,885,000. In a clear reflection of the gendered differences in migration patterns, 3,503,000 women and

---

3 For a discussion of the Popular Front that highlights the role of the Socialist Party, see Paul Drake, *Socialism and Populism in Chile, 1932–1952* (Urbana: University of Illinois Press, 1978), chapters 7–10.

4 For a description of the Popular Front's economic policies, see Simon Collier and William F. Sater, *A History of Chile, 1808–1994* (Cambridge: Cambridge University Press, 1996), 264–74, and Drake, *Socialism and Populism*, 180–81.

5 Peter Winn, *Weavers of Revolution: The Yarur Workers and Chile's Road to Socialism* (New York: Oxford University Press, 1986), 19.

6 Brian Loveman points out that this number is "well above the comparable figures for all major world areas except North America and Oceania." See Brian Loveman, *Chile: The Legacy of Hispanic Capitalism* (New York: Oxford University Press, 1988), 235.

7 Collier and Sater, *History of Chile*, 291, 312.

3,172,000 men lived in cities in 1970, and 1,039,000 women and 1,170,000 men lived in the countryside.[8] Women migrated to the cities because they could find work there in the service sector and as domestics.

Although the Popular Front governments were successful in increasing Chile's industrial capacity, they did not ameliorate the conditions in which the majority of Chileans lived, nor did they break Chile's dependency on foreign (principally U.S.) products and capital. As Brian Loveman notes, "most urban workers along with the rural labor force actually lost ground in real income from 1938 to 1952," and Chile "had become increasingly dependent upon private capital, loans, and marketing decisions made by the United States copper firms."[9] The Radical Party's inability to achieve its goals led simultaneously to a decline in the party's popularity and to increased support for the Christian Democratic Party in the late 1950s.

In the early 1960s, the Christian Democratic Party supplanted the Radical Party as the party of the center, successfully obtained the allegiance of Chile's middle class, and emerged as the largest party. Identifying itself as the party of both moderation and modernization, the PDC was also blessed with the backing of the Catholic Church, whose support the secular Radical Party had never obtained. The Christian Democratic Party sought to build popular support by organizing sectors of the population that the other parties had ignored—specifically, peasants and the urban poor.

In the 1960s, Santiago enjoyed a rich associational life and culture, thanks to the accumulated experiences of a broad spectrum of political parties, trade union organizations, and popular mobilizations. The massive population growth of the 1960s intensified people's demands for jobs, housing, and basic services and swelled the number of those willing to struggle to obtain them. Peasants who abandoned the rural estates dominated by autocratic landlords (estates on which they could not legally unionize until 1967)[10] arrived in Santiago with high hopes and rising expectations, but little political experience.

What the urban poor lacked in experience and organization, the PDC attempted to provide, along with structure and resources. The urban poor, in turn, offered the Christian Democratic Party what it most

---

8 Lucía Santa Cruz, Teresa Pereira, Isabel Zegers, and Valeria Maino, *Tres ensayos sobre la mujer chilena: Siglos XVIII–XIX–XX* (Santiago: Editorial Universitaria, 1978), 208.

9 Loveman, *Chile*, 260.

10 Arturo Valenzuela, *The Breakdown of Democratic Regimes: Chile* (Baltimore: The Johns Hopkins University Press, 1978), 26.

needed: a mass base. According to Jacques Chonchol, a leading member of the PDC during much of the 1960s, "the party had begun to grow as a result of the marginal urban sectors. Chile underwent a process of rapid urbanization as people moved from the countryside to the city. Most of these people went to the *poblaciones* [urban slums]. The party specialized in the organization and struggle of these sectors."[11]

In 1964, the Christian Democratic Party, led by Eduardo Frei, managed to capture the vote of those who supported change as well as those who steadfastly opposed it. The PDC promised the former a more modern society; to the latter, it offered the only realistic possibility of preventing Salvador Allende's victory and the substantial social transformations his presidency would entail. The breadth of support Frei received allowed him to win the presidential elections with 55.5 percent of the vote.[12] However, by the late 1960s, many Chileans believed that neither President Eduardo Frei nor the Christian Democratic Party had delivered on their campaign pledges. The Christian Democratic failure to improve substantially the conditions in which many Chileans lived—especially given its promises to do just that—encouraged workers, peasants, the poor, and sectors of the middle class to embrace, or at least be receptive to, more radical solutions to their problems.

The 1960s: The Radicalization of Chilean Politics

The late 1960s witnessed an unprecedented upsurge in popular urban struggles. Thousands of homeless people seized empty land and built homes and communities on it. In 1967, homeless people in Santiago organized thirteen land seizures; in 1969, on the eve of the 1970 presidential elections, the number of land takeovers had risen to seventy-three.[13] In addition, urban workers demanded higher pay, more benefits, and better working conditions. More workers joined unions and went out on strike in the 1960s than in any previous decade. For example, there were 2,049 unions and 305 strikes in 1954; by 1969, this number had grown to 3,749 unions and 977 strikes.[14]

The rural-to-urban migration converted rural peasants into urban workers (or urban poor). It simultaneously undercut the power of the landowners and weakened the rightist Conservative and Liberal parties.

11 Jacques Chonchol, interview by author, tape recording, Santiago, 13 December 1998.

12 For a discussion of the Christian Democratic Party's policies and program—and why the party won the 1964 elections—see Chapter 4.

13 Loveman, *Chile*, 286.

14 Arturo Valenzuela, *Breakdown*, 26.

For much of the twentieth century, these two parties had articulated the interests of the Chilean upper class. The Conservative Party primarily represented the large landowners and enjoyed close ties to the Catholic Church. The secular Liberal Party reflected the political perspective and economic demands of urban industrialists and the commercial sector. Although these parties had political differences, they shared a joint economic and political project: the maintenance of an export economy and their own class privileges and power. This bond encouraged them to settle their disagreements in order to preserve the status quo.[15]

The peasants' exodus from the countryside, along with changes in electoral procedures, undermined the large landowners' base of power and source of votes. During the 1940s and 1950s, the rightist parties "maintained over forty percent of the vote and a plurality in Congress."[16] A key reason why the Conservatives and Liberals were elected to Congress was that they controlled the votes of the *inquilinos* (tenant laborers) who worked their land and depended upon them for their livelihood. In a practice known as *cohecho*, landowners purchased the votes of the poor. In 1958 and 1962, Congress passed laws that made voting secret and ended *cohecho*. These laws, combined with the migration to the cities, meant that the right steadily lost power in the 1960s and partially explains the growth in electoral support for both the left and the Christian Democratic Party.[17]

In the first half of the 1960s, the political fortunes of the right reached their lowest point. Not only did the rightist parties lose some of their rural votes, but a large number of people also began to see the right as an obstacle to progress and development. Another factor that led to a decline in support for these conservative parties was that many Chileans associated the right with self-serving policies and outdated traditions, such as "semifeudal social relations in the countryside . . . and denationalization of national resources," that seemed out of step with the drive to modernize sweeping over much of the country.[18] In a clear indication of the

---

15 Ben G. Burnett, *Political Groups in Chile: The Dialogue Between Order and Change* (Austin: University of Texas Press, 1970), 196–98. For a discussion of these parties during this period, see Tomás Moulian and Isabel Torres Dujisin, *Discusiones entre honorables: Las candidaturas presidenciales de la derecha entre 1938 y 1946* (Santiago: FLACSO, n.d.), 324.

16 Smith, *Church and Politics*, 94.

17 Through *cohecho* and the landlord's control of his workers, the Conservative and Liberal parties "controlled thirty to forty percent of the popular vote" (Collier and Sater, *History of Chile*, 240). For a description of how *cohecho* worked, see Tomás Moulian, *La forja de ilusiones: El sistema de partidos 1932–1973* (Santiago: FLACSO, 1993), 53–54.

18 Moulian and Torres, *Discusiones entre honorables*, 324.

changing political climate, the Conservatives and the Liberals failed to win a plurality of seats in the 1961 congressional elections.[19] An even more pivotal loss followed this setback: a Socialist won the 1964 by-election in Curicó, a city located in the stronghold of the landed elite. These two astonishing defeats encouraged the Conservative and Liberal parties to support the centrist candidate, Eduardo Frei, in 1964 in order to prevent the electoral triumph of Salvador Allende. In 1966, the two parties dissolved and formed a new rightist party, the National Party.[20]

At the same time, while Conservative and Liberal parties were losing their voting bases, the Catholic Church underwent significant political changes of its own. Chile had traditionally been a Catholic country, and the church exerted considerable influence on both public discourse and people's thinking. For much of the twentieth century, the church aligned itself with the Conservative Party and publicly condemned Marxism and radical politics. In the early 1960s, a growing sector of the church began to espouse the new interpretations of the church's mission articulated in the Second Vatican Council (1962–65). This council, more commonly referred to as Vatican II, signified a substantial change in church policy—primarily that concerning the church's relationship to civil society. Instead of urging support for the status quo and encouraging the faithful to await their reward in heaven, Vatican II "committed the Church to an active role in the promotion of justice, human rights, and freedom."[21] Reformist members of the Catholic Church in Chile applauded these new interpretations and saw in them institutional backing for the policies then being expressed by the Christian Democratic Party. Other sectors in the church understood Vatican II as signaling support for more revolutionary solutions and worked directly with the Chilean left. In a dramatic demonstration of this belief, nine priests, three nuns and two hundred Catholic laypeople took over Santiago's main cathedral in 1968 and, among other things, prayed "for an end to exploitation in Latin America."[22] By the end of the 1960s, the church in Chile ceased its public denunciations of Marxism and voiced its ongoing support for social justice, a change that made it easier for Catholics to reconcile their religious faith with political support for the left.[23] However, not everyone in the church approved of these

19 Loveman, *Chile*, 265.

20 For further discussion of this period, see Chapter 3.

21 Smith, *Church and Politics*, 3–4.

22 José del Pozo, *Rebeldes, reformistas y revolucionarios* (Santiago: Ediciones Documentas, 1992), 62. They also prayed for "the dead Vietnamese who died in defense of their country . . . and the political prisoners in Brazil."

23 Smith, *Church and Politics*, 136.

changes. Conservative sectors in Chile rejected them and joined reactionary Catholic organizations, such as Tradition, Family, and Property (Tradición, Familia y Propiedad, TFP), in order to fight against them.[24]

Nor was the left untouched by the radicalism that characterized global politics during the 1960s. The Vietnamese people's ability to wage an increasingly successful war against the United States—one of the most powerful nations on earth—inspired hope in millions of people around the world that they, too, could vanquish their oppressors.

Even closer to home and more direct in its impact was the 1959 Cuban Revolution. This revolution profoundly convinced many in the Chilean left, particularly young people, that not only was it *possible* to seize state power through armed struggle (specifically, guerrilla warfare), but it was also the *only* way to do so. A number of Chileans began to believe that fundamental, structural changes were necessary, and that without them, their lives would not improve. Socialism became the system they aspired to create—the only economic model, they believed, that could end poverty and misery for the majority of Chileans. Che Guevara, the Argentine who joined with Cuban revolutionaries to topple the Batista dictatorship in 1959 and then unsuccessfully attempted to repeat the experience in Bolivia, became the most popular symbol of this new political perspective. His picture, featuring Che's intense gaze, long hair, and black beret, adorned the walls of universities and young people's rooms throughout Chile.

Nothing illustrates the radicalization of the Chilean left more clearly than the political changes adopted by the Socialist Party. The PS formed in 1933 (following the defeat of the Socialist Republic).[25] It operated squarely within the parameters of Chilean electoral politics and respected the established rules of the game. Most of its leaders were from middle-class backgrounds, as were its congressional representatives.[26] Political differences and divisions plagued the Socialist Party; in 1940, 1943, 1948, and 1952, various factions left the party and formed their own organizations. By 1957, though, the party had reunited—a process that explains, in part, the subsequent increase in the party's membership and its growing influence within the left.[27] Since 1952, the Socialist Party had

---

24 This response is examined more fully in Chapter 4.

25 In 1932, socialists led by Air Force Commander Marmaduque Grove (who was Salvador Allende's cousin) seized power and established the "Socialist Republic." The Republic lasted for one hundred days—until the army overthrew it. See Edy Kaufman, *Crisis in Allende's Chile: New Perspectives* (New York: Praeger, 1988), 127, and Drake, *Socialism and Populism*, 72–82.

26 Drake, *Socialism and Populism*, 310.

27 At its lowest point (in 1949), the Socialist Party received only 9.4 percent of the vote in congressional elections. However, by 1973 it obtained 18.7 percent of the vote, and the Communist

faithfully nominated Salvador Allende as its presidential candidate and worked diligently to ensure his election. At congresses held in 1965 and 1967, the Socialist Party declared itself to be Marxist-Leninist, rejected the party's traditional reliance on electoral politics, defined the acquisition of state power as its goal, and approved the use of armed struggle to achieve this end.[28] These changes reflected the Chilean left's stronger identification with revolutionary politics.[29]

The 1965 formation of the Movement of the Revolutionary Left by young leftists, many of them university students, further reflected the extent to which revolutionary ideas permeated Chilean politics. The MIR supported armed struggle and opposed the Chilean left's traditional participation in and reliance on elections as the means to gain power. As a result, the MIR did not campaign for Allende in the 1970 presidential elections, although it supported his victory.[30] As a former member of the MIR explains, "we supported the election of Salvador Allende because it offered the Chilean people the possibility of a popular government. But at the same time, the MIR supported armed struggle and the sharpening of class contradictions."[31] During the Popular Unity years, the MIR encouraged peasants to occupy rural estates, homeless city dwellers to seize land, workers to take over factories, and students to secure control of the universities. Their political perspective differed radically from that of the more moderate party of the Chilean left, the Partido Comunista (PC, Communist Party).

The Communist Party (during the Popular Unity years, the second-largest leftist party after the Socialist Party) did not experience the same process of radicalization that much of the Chilean left did. Since its origins in 1922, the PC had prioritized electoral work and involvement in and leadership of the trade union movement. The party built a tightly structured, unified, and effective organization and maintained a very close

---

Party received 16.2 percent. Kenneth Roberts, *Deepening Democracy: The Modern Left and Social Movements in Chile and Peru* (Stanford: Stanford University Press, 1998), 88–99.

28 Collier and Sater, *History of Chile*, 321, and Moulian, *La forja*, 60–62. According to Peter Winn, another factor that explains the Socialist Party's embrace of more radical politics was Allende's loss in the 1964 elections. In 1964, the left anticipated Allende's victory; his defeat raised questions in many supporters' minds about the practicality of pursuing an electoral strategy. See Winn, *Weavers*, 269.

29 For an example of the PS's endorsement of more radical politics, see Cristián Pérez, "Guerrilla rural en Chile: La batalla del Fundo San Miguel (1968)," *Estudios Públicos* 78 (Fall 2000).

30 MIR, *What Is the MIR? Notes on the History of the MIR* (Oakland, Calif.: Resistance, 1977), 43–44; Kaufman, *Crisis*, 161.

31 Ernesto Torres, interview by author, tape recording, Santiago, 6 August 1999.

relationship with the Soviet Union. This internal cohesiveness allowed the PC to concentrate on its strategy of electing a leftist president of Chile—and permitted its tactics to continue unchanged by the upsurge of revolutionary politics that swept over much of the world, particularly among young people.[32]

The radicalization of Chilean politics also affected both the rightist National Party and the centrist Christian Democratic Party and made it difficult for them to unite against Allende in 1970 (as they had done in the 1964 elections). In response to the left's embrace of more revolutionary politics, the National Party adopted increasingly vitriolic anticommunist positions. In addition, the agrarian reform carried out by the PDC antagonized the PN, many of whose members owned rural estates, and prevented the formation of a PDC-PN coalition against Allende.

The PDC pursued a very different path than that chosen by the PN. Much of its leadership supported an alliance with the left in order "to deepen the changes that had taken place during the Frei government." When they realized that the party rejected this alliance, several of these leaders left the party and formed MAPU (Movimiento de Acción Popular Unitario, Movement of Unified Popular Action). In addition, the 1969 congressional elections indicated people's growing dissatisfaction with Frei, starkly revealing the PDC's steady decline in popularity.[33] These electoral results encouraged the party to select Radomiro Tomic, a representative of the party's left wing, as its 1970 presidential candidate. The choice of Tomic reflected the party's assessment that a more leftist candidate would have greater appeal to the Chilean people; it also demonstrated the party's desire to prevent further internal divisions.[34] Tomic (and the tendency he represented) refused to ally with the PN, just as the PN rejected any alliance with the Christian Democrats. The parties' inability to form an anti-Allende bloc thus split the vote three ways and allowed Allende to obtain the plurality needed to win the election.

32 For a history of the Communist Party, see Carmelo Furci, *The Chilean Communist Party and the Road to Socialism* (London: Zed, 1984). For a description of the PC during the 1960s and early 1970s, see 97–103 and 105–30.

33 In the 1965 congressional elections, the PDC received 42.3 percent of the vote. In the 1969 congressional elections, their support fell to 29.8 percent. See Moulian, *La forja*, 123.

34 In 1969, many of the party's most important intellectuals left the party, formed their own party (MAPU), and subsequently joined the Popular Unity coalition. Reflecting upon the decision to leave the PDC and form MAPU, Jacques Chonchol noted that "when we formed MAPU we thought that a lot more people would join with us [but they did not]. Basically, what happened was the leadership of the party divided, but it didn't really affect much of the base of the party" (Chonchol, interview).

Popular Unity in Power

The Popular Unity government's three years in power (1970–73) can be divided into three distinct phases. From Allende's November 1970 inauguration until early 1972, the UP enjoyed its most successful period of governance. The standard of living for the majority of Chileans dramatically improved and popular support for the leftist government grew. The opposition, composed at that time of the rightist PN and the centrist PDC, was still divided. The second period began in early 1972 and ended with the massive truck owners' strike of October 1972. During this time, conflict between Popular Unity and the opposition—which now included the *gremio* (guild) movement[35] and the anti-Allende women's movement—increased but did not seriously threaten the government's existence. It did, however, limit the government's ability to implement its program and undermined many of the advances that Popular Unity had achieved in its first year. The third phase was one of escalating crisis: it culminated on 11 September 1973, when the Chilean military overthrew the Popular Unity government and seized power. The March 1973 parliamentary elections, the June 1973 failed coup attempt, talk of civil war, street confrontations, further political polarization, antigovernment strikes, and the government's inability to control the situation defined this third period.

September 1970–January 1972: Popular Unity Advances Its Program

The program of the UP outlined both the goals of the new government and the means by which it planned to achieve them. The basic goal of Popular Unity was "to end the domination of the imperialists, the monopolies, and the landed oligarchy and to begin the construction of socialism in Chile."[36] In order to carry out its plans, the UP pledged to uphold Chile's democratic traditions and to respect its legal structures in the process of socializing the economy, a policy that has come to be known as *la via chilena hacia el socialismo* (the peaceful road to socialism).[37] The government program called for

35 In Chile, the *gremio* movement consisted of small business owners and professionals; it represented an intermediary stratum of the population located between the industrial worker (or the rural peasant) and the large owner of capital. The *gremio* movement claimed that its sole purpose was to defend the economic interests of its members and that it had neither political ambitions nor party connections. Although it may have originated independently of the parties, by October 1972 it had the solid backing of both the National and Christian Democratic parties. *Gremio* literally means "guild," but "corporatism" is a more accurate translation. Chapter 4 discusses the *gremio* movement.

36 Unidad Popular, *Programa basico de la UP* (Santiago: Impresora Horizonte, n.d.), 10.

37 Although this is not the literal translation, it both accurately conveys the meaning of the phrase and is used most commonly.

an expansion of Chile's democracy through increased popular participation in government institutions, community groups, and workplace organizations and the redistribution of wealth to increase the working class's standard of living. The program proposed the formation of a mixed economy, with both private and state ownership of property. While foreign holdings and domestic monopolies would be nationalized, the majority of industry would be left in private hands. Thus, the program called for the state to take over the copper industry, large financial institutions, and foreign trade, but to permit private ownership of the smaller industries. It pledged to accelerate agrarian reform by expropriating landholdings larger than "eighty basic hectares."[38]

Allende's victory elated the members of the Popular Unity parties and the large number of independents who had voted for him. As news of his triumph spread through Santiago, Allende's supporters flocked to the streets to celebrate what for them was the realization of their dream for a better, more just life for themselves, their children, and their nation.

Not surprisingly, Allende's election inspired very different emotions among U.S. government officials and the Chilean industrialists, financiers, and landowners whose extensive holdings the government had promised to expropriate. On the day of the election, Edward Korry, U.S. ambassador to Chile, cabled Secretary of State Henry Kissinger to bemoan that "we have suffered a grievous defeat."[39] North American companies—including Anaconda and Kennecott, which owned much of Chile's copper, and International Telephone and Telegraph (ITT), which had invested heavily in Chile—vehemently opposed the Popular Unity victory.[40] The U.S. government, which saw this event through the lens of the Cold War, attributed Allende's triumph to the machinations of world communism and was determined to prevent his assumption of power.[41]

(margin note: US against PU)

---

38 Collier and Sater, *History of Chile*, 337. They explain that this applied to "80 hectares of irrigated Central Valley land [the most fertile agricultural region in Chile]" (313 n. 11). An area of 100 hectares is approximately 250 acres, so 80 hectares would equal roughly 200 acres.

39 Edward Korry, cables to the Department of State on the election of Salvador Allende and efforts to block his assumption of the presidency, 4 September 1970, National Security Archives, online: <http://www.gwu.edu/~nsarchiv/NSAEBB/NSAEBB8/ch18-01.htm>.

40 In 1970, "ITT owned all telephone works and took $38 million profit annually from Chile." See David F. Cusack, *Revolution and Reaction: The Internal and International Dynamics of Conflict and Confrontation in Chile* (Denver: University of Denver, Graduate School of International Studies, 1977), 103.

41 According to a recently released CIA memo, "President Nixon had decided that an Allende regime was not acceptable to the United States. The President asked the Agency [the CIA] to prevent Allende from coming to power or to unseat him. The President authorized ten million dollars for this purpose, if needed." Central Intelligence Agency, memo on the genesis of Project

Allende received a plurality of the vote, but not a majority; this meant that Congress had to confirm his election. The U.S. government was not able to convince the Christian Democrats to vote against Allende's confirmation, an action that would have violated Chile's tradition of automatically naming the candidate who receives the plurality of votes as president. During September and October 1970, the CIA encouraged anti-Allende officers to stage a coup, but the plan failed because the commander in chief, René Schneider, refused to violate the Constitution by intervening in the nation's political affairs.[42] However, on 22 October, a right-wing group kidnapped Schneider and killed him, using weapons supplied by the CIA. The outrage generated by his murder effectively ended the plans of the U.S. government and the Chilean elite to prevent Allende from assuming the presidency on 24 October.[43]

Once Allende became president, he moved rapidly to implement key points of the UP program. In December 1970, he presented a proposal to Congress to nationalize foreign copper holdings, and the amendment unanimously passed in July 1971.[44] No other measure he introduced met with such universal approval.

By the end of its first year in power the Allende government had nationalized the copper mines, taken control of 90 percent of the banks, and expropriated many of the large industries and the rural estates, redistributing wealth to workers, peasants, and the poor.[45] The UP attempted to realize its program using laws enacted during the Socialist Republic of 1932 and by the Frei government (1964–70). In his March 1971 message to Congress, Allende proudly reported the government's accomplishments. It had nationalized Bethlehem Steel's holdings and taken control of

---

FUBELT, 16 September 1970, National Security Archives, online: <http://www.gwu.edu/~nsarchiv/NSAEBB/NSAEBB8/cho3-01.htm>.

42 Despite its inability to convince the Christian Democrats to go along with its plans, one CIA memo stressed that it was the U.S. government's "firm and continuing policy that Allende be overthrown by a coup." Thomas Karamessines (CIA), operating guidance cable on coup plotting, 16 October 1970, National Security Archives, online: <http://www.gwu.edu/~nsarchiv/NSAEBB/NSAEBB8/cho5-01.htm>. To facilitate the efforts of those sectors of the Chilean military willing to overthrow Allende, U.S. government officials met clandestinely with "two Chilean Armed Forces officers" and offered them support and weapons. The CIA confirmed that "sub-machine guns and ammo [were] being sent by regular courier leaving Washington 0700 hours 19 October due [to] arrive Santiago late evening 20 October." Central Intelligence Agency, cable transmissions on coup plotting, 18 October 1970, National Security Archives, online: <http://www.gwu.edu/~nsarchiv/NSAEBB/NSAEBB8/ch27-01.htm>.

43 Senate Select Committee, *Covert Action: Report*, 10–11, 25–26.

44 Collier and Sater, *History of Chile*, 334.

45 Winn, *Weavers*, 227–28.

nine banks and several large industries, such as Purina, various textile factories, and Zig-Zag Press. Furthermore, it had effected these changes "with the decided support of the workers, immediate growth in productivity, and the active participation of workers, employees, and technicians in the management and administration [of the industry]." Allende added that by the end of the year, the government planned "to expropriate one thousand large estates."[46] In 1972, land seizures—some with government approval, many without—multiplied. By early 1972, "*campesinos* [peasants] temporarily or permanently occupied some 1700 rural properties."[47]

In order to redistribute Chile's wealth from the upper class to the working, peasant, and middle classes, the UP raised wages, froze prices, increased spending to social services, and expanded public works programs. These policies achieved results that surpassed the government's goals. Unemployment dropped; by July 1971, average salaries increased by almost 60 percent; the gross domestic product grew 8.6 percent; production expanded; and inflation decreased from almost 40 percent in 1970 to around 22 percent the following year.[48]

These programs gave workers, peasants, and the poor access to products and services about which they had only dreamed. The improved standard of living that resulted for this sector, along with the perception that this government was responsive to their needs, enhanced their sense of self-worth and well-being—sentiments that translated into direct popular support for the Popular Unity government. The 1971 municipal elections reflected Chileans' growing approval of the UP. In these elections, the UP received 50 percent of the vote (a figure substantially higher than the 36 percent it had obtained only eight months earlier, in the presidential elections).[49] This significant growth confirmed the UP's assessment that its policies were both just and efficient and bolstered its belief that the government represented the majority of the Chilean people.

Neither the PDC nor the PN shared this assessment of the situation. However, the lack of unity between the two opposition parties during this first period made it difficult for them to express their dissatisfaction in an effective way. Despite Tomic's poor showing in the presidential elections (he came in last, with only 27.8 percent of the vote), the left wing, which opposed an alliance with the PN, controlled the party apparatus. By early

46 Salvador Allende, *La via Chilena hacia al socialismo* (Santiago: Ediciones Palabra Escrita, 1989), 45–46.

47 Loveman, *Chile*, 300.

48 Arturo Valenzuela, *Breakdown*, 51–52.

49 Kaufman, *Crisis*, 183–84.

July, however, the balance of power within the party had shifted to the right. In June 1971, the VOP (Vanguardia Organizada Popular, Popular Organized Vanguard)[50] murdered Christian Democrat Edmundo Perez Zujovic, who was a close friend of Eduardo Frei and had been his interior minister.[51] His assassination angered many in the party, and they blamed Popular Unity for his death.[52] Perez Zujovic's murder strengthened the right wing of the party and allowed it both to build a closer relationship with the PN and to oppose attempts to work with Popular Unity. One consequence of this shift was that the PDC accepted the PN's backing for its candidate, Oscar Marín, in the July 1971 by-election in Valparaíso. Marín won the election in a close race. As had been true in previous elections, more women than men voted for the conservative candidate, and their vote gave him the victory.[53]

The party's decision to support Marín provoked much of its left wing to quit. They subsequently formed the Christian Left and joined the UP. The left wing's exit from the party weakened the voices of those who counseled support for (or at least a working relationship with) the UP and strengthened the position of those who opposed the government.

Women from the Christian Democratic and National parties drew two lessons from the July 1971 election in Valparaíso. They concluded that unity between the two opposition parties was critical to their success and that women's role in the process was pivotal. Fortified by these conclusions and by their growing hatred of the UP government, they organized the highly successful December 1971 March of the Empty Pots and Pans,[54] in which some five thousand women took over the streets in downtown Santiago to express their repudiation of the Allende government. The march

---

50 The VOP was a small organization whose members had been expelled from the MIR in 1969. During the Popular Unity years, the group carried out armed actions, several of which resulted in the deaths of its members. For a description of the VOP, see NACLA, *New Chile* (New York: NACLA, 1973), 32.

51 In 1968, landless people occupied land in the southern city of Puerto Montt. Police shot and killed nine of the participants in the takeover. Since Edmundo Perez Zujovic was minister of the interior at the time, much of the left held him responsible for the killings. See Kaufman, *Crisis*, 160.

52 It was speculated, but not proven, that the CIA was involved in Perez Zujovic's death. In any case, the greater rapprochement between the PDC and the PN that resulted from his murder certainly benefited U.S. government plans for Chile (ibid., 146).

53 Marín received votes from 80,610 women and 61,617 men; 63,143 women voted for Hernán del Canto, the Socialist candidate, and 74,057 men did. See "Elección extraordinaria de un diputado," Dirección del Registro Electoral, Santiago, 18 July 1971.

54 María Correa Morandé, *La guerra de las mujeres* (Santiago: Editorial Universidad Técnica del Estado, 1974), 27–40.

accomplished three things. It promoted women as central to the opposition movement, provided a concrete and convincing example of what unity could achieve, and encouraged the opposition to build an activist movement against the Allende government. It also brought the first phase of Allende's government to an end and foreshadowed some of the central developments of the second.

January–October 1972: Increased Conflict and Confrontation

Between January and October 1972, the working relationship between the National and Christian Democratic parties was strengthened, conflict between them and the UP heightened, and tension among the different parties (and political tendencies within the governing coalition) increased. The economic achievements of the first year began to fade; shortages, inflation, and resistance to the government multiplied.

An array of factors caused the economic problems that increasingly plagued the Popular Unity government from 1972 until the September 1973 military coup. The first was of a structural nature. Although previous governments had attempted to expand both domestic production and the internal market through import substitution and industrialization, Chile's productive capacity remained low. During the UP's first year, the government pumped unprecedented amounts of money into the hands of the poor and working class by raising their salaries and freezing prices. According to Pedro Vuskovic, minister of the economy, by July 1971 "the purchasing power of the workers [had] increased 30 percent and the consumption of the whole population [had] increased more than 20 percent." Demand soared, as many people could now afford to purchase goods that had previously been beyond their economic reach. However, the national industry—geared to a much smaller market—lacked the productive capacity to meet heightened demand. Consequently, although larger numbers of Chileans enjoyed the greater purchasing power that their higher incomes gave them, the goods they wished to buy often were in short supply or could not be found.[55]

Compounding the problem, owners of industries and rural estates felt threatened by the UP's policies of nationalization and expropriation and did what they could to undermine the government economically. The elite sabotaged their own industries and estates, hoarded what they produced or

causes for economic problems.

---

55 Pedro Vuskovic, "Conversations with the Women of Chile," in *The Chilean Road to Socialism* (Austin: University of Texas, 1973), 460–61. Vuskovic adds that the nature of the system developed to distribute goods in Santiago exacerbated the problem as well: "The [distribution] system has been organized, designed, and directed to serve that part of the city where the rich people live and to give bad service to the people who work" (ibid., 469).

sold it on the black market, and decapitalized their own holdings. This was both a rational response on their part to the UP's plans to strip them of their economic and political power and a politically effective strategy to lessen popular support for the government.

Nor was the Popular Unity government blameless. Once it took over an industry, financial institution, or agricultural estate, it appointed one of its members to supervise the property. Following the established tradition of Chilean politics, the UP assigned people to these positions based on party affiliation. While the individuals delegated to any particular industry might have been very politically committed, they did not necessarily possess the skills needed to ensure either a smoothly running operation or maximum production. In addition, since government economic policies stressed popular consumption—and the increased demand thus outstripped production—inflation swelled. In July 1972, inflation rose to 45.9 percent, and by December it practically quadrupled to 163.4 percent.[56] The skyrocketing inflation undercut the positive impact of increased wages for most Chileans, produced anxiety among consumers, and undermined confidence in the government's economic policies. Aggravating the situation was the fact that the government financed its programs by spending money, not by raising taxes. As a result, it spent more money than it took in, which depleted the national treasury. The UP was unable to raise taxes because, as José Cademartori explains, "despite the fact that we [the UP] had plans and projects, we could not carry out any tax reform because the opposition dominated Congress and it rejected all our proposals."[57] Instead, the government drew on its reserves and increased the money supply by 100 percent, a policy that rapidly exhausted the treasury. By December 1972, "Chile's reserve situation showed a net deficit of $288.7 million and its balance of payments deficit had increased four-fold over the previous year to $538 million."[58]

In addition, the U.S. government and corporations joined with the Chilean elite to subvert UP policies. Following the directives of then President Nixon to "make the [Chilean] economy scream,"[59] the U.S.

56 Arturo Valenzuela, *Breakdown*, 55.

57 José Cademartori, interview by author, tape recording, Chicago, 19 March 1999. Cademartori was an economist, a Communist Party deputy from 1957 to May 1973, and minister of the economy from June 1973 to 11 September 1973.

58 Arturo Valenzuela, *Breakdown*, 55.

59 CIA Director Richard Helms recorded Nixon's apocryphal words in a meeting in which they discussed how to prevent Allende from becoming Chile's next president. In that meeting, according to Helms's notes, Nixon promised that "$10,000,000 [was] available, more if necessary."

[handwritten margin note: Still somewhat of a caudillo mindset.]

government cut aid to the Popular Unity government (but not to the military), made sure that no spare parts reached Chile, and pressured international financial institutions not to make loans to it. These policies had direct and devastating results. According to the U.S. Senate, "by late 1972, the Chilean Ministry of the Economy estimated that almost one-third of the diesel trucks at Chuquicamata Copper Mine, 30 percent of the privately owned city buses, 21 percent of all taxis, and 33 percent of state-owned buses in Chile could not operate because of the lack of spare parts or tires."[60]

The parties that constituted the UP coalition had managed to submerge their political disagreements for the sake of electoral victory in 1970. However, the reality of governmental power—and the opportunities it presented each party to achieve its goals—highlighted and intensified their disparate political approaches. Popular Unity was, in fact, not all that united. Divisions within the UP were exacerbated as economic problems spread, conflicts with the opposition worsened, and mass mobilizations escalated. This disunity weakened the government's ability to rule successfully (and favored the opposition's campaign against the UP). Two distinct tendencies emerged within the left; each was grounded in a distinct analysis of the situation, definition of the goals to be achieved, and strategy for realizing those goals. One grouping, which consisted of much of the Socialist Party (but not Allende), the MIR, the Christian Left, and a section of MAPU,[61] emphasized class struggle, believed that conflict with the bourgeoisie was inevitable, and argued that the UP and its supporters should prepare for the impending fight. Instead of relying on congressional compromises, the passing of laws, or approval from party officials and ministers, these sectors counted on and worked to build *poder popular* (people power). They encouraged peasants to seize the estates they worked, workers to take control of their factories, and *pobladores* (inhabitants of the urban slums) to grab empty land and build revolutionary communities on it.

The Communist and Radical parties, leaders and members of the PS (including Allende), and a part of MAPU made up the other sector. Influenced

---

Richard Helms, notes on meeting with President on Chile, 15 September 1970, National Security Archives, online: <http://www.gwu.edu/~nsarchiv/NSAEBB/NSAEBB8/ch26-01.htm>.

60 See Senate Select Committee, *Covert Action: Report*, 32–33.

61 Both MAPU and the Christian Left came out of the left wing of the Christian Democratic Party. MAPU formed in 1969 during the Frei presidency. The Christian Left formed in July 1971, after the PDC accepted the PN's support of its candidate in the elections in Valparaíso. Like MAPU before it, the Christian Left affiliated itself with the UP.

in part by their long history of working within Congress to achieve compromises and by their assessment both of their own strength and that of
the political opposition, they urged pragmatism, not confrontation—the
accumulation of forces, not polarization. Instead of encouraging
takeovers by peasants, workers, and *pobladores*, they advocated the nationalization of monopolies and foreign holdings. In order to avoid a showdown with the opposition (which they believed they would lose), they
supported a more conciliatory approach that would lessen antagonism.
For example, the MIR and sectors of the PS called on members of the
armed forces to democratize the military and oppose a military coup
against the government. While this policy bore some fruit among the
troops, it greatly outraged many of the officers. Employing a very different approach, the PC, Allende, and other UP leaders worked to maintain
good relations with military commanders and, after October 1972, incorporated officers into the cabinet. While much of the PS and the MIR characterized the PDC as a bourgeois party and therefore in the enemy camp,
Allende and the PC believed that it was critical not to antagonize what
continued to be the single largest political party in Chile. While the first
tendency called on the working-class base of the PDC to join with it in
building *poder popular*, leaders of the second sector employed a more top-
down strategy. They met with PDC leaders in an effort to build a working
relationship and to prevent the PDC from aligning itself with the rightist
PN against the government.

Unfortunately for the UP, neither strategy succeeded. As Chilean politics polarized, the PN—which had never vacillated in its goal to get rid of
the UP government—established itself as the dominant ideological force
in the opposition. Although the PDC attempted to maintain its independent identity as a party of the center, the determination and political clarity of the PN, coupled with the left wing's decision to abandon the PDC
and join the UP, pulled the PDC toward the right. The transportation
strike of October 1972 united the PN and the PDC, and it brought to an
end the second period of the UP government and set into motion the
dynamic that would characterize much of the third and final period.

October 1972–11 September 1973:
Polarization, Heightened Class Struggle, and the Coup

The strike of the truck owners, which soon escalated into the most severe crisis faced by the UP to date, began in response to the government's announcement that it planned to organize a state-run association of truck drivers. Many
truck drivers and owners believed that this plan represented the government's

attempt to nationalize the transportation industry. Since most truck drivers owned their trucks, they also interpreted the government-run organization as a direct attack on their property and livelihood. In order to prevent the UP from carrying out its plan, Leon Vilarín, head of the Chilean Truck Owners' Association (which included some 165 union locals), called on truckers to strike on 9 October 1972. Forty thousand truck drivers, who owned some 56,000 trucks, responded to his call, went out on strike, and practically shut down most of Chile's transportation system.[62] The *gremio* movement supported the strike, which now included thousands of small shop owners, middle- and upper-class professionals, and many white-collar employees. The number of people participating in the strike grew to somewhere between six hundred thousand and seven hundred thousand.[63]

The enormous strike threatened to paralyze the Chilean economy and seriously undermine support for the Allende government. It was also, as Peter Winn points out, "the most naked and intense class conflict that Chile had ever seen."[64] Realizing what a critical challenge the strike posed to the government, workers in Santiago organized to protect it and to defend their gains and their workplaces. Taking matters into their own hands, workers in centers of high industrial concentration—such as the Vicuña Mackenna district in Santiago and the suburbs of Puente Alto, Maipú, and Cerrillos—set up *cordones industriales* (industrial belts). They took over and defended their factories against the owners, organized transportation to ensure that workers would be able to get to and from work, established networks to deliver needed supplies and food to factories and neighborhoods, and built political ties with the surrounding working-class communities. Led by the workers themselves and by the more radical sectors of the UP, the *cordones industriales* represented both a concrete expression of *poder popular* and a rejection of the more conciliatory policy advocated by Allende and the PC.[65]

The strike proved to be very costly to the government, both economically and politically. Losses incurred as a result of the strike reached at

---

62 *¿Qué Pasa?* 19 October 1972.

63 Collier and Sater, *History of Chile*, 349. For a list of seventy organizations (most of them middle-class and professional *gremios*) that supported the strike, see *La Prensa*, 20 October 1972.

64 Winn, *Weavers*, 238.

65 Ibid.; Loveman, *Chile*, 303–4. One of the best sources on the *cordones industriales* is a documentary film called *The Battle of Chile*. Filmed between the March 1973 elections and the 11 September 1973 coup, this movie depicts the political struggle between the UP government and the opposition as well as the conflicts between more radicalized sectors of the working class and UP officials.

least three million U.S. dollars.[66] Since trucks carried most of Chile's goods to market, the near total transportation stoppage also worsened shortages, led to higher inflation, and made normal business transactions very difficult. Politically, the strike demonstrated the power of the opposition and highlighted the importance of the anti-Allende *gremios*. It also intensified the political polarization that had beset the country and cemented the working alliance between the PDC and the PN.

Just as in many of the conflicts that raged during the Popular Unity period, the strike had no clear winners or losers, but it did have a very direct impact on future political developments. In order to settle the strike, Allende appointed military officers, including Army General Carlos Prats, to his cabinet on 5 November 1972. Although Prats was loyal to the elected government and fully abided by the military's mandate to respect the Constitution, the inclusion of an army officer in the government further spread the idea that the military had the right and the duty to intervene in politics. In fact, it suggested that without the military's help, the political problems facing the nation could not be resolved.[67]

From November 1972 until March 1973, politics centered on the upcoming congressional elections. Both the UP and the opposition saw the elections as critical. The National Party and the Christian Democratic Party, united in CODE (Confederación de la Democracia, Democratic Confederation), pledged to win a two-thirds majority in the March 1972 congressional elections and thereby obtain sufficient votes to impeach President Allende.[68] Popular Unity, in turn, vowed to increase its percentage of votes and thereby counter the opposition's claims that its popularity was on the decline. As a result, the March 1973 elections took on the character of a national plebiscite on the Allende government.

Neither side achieved its goal. Although CODE received the majority of the votes, 54.6 percent, it did not obtain enough deputies to impeach Allende.[69] The UP received 43.5 percent[70]—more votes than it had

66 Loveman, *Chile*, 303.

67 Arturo Valenzuela, *Breakdown*, 82.

68 Their goal was feasible. As Robert Moss argues, "the opposition was only two votes away from a two-thirds majority in the Senate." See Robert Moss, *Chile's Marxist Experiment* (New York: John Wiley & Sons, 1974), 176–77. For a discussion of the parties' perspective and rhetoric on the March 1973 elections, see Paul E. Sigmund, *The Overthrow of Allende and the Politics of Chile, 1964–1976* (Pittsburgh: University of Pittsburgh Press, 1977), 197.

69 Germán Urzúa, *Historia política electoral de Chile 1931–1973* (Santiago: Tamarcos-Van, 1974), 179.

70 "Elección ordinaria de Congreso Nacional," Dirección del Registro Electoral, Santiago, n.d. The rest of the votes were either cast for a small party, marked incorrectly, or left blank.

obtained in the 1970 presidential elections (36.3 percent), but less than it had received in the 1971 municipal elections (49.8 percent).[71] Given the severe economic crisis facing the nation, leftist leaders interpreted these results favorably.

What they did not realize at the time was that the March elections and the UP's ability to maintain widespread popular support signaled the beginning of the end for Popular Unity's peaceful road to socialism. The PN had no intention of waiting until the 1976 presidential elections to get rid of Allende. It urged the military to overthrow the Allende government, a position it had earlier advocated during the October 1972 truckers' strike. The opposition's failure to obtain the necessary votes to impeach Allende convinced the conservative wing of the Christian Democrats that military intervention was indeed necessary. In April 1973, Patricio Aylwin replaced the more moderate Renán Fuentealba as head of the party, a change that both presaged and accelerated the PDC's willingness to support the coup.[72]

The government's proposals for changes in the education system sparked the next round of conflict between the UP and the opposition. Buoyed by its favorable showing in the election, in March 1973 the UP government introduced its plan to reform the educational system—a project known as ENU (Escuela Nacional Unificada, National Unified Education).[73] The opposition parties had a field day with the plan. Ignoring most of the specific proposals, they concentrated on the "ideological content of the project" and lambasted ENU as an attempt to brainwash

---

71 The interpretation of these results has been the subject of much debate. Scholars disagree over the best basis of comparison in order to gauge whether support for the UP increased or declined—the 1969 parliamentary elections, the 1970 presidential election, or the 1971 municipal elections. The UP received roughly the same percentage in the 1973 parliamentary elections as it had in the 1969 ones. If the 1969 parliamentary elections are used as a basis of comparison, the UP maintained—but did not increase—its percentage of the vote. However, as Allende pointed out, it was unprecedented in Chilean political history for a ruling party to increase its parliamentary vote over and above the percentage it received in the presidential vote. If the 1971 municipal elections are used, then the UP's percentage of the votes declined from 50 percent to 43.5 percent, indicating a loss of popularity from that date. For a discussion of this issue, see Manuel A. Garreton and Tomás Moulian, *Análisis coyuntural y proceso político: Las fases del conflicto en Chile, 1970–1973* (San José, Costa Rica: Editorial Universitaria Centroamericana Educa, 1978), 94–95, and Urzúa, *Historia política electoral*, 177–80.

72 Arturo Valenzuela summarizes this change by noting that "any attempts at reopening a dialogue . . . [between the UP and] the Christian Democrats, . . . received a further setback in the third week of May when the Christian Democratic party elected a 'hard line' slate to preside over the party's fortunes." See Valenzuela, *Breakdown*, 92.

73 For a description of ENU, see Kathleen B. Fischer, *Political Ideology and Educational Reform in Chile, 1964–1976* (Los Angeles: UCLA Latin American Center, 1979), 114–19.

children and impose totalitarianism and atheism on young people.[74] Conservative women opposed the ENU because they perceived it as an attempt on the part of the "communist state" to invade their homes and take control of their children. The PN attempted to stir up fear among Chilean mothers. In a typical PN advertisement, a pensive and pregnant woman stares out a window below the headline, "What can you expect for your child?" The caption reads, "Liberty or Communism?" and calls on Chileans to "reject [ENU]."[75]

For the first time since the UP's electoral victory, both the armed forces and the Catholic Church publicly criticized the government. Up until this point, the military had openly backed the government, and officers had served in Allende's cabinet. Nor had the church leadership previously indicated any disagreements with government policy; in fact, church-state relations were friendly. The level and sources of hostility to ENU convinced the government that it would gain little, and lose a lot, if it proceeded with the proposal. As a result, ENU was "shelved," and it was not advocated again during Allende's term.[76]

June, July, August, and the first weeks of September 1973 were months of extreme polarization and escalating conflicts. The cold weather only made people's lives more difficult. (Chile is in the southern hemisphere, so its seasons are opposite those in the United States.) Food was harder to come by, as was heating fuel. Cold rains made standing in lines for food—primarily a woman's job—all the more unpleasant, and the dampness increased the dreariness of homes that lacked sufficient heat. While these environmental factors did not define this period, they certainly exacerbated already frayed tempers and did nothing to alleviate the tension that permeated Santiago.

June opened with the strike of copper workers in the El Teniente mine in full swing, and it ended with the failed coup attempt on the 29th—the *tancazo*.[77] The miners' strike revealed that the left did not control all the unions and that a significant segment of the working class identified with the Christian Democrats.[78] On 29 June, an army regiment attempted a

74 Garreton and Moulian, *Análisis coyuntural*, 96.

75 *El Mercurio*, 11 May 1973.

76 Smith, *Church and Politics*, 197–99.

77 Miners in El Teniente, the huge copper mine located south of Santiago, went out on strike in April. Although they were among the most highly paid workers in Chile, they demanded even higher wages, which the government initially refused to grant them. See Chapter 6 for further discussion of the strike.

78 In mid-1972, the Christian Democrats won one-quarter of the votes in the CUT (Central Única de Trabajadores, National Labor Confederation): see Winn, *Weavers*, 233.

coup in conjunction with members of Patria y Libertad (Fatherland and Liberty), a neofascist organization. Tanks surrounded government buildings in downtown Santiago and fired shots at La Moneda, the presidential palace. General Prats intervened and convinced the leaders of the uprising to surrender, which they did after a few hours.[79]

The failed coup indicated several facts that the anti-Allende forces took into serious consideration. First, for the coup to be successful, the military needed to be united and to work together in a coordinated fashion. Second, workers in the *cordones industriales* had taken over 350 factories,[80] but they were unable to protect their government against the military. The forces that supported the Popular Unity government did not offer any real resistance to the attempted coup; the government had to rely on the military to defend it and to restore order.[81] Third, General Prats's pivotal role in suppressing the rebellion demonstrated that he had to be removed as commander in chief in order for the next coup to be a success.

The attempted coup added to people's growing sense of insecurity and fear. The second strike by the transportation workers, which began in late July, heightened these feelings and made people's lives intolerable. It aggravated the shortages of goods that plagued the nation and made life more difficult for women, who were responsible for providing food and other necessities for their families. The opposition (especially the *gremio* movement) joined the strike and effectively paralyzed huge sectors of the economy. By early September, one million people were on strike. Although this number did not include the industrial working class, it did involve most of the professional unions, such as doctors, and large numbers of the middle class.[82]

On 4 September 1973, the third anniversary of Allende's election, Popular Unity held a massive march to demonstrate the breadth of support that the government had. Hundreds of thousands of enthusiastic Chileans marched through the streets of downtown Santiago for hours. As they marched, they chanted "Allende, Allende, el pueblo te defiende" ("Allende, Allende, the people will defend you") and "luchando, creando, poder popular" ("fighting, creating, people power").[83] This enormous

79 *El Mercurio*, Edición Internacional, 25 June–1 July 1973; *¿Qué Pasa?* 5 July 1973; *Ercilla*, 4 July 1973. One important factor that made Prats's arguments persuasive was that no other army regiments or branches of the Armed Forces joined in the coup. It thus became clear to the coup leaders that they had no chance of success.

80 Collier and Sater, *History of Chile*, 354.

81 Garreton and Moulian, *Análisis coyuntural*, 101.

82 *El Mercurio*, 5 September 1973.

83 See *The Battle of Chile*, part 2, for excellent footage of the final march in support of the UP.

public confirmation of Allende's popularity did not deter the military. Seven days later, the Chilean armed forces overthrew the UP government and imposed the military dictatorship that lasted for almost two decades. In the next few weeks—and over the next seventeen years—the military imprisoned, tortured, exiled, murdered, and disappeared many who had marched that day in Santiago and hundreds of thousands of those throughout Chile who had supported the UP government.

The United States and Chile

The United States government actively opposed the Popular Unity government. It did so because it believed that the UP government directly threatened U.S. economic and political interests in Chile and the region. Following World War I, the United States had greatly expanded its economic interests in and political control over Latin America. After the war, England—which had dominated the world throughout the nineteenth century—ceased to be the global superpower it had been. Spared the destruction that six years of fighting had inflicted on Europe and confident from its 1898 conquest of Hawai'i, Guam, the Philippines, Cuba, and Puerto Rico, the United States emerged from the First World War with a developed infrastructure, unparalleled industrial capacity, surplus capital, a powerful military, and an expansionist spirit. With England in economic decline, U.S. capitalists freely invested in Latin America, taking over or expanding upon what the English had already developed.[84]

As England faded in importance, U.S. investments in Chile soared. The lion's share of North American money went into Chile's abundant mineral resources, the most profitable branch of the economy. Loveman estimates that by 1918—the end of the First World War—North American capitalists held "over 87 percent by value of Chilean copper production." As the century progressed, U.S. investment grew, deepening Chile's economic dependence on the United States; by 1930, as Loveman puts it, "United States capital would account for some 70 percent of all foreign investment in Chile."[85] U.S. corporate and financial involvement in Chile expanded up until Allende won the 1970 elections. In that year, international investment in Chile reached $1.67 billion, and most of that capital—$1.1 billion—originated in private investments by the United States. Not only was the United States the principal foreign investor in Chile, but its money was

84 For figures on U.S. and English investments in Latin America and a discussion of their significance, see James Dunkerly, "The United States and Latin America in the Long Run (1800–1945)," in *The United States and Latin America: The New Agenda*, ed. Victor Bulmer-Thomas and James Dunkerly (Cambridge: Harvard University Press, 1999), 3–31.

85 Loveman, *Chile*, 213.

also in the most strategic sectors of the economy—ranging from the copper, iron, and steel industries to radio and television.[86]

The enormity of U.S. economic power in Chile allowed the U.S. government to exert an inordinate amount of political influence as well. The end of World War II witnessed the beginning of the Cold War. During those years, U.S. government officials envisioned the world as a continuous (if frequently undeclared) battlefield in the war between the United States and the USSR for the hearts, minds, allegiances, and resources of the world's population. To be a friend of the United States meant being an enemy of the USSR, which required that a government treat the USSR's domestic representatives, the local communist party, with hostility.[87] The 1948 outlawing of the Chilean Communist Party provides one example of how the U.S. government used its economic power to influence internal Chilean politics.

In 1947, Gabriel González Videla, a member of the Radical Party, was elected president with the active backing of the Communist and Liberal parties.[88] In the eyes of the U.S. government, the presence of Communists in the González Videla government was the political equivalent of the USSR establishing a military beachhead in this southern nation. The United States made it clear that as long as Communists were members of the government, Chile could expect none of the loans the country urgently needed. In 1948, González Videla's government passed the inappropriately named Law for the Permanent Defense of Democracy, which outlawed the PC and relegated party members to camps in the arid north of Chile.[89]

The 1959 Cuban Revolution caused foreign policy experts in the United States to view Latin America with increased concern and alarm.

---

86 Cusack, *Revolution and Reaction*, 102–3.

87 For a speech that exemplifies this Cold War mentality, see Roy R. Rubottom Jr., Department of State Bulletin 6601, 3 March 1958.

88 This coalition of the left and right fully justifies the political—but perhaps not the literal—expression that politics makes strange bedfellows!

89 Although this law reflected U.S. government influence, it also responded to the domestic political needs of González Videla. In the late 1940s, the Communist Party enjoyed growing popularity, had significant influence in the labor movement, and encouraged workers to strike for higher wages and better conditions. This situation angered the right, which in turn pressured the González Videla government to bring the strikes—and Communist Party leadership—to an end. The passage of the law, therefore, reflects a confluence of domestic and international interests. See Collier and Sater, *History of Chile*, 246–51, and Loveman, *Chile*, 254–59, for a fuller discussion of this incident. For insight into the fate suffered by those the González Videla government sent into exile, see Lessie Jo Frazier, "Memory and State Violence in Chile: A Historical Ethnography of Tarapaca, 1890–1995" (Ph.D. diss., University of Michigan, 1998), 261–69.

The U.S. government wanted to prevent the spread of revolution to other Latin American nations at all costs. To accomplish this, the United States developed a two-pronged strategy: counterinsurgency training and the Alliance for Progress.[90] Through the counterinsurgency programs, the U.S. military taught the Latin American armed forces to oppose both domestic guerrilla forces and those sectors that could potentially become revolutionaries or provide support for them. From this perspective, the Latin American military was taught to view internal forces, not neighboring nations, as its prime enemy.

The Alliance for Progress was a highly ambitious program launched by President Kennedy with much fanfare in 1961. The U.S. government budgeted $20 billion to finance the project.[91] Like the counterinsurgency warfare strategy, the Alliance for Progress aimed at preventing the spread of revolution—but through reform and economic growth, not warfare. Those who formulated the Alliance for Progress believed that socioeconomic changes would generate increased development, create greater popular approval for the established government, and undercut the appeal of revolution. In order to achieve its goals, the Alliance preached the need for significant structural reforms (specifically, agrarian reform and industrial development). In practice, the programs suggested by the Alliance were seldom implemented. Moreover, instead of breaking up the landed estates that dominated Latin America and redistributing the land to the peasants, the Alliance supported the "technical modernization and the commercialization of Latin America's agricultural economy."[92] Jorge Alessandri was the Chilean president during the opening years of the Alliance for Progress. Although his government had passed an agrarian reform law in 1962, by November 1964, only 1,000 to 1,200 peasant families had received any land.[93]

Unlike Alessandri, President Frei enthusiastically embraced the Alliance for Progress, and he proclaimed his intentions to implement a more meaningful agrarian reform policy than Alessandri had. With Christian Democrat Frei as president, Chile became the showcase nation for the Alliance for Progress.[94] A long history of political stability, a highly

90 Stephen G. Rabe, *The Most Dangerous Area in the World: John F. Kennedy Confronts Communist Revolution in Latin America* (Chapel Hill: University of North Carolina Press, 1999), chapters 6 and 7.

91 John Gerassi, *The Great Fear in Latin America* (New York: Collier Books, 1965), 251.

92 Rabe, *Most Dangerous Area*, 169.

93 Paul E. Sigmund, *The United States and Democracy in Chile* (Baltimore: The Johns Hopkins University Press, 1993), 17.

94 James F. Petras and Robert LaPorte Jr., *Cultivating Revolution: The United States and Agrarian Reform in Latin America* (New York : Random House, 1971), 136.

educated and politicized population, a comparatively large middle class, strong leftist parties, and the growing popularity of the centrist and reformist PDC made it particularly attractive to the U.S. government. In order to finance these reforms, the United States spent, over the period from 1961 to 1970, $720 million in Chile—a figure that, per capita, exceeded expenditures on any other country in Latin America.[95] Despite the enormous expense and the tremendous political and moral backing the U.S. government extended to the PDC, Frei's party was simply unable to engineer the necessary reforms. The failure of the PDC to ameliorate the hardships endured by the majority of Chileans helped radicalize the population and bring about, in part, the presidential victory of Salvador Allende in 1970.

The U.S. Government and Allende's Presidential Victory

Several factors explain the U.S. government's implacable hostility to the Popular Unity government. First, as discussed above, the United States had invested a tremendous amount of economic and political capital in Chile by 1970. According to CIA Director Richard Helms, "U.S. private assets in Chile [totaled] about one and a half billion dollars."[96] Neither President Nixon nor Secretary of State Henry Kissinger had any desire to see this squandered, which is what they believed would happen if Allende won the election. Second, the practices adopted by the UP government in its first year in office confirmed the fears of U.S. government officials. Under Allende's leadership, the Chilean Congress voted unanimously in 1971 to nationalize U.S. mining companies' extensive copper holdings in Chile. To leaders and economic interests in the United States, this action represented both a hazardous precedent and a harbinger of future UP policies that they would adamantly oppose.

What made the Popular Unity government dangerous to the United States, however, was not its failure, but its success. The democratic election of Allende, a Marxist, directly contradicted Cold War propaganda in the United States that equated communism with totalitarianism and dictatorship. Not only did a plurality of the population choose Allende for president in 1970, but a majority of Chileans also voted for the UP in the 1971 municipal elections. Moreover, the Allende government offered an alternative to the peoples of Latin America, one that promised to respect the democratic process and to bring about profound economic and social

---

95 Collier and Sater, *History of Chile*, 310.

96 Richard Helms, briefing for the National Security Council, 6 November 1970, National Security Archives, online: <http://www.gwu.edu/~nsarchiv/NSAEBB/NSAEBB8/ch08-01.htm>.

changes peacefully. As a result, the Popular Unity government generated widespread enthusiasm and support throughout Latin America. This meant that U.S. government opposition to Allende was generally repudiated, and as a result, the United States could not isolate Chile as easily and successfully as it had Cuba. In addition, the U.S. government feared that Chile would provide support for Latin American revolutionary forces. As an "Options Paper" for the U.S. National Security Council warned, "Chile will probably become a haven for Latin American subversives and a staging ground for subversive movements in other countries despite Allende's desire to maintain normal relations within the hemisphere."[97]

A final factor explains the U.S. government's opposition to the UP. Despite their public show of optimism, it was fairly clear to U.S. policymakers by the early 1970s that this country could not win the war in Vietnam. The probable "loss" of Vietnam, the first serious military defeat of the United States in the twentieth century, caused the government to look upon Latin America with increased concern and possessiveness. Another socialist nation in Latin America would, according to U.S. diplomats, provide a second nearby base for the Soviet Union and threaten North American interests in the region. Henry Kissinger fully understood the geopolitical implications of a successful Popular Unity government. Speaking before the 1970 elections, Kissinger noted that

if Allende wins, there is a good chance that he will establish over a period of years some sort of communist government. In that case, we would have one not on an island off the coast (Cuba) which has not a traditional relationship and impact on Latin America, but in a major Latin American country you would have a communist government, joining, for example, Argentine [sic] . . . Peru . . . and Bolivia . . . so I don't think we should delude ourselves on an Allende takeover [sic] and Chile would not present massive problems for us, and for democratic forces for pro-U.S. forces in Latin America, and indeed to the whole Western Hemisphere.[98]

After Allende became president, the U.S. government employed a variety of measures to sabotage and weaken the Popular Unity government. In order to undermine popular support for Allende, the United States helped

97 For an interesting discussion of these issues from the U.S. government's perspective, see National Security Council, "Options Paper on Chile (NSSM 97)," 3 November 1970, National Security Archives, online: <http://www.gwu.edu/~nsarchiv/NSAEBB/NSAEBB8/ch24-01.htm>. Although the UP government did offer political asylum for those who faced persecution in their own countries, there is no indication that the government ever supported revolutionary forces acting in other nations.

98 Senate Select Committee, *Covert Action: Report*, 52.

exacerbate the economic problems that increasingly plagued Chile from the end of 1971 until the September 1973 coup. It cut aid to the Popular Unity government, made sure that no spare parts reached Chile, and pressured international financial institutions not to make loans to Chile. In order to intensify political pressure on the UP, the Nixon administration financed the opposition parties, organizations, and media.[99]

Although much of what the U.S. government did to destabilize the Allende government is known, much critical information has not yet been revealed. In 1998, the Clinton administration began to declassify documents relating to U.S. government involvement in Chilean internal affairs. It is important that all pertinent literature be declassified and released to the public in order to determine both the precise nature of U.S. intervention against the UP government and the extent of U.S. involvement in the 1973 coup that overthrew Allende. A better understanding of the means adopted by the United States to bring down the democratically elected government in Chile will hopefully ensure that such illegal practices cease to be part of U.S. foreign policy.

Conclusion

Salvador Allende's 1970 presidential victory was unprecedented: for the first time, a Marxist leader was made president as a result of democratic elections. The structural and political transformations that took place in Chile during the twentieth century help explain why Chileans voted for Allende. The economy evolved from a rural, agricultural base to an urban, industrialized one. Chilean peasants and workers both responded to these fundamental changes and promoted their development. Thousands of peasants abandoned the countryside to seek a better life and future in the cities, attracted by the promises of expanded economic and political possibilities, more freedom, better jobs—in a word, the shimmering allure of modernity.

The rise of an urban lifestyle, the emergence and concentration of working-class and popular organizations, and the intensification of political struggle helped create new identities among the poor, who increasingly saw themselves as people with rights and the ability to fight to obtain them. People's demands for inclusion in the economic, political, social, and cultural life of the nation hastened the demise of the traditional rightist Liberal and Conservative parties, fostered the growth of the centrist PDC, and increased support for the Socialist and Communist parties.

99 Ibid., 28–35.

In 1970, the Popular Unity coalition rode this wave of disappointment with the PDC to secure the electoral victory of Salvador Allende. The three years of the UP government were marked by intense and passionate conflict. The economic and political advances achieved during the UP's first year slowed in the second and ground to a halt by the third. This was neither inevitable nor irreversible. It was, instead, the concrete result of the decisions taken by all the major actors discussed above.

Anti-Allende women contributed materially and politically to the defeat of the UP. In order to understand why so many women mobilized against the progressive government, the next chapter examines the history of rightist women's political involvement in twentieth-century Chile.

2

Women's Political Incorporation and the Right

A Success Story

ONE OF THE outstanding features of the Chilean right has been its ability to appeal to and win the support of women. Much of the right's success is due in large part to the fact that it, unlike the left, has prioritized the organization of women. Women, in turn, have embraced the right and enthusiastically volunteered their services and time to help ensure its victory. The participation of many women as members of, campaigners for, or candidates of rightist parties has had an important impact on these parties. Their articulation of women's demands and aspirations has enabled the rightist parties to fashion programs that include women's concerns and to earn further support among women.

One factor that facilitated the right's success with women is that it affirmed the idea that women's primary functions in life were to be mothers and wives. Far from challenging this notion of what it meant to be a woman, the right defended it and geared its political discourse and policy to sustain it. The right was particularly skillful at developing platforms that spoke to women's needs in the domestic and public arenas: it simultaneously offered them concrete solutions to their problems and rejected the argument that women were oppressed.

The first part of this chapter explores Chilean women's involvement with politics during the twentieth century, focusing on women's participation with the right. The right's identification of women as mothers and housewives dovetailed with many Chileans' ideas about gender. In order to illustrate how conceptions of masculinity and femininity affected the lives—and the political choices—of many Chilean women, the second section of this chapter examines women and work in twentieth-century Chile. Women's relationship to work both stemmed from and reinforced the belief that women were mothers, first and foremost. For most of the twentieth century, the majority of women did not work outside the house. Instead, they dedicated themselves to their families and homes, while men labored to support their families financially. This reality favored the right's efforts to win and maintain women's support—just as it undercut the left's attempts to organize women. Women were much less likely than men to come into contact with leftist politics and organizing efforts, because the left largely concentrated on the industrial labor force, not on housewives and mothers. The right, on the other hand, directly and specifically targeted housewives and mothers in its campaigns.

This chapter's emphasis on the right and women should not obscure the fact that throughout much of the twentieth century, the centrist Radical Party and the leftist Communist and Socialist parties also waged active campaigns to organize women, developed programs directed toward them, and benefited from energetic female members and leaders who spoke for and to women.[1] However, since this book emphasizes women and the right, the following chapter will refer only briefly to these parties' policies and practices toward women. It does so primarily to illustrate that alternatives to the right did exist and to explain why the right had the degree of success in organizing women that it did.

Women Enter the Political Arena

During the nineteenth century and the first half of the twentieth, the male-led political parties denied women the right to vote in national or local elections. Because Chilean political life revolved around elections, women's exclusion from the voting process prevented them from enjoying formal and effective participation in national politics. Women finally gained the right to vote in congressional and presidential elections in 1949, after decades of struggle. One reason why many men and quite a few women accepted the parties' refusal to permit women to vote was that they concurred with the essentialist notion that women were fundamentally apolitical—that politics was men's business. They believed that women's hearts and minds were naturally attuned to domestic duties, which left them with little time or inclination to sully their purer nature in the dirty business of politics.

Women's first attempts to obtain the vote took place in the late 1800s and were carried out by individuals who apparently acted independently of each other. What is particularly notable about the women who first

1 For an insightful discussion of the left's relationship to women and women's political participation, see Karin Rosemblatt, *Gendered Compromises: Political Cultures and the State in Chile, 1920–1950* (Durham: University of North Carolina Press, 2000).

[handwritten margin note: Poder Femenino definitely disproves this]

struggled for the vote is their motivation to do so. Their religious beliefs and support for the Catholic Church, not a desire to be granted their rights as citizens, inspired these women to seek the vote. As Erika Valenzuela notes, they wanted to vote in order to defend the Catholic Church, which they believed was under attack by the anticlerical Liberal Party. Therefore, although these women acted as individuals (not as members of any organization), their efforts reflected the political goals of the Conservative Party, which was closely aligned with the Catholic Church.[2]

Domitila Silva y Lepe, a member of the elite, was the first woman to register to vote in 1875. A law passed the previous year had established "literacy as the only requirement for the enfranchisement of adult 'Chileans,'" which encouraged Silva y Lepe to act. Because the wording did not directly deny women the right to vote, several other women in Chile followed her example and registered to vote, also to defend the Catholic Church.[3] In order to prevent a repetition of this challenging behavior, the Congress, then dominated by the anticlerical Liberal Party, passed a law in 1884 that explicitly denied women the right to vote.[4] Women's connections with two of the more conservative institutions in nineteenth-century Chile—the church and the Conservative Party—led more progressive sectors to assume that granting women the vote was tantamount to enfranchising supporters of the Conservative Party. These women's actions also offer an early example of conservative women undertaking innovative actions to protect what they esteemed (in this case, the Catholic Church), just as during the UP years they did so in defense of the home and family.

Through its policy of Social Catholicism, the Catholic Church also provided the impetus for upper-class women to organize working-class women. This program, as Sandra McGee Deutsch describes it, "was the

---

2 See Erika Maza Valenzuela, "Catholicism, Anticlericalism, and the Quest for Women's Suffrage in Chile" (working paper 214, The Helen Kellogg Institute for International Studies, University of Notre Dame, 1995), 15–18. During the 1870s and 1880s, the anticlerical Liberal and Radical parties controlled the government. Under their rule, "reform laws were passed subjecting clerics to public trials and penalties in civil and criminal courts, releasing cemeteries from exclusive Church control, making civil marriage compulsory, and placing all civil records in the hands of the state." Both the church and the Conservative Party opposed these policies. For a further discussion of the ties between the Catholic Church and the Conservative Party, see Smith, *Church and Politics*, 71–72. Although the Liberal Party was anticlerical, it represented the interests of the Chilean elite and worked to maintain the social order.

3 Erika Valenzuela, "Catholicism, Anticlericalism," 15.

4 Edda Gaviola Artigas, Ximena Jiles Moreno, Lorella Lopresti Martínez, and Claudia Rojas Mira, *"Queremos votar en las próximas elecciones": Historia del movimiento femenino chileno 1913–1952* (Santiago: Centro de Análisis y Difusión de la Condición de la Mujer, 1986), 19.

church's attempt . . . to win workers away from religious indifference, liberalism, and socialism by proposing reforms that would not endanger the class hierarchy."[5] Upper-class Catholic women had long occupied themselves with charitable works. Now, the church's efforts to retain its hold on the increasingly organized and secular workers encouraged these women to direct their attention specifically toward this sector of the population. In order to facilitate their efforts, 450 of these women, led by Amalia Errázuriz de Subercaseaux and backed by the church hierarchy, started the Liga de Damas Chilenas (League of Chilean Ladies) in 1912.[6] The Liga organized working women into Catholic unions that would "uphold and defend the interests of those women who worked for a living without attacking the principles of order and authority." In 1914, the group formed a union of female store clerks and office employees, and in 1915, a union of seamstresses.[7] Through their work, these elite women better understood the lives of poor and working-class women and gained insight into how to organize them. After women obtained the right to vote, many of these upper-class women applied what they had learned from their experience in the Liga to their political organizing on behalf of the conservative parties.

A plethora of elite women's associations formed in Santiago in the early 1900s. Two of the first were the Santiago-based Círculo de Lectura de Señoras (Ladies' Reading Club) and the Club de Señoras (Ladies' Club), whose members were middle- and upper-class women. The upper-class women who formed the Club de Señoras, which they modeled on a U.S.-style reading club,[8] felt the need to educate themselves in order to better defend their social position from the inroads then being made by the growing, increasingly well-informed, and assertive middle class. Inés Echevarría, one of the members, explicitly expressed this sentiment when she explained the club's origins: "we were terrified that if our class continued to be ignorant, in two more generations our grandchildren would become lower class and the lower class would become the upper class."[9]

5 McGee Deutsch, *Las Derechas*, 23.

6 Ericka Kim Verba, "The Liga de Damas Chilenas [League of Chilean Ladies]: Angels of Peace and Harmony of the Social Question" (paper presented at the Latin American Studies Association meeting, Guadalajara, April 1997); Virginia Vidal, *La emancipación de la mujer* (Santiago: Editora Nacional Quimantú, 1972), 22.

7 Verba, "The Liga de Damas Chilenas," 9.

8 Paz Covarrubias, "El movimiento feminista chileno," in *Chile: Mujer y sociedad* (Santiago: UNICEF, 1978), 624–25.

9 Julieta Kirkwood, *Ser política en Chile: Los nudos de la sabiduria feminista* (Santiago: Editorial Cuarto Propio, 1990), 114.

Although these words reflect the sentiments of most of the club's members, it is interesting to note that some women promoted women's education in order to encourage their participation in civil society. Amanda Labarca—one of Chile's leading feminists, an anticlerical member of the Radical Party, and a founder of the Ladies' Reading Club—had such goals in mind for this women's group.[10] She firmly believed that women needed to be educated in order to play a more productive role in society. Instead of understanding education as a means by which to maintain class privilege, she held that "intellectual pursuits should be accompanied by greater involvement in social reform."[11]

These groups were not feminist, because most of their members neither believed that women were oppressed nor envisioned the need for any fundamental change in women's position in society. They were, however, some of the first organizations for women that were not under the direction of either the church or of men. They were unique because they consciously sought to enrich women's lives. As Ericka Verba points out, "they were the first secular, all-women associations of women from middle- and upper-class backgrounds organized around the gender-centered goal of promoting the cultural, social, and political uplift of women within Chilean society."[12]

In 1917, the Conservative Party introduced a law into Congress that called for women's voting rights—and thus became the first party to do so. (The law did not pass.) Reportedly, the Club de Señoras influenced the youth section of the Conservative Party to present this law to Congress.[13] The Conservative Party's sponsorship of this law, along with the action undertaken by the pious women who registered to vote in the 1870s, highlights a quality that has characterized the relationship between the rightist parties and women throughout much of the twentieth century: the right's willingness to undertake innovative actions that simultaneously promise to improve women's lives while maintaining women's subordinate position in society. For example, the Conservative Party was willing to extend voting rights to women; it did not plan, though, to relinquish men's control of either the party or the political system.

10 In the 1930s, Amanda Labarca was on the directorate of Acción Republicana (Republican Action), a rightist party composed of many members of the militia movement. See McGee Deutsch, *Las Derechas*, 154, 368 n 42.

11 Lavrin, *Women, Feminism, and Social Change*, 287.

12 Ericka Kim Verba, "The Círculo de Lectura de Señoras [Ladies' Reading Circle] and the Club de Señoras [Ladies' Club] of Santiago, Chile," *Journal of Women's History* 7, no. 3 (September 1995): 7.

13 Lavrin, *Women, Feminism, and Social Change*, 288; Gaviola Artigas et al., *"Queremos votar en las próximas elecciones,"* 35.

One fairly constant feature of the right in the twentieth century is that it did not hesitate to promote women's political activity when it found such activity beneficial. The Conservative Party was the first political party to actively pursue women's suffrage, just as during the Allende years the rightist National Party vociferously hailed women as the key political opponents of the Popular Unity government. That the Conservative Party supported voting rights for women should not, however, suggest that a desire to achieve women's equality guided its actions. Instead, the Conservative Party accurately understood that those sectors of women eligible and likely to vote would cast their ballots for the Conservatives.[14] One reason for this is that according to the law, only literate women could vote—a requirement that effectively limited the potential pool of female voters to upper- and middle-class women who could afford an education. In addition, the time and expense involved in securing the documents required to register, registering to vote, and actually voting discouraged poor women from participating in the electoral process.

A second similarity that emerges among conservative female activists in the early 1900s and during the Popular Unity government is that neither questioned a woman's role as wife and mother. In fact, many of the conservative forces saw women's voting rights as a means by which to expand the number of supporters of the status quo and of traditional gender roles. Similarly, the women who acted against the Popular Unity government mobilized to preserve their roles as wives and mothers in opposition to the government, which, they proclaimed, made it difficult for women to fulfill those roles.[15]

Third, in order to defend that which they held sacred, conservative women proved willing to undertake bold, unprecedented actions. They registered to vote at a time when no other women dared publicly to defy women's marginalization from politics. During the Popular Unity years, the granddaughters and great-granddaughters of these women took to the streets of Santiago and waved pots and pans to indicate their repudiation of the Allende government. They then used these same pots and pans to assault both government supporters and the police that opposed them.

Women and Local Elections

Women's first official foray into electoral politics took place on the local level in 1935, one year after women were granted the right to vote in

14 Lavrin, *Women, Feminism, and Social Change*, 300–301.

15 Conservative forces were not the only ones to accept these ideas about womanhood; feminists did, too. For a discussion of early Chilean feminist perspectives on women's roles, see Lavrin, *Women, Feminism, and Social Change*, 289–90.

municipal elections. Since the 1920s, a variety of women's organizations had advocated voting rights for women. Their work helped popularize the idea that educated women of the middle and upper classes deserved the opportunity to express their political views formally.

Several factors explain why the political parties decided to grant municipal voting rights to women and allow women to run in local elections. The parties understood the municipality to be an extension of the female domestic sphere because it primarily dealt with local, neighborhood issues.[16] Thus, granting female suffrage on this level did not violate a woman's primary role as wife and mother; it merely offered her the opportunity to vote on matters that directly affected her family's well-being.

In addition, the political parties could allow women to vote on the municipal level without risking their intrusion into any significant political issue that would substantially affect the nation. Granting women the municipal vote, then, allowed the parties to determine women's voting patterns *and* maintain control over national politics. A final element to consider here is the growing appeal exerted by the left at that time (as evinced, for example, in the attempt of military officers and other supporters to establish the Socialist Republic in 1932). One way to counter the left's appeal was to expand the voting public to include women. Conservative parties believed that they could count on women to vote for them and help defeat the Communist and Socialist parties.

They were right. In the 1935 municipal elections, the majority of women who voted cast their ballots for either the Conservative or the Liberal party.[17] However, it should be noted, so did the male voters. Not only did a large number of women vote for the conservative parties, but these parties also succeeded in electing the largest number of female candidates. Of the twenty-five women elected, sixteen were linked to the Conservative Party and five had ties to the Liberal Party.[18]

In acknowledgment of women's increased political importance, many of the parties established women's sections during the 1930s.[19] Each party hoped to use these formations to mobilize women to join and thereby

16 Elsa M. Chaney, *Supermadre: Women in Politics in Latin America* (Austin: The University of Texas Press, 1979), 21–24; Kirkwood, *Ser política*, 119–20.

17 Since the number of new voters (850,000) included both women and foreigners, it is hard to determine how many were women and how they voted. Of the newly added voters, only 76,049 (9 percent) voted, whereas 302,541 men, or 39 percent of a potential electorate of 770,000, voted. See Gaviola Artigas et al., *"Queremos votar en las próximas elecciones,"* 61.

18 In addition, "two Radicals, one Democrat, and one Independent" were elected (ibid.).

19 The Radical Party opened its membership to women in 1888. Only the Communist Party did not maintain a women's section in the 1930s. See Corinne Antezana-Pernet, "Mobilizing Women in the Popular Front Era: Feminism, Class, and Politics in the Movimiento

expand its electoral base. The sections served more as auxiliaries than as structures for empowerment: they offered women the facade of participation. Instead of encouraging their full integration, however, they isolated women from the upper echelons of power and committees in which the important political decisions were made.[20] While it caused some political parties to pursue women's votes with more energy, women's increased electoral weight did little to shake up the fundamentally male *modus operandi* of Chilean politics.

From the 1930s through the 1950s, the parties that most assiduously sought women's support were those on the right, especially the Conservative Party.[21] The Conservative Party devoted a great deal of energy and resources to winning women's allegiance, because it understood that women were one of its surest sources of support. Its close ties to the Catholic Church served to heighten the party's appeal to women whose religiosity was a primary feature of their lives and identities. In addition, the party presented itself as the most steadfast defender of the Chilean mother and family. It upheld women's primary function (as mothers) and defined itself as the party most able to obtain the order and security that women needed in order to fulfill that role.[22] Hoping to appeal directly to women's maternal identity, the Conservative Party peppered its campaign propaganda in the late 1930s with slogans such as "only the right will take care of your children" and "only the right will protect your families."[23] Their strategic targeting of women paid off. In the 1941 elections, two-thirds of female voters cast their votes for conservative candidates.[24]

An additional element that explains the high percentage of women who identified with the right was rightist women's ability to organize diverse

---

Pro-Emancipación de la Mujer Chilena (MEMCh), 1935–1950" (Ph.D. diss., University of California, 1996), 62.

20 For the dates on which the parties established their women's sections, see Santa Cruz et al., *Tres ensayos*, 244–45. As Corinne A. Pernet points out, "even in the Communist Party, where there was no women's section, women did not hold any leading positions" (personal correspondence, 8 December 1999).

21 The Chilean Naci Party proved to be the exception in that it did not, at least initially, attempt to organize women: as Sandra McGee Deutsch points out, "its vision of life was essentially 'virile and manly.'" However, in 1935, after women received the right to vote in the municipal elections, the Naci Party changed its position and allowed women to join. They were not particularly successful in recruiting women. At most, only several hundred women joined the party. For a discussion of both the Chilean Naci party and women's involvement in it, see McGee Deutsch, *Las Derechas*, 171–75.

22 Gaviola Artigas et al., *"Queremos votar en las próximas elecciones,"* 65.

23 Antezana-Pernet, "Mobilizing Women," 64.

24 Lavrin, *Women, Feminism, and Social Change*, 317.

groups of women in support of their politics—including women from other social classes. Several factors allowed the elite women who usually began and led the conservative women's organizations to extend their appeal. Many conservative women were well-to-do, and as a result, they had both disposable time and resources to dedicate to their causes. They offered no ideological challenge to traditional gender roles, even if their extensive activity did take them away from the home and their domestic responsibilities. In fact, they affirmed women's identities as wives and mothers and did not question women's subordinate status in society, which enhanced their appeal to other women who were content with their roles as wives and mothers. (This also meant that they represented no overt threat to men who wanted to preserve gender traditions as well.) The close connection between these women's organizations and the rightist parties illustrates the mutual support and shared understandings that defined their relationship. Equally important was the profound faith in the teachings of the Catholic Church and respect for its institutions and hierarchy that many women of all classes shared. Conservative women not only had the backing of the church, but they also typically carried out their political work in the name of the church, Christian ethics, and family values.

Along with guaranteeing the gender status quo, women and parties on the right articulated demands that would improve women's lives in concrete ways. For example, as part of their campaign to win the 1935 municipal elections, three members of a conservative women's organization, Acción Nacional de Mujeres (Women's National Action), called for "improved educational conditions for the population [and] better hygiene, . . . and [supported] the struggle against alcoholism."[25] Their demands did not suggest the need for any fundamental changes in women's position as mothers or in Chile's economic and social structure. However, the group did attempt to deal with some of the pressing problems that affected women—especially poor women, who wanted better schools for their children and suffered most from the diseases caused by poor sanitation and unhealthy water.

Acción Nacional de Mujeres exemplified conservative women's ability to build support beyond the elite and to struggle for women's rights while upholding a traditional view of womanhood. Adela Edwards de Salas, an upper-class woman with ties to both the Conservative Party and the Catholic Church (she had been active in the Liga de Damas Chilenas),[26]

25 Gaviola Artigas et al., "Queremos votar en las próximas elecciones," 62.

26 I thank Sandra McGee Deutsch for bringing her membership in this organization to my attention.

organized this group in 1934. The group's platform called for "full civil and political rights for women, . . . unity among women to oppose the legalization of divorce, which will destroy the family, and the passage of laws to provide maintenance, [as well as] a law that will suppress . . . alcoholism, and the corruption of minors."[27] In 1935, one year after the formation of Acción Nacional de Mujeres, thirty-five thousand women belonged to it.[28] And in that same year, Edwards, along with two other members (Elena Doll and Natalia Rubio), ran in the local elections in Santiago and won seats in the municipal government.[29]

Acción Nacional de Mujeres both appealed to and promoted the participation of working-class women, just as Feminine Power would do in the 1970s. At the second anniversary celebration for Acción Nacional de Mujeres in 1935, women workers spoke to the crowd and called for "a minimum wage, equal pay for women and men." They also encouraged the election of "women representatives in the Caja de Seguro Obligatorio [Obligatory Insurance Fund][30] and in the leadership of unions, in order to make sure [that these institutions] defend the proletarian woman." The assembled women enthusiastically adopted their demands and incorporated them into their program.[31]

Women, Politics, and the National Elections

Given the reluctance of many male politicians to grant women the right to vote, women from across the political spectrum formed their own groups in order to win full suffrage in national elections in the 1920s. Their determined efforts secured women's right to vote in national elections in 1949. In 1922, Graciela Mandujano and other women formed the Partido Cívico Femenino (Women's Civic Party), which included the vote among its goals.[32] In that same year the Consejo Nacional de Mujeres (National Women's Council), which had formed in 1919, publicized its program and called for "civil and political rights for women and explicitly advocated the vote for women." The Council believed that women should vote—not because they were citizens, but because their participation would clean up the electoral proceedings. Accordingly, the

27 *El Mercurio*, 23 June 1935.

28 Lavrin, *Women, Feminism, and Social Change*, 305. Because the source for these numbers is Adela Edwards de Salas, it is possible that the figures are exaggerated.

29 Gaviola Artigas et al., *"Queremos votar en las próximas elecciones,"* 62.

30 This was a government agency that dealt with workers' retirement and health insurance.

31 *El Mercurio*, 22 June 1935.

32 Lavrin, *Women, Feminism, and Social Change*, 292.

group argued that women should be granted the vote because they would "both purify and ennoble" the electoral process.[33]

The Council's voice, however, was not the only voice that supported voting rights for women. In 1935, the Movimiento Pro-Emancipación de la Mujer de Chile (MEMCh, Movement for the Emancipation of Chilean Women) was formed by women, many of whom were members or sympathizers of the Partido Comunista (Communist Party).[34] MEMCh was a unique organization, because it both struggled wholeheartedly for women's suffrage and advanced a radical program that envisioned, as its name indicates, the emancipation of women. Unlike most of the women's organizations then existing in Chile, MEMCh's members were predominantly working-class. They helped define the organization's political agenda, which, among other things, called for equal pay for female workers and demanded that "pregnant women and new mothers be paid their full salaries by the state, and that maternity benefits be extended to all working women."[35] Even as the organization fought for better conditions for mothers, it also advocated the right of women to choose or reject motherhood. In its 1935 program, MEMCh stated that "in order to emancipate women from unwanted maternity," the state should "make known and available contraceptive methods and [sponsor] scientific regulations that will allow us to combat the clandestine abortions and all the dangers they entail."[36]

During the 1940s, the movement for women's suffrage intensified and broadened. One clear indication of the growing appeal that voting had for women was the 1944 formation of the Federación Chilena de Instituciones Femeninas (FEChIF, Chilean Federation of Women's Institutions).[37] FEChIF included women from across the political spectrum and featured many of the more outstanding women who had struggled for the vote since the 1920s, such as Amanda Labarca and Graciela Mandujano.[38]

33 Covarrubias, "El movimiento feminista chileno," 626, 627.

34 For an excellent discussion of the history, politics, constituency, and programs of MEMCh, see Rosemblatt, *Gendered Compromises*, and Antezana-Pernet, "Mobilizing Women."

35 Ibid., 48, 131, 165.

36 As cited in Ximena Jiles Moreno and Claudia Rojas Mira, *De la miel a los implantes* (Santiago: Corporación de Salud y Políticas Sociales, 1992), 103.

37 Lavrin, *Women, Feminism, and Social Change*, 319.

38 In addition to founding the Ladies' Reading Club, Labarca contributed articles to *Nosotras* (*We Women*), the magazine of the Unión Femenina de Chile (The Chilean Women's Union), and argued that the Chilean practice of allowing annulments to occur—but not divorce—was hypocritical and unjust. It allowed the wealthy who could afford the expenses entailed by annulment to end their marriages, but not the poor who lacked the money to do so. See Lavrin, *Women, Feminism, and Social Change*, 286. Divorce is still illegal in Chile today, and the wealthy are still the only sector of society capable of financing an annulment.

Table 2.1 Results of the 1952 presidential elections, by gender

Candidate	Women's Vote	Men's Vote	Total
Carlos Ibáñez	**43%**	**48%**	**47%**
Arturo Matte	32	26	28
Pedro Alfonso	20	20	20
Salvador Allende	5	6	5

Note: Boldface type indicates the candidates who received the most votes.
Source: República de Chile, Servicio Electoral (Santiago: Servicio Electoral, n.d.).

However, as we shall see below, the breadth of political representation in FEChIF strengthened the pro-suffrage movement even as political differences among the diverse members led to internal divisions. After fighting for decades, Chilean women obtained the right to full suffrage in 1949 and first voted in national elections in 1952.

Since only 20 percent of women eligible to vote cast their ballots, the electoral results grant us only a partial insight into what women's political tendencies were at the time.[39] The most marked difference between women's and men's votes is that more women voted for Arturo Matte, the rightist Liberal Party candidate, than men. (See Table 2.1.[40]) More men voted for General Carlos Ibáñez than women did—by 5 percent—but he received a very high plurality from both genders and was elected president. An equal percentage of men and women cast their ballots for Pedro Alfonso, the Radical Party candidate. And while only 5 percent of women chose Salvador Allende, the Socialist Party candidate, only 6 percent of men did (a difference that is not significant).

All the candidates, except leftist Salvador Allende, made particular appeals to women. Carlos Ibáñez del Campo held a special event for women in the Caupolicán theater, in which he both extolled women as wives and mothers and promised that he would clean up politics.[41] Continuing the

---

39 In 1950, there were 6,081,931 Chileans, of whom 3,069,471 (50.5 percent) were women and 3,012,460 were men. See Teresa Valdés and Enrique Gomariz, *Mujeres latinoamericanas en cifras* (Santiago: FLACSO, 1992), 21, 99; Valdés and Weinstein, *Mujeres que sueñan*, 53.

40 The early electoral results primarily reflect the voting patterns of the elite in Chile. The electorate expanded when larger numbers of middle- and working-class Chileans began to vote in the late 1950s and early 1960s. It is at this point that we see a more pronounced gender gap between the male and female votes. Women of all classes continued to choose the more conservative candidate, while the additional votes of some middle- and many working-class men increased the number of ballots cast for the centrist or leftist candidates.

41 For an insightful discussion of gender politics and Ibáñez, see Elisa Fernández, "Beyond Partisan Politics in Chile: The Carlos Ibáñez Period and the Politics of Ultranationalism Between 1952–1958," (Ph.D. diss., University of Miami, 1996).

right's well-established practice of emphasizing the importance of women and their specific issues, the Liberal Party established a Women's Committee to support party candidate Arturo Matte Larraín. Matte appealed to women's religious and maternal identities, guaranteed them a better life, and offered them a grandiose vision of their role in Chilean society. Specifically, he condemned the Radical Party because it "poisoned your children with a secular and atheistic education," promised that under his presidency every woman would receive the home she deserved, and called on women to "join the cause of national salvation."[42]

The Dissolution of the Women's Movement

The pro–voting rights organizations that women had built generally ceased to function by the early 1950s, if not before.[43] Most female suffrage activists believed that they had achieved their goal and that the groups they had formed to obtain the vote were no longer needed. More particular factors led to the demise of MEMCh: internal conflicts, opposition from male leftists, and the heightened atmosphere of anticommunism that strongly marked the González Videla presidency beginning in 1947. Political and class differences within MEMCh weakened the organization. For example, while much of the middle-class leadership opposed women's dependence on men and challenged women's subordinate status to men within the family, many working-class members found marriage to be a positive alternative and supported their husbands' struggle for a higher wage. In addition, many leftist men rejected feminism, which they characterized as "stupid," and were less than enthusiastic about MEMCh.[44]

The intensification of the Cold War and the growing hostility toward communism expressed both by the United States and by President González Videla led to greater repression against members and sympathizers of the Chilean Communist Party. González Videla's sharp attack on communists extended beyond the party and affected the women's movement by fostering mistrust and division within and among organizations. For example, at a 1974 FEChIF congress, González Videla threatened to use force against communists. His provocative statement infuriated Elena Caffarena, a MEMCh leader, who "stormed out of the proceedings with other MEMCh members following."[45] In 1948, the

---

42 Gaviola Artigas et al., *"Queremos votar en las próximas elecciones,"* 82–83.

43 See Covarrubias, "El movimiento feminista chileno," 645–46, for a discussion of what happened to the different women's organizations.

44 Rosemblatt, *Gendered Compromises*, 80, 95–99.

45 Ibid., 248.

executive committee of FEChIF—many of whose members supported either the Radical Party and President González Videla or the anticommunist rightist parties—"expel[led] all member institutions that were affiliated with the Communist Party." As a protest against this undemocratic behavior, MEMCh withdrew from FEChIF, a move that simultaneously isolated MEMCh from the broader suffrage movement and deprived FEChIF of much of its base.[46]

The growing anticommunist sentiment that permeated Chilean politics in the late 1940s had a severe impact on MEMCh. As Corinne Antezana-Pernet points out, "While MEMCh in Santiago faced formal marginalization within the women's movement and in the mainstream political circles, the committees in the provinces suffered the brunt of direct persecution by the government."[47] The government sent the leadership of some provincial MEMCh chapters to Pisagua, a prison camp in northern Chile that housed many communists who were victims of government repression. In some of the northern mining towns, where both the Communist Party and MEMCh were strong, the government prohibited the women's group from holding any meetings.[48] The external attacks and internal weaknesses undermined MEMCh's ability to project a more progressive vision of women and politics—and allowed more conservative ideas about both to dominate. By the end of the 1940s, MEMCh and FEChIF (two of the most important women's organizations in Chile) could not possibly maintain an ongoing women's movement.

Once they obtained the vote, the female activists lacked a shared purpose. In its absence, political and class divisions came to the foreground and separated the activists who had fought together so determinedly for the vote. In response, most women returned to or continued their roles as wives and mothers, limiting their political participation to voting. Their struggle for political and social rights as women had temporarily ended. A small number of women joined the political parties,[49] but they were usually absorbed into the rank and file and carried out programs designed by the predominantly male party leadership.

Not only did few women achieve leadership positions within their respective parties, but a very small number of them ever held elected

46 Antezana-Pernet, "Mobilizing Women," 362.

47 Ibid., 365.

48 For a vivid description of the various measures of repression that the government—in conjunction with mining companies and merchants—enacted against MEMCh, see ibid., 365–74.

49 According to Kirkwood, women constituted no more than 10 percent of the membership of the political parties. See Kirkwood, *Ser política*, 148.

office. According to a recent study, "between 1949 and 1973, women on average held only four percent of the seats in Congress. . . . At the municipal level (between 1944 and 1973), women on average occupied only four percent of the municipal council seats."[50]

Women's Political and Social Activity from the Late 1940s to the Early 1960s

Although most women's independent organizations dissolved once suffrage was granted, the Partido Femenino Chileno (Chilean Women's Party) continued its work. Founded in 1946 by María de la Cruz, the party grew to have twenty-seven thousand members in the early 1950s.[51] De la Cruz's leadership of this independent women's party reflected her belief that gender differences defined women and men, a distinction she was not inclined to challenge. According to de la Cruz, "ideas divide men, while feelings unite women."[52] Like many other women who struggled for universal suffrage, de la Cruz professed women's moral superiority to men, a quality that both entitled women to vote and promoted a cleaner electoral process.

In the early 1950s, María de la Cruz allied herself with Carlos Ibáñez, who—after having ruled Chile dictatorially from 1927 to 1931—was elected president in 1952. He received the plurality of votes as a result of the populist promises he made, the mass appeal he generated, and the divisions that existed in some of the other parties.[53] Ibáñez, in turn, supported de la Cruz and her party. In 1953 she ran for his vacant senatorial seat and, upon winning, became the first female senator in Chile. Shortly thereafter, the Senate disqualified her and threw her out of the Senate. Why did this happen, and how did it affect women's political involvement?

50 Mark P. Jones and Patricio Navia, "Assessing the Effectiveness of Gender Quotas in Open-List Proportional Representation Electoral Systems," *Social Science Quarterly* 80 (June 1989): 346.

51 Gaviola Artigas et al., "*Queremos votar en las próximas elecciones,*" 73. Prior to founding the party, María de la Cruz had not been politically active. In fact, according to Elisa Fernández, "she was considered extraordinary, in part, because she survived the loss of two husbands" whom she had nursed during their illnesses. Thus, what qualified her to participate in politics was not experience but the ability to care for and nurture others—in her case, men. See Fernández, "Beyond Partisan Politics," 301.

52 Ibid. Similarly, during the Popular Unity government, the women of Feminine Power maintained that women's ability to unite—as opposed to men's divisive struggles for political power—strengthened the opposition to Allende. During the Allende years, de la Cruz supported the rightist National Party and participated in women's activities against the Popular Unity government. See *¿Qué pasa?* 1 February 1973.

53 Divisions existed both within the Socialist Party and between it and the Communist Party.

In 1953, three women accused de la Cruz of "ideological commitments" to Peronism and of having "illegally imported watches."[54] Although a special committee established by the Senate subsequently found her innocent, a majority of senators voted to remove her from the Senate.[55] According to Julieta Kirkwood, the public accusations of guilt lodged against Chile's first female senator had a profound impact on women's political involvement and self-perception. It made them feel less secure about their capacity to hold elected office and undermined their belief that women would make better politicians than men did. Many women left the Partido Femenino Chileno, apparently believing that de la Cruz's fall revealed that "women were 'not sufficiently prepared' for politics." Regardless of whether this was the goal of male politicians—and Kirkwood suspects that it was—it effectively decimated the party, offering those women who did want to be politically active no alternative but to join the already constituted and male-dominated political parties. Moreover, it left female voters no choice but to cast their votes for the predominantly male candidates. As Kirkwood notes, "in other words, [male politicians] allowed women to participate in politics. They called upon them [to be active politically]. All the parties directed their propaganda at them, but as backroom allies, not as contenders."[56]

The organizations that attracted the largest number of women from the late 1940s to the mid-1960s revolved around social issues that primarily affected the Chilean woman as wife and mother. While their initiatives worked to improve women's lives, they did not undermine women's subordination to men. Instead of questioning a woman's role as wife and mother, they were both based upon it and served to reinforce it. One such formation was the Asociación de Dueñas de Casa (Housewives' Association). The Housewives' Association adopted some of the ideas and tactics first established by the progressive female consumers' movement. (This movement, which began in the mid-1930s, mobilized women to demand that local retailers sell their products at the price set by the Commissariat for Subsistence Goods and Prices.[57] When the González Videla government brought the consumers' movement under state control, it stripped

---

54 Kirkwood, *Ser política*, 169–70. De la Cruz enthusiastically supported Argentine president Juan Perón and declared herself a "Justicialista diehard." (The Justicialist Party was the party of Perón.) See *¿Qué pasa?* 1 February 1973.

55 Fernández, "Beyond Partisan Politics," 291–305.

56 Kirkwood, *Ser política*, 170–73.

57 For a discussion of the politics of the consumers' movement and the various organizations that were part of it, see Rosemblatt, *Gendered Compromises*, 116–21.

the movement of any autonomy and militancy and undercut leftist and feminist attempts to organize women against the high cost of living.)

In 1947, First Lady Rosa Markmann sponsored the Association in order to educate women, especially poor ones, about how to be better homemakers. The organization trained women to manage their resources more carefully and inspect prices charged by local businesspeople to determine whether they were too high. The combination of government support for the project and women's economic needs generated enthusiasm for the group. By 1948, "more than 200 housewives' groups were formed across Chile with over 1,500 participating ad-honorem price inspectors."[58] According to one estimate, two hundred thousand women belonged to the organization.[59] As Markmann recounts, "a group of women with their children began to check the prices of goods." The inspectors reported their findings to the government, which pledged to fine any business whose prices were excessive.[60] Although they had quite different political perspectives on many issues, it is notable that the Radical Party-led Housewives' Association *and* the progressive female consumers' movement that preceded it both responded to and reinscribed women's position within the home and family.

Homeless women also participated in (and many times, directed) land seizures, the subsequent construction of their homes, and the establishment of communities. The growth in the urban population described in Chapter 1 meant that many people living in Santiago in the 1950s and 1960s lacked homes, running water, and electricity. In order to obtain these basic necessities, homeless people—often working in conjunction with leftist parties—occupied land and proceeded to construct their homes on it. In 1957, for example, poor people took over land in the southwest part of Santiago and built the community of La Victoria. The women's committee that formed after the takeover assumed charge of the medical clinic and worked to ensure that the inhabitants respected the rules of the community. Because they believed that alcoholism frequently led to sexual and physical abuse as well as the spending of scarce household money, they made sure that no liquor was sold in La Victoria.[61]

Many women perceived their political activity as an extension of their female identity as wife and mother. As a result, conservative forces'

---

58 Antezana-Pernet, "Mobilizing Women," 363.

59 "Madre Universal" (n.p.: IBM World Trade, 1952), 2.

60 Rosa Markmann de González Videla, interview by author, tape recording, Santiago, 5 January 1994.

61 Valdés and Weinstein, *Mujeres que sueñan*, 49–50.

appeals to women as wives and mothers resonated with them, because such appeals confirmed their fundamental belief in who they were. While most men worked outside the home, coming into contact with a variety of situations and people, the majority of women spent long hours of the day in the relative isolation of their homes. There they cleaned, prepared the food, washed and ironed the clothes, and took care of their families. Their lives revolved around their domestic responsibilities, just as men's were organized to fulfill their role as economic providers. In order to understand the impact of this reality on women's political consciousness, the next section discusses women and work.

Women and Work: Reflecting and Reinforcing a Conservative Definition of Womanhood

The fact that most Chilean women did not work outside the home made them more susceptible to rightist politics than men were. Men were more likely to be exposed to new ideas and involved in political debates, while women more typically spent much of each day working alone or chatting with neighbors, listening to romantic music or watching soap operas (two forms of entertainment that have seldom been associated with the propagation of radical ideas). While working-class men came into contact with leftist politics at the workplace, the primary outside influences for many working-class women were the Catholic Church or, after 1964, the Christian Democratic Party-controlled Mothers' Centers.

Ideas about womanhood shaped women's participation in the labor force, as did the demands of their domestic roles. For women who lacked maids or nannies, working outside the home—in addition to doing the cooking, cleaning, laundry, and childcare within the home—represented an additional burden, not liberation. Only a minority of women held paying jobs (although the percentage of women who received a salary varied throughout the twentieth century), but a majority of men did. Women took care of the home and family, and men held financially responsibility. Social attitudes and economic factors both shaped this reality and, in turn, were influenced by it: the gendered division of labor discouraged women from working outside the home, even when economic necessity or personal preference might have encouraged them to do so. Definitions of womanhood also affected the types of jobs available to women, the salaries and wages they received, and their families' attitudes toward their outside work.

In 1907, women accounted for 28 percent of the paid labor force (a figure that was not surpassed until 1978, when 29 percent of the labor force was female).[62] The numbers fluctuated, though: women constituted 27 percent of the labor force in 1920, only 20 percent in 1930, and 25 percent in 1952.[63] During the 1950s, this figure decreased again, reaching a low of 22.4 percent in 1960 and growing only slightly during the decade to reach 22.8 percent in 1970. From the 1970s through the 1980s, women's participation in the labor force demonstrated a slow but steady climb.[64] However, the percentage of women in the labor force did not exceed 30 percent until the 1980s.[65]

A large number of women who worked outside the home were domestic servants in the homes of the middle and upper classes. As a result, many female workers were not part of the industrial workforce, the labor sector where the left concentrated most of its organizing efforts. Instead of spending their working hours in the company of other workers whose experiences mirrored those of their own, these women lived surrounded by the families of Chile's elite and middle class. From the 1920s to the 1970s, somewhere between 25 to 40 percent of working women were employed as servants.[66] In 1970, 655,000 women worked outside the home, approximately one-quarter of them as domestic servants.[67] As domestic employees, many of these women experienced relationships with their employers that were individualized, isolated, and intimate. Their work had a degree of ambiguity that was usually absent from jobs in large factories. Proximity to their employers' families also exposed these women to both the possibility of friendship and love and the likelihood of abuse. Although the disparity between their conditions and those of their employers could exacerbate feelings of class-based resentment, it could also produce a blurring of differences and a sense of identification with a higher class.[68] In either case, it meant that women who worked as domestic servants were unorganized, positioned outside the union

62 Elizabeth Quay Hutchinson, "'*El fruto envenenado del arbol capitalista*': Women Workers and the Prostitution of Labor in Urban Chile, 1896–1925," *Journal of Women's History* 9 (Winter 1998): 131; for the 1978 figure, see Valdés and Gomariz, *Mujeres latinoamericanas*, 39.

63 Antezana-Pernet, "Mobilizing Women," 46.

64 Centro de Estudios de la Mujer, *Mundo de mujer: Continuidad y cambio* (Santiago: Centro de Estudios de la Mujer, 1988), 198, 203.

65 Valdés and Gomariz, *Mujeres latinoamericanas*, 39.

66 Antezana-Pernet, "Mobilizing Women," 45; Covarrubias, "El movimiento feminista chileno," 207.

67 *Chile Hoy*, 27 October–2 November 1972.

68 For a perceptive discussion of this situation, see Vidal, *La emancipación*, 59–61.

movement, and not possessed of effective means by which to air and remedy their grievances.[69]

Professional women, whose numbers increased during the twentieth century, constituted a second important category of women who worked outside the home.[70] Although some women were lawyers, architects, and agronomists, most professional women were teachers, nurses, and social workers. One outstanding feature of Chile's educational system is that it was the first one in Latin American to allow women to be trained professionally. In 1877, Miguel Luis Amunátegui, the minister of public education, declared that women "could advantageously practice some of the scientific professions" and that it is "important to provide women with the means by which they can earn their own living."[71] As a result of this liberal attitude, in 1886 the Chilean Eloísa Díaz became the first Latin American woman to receive a degree as a medical doctor.[72]

The educational opportunities open to women in Chile allowed some women to pursue intellectual paths and prepare for careers that had been denied their mothers and grandmothers. At the same time, both the educational system and the women who obtained a university diploma reflected specific class realities and gender perceptions. A college degree was a privilege enjoyed by only the small number of Chileans whose families could afford to pay for their education. In 1970, roughly 77,000 Chileans—not even 1 percent of the total population of 8,885,000—attended the university. Of that number, 62 percent were men and 38 percent were women.[73]

Women's access to higher education allowed them to obtain paid positions as professionals. However, their presence in the workforce does not appear to have altered conceptions of gender. The academic careers women pursued usually extended their roles as wives and mothers into the workplace. The top three professions taken up by women in the twentieth century were in the fields of education, health, and the social sciences.[74]

69 In (and after) 1926, diverse unions formed to represent household workers. Their efforts reached a high point during the Popular Unity government, but the military coup brought them to a sudden end. For a history of their work, see Aída Moreno de Valenzuela, "History of the Household Workers' Movement in Chile, 1926–1983," in *Muchachas No More: Household Workers in Latin America and the Caribbean*, ed. Elsa M. Chaney and Mary García Castro (Philadelphia: Temple University Press, 1989).

70 In 1972, 16 percent of the women who worked held professional positions. See Michèle Mattelart, "Feminine Side," 31 n. 13.

71 Felicitas Klimpel, *La mujer chilena: El aporte femenino al progreso de Chile, 1910–1960* (Santiago: Editorial Andrés Bello, 1992), 232.

72 Vidal, *La emancipación*, 31–32.

73 Santa Cruz et al., *Tres ensayos*, 211; Valdés and Gomariz, *Mujeres latinoamericanas*, 66.

74 Santa Cruz et al., *Tres ensayos*, 222–25.

The availability of domestic servants who worked for low wages made these women's labor outside the home both possible and socially acceptable. Professional women considered themselves responsible for the functioning of their households; their economic status made it possible for them to hire other women to carry out their domestic duties. One study found that in the late 1960s, 100 percent of wealthy women and 88 percent of middle-class women who worked outside the home had maids.[75]

Because most women and men accepted that a woman was destined to be a wife and mother, the variety and number of jobs open to women were more limited than those available to men. In 1970, close to 75 percent of women did not work outside the home. About 24 percent of women who did work outside the home held factory jobs, compared with 61 percent of men.[76] A large number of these women were concentrated in textile, food, chemical, and pharmaceutical production.[77] Since only 23 percent of all the women in Chile worked for wages at that time, no more than 5 to 6 percent of Chilean women were part of the industrial labor force in the early 1970s. Seventy-three percent of working women (and only 39 percent of men) worked in the service sector.[78]

Women's position in the workforce, combined with the union's traditional emphasis on organizing the male worker, marginalized most women from the union movement during the Popular Unity years. The leftist parties and the Christian Democratic Party all concentrated their organizing efforts on the industrial workforce and on miners (and the latter group excluded women). By and large, they ignored or at least failed to focus on those areas of work that attracted female workers. As a result, most women in the workforce were not unionized during this period.

The belief that women did not and should not work outside the home helped keep women's wages lower than men's. In addition, women's household labor was both unpaid and unrecognized as work. Therefore, as the majority of jobs available to women outside the home consisted of occupations that reflected their domestic duties, it is not surprising that their services continued to be undervalued and underpaid. Women's limited access to jobs, the large number of low-paying service jobs they held, the fact that most female workers were not unionized, and the idea that a man was the family's main breadwinner all explain why so few women worked outside the home and why they earned substantially less money than men did.

75 Michèle Mattelart, "Feminine Side," 31 n. 13.

76 Ibid., 209.

77 Vidal, *La emancipación*, 58.

78 Covarrubias, "El movimiento feminista chileno," 208.

Table 2.2 Wages and salaries in Santiago, by gender

Year	Men's Earnings, Using 1970 as Base Year	Women's Earnings, Using 1970 as Base Year	Women's Earnings, Compared with Men's
1960	66.75%	30.78%	46%
1965	69.73	36.95	53
1970	100.81	60.95	61
1971	127.59	73.16	57
1972	87.21	52.34	60
1973	41.12	24.58	60

Note: The table takes 1970 as the base year for comparison; in the first two columns, wages are represented as a percentage of earnings in 1970. Salary and wage figures were calculated on the value of the peso in 1980.
Source: Pardo Vásquez, *Una interpretación de la evidencia*, 9.

The fact that men earned more than women helped to reinforce and maintain a gendered division of labor. Table 2.2 illustrates several important points regarding wages and salaries. Taking salary levels in 1970 as the basis of comparison, the table indicates that both women's and men's pay rose substantially in 1970 and 1971 (compared with salary and wage levels in the 1960s), dropped in 1972 as the economy worsened, and sank again in 1973 when the economic situation deteriorated. It also shows that women's pay lagged far behind men's. It is notable, however, that the difference between women's and men's salaries lessened in 1970 and remained relatively stable during these years of economic crisis. Such improvements in women's salaries were due, in part, to the UP government's efforts to increase general wages and equalize those of women and men.[79]

A woman's lower earnings made it less economically worthwhile for her to work outside the home and increased the family's dependence on the man's income for survival. As a result, married women or women who lived in stable relationships with men were far less likely to hold paying jobs than single ones were. Although married women outnumbered single ones in the overall population, far more single women worked outside the home than married ones did.[80] According to the 1970 census, single women were

79 Pardo points to women's increased levels of education—and the corresponding drop in both fertility and infant mortality—to explain the smaller wage gap between women and men. These developments meant that women had increased leisure time around the home and a heightened ability to access better jobs. See Lucía Pardo Vásquez, *Una interpretación de la evidencia en la participación de las mujeres en la fuerza de trabajo: Gran Santiago 1957–1987* (Santiago: Universidad de Chile, 1989), 1–2.

80 Employers' preference for single women also affected this figure. Employers favored single women over married women because they believed that married women were more likely to

almost twice as likely as married ones to work outside the home. Approximately 87 percent of formally married women (or those in common-law marriages) did not work outside the home; only about 12 percent— 177,960 out of 1,444,360—did. By comparison, roughly 26 percent of single women worked outside the home.

Many Chileans accepted this gendered division of labor because they believed that men and women were fundamentally different and, as a result, had separate functions to fulfill within society. A study of Chileans' attitudes toward women—and, by implication, toward men—entitled *La mujer chilena en una nueva sociedad (The Chilean Woman in a New Society)* sheds light on how people thought about men and women and their respective social roles in the late 1960s. The study, which is based on surveys carried out with women and men of all classes and in urban, rural, and fishing communities, confirms the gendered division of responsibilities and identities.[81] With the sole exception of upper-class women, who relied on servants to carry out the household chores, the majority of women believed that in order to be a good mother and wife, a married woman must "devote herself to her home . . . await the arrival of her husband, take care of her children, [and] know how to run her home."[82]

If a married woman's primary responsibility was to be at home, then a man's chief duty was "to sustain the home." When asked, "Do you believe that a married woman should work outside the home?" men responded in a way that paralleled this perception of what each gender's role within the family should be. Although 52 percent of upper-middle-class men said

---

become pregnant. According to Chilean labor laws, employers had to grant women six weeks of rest before and after they gave birth, a reality that explains the tendency of employers to hire single women. See *El Mercurio*, 4 June 1972. For the figures from the 1970 census on married and single female workers, see *Chile Hoy*, 27 October–2 November 1972. Even though single women were more likely than married women to work outside the home, they generally did not do so (approximately 72 percent of single women—923,420 of 1,280,220—did not engage in outside work).

81 One of the authors of the book, Michèle Mattelart, concluded that "women are a very valuable element within Chilean society. I was struck by their greater ability to adapt to changes, even the most profound ones, than men. But, at the same time, . . . it is perhaps women's sense of tradition that stops them from visualizing these changes. They therefore adapt themselves in an almost instinctive fashion" (*Eva*, 5 July 1968, 11).

82 Armand Mattelart and Michèle Mattelart, *La mujer chilena en una nueva sociedad: Un estudio exploratorio acerca de la situación e imagen de la mujer en Chile* (Santiago: Editorial del Pacifico, 1968), 59. The study offers no explanation for why only 40 percent of upper-class women said that married women should be "good mothers and wives" (as opposed to much higher percentages of women from all other classes). I believe, however, that their response is due to the fact that these women relied on domestic servants to carry out most of their household duties and were more inclined to spend their time in social activities, which took them out of the home and away from their children.

that women *should* be able to work outside the home, urban men of all other classes were unequivocal in saying "No." However, the majority of urban women—of *all* classes—responded with a resounding "Yes." In order to explain their firm opposition to women working outside the home, the men claimed that a working wife would neglect her domestic duties and her children. Some expressed fear that having a job would offer a woman increased opportunity for sexual relations with other men. Most women did not express these concerns. Perhaps they considered the latter possibility unlikely—or perhaps they considered it likely, viewing it as a further enticement to obtain work outside the home.[83]

The Popular Unity government did not effect a substantial change in attitudes among men and children. According to a study done by the Ministry of Labor in 1973, the majority of husbands and children opposed the idea of their wives and mothers being part of the paid workforce; they expected them to be at home, caring for them. (Unfortunately, there are not comparable figures for what women thought.) Roughly 60 percent of the husbands and 59 percent of the children surveyed reported an unfavorable attitude toward women working outside the home; only 37 percent of husbands (and 35 percent of children) perceived women's outside work favorably.[84]

Conclusion

During the first half of the twentieth century, the struggle for the vote absorbed much of Chilean women's political energies. However, neither women's fight for full suffrage nor their involvement in other activities, such as the Housewives' Association or land takeovers, led them to question their role as mothers and wives. In fact, most of the work they undertook was both premised on this definition of themselves and served to reinforce it. As a result, women's half-century struggle for the vote and other political activities left gender roles in Chile largely unchallenged and intact.

The right both affirmed this definition of womanhood and used it to build support for itself among women. Conservative Catholic women were the first Chilean women who attempted to register to vote, just as

83 Ibid., 63, 114–20. To the question posed by the study, 70 percent of upper-class men, 48 percent of upper-middle-class men, 76 percent of lower-middle-class men, and 80 percent of lower-class men said "No." Women disagreed. Of upper-class women, 80 percent said "Yes," and that answer was echoed by 70 percent of upper-middle-class women, 74 percent of lower-middle-class women, and 52 percent of lower-class women.

84 For the 1973 Ministry of Labor study figures, see *Ramona*, 13 February 1973. In the study, only 2.7 percent of husbands and 5.78 percent of children reported an "indifferent" attitude toward the idea of women working outside the home.

the rightist Conservative Party was the first party to sponsor a bill in Congress to grant women that right. Conservatives promised female voters that they would protect women and children from all danger by defending the family and women's role within it. And many women believed them! From the 1930s until the 1960s, the majority of voting women cast their ballots for conservative candidates. One factor that facilitated the right's capacity to organize women was the enthusiastic involvement of its many female supporters. Not only were they some of the most visible spokespersons on the right, but they were also able to articulate clearly issues of deep concern to many women.

The right proved adept at devising political programs that proposed specific improvements in women's lives without fundamentally questioning women's subordinate position within society. Acción Nacional de Mujeres, for example, opposed alcoholism, because liquor made men more likely to abuse women and children and to waste money their families needed. At the same time, because the group firmly believed that the family was one of the fundamental pillars of society, it fought legislation to make divorce legal—legislation that would have made it easier for women to sever their ties to the men who abused them.

The most significant attempt undertaken by leftist women to build an alternative political organization for women, MEMCh, was ultimately unable to sustain itself. Attacked by an increasingly conservative and anti-communist government and weakened by internal divisions, MEMCh disbanded at a time when its progressive vision appeared to be reaching growing numbers of Chilean women. The demise of MEMCh left the political space wide open for more conservative discourses on women and politics. Organizations like the Housewives' Association (headed by First Lady Rosa Markmann) stepped in to fill the gap and to organize women as wives and mothers, not as political activists or as citizens.

In Chile, politics, work, and ideas about gender shaped and reinforced each other. When women entered the political arena, they did so in their traditional roles, not as citizens who had just as much right to determine the politics of their nation as men did. Women's acceptance of their gendered identities helped define both their relationship to politics and male politicians' perceptions of their involvement in the public sphere. The parties were willing to establish women's sections; the primary function of those sections, however, was to expand the electoral base and incorporate women into the parties, not to facilitate women's access to political power. By and large, women were neither party leaders nor elected officials. In short, the public face of politics in Chile continued to belong to men.

Being a woman meant taking care of children, husband, and home; being a man meant being the family's economic mainstay. Most women worked in their own households, a form of labor that was both individualized and isolating. Men, on the other hand, worked in more socialized forms of production and shared their daily work experiences with other men. This gendered division of labor encouraged women to view their family's well-being as their fundamental concern and reinforced the idea that ensuring its welfare was their overriding mission in life. This attitude also defined women's role in politics, which they interpreted in the context of their domestic responsibilities. Women's devotion to their homes and families removed them from the mainstream of left organizing efforts and political battles—many of which took place in the unions and the workplaces where men spent the better part of their days. As we shall see in subsequent chapters, the confluence of women's emphasis on the family and home and their distance from leftist organizing greatly facilitated the right's attempts to coordinate women to contest the Allende government.

3

Anticommunism and the Mobilization of Women

The 1964 Presidential Campaign

AS THE CHILEAN political spectrum shifted to the left during the 1960s, the right declined in strength. This political turn led to the demise of the Conservative and Liberal parties, the traditional parties of the right. However, the passing of these parties did not mean the disappearance of the Chilean right; instead, it forced the right to reformulate itself, an important process that is frequently obscured by the attention paid to the centrist and leftist parties in these years. During the 1960s, the right formed a new, more modern party, the National Party, and it influenced the development of a new type of organization—the *gremios*, or guilds.

Women figured prominently in both the development and projection of the Chilean right during the 1960s. Indeed, the right's focus on women was central to its efforts to reconstitute itself in a challenging political landscape. The right believed that by prioritizing women, it would broaden its appeal to the growing electorate (in which women were increasingly represented). In order to illustrate the relationship between the right, women, and Chilean politics during these years, this chapter examines the conservative women's group Acción Mujeres de Chile (Women's Action of Chile), which formed in 1963, and the Scare Campaign, which took place during the 1964 presidential elections.

The U.S. government helped design and finance the Scare Campaign. Drawing on ideas about gender and anticommunism prevalent in the United States—as well as their knowledge that in Chile, women voted more conservatively than men did—U.S. government officials worked with Chilean politicians to develop the Scare Campaign. Washington's sponsorship of this anti-Allende and anticommunist propaganda campaign reveals that in the 1960s, and perhaps before, U.S. foreign policy incorporated a sophisticated understanding of gender in its attacks against the Latin American left. Two important models served to inspire this campaign: Operation Pedro Pan in Cuba in the early 1960s and the work of the conservative women in Brazil who opposed President João Goulart in 1964 and called for military intervention against him.

Alessandri's 1958 Presidential Victory and the Increased Popularity of the Left

Decades of electoral struggle fostered a political culture among Socialists and Communists that led them to identify politics with elections, Congress, and candidates—and to see power as winning votes, offices, and government positions. By the late 1950s and early 1960s the two principal parties of the Chilean left, the Socialist Party (PS) and the Communist Party (PC), had weathered repression (and, in the case of the PS, internal disunity) to emerge as "the best organized Marxist parties in the hemisphere."[1] While much of the left around the world took up armed struggle in the 1960s in order to achieve socialism, most of the Chilean left chose the ballot, not the bullet. Over the years, both the Communist and Socialist parties had members elected to national and local office, participated in coalition governments (which garnered them ministerial positions), and amassed a large electoral base.

In 1956, the Communist and Socialist parties formed the FRAP (Frente de Acción Popular, Popular Action Front) in order to advance their electoral aspirations.[2] The alliance proved successful. Between 1957 and 1963, the FRAP increased its percentage of votes from 10.7 to 23.5, a fact that reinforced its reliance on elections as a strategy for obtaining power. And in 1958 the FRAP, with Salvador Allende as its candidate, came within a hairsbreadth of winning the presidential elections (Alessandri beat Allende by only 33,416 votes). Men's and women's electoral choices continued to reflect gender differences: 34 percent of women, the plurality, voted for Jorge Alessandri, while the plurality of men, 32 percent, voted for Salvador Allende (see Table 3.1). In marked contrast to men, only 22 percent of women cast their ballots for Allende. The large number of women who

---

1 Bernard Collier, "Eduardo Frei Is Trying 'A Revolution Without the Execution Wall,'" *The New York Times Magazine*, 19 February 1967. For a thorough history of the earlier years of the PS, see Drake, *Socialism and Populism*. For interpretations of the PS's history and ideology, written by a leader of the party, see Jorge Arrate and Paulo Hidalgo, *Pasión y razón del socialismo chileno* (Santiago: Las Ediciones del Ornitorrinco, 1989), and Jorge Arrate, *La fuerza democrática de la idea socialista* (Santiago: Las Ediciones del Ornitorrinco, 1985). Also see Benny Pollack and Hernan Rosenkranz, *Revolutionary Social Democracy: The Chilean Socialist Party* (London: Frances Pinter, 1986), and Carmelo Furci, *Chilean Communist Party*, 98–99.

2 Timothy R. Scully, *Rethinking the Center: Party Politics in Nineteenth- and Twentieth-Century Chile* (Stanford: Stanford University Press, 1992), 133; Moulian, *La forja*, 99.

Table 3.1 Results of the 1958 presidential elections, by gender

Candidate and Party	Women's Vote		Men's Vote		Total	
	#	%	#	%	#	%
Alessandri (Conservative/Liberal)	**148,009**	**34%**	241,900	30%	**389,909**	**31%**
Allende (FRAP)	97,084	22	**259,409**	**32**	356,493	29
Frei (PDC)	103,899	24	151,870	19	255,769	20
Bossay (Radical)	70,077	16	122,000	15	192,077	15
Zamorano (Independent)	15,494	4	25,810	3	41,304	3

Note: Boldface type indicates the candidates who received the most votes.
Source: República de Chile, Servicio Electoral (Santiago: Servicio Electoral, n.d.).

voted for Jorge Alessandri swung the elections in favor of the conservative candidate.[3] These election results confirmed for many the perception that Chilean women were more conservative than Chilean men. They also encouraged the right to prioritize women during the 1964 and 1970 presidential elections.[4]

As the 1960s opened, President Jorge Alessandri led a nation headed for profound changes, most of which he opposed. The right, along with the conservative business and landowning interests it represented, hoped to rest secure in its 1958 victory. However, events of the 1960s showed that the winds of change would blow more fiercely than before.

Elections in Curicó: *El Naranjazo*

On 15 March 1964, a by-election in the province of Curicó—an agricultural province located several hours south of Santiago—shook up politics in Chile.[5] Both the Christian Democrats and the Democratic Front (the electoral alliance between the Radical, Conservative, and Liberal parties)

3 There are two main interpretations of Allende's defeat in the 1958 elections. The first blames or credits women for voting for Alessandri. See Francis and Kyle, "Chile: The Power of Women at the Polls." See also *SEPA*, 7–13 December 1971, 22, and Santa Cruz et al., *Tres ensayos*, 245. The other interpretation attributes Allende's loss to the candidacy of the "maverick" ex-priest, Antonio Zamorano. According to Scully, had Zamorano not run as a fifth presidential candidate, "it is likely that Allende would have emerged the winner of the 1958 contest." See Scully, *Rethinking the Center*, 138.

4 Elsa Chaney disagrees that women are "makers of Presidents" in Chile. However, she does acknowledge that their vote in the 1958 election gave Jorge Alessandri the plurality. She writes that "if women had not voted in that election, Salvador Allende would have won the election with the 18,000 majority the men gave him over Alessandri." See Chaney, *Supermadre*, 96.

5 The by-elections resulted from the death of Socialist Deputy Oscar Naranjo. The PS brought Naranjo's son—who bore the same name—forward as its candidate to replace him.

Table 3.2 Results of the 1964 by-election in Curicó, by gender

Candidate and Party	Women's Vote		Men's Vote		Total
	#	%	#	%	#
Naranjo (PS)	3,476	36%	**6,080**	**64%**	**9,556**
Fuenzalida (PDC)	3,197	48	3,424	52	6,621
Ramírez (FD)	**3,833**	**48**	4,117	52	7,950

Note: Boldface type indicates the candidates who received the most votes.
Source: República de Chile, Servicio Electoral, "Resultados generales de la elección extraordinaria de un diputado por la Provincia de Curicó, efectuada el 15 de marzo de 1964" (Santiago: Servicio Electoral, n.d.).

viewed the by-election as a trial run for the upcoming presidential elections, which compounded its importance.[6] Curicó was one of the strongholds of the landowning class and of the Conservative and Liberal parties. The Democratic Front fully expected that its candidate, Rodolfo Ramírez, would win the election for deputy. (It felt confident of victory: much to its later chagrin, the Democratic Front even boasted that its candidate would win by 56 percent of the vote.[7]) But Oscar Naranjo Jr., the Socialist candidate, came in first; Rodolfo Ramírez, the Democratic Front candidate, second; and Mario Fuenzalida, the Christian Democratic candidate, third (see Table 3.2). Consistent with the voting trends of the period, the plurality of women voted for the conservative candidate, Ramírez, while the plurality of men—who made up the majority of voters—cast their votes for the Socialist, Naranjo.

The victory of Socialist Oscar Naranjo, an event subsequently known in Chilean history as *el naranjazo*, caused a major realignment in Chilean politics. The Liberal and Conservative parties realized that if their candidate could lose in a region considered their stronghold, then a similar fate might befall their candidate in the upcoming presidential elections. As a result, both parties withdrew from their alliance with the Radical Party and gave their support to Eduardo Frei, the candidate of the Christian Democratic Party and the "lesser of two evils."[8]

6 Scully, *Rethinking the Center,* 139.

7 Federico G. Gil and Charles J. Parrish, *The Chilean Presidential Election of September 4, 1964: An Analysis* (Washington, D.C.: Institute for the Comparative Study of Political Systems, 1965), 32.

8 Neither the Conservative Party nor the Liberal Party bore much love for Frei. During the Alessandri government, the Christian Democrats in general (and Eduardo Frei in particular) sharply criticized Alessandri's focus on business interests. For a discussion of this issue, see Tomás Moulian, "Desarrollo político y estado de compromiso. Desajustes y crisis estatal en Chile," *Estudios CIEPLAN* 8 (July 1982): 120.

The Formation of Acción Mujeres de Chile
(Women's Action of Chile)

The victory of the Cuban Revolution, combined with the growing strength of the Chilean left, exacerbated rightists' apprehension about a "communist takeover" of Chile and spurred them to action.[9] As part of this response, a group of elite conservative women formed Acción Mujeres de Chile in 1963. While the number of women who composed this anticommunist women's group was never large, the group's existence was highly significant. It mobilized women against Allende during both the 1964 and 1970 presidential elections, and one of its founders, Elena Larraín, participated in the formation of Poder Femenino (Feminine Power), the group that organized women against Allende in the early 1970s. Because Larraín played such a central role in organizing conservative women against the left, this section begins with a brief description of her.

Elena Larraín's family owned an extensive estate south of Rancagua. She lived there until she was eleven years old, at which time her parents sent her to school in Santiago. During the 1930s her father, Jaime Larraín, belonged to the conservative Integralistas (Integralists), a group that defined itself as "an alternative to liberal capitalism and Marxist socialism." The group "proposed a type of Catholic corporatism, with a system of guilds (*gremios*), vertically orchestrated by the state." He was also a founding member of the Agrarian Labor Party (PAL).[10] Her mother did not participate in politics.[11]

Larraín never held a paying job, but did volunteer work in insane asylums. She had several children with her husband, a medical doctor. He neither belonged to a political party nor was politically active, but "he was happy that I was. Of course sometimes he thought I went a bit too far, but what could I do? I was so involved!" During the UP years, he kept scrapbooks that documented her (and the opposition's) activities against Allende.[12] Larraín never joined a political party either. She was a conservative activist who was critical of the parties because, she believed, they

---

9 Until the 1990s, the Chilean right routinely referred to the left as communist, ignoring the presence and independence of the PS. This changed during the 1999 presidential elections. The breakup of the Soviet Union, the fall of the Berlin Wall, the lesser importance of the PC, and the candidacy of Ricardo Lagos (a member of the PS) led the right to refer to the "socialist conspiracy" instead of the "communist conspiracy."

10 PAL existed from 1945 to 1958. The PAL was a populist party that "advocated corporatism, Hispanism, a third way between socialism and capitalism. . . . Although some of [its members] were traditionally rightist, others smacked of Nacismo [the Chilean Nazi Party]." See McGee Deutsch, *Las Derechas*, 317, 328.

11 Elena Larraín, interview by author, tape recording, Providencia, 16 March 1994.

12 Ibid.

spent an inordinate amount of time fighting for power among themselves and not enough time on getting things done.[13] Her political activism began in the early 1960s, when she joined Chile Libre (Free Chile).

Eduardo Boetsch—a civil engineer, landowner, and political independent with strong anticommunist convictions—started Chile Libre in 1960 with several other conservative, upper-class friends. These independent conservatives formed Chile Libre "in order to warn others of the dangers of communism," he wrote. They had long been on the alert for Soviet infiltration through the PC of Chile. Now they also had to contend with the presence of socialist Cuba in their own hemisphere. Spurred on by this threat to their way of life and fully prepared to meet it head-on, these conservative Chileans began to organize "against the sweeping advance of communism" in order to defend "the Christian heritage of Western civilization." Chile Libre brought together political independents with strong anticommunist beliefs who chose not to work through any of the existing conservative parties. In fact, despite Chile Libre's decided political beliefs, Boetsch defined the organization as "apolitical."[14] Along with the rightist parties, it supported Frei in the 1964 elections in order to ensure Allende's defeat.[15] According to Eduardo Labarca Goddard (political editor of the Communist Party paper, *El Siglo*), the United States channeled some of its generous donations to the Frei campaign through Chile Libre.[16]

Membership in Chile Libre appears to have been the point of departure for Elena Larraín's political activism. Although she speaks highly of the group, and retains a close friendship with Eduardo Boetsch, Larraín did not remain long in the organization. After participating in it for about one year, she concluded that the men "got lost in a lot of useless discussions," so she, along with several other women, "chose to separate" from Chile Libre and form Acción Mujeres de Chile.[17]

13 This antiparty strand has long existed within the Chilean right. For an excellent history of the Chilean right in an earlier period, see McGee Deutsch, *Las Derechas*.

14 Eduardo Boetsch, *Memoirs* (Santiago: n.p., n.d.), 45, 44.

15 Eduardo Boetsch, interview by author, tape recording, Providencia, 20 June 1994. Boetsch added that sectors of the right now believe that it would have been better if Allende had won in 1964. At the time, Boetsch argued against that position; in hindsight, however, he thinks that it was the correct one, because "if Allende had tried to impose communism in Chile in 1964 [without the benefit of] the golden bridge built for him by Frei in his six years as president, he would have failed miserably."

16 Eduardo Labarca Goddard, *Chile invadido: Reportaje a la intromisión extranjera en Chile* (Santiago: Empresa Editora Austral, 1968), 72.

17 Elena Larraín, interview by author, tape recording, Providencia, 8 July 1994.

Acción Mujeres de Chile acquired legal status on 20 August 1963.[18] The names of its founding members read like a list of the illustrious families of Chile: María Elena Valdés Cruz, Elena Larraín Valdés, Graciela Ibáñez Ojeda, Dora Sierra Espinoza, and Olga Irarrázaval Larraín.[19] The extent of the organization's activities in the early 1960s is a matter of conjecture, to some extent. It produced no public statements, no press conferences, and no leaflets. However, Acción Mujeres de Chile did serve two vital purposes. It provided an entrée for elite conservative women into modern Chilean politics, and it participated in the Scare Campaign during the 1964 elections.

Neither Elena Larraín nor the other leaders of Acción Mujeres de Chile trusted Eduardo Frei. Since Larraín came from a landowning family, his promises of agrarian reform concerned her. Nevertheless, she voted for him—a fact she now deeply regrets. When I interviewed her in 1994, she, like so many other conservative women, harbored feelings of betrayal and bitterness for Frei and the Christian Democrats. Larraín commented that "we [members of the landowning class] didn't like him. We knew he would sell us out to the left in the long run." Despite her misgivings about Frei, she and Acción Mujeres de Chile worked to organize women to vote for him because he was preferable to Salvador Allende. As part of its effort to mobilize women, the group sponsored "important people who came from France and Venezuela to have meetings with us. They told us that we had to vote for Frei because purgatory was better than hell, given that the other candidate was Allende." According to Larraín, Acción Mujeres de Chile was well organized, had an office, and could mobilize up to one hundred women to go out at 2:00 A.M. to post anti-Allende propaganda or slip it under people's doors. She claims that ten thousand women—most likely an inflated figure—belonged to the group throughout Chile.[20]

Larraín's reasons for leaving Chile Libre and forming Acción Mujeres de Chile reflect her perception that men and women are essentially dif-

18 *Diario Oficial de la República de Chile*, 6 September 1963, 3.

19 Congreso Chileno, Cámara de Diputados, legislatura ordinaria, *Informe de la Comisión Especial Investigadora . . .* , sesión 25, 19 August 1970, 2422. See also Mariana Aylwin, Sofía Correa, and Magdalena Piñera, *Percepción del rol político de la mujer: Una aproximación histórica* (Santiago: Instituto Chileno de Estudios Humanísticos, 1986), 50.

20 Larraín, interview by author, 8 July 1994. She did not name the people from France or Venezuela. Echoing many of the rightists with whom I spoke, she claimed to have liked Salvador Allende: "He was a very nice man. He would have much preferred to be a candidate of the right than the left. However, since he couldn't have been a candidate of the right, he went to the left." When I asked her why Allende couldn't have been a candidate of the right, she replied, "The right had many more educated people than the left, so it was easier to get ahead

ferent. Larraín shared the belief (held by many other conservative women) that women are morally superior to men. They do not believe that men can change and they make no attempt to change them.[21] These assumptions about men and women shaped the political culture of both Acción Mujeres de Chile and Poder Femenino, and they also echo many rightist women's attitudes toward men and the male-dominated parties. Larraín inverts the stereotype of the passive and dominated Chilean woman and identifies women as important, even key, political actors. She rejects the idea that men are naturally better at practicing politics and performing public duties, while women are biologically suited for a peaceful life in the home, an idea then commonplace in Chile. According to Larraín, self-interest and "the need to have power" motivate men, and these qualities are counterproductive in political work. Women are much more effective political activists, because they are better able to work together to achieve a common goal. Simultaneously infantilizing men and elevating women, she stated that men "can't do anything alone. . . . They make plans that are larger than their minds. They have ambitions." Women, on the other hand, "lack political ambitions" and, as a result, "are able to unite and get things done."[22]

It is very possible that the CIA used Acción Mujeres de Chile as a conduit for funds to support Frei's presidential bid and to finance the Scare Campaign. In 1963, the year that the women listed above founded Acción Mujeres de Chile, the CIA began to fund a "right-wing" women's group in Chile. The Church Committee, which investigated CIA covert actions in Chile, concluded that "in the mid-1960s the CIA supported an anti-communist women's group active in Chilean political and intellectual life."[23] Although the report does not name the group, it is likely that it was Acción Mujeres de Chile, because it was the most prominent and active right-wing women's organization in existence at that time.

---

in the left." Her husband had been a doctor and had studied with Allende. She added that when Allende was president, "he called and asked me to come talk with him about this organization of women [Poder Femenino]. I consulted [with the group] and they said no, it would be very strange for you to talk with him since I was in an organization that opposed him."

21 This attitude differs markedly from that of feminists, who contend that society constructs masculinity and femininity. As a result, many feminists believe that men can (and indeed should) change themselves in order to end their oppressive attitudes and practices toward women and to free themselves from restrictive gender roles.

22 Larraín, interview by author, 16 March 1994. When I spoke with her, Larraín occasionally confused the activities of Acción Mujeres de Chile with those of Poder Femenino. Her mental conflation of these two organizations indicates her perception of the continuity between them.

23 Senate Select Committee, *Covert Action*, Hearings, 16.

The 1964 Scare Campaign

The closeness of Alessandri's 1958 victory and the left's growing strength made Allende's success in the 1964 presidential elections appear a very real possibility. The Frei campaign developed a two-pronged strategy to counter Allende's appeal to the Chilean electorate. This chapter discusses one aspect of the plan: the attempt to convince Chileans that a vote for Allende meant a vote for dictatorship, while one for Frei assured the continuation of Chilean democracy. This strategy has come to be known as the Scare Campaign. (The other angle adopted by Frei's supporters stressed the positive benefits that would result from his victory. This strategy is examined in Chap. 4.)

While both approaches used powerful imagery to convince Chileans to vote for Frei, the sensationalist character of the Scare Campaign guaranteed that it would have a profound impact. As part of this campaign, anticommunist propaganda filled the airwaves and newspapers of Chile. Although the specific ads varied, a consistent message ran through them: Chileans must act now to defend their nation and their traditions from the communists. They must vote against Allende in order to prevent Chile from falling into the morass of totalitarianism (which is how the right characterized the Soviet and Cuban systems).

This anticommunist propaganda promoted an atmosphere of hysteria. It portrayed the 1964 presidential elections as a showdown between Frei, the valiant hero fighting to preserve Chile's democratic traditions, and Allende, the nefarious representative of the international Marxist conspiracy. For example, on 1 August—and every day thereafter until 4 September—blaring ads appeared in *El Mercurio* that counted down the days remaining until the elections, which were defined as a battle between the forces of good and evil, between patriotism and national betrayal. One ad, calculated to instill a sense of doom in the reader, screamed in large type, "Only thirty-four more days!" Beneath the headline, the text read, "Can we allow international Marxism to take over a part of our territory, land that has belonged to all Chileans? To them [the communists], we free men respond: After September 4th, Chile will continue to be Chilean."[24]

The Scare Campaign was a massive and sophisticated propaganda production that utilized accepted concepts of gender to communicate its message. It consisted of a series of posters, leaflets, letters, and radio announcements that attempted to terrorize Chileans into voting against

24 *El Mercurio,* 1 August 1964.

Allende and for Frei.[25] The U.S. government was heavily involved in the Scare Campaign and provided many of the propaganda skills, resources, and monies needed to develop it. The campaign began toward the end of June 1964. During that week alone, according to the U.S. Senate report on covert action in Chile, "a CIA-funded propaganda group produced twenty radio spots per day in Santiago and on 44 provincial stations; twelve-minute news broadcasts five times daily on three Santiago stations and 24 provincial outlets; thousands of cartoons, and much paid press advertising." As the presidential campaign progressed, the propaganda escalated. The U.S. Senate report further stated that "by the end of June, the group produced 24 daily newscasts in Santiago and the provinces, 26 weekly 'commentary' programs, and distributed 3,000 posters daily."[26]

Given the extent of the available funds, the campaign was able to design specific messages for a diverse set of target groups. In an attempt to refute Allende's campaign promises of agrarian reform, which appealed to many peasants, the campaign prepared ads specifically for rural workers. These ads ignored the material conditions in which the peasants lived and appealed instead to their sense of nationalism; they substituted vague references to cultural identity for concrete promises to improve the living conditions of the rural poor. A typical ad read, "You [the peasant] embody the best tradition of the Fatherland. You are the symbol of *chilenidad* [the essence of what it means to be Chilean]."[27]

Some of the ads specifically addressed men as husbands and fathers, the patriarchal heads of their families who were responsible for ensuring the survival and sustenance of their wives and children. One such ad, entitled "Chile at the Crossroads," pictured a heterosexual nuclear family, with the husband in the foreground and his wife and daughter in the background, both dominated *and* protected by him. Reflecting the idea that a man worked to provide for his family—and that the family's well-being depended

25 In the early 1960s, most Chileans could not afford televisions. However, many—if not most—homes had radios. As a result, almost all the electoral propaganda was carried by radios and newspapers. Jack Webster, who was then manager of the J. Walter Thompson advertising agency in Santiago, pointed out to me that at that time, more men than women read newspapers. Therefore, the best way to reach women was through the radio. Jack Webster, telephone interview by author, Southern Pines, N.C., 8 November 1994.

26 Senate Select Committee, *Covert Action: Report*, 15–16.

27 *El Mercurio*, 10 August 1964. Compounding the irony, of course, is the fact that it was highly unlikely that a Chilean peasant would read *El Mercurio*. Though these advertisements ostensibly spoke to the peasants, it is likely that they were in fact directed toward the upper- and middle-class readership of the newspaper—readers who could use the arguments presented in the ads to oppose Allende.

on him—the ad said, "for you, the word FREEDOM means the right to work, to express your opinion, to live with your family, to develop your children spiritually. Are you willing to sacrifice the rights to which freedom entitles you for the Marxist adventure? Think of your children's future."[28]

Women were the campaign's prime targets, because the Frei campaign understood that in order to win, it had to receive their votes. As both the 1958 presidential campaign (see Table 3.1) and the Curicó by-election (see Table 3.2) indicated, men were much more likely to vote for the left, and women tended to choose the more conservative candidate. An additional factor that encouraged the Frei campaign to seek women's votes is that the number of women voting had steadily increased since 1952, the first year in which they were able to vote in national elections.[29] Their vote, then, would mean the difference between Frei's victory or his defeat.

Although the male figures that appeared in the ads assumed a variety of identities—visually, they were portrayed as businessmen, workers, peasants, or fathers—women were primarily represented as mothers. It was to the mothers of Chile that the Scare Campaign directed much of its publicity. Over and over again, the ads warned Chilean women that an Allende victory would mean the loss of their children, the destruction of their homes, and the end of motherhood as they knew it. Beneath a picture of three middle-class women, one ad called on Chilean women to "Listen, as a mother, as a wife, as a daughter. Today you have a great responsibility. Have you thought of the unity of your home? The future of your children? Your children's happiness? Remember that that which you value most in your life is in danger. And remember that the choice is Democracy or Marxism!"[30]

The Scare Campaign fused motherhood and nationalism and defined Allende as a threat to both. Many of the ads implied that if Allende won, he would send Chilean children to Cuba to be indoctrinated in communist propaganda and denationalized. An Allende government would take children away from their mothers and their nation and destroy their feelings of filial love and patriotism.[31]

28 *El Mercurio*, 2 August 1964.

29 When Chilean women first voted in presidential elections in 1952, their votes represented 30 percent of all valid votes cast. By 1958, women's percentage of the vote had increased to 35, and in the 1964 presidential elections, the figure rose to 46 percent. See Operations and Policy Research, *Chile Election Handbook* (Washington, D.C.: Operations and Policy Research, 1963), 33, and Gil and Parrish, *Chilean Presidential Election*, 18.

30 *El Mercurio*, 5 August 1964.

31 I would like to thank Melinda Power for this insight.

One variation on this theme is that an Allende victory and the subsequent imposition of communism would sound the death knell for femininity, which meant being a good wife and mother, physically attractive to and dependent upon men. Communism desexes women and converts them into dull robots whose energies are absorbed by the tasks delegated to them by the communist authorities. As a result, they no longer spend their time loving their husbands and children and making themselves appealing to men.[32] Using Cuba as the paradigm of what "communism" would mean for women, one ad shows several young Cuban women being forcibly recruited into the militias. The caption asks, "Chileans, is this how you want to see your daughter?"[33] Pictures frequently show Cuban women with guns, an image that is not in keeping with the traditional gender assignments (weapons are for men, and purses are for women).[34] Cuban women in Miami wrote to Chilean women urging them to vote for Frei. They implored Chilean women to vote against Allende because under Castro, according to them, Cuban women "have lost their femininity. Today, a Cuban woman's only accessory is a machine gun."[35]

Whatever the medium—"press, radio, films, pamphlets, posters, leaflets, direct mailings, paper streamers, and wall paintings"—the message directed to women was the same: if communism wins, your way of life will be destroyed.[36] In 1964, most Chilean women did not work outside the home, and a large number of those who did worked as maids in other people's homes. Since they were inside much of the day and frequently listened to the radio, ads broadcast through this medium were particularly effective in reaching women.[37] One radio ad, for example, opened with the sound of a machine gun, followed by a woman shouting, "They have killed my son. The Communists!" With feeling in his voice, the radio announcer then said, "Communism only offers blood and pain. To make sure this does not happen in Chile, elect Eduardo Frei president."[38]

The ads were powerful because they reflected, appealed to, and constructed ideas about gender then prevalent in Chilean society. As a result,

---

32 Nothing represents this image of what communism means to femininity better than the difference between Julie Christie and Rita Tushingham in the film *Doctor Zhivago*. The glamorous and romantic Christie represents women in Tsarist Russia, while the drab and serious Tushingham (her daughter) embodies the new Soviet woman. Which would most women rather be?

33 *El Mercurio*, 9 August 1964.

34 *El Mercurio*, 13 August 1964; *El Mercurio*, 14 August 1964.

35 *El Mercurio*, 25 August 1964.

36 Senate Select Committee, *Covert Action: Report*, 15.

37 I would like to thank Temma Kaplan for pointing out this connection.

38 Labarca Goddard, *Chile invadido*, 66.

it is likely that the ads affected both women and men.[39] A woman who depended upon her husband's salary for her and her family's survival would feel threatened by the idea that an Allende victory would mean her husband's loss of a job. Equally, a man who viewed his wife and family as his dependents would be distressed by the suggestion that his children would be taken from him if Allende won. At the same time, because so much of a Chilean woman's life centered on her children, the emotional thrust of the ads that equated an Allende presidency with the destruction of the family had a particularly strong and negative impact on women.

On 2 September, advertisements announced that three radio stations would play a message to Chilean women from Juana Castro, Fidel Castro's anticommunist sister, on 3 September, election eve.[40] Juana Castro had "defected" from Cuba in June 1964, and during the month of August, she was on a "propaganda tour of South America" organized by the CIA.[41] The tape was brought to Chile from Brazil only two days prior to the elections, played on Chilean radios, and transcribed and printed in Chilean newspapers. The timing of the tape's arrival posed a problem for the rightist forces who brought it, because Chilean law forbade the printing or airing of any political propaganda beginning forty-eight hours before the elections. Elena Larraín gleefully recounted to me the role she played in making sure the tape aired. Using her personal connections, she convinced the managers of the three radio stations to play the tape, which she personally delivered to them. She is sure that the message on the tape convinced many women to vote for Frei.[42]

In her message, Juana Castro told Chileans not to believe the false promises of Salvador Allende, since "they are all lies." She warned Chileans that "in Chile you will not be able to carry out any type of religious activity if the Reds win. The new Gods will be Marx, Lenin, and the Communist Party." She also spoke specifically to women: "Chilean mothers, I am sure that you will not allow your small children to be taken from you and sent to the Communist bloc, such as happened in Cuba. . . . The enemy is stalking, it is at your doors. I repeat once again: Don't let yourselves be deceived! Don't be confused! Be alert! . . . Remember your families. Remember your children."[43]

39 I would like to thank Gil Joseph for this observation.

40 *El Mercurio*, 2 September 1964. The three radio stations were Radio Sociedad Nacional de Mineria, La Voz de Chile, and Radio Corporación.

41 Philip Agee, *Inside the Company: CIA Diary* (New York: Stonehill, 1975), 387.

42 Larraín, interview by author, 16 March 1994. According to Larraín, Frei "didn't want the tape to be played because leftist groups pressured him to oppose it." Larraín did not name the groups involved.

43 Labarca Goddard, *Chile invadido*, 70.

Because he realized how potentially damaging the Scare Campaign was, Allende criticized it vehemently. In one speech, he angrily pointed out that "the country is witnessing an unprecedented squandering of money, a saturation of the media, a colossal disinformation attempt. This is no longer a simple case of propaganda; this is an example of violent, psychological repression. . . . They say we are enemies of the family, the home, the fatherland, religion, freedom, culture, and the spirit. These are all anticommunist lies."[44] Because they were so disturbing, Allende devoted a large portion of his final speech before the elections to countering the charges made by the Scare Campaign and to registering his outrage with Juana Castro's message. He pointed out that "the words of Juana Castro are not an isolated incident. They are part of an international conspiracy that began months ago, with articles published in newspapers and foreign magazines." Directing his message specifically to women, he proclaimed that "the Chilean woman understands clearly what her position is in this struggle we are waging. I know that she will act . . . according to her own conscience. For this reason, the words spoken yesterday [in Juana Castro's taped message] constitute an offense to our [female] compatriots."[45]

Mireya Baltra is very familiar with the Scare Campaign. In 1964, as a member of the Communist Party, she was negatively affected by it. In the 1970s, she served as a deputy in the Chilean Congress and helped lead the investigation into the 1970 Scare Campaign. She believes that despite the efforts of the left to organize them, "women stayed behind. Allende lost in 1964 because of women. He won men's votes. But he lost with women. This showed that women were a fertile terrain and their consciousness could be manipulated [by the Scare Campaign] so they would not vote for Allende. Women played the decisive role . . . in the struggle for power."[46]

International Connections and Precedents to the Scare Campaign

When I first read the U.S. Senate's report, *Covert Action in Chile, 1963–1973,* I was struck by its scattered references to U.S. government money and propaganda directed specifically at women.[47] Since 1993, I have repeatedly attempted to obtain more information on CIA and other U.S. government programs designed to convince women in Chile that an Allende victory would harm them and their families. To date, the U.S.

44 *Aurora,* 23 August 1964.
45 *El Mercurio,* 4 September 1964.
46 Mireya Baltra, interview by author, tape recording, Santiago, 31 January 1994.
47 Senate Select Committee, *Covert Action: Report,* 7, 9, 15, 6, 18, 21, and 60.

government has refused my requests for documents and information. However, I believe that several factors explain the U.S. government's development of a highly sophisticated strategy that targeted Chilean women. First, during the late 1940s and 1950s, the political culture of the United States assumed a direct link between fighting communism (at home *and* abroad) and the American family. As Elaine Tyler May points out in *Homeward Bound,* during the Cold War, Americans believed that "American superiority rested on the ideal of the suburban home . . . and distinct gender roles for family members." A man was the "breadwinner" and a woman was "a full-time . . . homemaker."[48] U.S. government officials drew upon these gendered perceptions when they developed their work in Chile. In addition, it is probable that U.S. policymakers, like Chilean politicians, had analyzed the results of the 1952 and 1958 presidential elections and were aware that women had voted more conservatively than men. Therefore, faced with the very real possibility that Allende would win the 1964 presidential elections, it is reasonable to conclude that the U.S. government would target women as the most likely source of anti-Allende votes. The Scare Campaign is the concrete manifestation of U.S. government efforts to use gender to prevent Allende's election.

The Scare Campaign suggests two important aspects of U.S.–Latin American relations that previously have not received much attention. The first is that in the early 1960s, and possibly before, the U.S. government used ideas about gender to foment anticommunist sentiment among women in Latin America. The second is that the U.S. government and conservative forces in Latin America learned from each other's experiences in mobilizing women against progressive or leftist governments and applied these lessons to their own situations. The following pages examine Operation Pedro Pan in Cuba and the mobilization of women against President João Goulart in Brazil to illuminate these international connections.

Operation Pedro Pan (1960–62) was "a clandestine operation set up specifically to get children out of Cuba."[49] It offered "a safe conduit out of Cuba for children under sixteen and supposedly in imminent danger of being taken away from their parents." Just as would subsequently happen in Chile, a combination of factors convinced some Cuban parents that "their children were about to be taken away, probably to the Soviet Union

---

48 Elaine Tyler May, *Homeward Bound: American Families in the Cold War Era* (New York: Basic Books, 1999), 11.

49 Yvonne M. Conde, *Operation Pedro Pan: The Untold Exodus of 14,048 Cuban Children* (New York: Routledge, 1999), 47.

for brainwashing and indoctrination."[50] Anti-Castro Cubans, Catholic priests, U.S. citizens, and the U.S. government all played a role in Operation Pedro Pan.

Cuban parents' desire to send their children out of Cuba stemmed both from certain measures that the revolutionary government took once it came to power and from rumors spread by anti-Castro forces about what the government planned to do. For example, some parents opposed the idea of their children being sent to the countryside to teach illiterate peasants how to read. They were fearful about what could happen to the children away from the shelter of their homes, and they disagreed with the pro-revolutionary politics that were integral to the literacy campaign. Parents also reacted with concern to the rumors (very likely spread by those who opposed the revolution) that the government "was going to take over legal guardianship of the children from their parents."[51]

According to María Torres, whose parents sent her to the United States when she was a child as part of Operation Pedro Pan, the campaign "collapsed communism and fascism and played on people's fears of what had happened to Jewish children during World War Two." Torres, who has met with government officials in an effort to secure documents about and information on Operation Pedro Pan, believes that the success of this project in Cuba encouraged the U.S. government to repeat it throughout Latin America.[52] One thing is clear: the fact that Cuban parents sent over 14,000 of their children out of Cuba in order to save them and preserve the family offered the U.S. government and conservative forces in Latin America dramatic "proof" that communism destroys the family. What made this image even more potent was that it happened in this hemisphere. It therefore made the threat to other Latin American nations and families appear very real.

Another apparent threat came in the figure of Brazilian President João Goulart, although Goulart—who became president in 1961—was more a populist than a revolutionary.[53] In the early 1960s, conservative women

50 "Operation Pedro Pan's Code of Silence," *Chicago Tribune*, 15 January 1998, 23.

51 Conde, *Operation Pedro Pan*, 31–33, 40.

52 María Torres, interview by author, notes, Chicago, 9 March 1998.

53 João Goulart, the vice president, assumed the presidency of Brazil in 1961 when President Jânio Quadros resigned. Goulart, who came out of the populist tradition established by President Getúlio Vargas (1934–37 and 1951–54), gave the working class an increased say in his government and favored key reforms that the wealthy and much of the middle class in Brazil perceived as communist. Goulart supported agrarian reform, electoral reforms (including the extension of voting rights to the illiterate), more student control in the universities, and constitutional reforms that would give the president more power. See Solange de Deus Simoes, *Deus, Pátria e Familia: As mulheres no golpe de 1964* (Petrópolis, Brazil: Vozes, 1985), 24.

organized in opposition to him.[54] Their mobilization against his government was a critical part of the strategy pursued by the U.S. government and conservative sectors in Brazil: these forces hoped to undermine popular support for him and to create the image that his presidency menaced the Brazilian woman, the family, and the Catholic Church.[55]

As was later true in Chile during the Popular Unity years, the mobilization of Brazilian women against Goulart reflected both careful planning by organizations on the right *and* women's spontaneous response to a situation they feared and disliked. In 1961, a group of Brazilian businessmen set up Instituto de Pesquisas e Estudos Sociais (IPES, the Institute of Research and Social Studies), an organization that Marlise Simons labeled "a political think tank with the specific object of preparing to overthrow Brazil's 'communist-infiltrated' civilian government."[56] Of particular note was the importance that IPES gave to organizing women. Beginning in mid-1962, IPES offered courses on democracy to women who "had decided to organize actively after coming to feel that children were falling under the control of Communist student leaders."[57]

Over the next two years, women took the lessons they had learned in these classes and applied them to the anti-Goulart struggle. Six anti-Goulart women's organizations developed in different parts of Brazil between 1962 and 1964. The two principal organizations were União Cívica Femenina (UCF, Feminine Civic Union), based in São Paulo, and Campanha de Mulher pela Democracia (CAMDE, Women's Campaign for Democracy), based in Rio de Janeiro. In 1962, Brazil held congressional and state elections. As Acción Mujeres de Chile would later do in Santiago,

54 In order to convey the sense that opposition to Goulart was an autochthonous Brazilian reaction to which the United States merely responded, Vernon Walters, who was both a military officer and deputy director of the CIA, quotes unnamed Brazilian military officers who expressed this sentiment to him during his 1964 visit to the country. When he was alone with his "old friends" in the Brazilian military (he had worked with the Brazilian military during WWII), they "would pour out their worry at seeing their country drifting toward becoming what so many called 'another Cuba.'" In fairly typical language of the period, Waters builds his case that President Goulart is leading Brazil down the path taken by Cuba, that most Brazilians oppose the political direction taken by Goulart, that Goulart's military overthrow is therefore necessary and understandable—and that the United States had absolutely nothing to do with it. See Vernon A. Waters, *Silent Missions* (Garden City, N.Y.: Doubleday, 1978), 374–406.

55 See A. J. Langguth, *Hidden Terrors* (New York: Pantheon, 1978), 77, 86–97.

56 *Washington Post*, 6 January 1974. IPES worked very closely with IBAD (Instituto Brasileiro de Ação Democrática, Brazilian Institute for Democratic Action). According to Solange de Deus Simoes, the leadership of both institutions came from the "elite" and consisted of "technocrats, businessmen, and the intellectual sectors of the military, [who were] organized in the interests of the ruling classes." See de Deus Simoes, *Deus, Pátria e Familia*, 26.

57 John F. W. Dulles, *Unrest in Brazil: Political-Military Crisis 1955–1964* (Austin: University of Texas Press, 1970), 173.

CAMDE plastered the walls of the city with anticommunist posters. Addressing women as "housewives," CAMDE called on them to "defend their homes and their children, who are being threatened by a subversive minority."[58]

Unlike the anticommunist women's organizations in Chile, however, the conservative women's groups in Brazil highlighted religion as part of their anti-Goulart drive. During one action in Belo Horizonte in February 1964, women successfully prevented Goulart's brother-in-law, Leonel Brizola—a federal deputy and a "dynamic left-wing populist"[59]—from speaking by "rattling their rosaries and praying loudly." Women did not just pray to disrupt the rally. They also attacked supporters physically, using their umbrellas and the chairs set up for listeners. The attack was so violent that Brizola was forced to flee from the rally.[60] A few weeks later, pro-Goulart forces held a mammoth rally to demonstrate support for the reforms the government was attempting to implement. When he spoke, Goulart criticized the women's use of rosaries, saying, "Christianity never was a shield for the privileged . . . , nor, Brazilians, can rosaries be raised against the people's will and against their most legitimate aspirations."[61] Claiming that Goulart's remarks had insulted the rosary and shamed Brazil, a nun in São Paulo called for a "March to Make Amends to the Rosary." Civic leaders and politicians took up her suggestion and made plans to hold a massive anti-Goulart march. They changed the name of the demonstration to "March of the Family with God for Liberty" so that non-Catholics would be encouraged to participate.[62] Estimates of the number of participants in the march run from five hundred thousand to eight hundred thousand; its success inspired women in all the major cities of Brazil to plan similar events. Held two weeks before the military overthrew Goulart, the march both encouraged the armed forces to intervene and provided it with justification for the coup.[63] On 1 April 1964, the Brazilian military deposed the populist government of João Goulart and installed itself in power.

58 See de Deus Simoes, *Deus, Pátria e Familia*, 27–29, 32.

59 Thomas E. Skidmore, *Politics in Brazil 1930–1964: An Experiment in Democracy* (London: Oxford University Press, 1967), 281.

60 Leacock, *Requiem for Revolution*, 189. According to Dulles, the women's husbands and sons also joined in the fight. For his account, which is similar to Leacock's, see Dulles, *Unrest in Brazil*, 261–62.

61 Leacock, *Requiem for Revolution*, 193.

62 Dulles, *Unrest in Brazil*, 275.

63 Skidmore, *Politics in Brazil*, 298. Skidmore places the number of participants at five hundred thousand. For a description of other women's organizations and marches, see Dulles, *Unrest in Brazil*, 193.

The U.S. media helped diffuse the story of the Brazilian women who had acted against communism. In November 1964, *Reader's Digest* published a lengthy article about Brazil entitled "The Country That Saved Itself." The article highlights the organization and activities of women and features Dona Amélia Bustos, the leader of CAMDE. In an eerie foreshadowing of the discourse adopted by the right in Chile after the coup, the article quotes "one leader of the counterrevolution" who says that "without the women, we could never have halted Brazil's plunge toward communism. While many of our men's groups had to work undercover, the women could work in the open—and how they worked!"[64]

Similarities between the women's anti-Goulart and anti-Allende movements suggest the strong possibility of a political link between them. In both Chile and Brazil, the conservative opposition to the elected governments sponsored the development of anticommunist civic movements that promoted the leadership and involvement of women. Conservative women in both countries supported the overthrow of democratically elected governments and applauded the military's seizure of power. Finally, female activists in both Brazil and Chile attributed the military's ability to stage a successful coup to their demands that it do so. The women further claimed that their actions were motivated by a desire to protect democracy and their families—both of which, they asserted, were threatened by the communists.

Although precise data on the relationship between the U.S. government and the women's anti-Goulart marches has not been revealed, informed sources state that "During the week before the military moved to oust Goulart, two huge civic marches for 'God, nation, and family' took place in São Paulo and Belo Horizonte, the capitals of the states where the insurrection began. U.S. businessmen resident in Brazil, who were in close contact with the CIA representatives there, helped organize and finance these demonstrations."[65]

64 In their enthusiasm, the editors of *Reader's Digest* went to rather unusual lengths to broadcast their support for the military coup and the civic movement that urged it to take place. Proclaiming that the article "provides a blueprint for action by *concerned citizens in other nations threatened by communism*" (emphasis added), they urged their readers to "mail this article to some friend living abroad, either in such sensitive areas as the newly developing countries, or in older countries confronting communist threats. . . . Obtain additional reprints . . . for sending to relatives and friends working abroad, such as government or Peace Corps representatives" (see *Reader's Digest*, November 1964).

65 Jerome Levinson and Juan de Onis, *The Alliance That Lost Its Way: A Critical Report on the Alliance for Progress* (Chicago: Quadrangle, 1970), 89. Levinson was assistant director of the USAID mission to Brazil, and de Onis was a reporter with *The New York Times*. Levinson later served as a staff member for the 1975 Church hearings on U.S. covert action in Chile.

Ruth Leacock believes that Brazil served as an important laboratory for future U.S. intervention in Latin American elections, including the upcoming Chilean ones. She writes that "honing skills already partially tried out in other underdeveloped countries, the CIA, with assistance from the State Department, developed a model that could be used a little later in Chile."[66] One lesson was clear: in societies that conflate womanhood with motherhood, women respond decisively to what they perceive to be a threat to their children and their families.

U.S. Government Involvement in Chile's 1964 Elections

The Cuban Revolution alarmed the U.S. government as well as conservative forces in Chile. In response, Washington devised a foreign policy for Latin America that had one main goal: to prevent another Cuba. Although Chile lacked a guerrilla movement (such as those U.S.-backed counterinsurgency forces confronted in Venezuela, Guatemala, and Peru), U.S. officials did not accept with equanimity the possibility of the Chilean left winning in free and democratic elections.[67] In fact, the United States viewed the increased electoral strength of the Chilean left with concern. The left's victory in Curicó encouraged the U.S. government to drop its traditional support for the Conservative and Liberal parties and to back the Christian Democratic Party. It defined the PDC as the best vehicle to respond to and contain the Chilean people's demands for land reform, increased political participation, higher wages, and the nationalization of Chile's resources. Convinced that it was the party most likely to defeat the left, the U.S. government extended considerable financial and political support to the PDC.[68]

Although the precise figures spent by the Johnson administration (1964–68) to ensure Frei's electoral victory and Allende's defeat are not known, there is no doubt that they ranged in the millions. This sum may sound rather paltry nowadays, when we hear of the millions spent in U.S. congressional and presidential elections, but it was unprecedented in 1964 in Chile. The *Washington Post* quoted one unnamed "former intelligence official deeply involved in the 1964 effort" who claimed that "up

66 Leacock, *Requiem for Revolution*, 118–22.

67 In 1967, Barnard Collier, the *New York Times* correspondent in Latin America, wrote that Frei's victory "had preserved the keystone of United States cold-war diplomacy: no Communist ever gets elected head of a nation in free elections in the free world." See Collier, "Eduardo Frei."

68 Eduardo Labarca Goddard writes that in 1962, President Kennedy sent Richard Goodwin and Teodoro Moscoso (then head of the Alliance for Progress) to Chile to convey his support for the Christian Democrats. He adds that "the White House recommended that the Right support a Christian Democrat for president." See Labarca Goddard, *Chile invadido*, 54, 60.

to $20 million in U.S. funds . . . and as many as 100 U.S. personnel" were involved.[69] The figures cited in the U.S. Senate report, *Covert Action*, add up to somewhere between $3 and $4 million.[70] Philip Agee, who was a CIA operative based in Montevideo, Uruguay, at the time, confirms this. In his memoirs, Agee recalls thinking that "the Santiago station has a really big operation going to keep Salvador Allende from being elected. He was almost elected at the last elections in 1958, and this time nobody's taking any chance."[71]

Apparently, the scope of the operation was so great that the CIA had to develop diverse channels to smuggle the money into Chile, because "the Office of Finance in [CIA] headquarters couldn't get enough Chilean *escudos* [the Chilean currency] from the New York banks."[72] One former CIA agent claims that the United States funneled in $20 million, in part through "an ostensibly private organization called the International Development Foundation."[73] Philip Agee helped send money to Chile through the Montevideo branch of the First National City Bank, with the help of the assistant manager, John M. Hennessy. A CIA finance officer in charge of ensuring that the funds reached Chile commented to Agee, "we are spending money in the Chilean election practically like we did in Brazil two years ago."[74]

When the U.S. Senate investigated covert action in Chile, it found very direct evidence of U.S. participation in the Scare Campaign. The report first established that in 1964, "the Central Intelligence Agency . . . spent over $3 million in election programs, financing in this process over half of the Christian Democratic campaigns." In order to develop a comparative perspective on how much money was spent, Karl Inderfurth, a staff member of the Senate Select Committee, pointed out that "the $3 million spent by the CIA in Chile in 1964 represents about 30 cents for every man, woman, and child in Chile. Now if a foreign government had spent an equivalent amount per capita in our 1964 election, that government would have spent about $60 million. . . . President Johnson and

---

69 *Washington Post*, 6 April 1973.

70 Senate Select Committee, *Covert Action: Report*, 57.

71 Agee, *Inside the Company*, 371.

72 Ibid.

73 Victor Marchetti and John D. Marks, *The CIA and the Cult of Intelligence* (New York: Knopf, 1974), 15.

74 Agee, *Inside the Company*, 372, 382. During the Popular Unity years, Hennessy was the assistant secretary of the treasury for international affairs and "in that post helped to coordinate the economic aspect of the Nixon administration's anti-Allende campaign."

Senator Goldwater spent $25 million combined, so this would have been about $35 million more."[75]

Inderfurth further specified just how this money was spent. He began by pointing out that "the 1964 Presidential election . . . was the first major U.S. covert action in Chile," and he then noted that "the CIA mounted a massive anti-Communist propaganda campaign. . . . The propaganda campaign was, in fact, a scare campaign. It relied heavily on images of Soviet tanks and Cuban firing squads and *was pitched especially to women* [emphasis added]".[76]

During the hearings, Frank Church (the committee chairman) commented to Charles Meyer, the assistant secretary of state for Latin American affairs, that "as the facts clearly establish, we were deeply involved in Chilean politics. We have been so ever since 1964. We had pumped millions of dollars into Chile to try to influence the results of those elections. We had helped secretly finance certain political parties. We had helped to support certain newspapers, commentators, columnists, radio stations, and you were aware of all that." Meyer agreed with Church's comment and nodded his head to indicate that it was true.[77]

U.S. involvement in Chilean politics was not limited to government agencies. Members of U.S. advertising agencies based in Chile helped design parts of the Frei campaign. Two of the largest were McCann-Erickson and J. Walter Thompson.[78] According to Jon Frappier in a special issue of the *North American Congress on Latin America (NACLA) Newsletter* on ad agencies in Latin America, McCann-Erickson "played an important and controversial role in getting Christian Democrat Eduardo Frei elected president of Chile in 1964. Several groups and reporters charged that Frei was receiving $1 million each month during the campaign from the CIA Some suspected that the money was being channeled through McCann-Erickson, since the CIA has been known to use ad agencies and public relations firms as covers."[79]

In a recent conversation with me, Jack Webster, manager of the Chilean office of the J. Walter Thompson ad agency during the 1960s,

75 Senate Select Committee, *Covert Action*, Hearings, 9, 10.

76 Ibid., 11.

77 Ibid., 36.

78 In 1968, McCann-Erickson had $2.5 million worth of business in Chile, and J. Walter Thompson had $2.8 million. They both advertised for a host of U.S. businesses. For a complete listing of U.S. companies they carried, see NACLA *Newsletter* 3, no. 4 (July–August 1969): 3. For a similar perspective, see Fred Landis, "The CIA Makes Headlines, Psychological Warfare in Chile," *Liberation*, March/April 1975.

79 NACLA *Newsletter* 3, no. 4 (July–August 1969): 10.

stressed that J. Walter Thompson's official policy was that the agency could neither design nor get involved with political campaigns, since it could back the wrong candidate—and could therefore weaken the agency's chances of carrying out successful commercial operations in that country. However, Webster pointed out, J. Walter Thompson encouraged individuals working in the ad agencies to take a leave of absence and to donate their skills to the candidate of their choice. In 1964, that candidate was Eduardo Frei; in 1970, it was Jorge Alessandri. Webster also pointed out that in Chile in the 1960s there were "precious few" televisions, so "everything was radio." As part of its advertising work, J. Walter Thompson purchased blocks of radio time for its clients. During the campaign period, J. Walter Thompson refused to relinquish these blocks of time—which were legally allotted to the Allende campaign—and thus prevented FRAP supporters from making political announcements.[80]

It seems quite feasible that some of the ad agencies' skill went into producing the hard-hitting poster ads that served to scare women into voting against Allende.[81] One *Washington Post* article cites the comments of a "State Department veteran of the campaign," who discussed an unidentified "newspaper friendly to the political interests of Christian Democrat Frei" that was covertly financed by the United States. The State Department official said that "the layout was magnificent. The photographs were superb. It was a Madison Avenue product far above the standards of Chilean publications."[82]

The Role of the Catholic Church

One reason why women responded so favorably to the message of the Scare Campaign was that it repeated the familiar anticommunist litany

---

80 Webster, interview; Tom LaPorte, telephone interview by author, Chapel Hill, N.C., 28 October 1994. LaPorte illustrated Mr. Webster's point about people leaving J. Walter Thompson to become involved in politics with the example of H. R. Haldeman. Haldeman, Nixon's chief of staff, was general manager in the San Francisco office of J. Walter Thompson before he left to work on the Nixon campaign.

81 According to Elizabeth McIntosh, who was a member of the OSS (the precursor to the CIA) and wrote the only book about women in the organization, J. Walter Thompson has a history of involvement with the CIA stretching back to the days of the OSS. During WWII, "a dummy corporation was set up [by the CIA] through the J. Walter Thompson advertising agency to handle negotiations with the Musicians Union, hiring an orchestra, and renting rehearsal and recording studios." The musicians produced music as part of the Musac project, a program that was part of a "Morale Operation" that worked to demoralize German soldiers by beaming "slanted news" and "entertainment features" at them. Elizabeth P. McIntosh, *Sisterhood of Spies: The Women of the OSS* (Annapolis: Naval Institute Press, 1998), 56–58.

82 *Washington Post*, 6 June 1973.

that much of the Catholic hierarchy preached in churches throughout Chile. Since women and children constituted the majority of those who attended Mass, they were exposed more consistently to the priests' sermons. According to a study carried out in Santiago one month before the presidential elections, a high percentage of devout Catholics feared Allende and communism. Seventy-four percent of regularly practicing Chileans living in Santiago (of whom the majority were women) believed that "communism is a real danger" to Chile, and they rejected the idea that "anticommunist propaganda is a means to avoid the reforms the country needs."[83]

During the early 1960s, the Catholic Church in Chile warned its congregation of the perils that communism posed to it. In 1962, it formulated an important statement, "El deber social y político en la hora presente" ("The Current Social and Political Duty"), which was read at masses "in all the chapels of Chile." While a portion of the pastoral letter called for "agrarian, tax, and industrial reforms," the bulk of the letter was devoted to pointing out "the dangers inherent in Marxism and the possible evils that could result if Marxists gained power in Chile." Like the Scare Campaign, this document warned that "if communism triumphs in Chile, the Church and all its children can expect only persecution, tears, and blood."[84] Knowing the important role that family played in the lives of Chilean women, the Chilean Catholic Church reproduced and propagated the encyclical written by Pope Pius XI against communism in 1937, *Divini Redemptoris*. The encyclical warned that communism "makes of marriage and the family a purely artificial and civil institution, the outcome of a specific economic system. . . . Communism is particularly characterized by the rejection of any link that binds women to the family and the home, and her emancipation is proclaimed as a basic principle. She is withdrawn from the family and the care of her children, to be thrust instead into public life and collective production under the same conditions as man."[85]

According to the U.S. Senate, the CIA helped pay for the cost of hundreds of thousands of copies of an anticommunist pastoral letter from Pope Pius XI (most likely the encyclical cited above) distributed throughout Chile by Christian Democratic organizations.[86] The church's teachings had their

---

83 Smith, *Church and Politics*, 116, 118.

84 Labarca Goddard, *Chile invadido*, 65.

85 Pope Pius XI, "Atheistic Communism," in *Five Great Encyclicals*, by Gerald C. Treacy, S.J. (New York: Paulist Press, 1939), 181.

86 Senate Select Committee, *Covert Action: Report*, 15.

Table 3.3 Results of the 1964 presidential elections, by gender

Candidate and Party	Women's Vote		Men's Vote	
	#	%	#	%
Frei (PDC)	**756,117**	**63%**	**652,895**	**49%**
Allende (FRAP)	384,132	32	593,770	45
Durán (Radical)	57,162	5	68,071	5
Null and blank	7,342	<1	11,208	<1
Total	1,204,753		1,325,944	

Note: Boldface type indicates the candidates who received the most votes. Women's votes accounted for 48 percent of the total vote in the presidential election; men's votes accounted for 52 percent.
Source: República de Chile, Dirección del Registro Electoral, Servicio Electoral (Santiago: Servicio Electoral, 1964).

desired effect. Only 10 percent of those who regularly attended Mass voted for Allende.[87]

Results of the 1964 Elections

Frei won the 1964 presidential elections (see Table 3.3). Although Frei won among both women and men, a much higher percentage of women (62.8 percent) voted for him; by comparison, 49.3 percent of men chose Frei. And many more men voted for Allende (44.8 percent) than women did (31.9 percent). In fact, almost twice as many women voted for Frei than for Allende. Allende received the majority of women's vote in only one region—the southern coal-mining province of Arauco.[88] In order to determine the impact of class on men and women's voting patterns, several representative voting districts from Santiago are presented below (see Table 3.4).

The voting patterns in the poor and working-class neighborhoods reflect results typical for other districts in the same category. In no working-class or poor neighborhood in Santiago did more women vote for Allende than for Frei. However, in several working-class and poor neighborhoods (Barrancas, Renca, San Miguel, and La Granja), more men voted for Allende than for Frei. Women in Barrancas voted for Frei, but did so to a lesser degree than they did in most other working-class communities. In all cases, women voted for Frei—or against Allende—in disproportionately higher numbers than men did. On the average, Frei

87 Smith, *Church and Politics*, 107.

88 James F. Petras, *Political and Social Forces in Chilean Development* (Berkeley and Los Angeles: University of California Press, 1969), 105.

Table 3.4 Results of the 1964 presidential elections in selected Santiago districts, by gender

Neighborhood	Women's Vote				Men's Vote			
	Frei		Allende		Frei		Allende	
	#	%	#	%	#	%	#	%
Working-class								
Barrancas	**6,866**	**55%**	5,290	42%	5,409	44%	**6,742**	**54%**
Conchalí	**16,915**	**61**	9,799	36	**13,159**	**50**	12,394	47
Renca	**6,434**	**60**	4,087	38	4,741	48	**4,870**	**49**
Quinta Normal	**18,203**	**62**	10,338	35	**14,579**	**49**	14,056	47
San Miguel	**28,322**	**57**	19,638	40	20,537	45	**23,877**	**52**
La Cisterna	**17,500**	**62**	9,683	35	**12,676**	**51**	11,494	47
La Granja	**7,031**	**54**	5,611	43	5,100	43	**6,570**	**55**
Middle-class								
Ñuñoa	**31,284**	**72**	10,306	24	**20,869**	**60**	12,286	35
La Reina	**2,310**	**73**	770	24	**1,163**	**59**	707	36
Upper-class								
Providencia	**20,868**	**83**	3,481	14	**11,539**	**73**	3,401	22
Las Condes	**17,182**	**80**	3,666	17	**9,552**	**68**	4,053	29

Note: Boldface type indicates the candidates who received the most votes. The total vote includes votes cast for Radical Party candidate Julio Durán, and both blank and incorrect votes: in order to highlight the results for the two principal rivals in the elections, I have not included these three additional categories. The totals, therefore, will not add up to 100 percent.
Source: República de Chile, Dirección del Registro Electoral (Santiago: Servicio Electoral, n.d.).

received 59 percent of the votes of working-class women, a substantial majority.[89]

Although the majority of all Chilean women preferred Frei to Allende, class differences are apparent in women's votes. Women in the middle-class neighborhoods of La Reina and Ñuñoa voted at a rate of three to one for Frei and against Allende. This is proportionately much higher than the number of women in the working-class neighborhoods who voted for Frei. The votes of women for Frei in the upper-class neighborhoods far outstrip those of women from middle- and working-class neighborhoods. They voted for Frei and against Allende at rates of five or six to one. Gender differences also emerge among the middle and upper classes. As Table 3.4 indicates, middle- and upper-class men certainly voted for Frei—but they were less likely to do so than their female peers.

Conclusion

The margin of Frei's victory was unprecedented. As Jacques Chonchol points out, "This was the first time in this century that a candidate was elected in the first round of voting with 56 percent of the votes."[90] Although it is difficult to determine the precise effect that the Scare Campaign had on voting patterns, forces across the political spectrum in Chile credit it with swinging the election in Frei's favor.

Eduardo Labarca Goddard attributes much of Frei's success among women voters to the Scare Campaign. He writes that "the effects of the propaganda were revealed by the fact that twice as many women voted for Frei as they did for Allende."[91] Elena Larraín proudly asserts that the work of Acción Mujeres de Chile was decisive in delivering women's votes to Frei.[92] In 1964, Bernardo Leighton was Frei's campaign manager and, as a result, he was very aware of the impact and purpose of the Scare Campaign. As a Christian Democratic deputy, Leighton led the congressional investigation into the 1970 Scare Campaign. He warned his colleagues to beware of this campaign, because the one in 1964 had "left a deep imprint that helps no one in terms of either our political struggles or our democratic system."[93]

89 Germán Urzúa believes that workers "apparently [were] more affected than others" by the Scare Campaign. See Urzúa, *Historia política electoral*, 122.

90 Chonchol, interview.

91 Labarca Goddard, *Chile invadido*, 73.

92 Larraín, interview by author, 16 March 1994.

93 Cámara de Diputados, *Informe de la Comisión Especial Investigadora*, 2624.

The Scare Campaign was so effective because it touched people—especially women—on a deep emotional level. It told them that if Allende won the elections, then their families, that which they held most dear, would be taken from them. Dramatic images of grieving mothers and young children seared this message into women's hearts and minds.

The legacy of the Scare Campaign continued long after the elections. It left a lasting association in many Chileans' minds between communism and the loss of their children. It gendered anticommunism in Chile, most closely linking it with women. Because the Scare Campaign was so successful, the right—aided by its allies within the U.S. government—redeployed it against Allende during the 1970 presidential elections.[94] The basic message it conveyed—that Allende equals communism, and communism means the destruction of the family—became one of the anti-Allende women's main *leitmotivs* during the Popular Unity years.

94 The United States subsequently used the Scare Campaign as a model for other anticommunist projects in Latin America. One clear example of this took place during the 1990 presidential elections in Nicaragua. See William I. Robinson, *A Faustian Bargain: U.S. Intervention in the Nicaraguan Elections and American Foreign Policy in the Post–Cold War Era* (Boulder: Westview, 1992).

4

The Christian Democratic
Party and Women

1964–1970

THE CHRISTIAN DEMOCRATIC Party swept into power in 1964 with 55.7 percent of the vote in the presidential elections. Presenting itself as the party of youthful idealism, Christian morality, and democratic reforms, the newly elected Christian Democrats promised a "Revolution in Liberty." Captivated by this image of moderation and modernization, enthusiasm and eloquence, the Chilean electorate endorsed the Christian Democrats' program. In the 1965 congressional elections, the PDC received 41.1 percent of the votes and gained eleven senators.[1]

Chapter 3 examined how and why the Scare Campaign—a classic example of negative campaigning—bolstered support for the PDC among women. This chapter looks at the positive appeal the PDC had for women.[2] It analyzes why women joined the party and what programs the PDC designed for them, and it focuses specifically on the centerpiece of PDC policy toward women: the Mothers' Centers.

The Mothers' Centers are a prism through which we can evaluate the policies and practices of the PDC toward women. These neighborhood-based women's organizations have been defined as "probably the only instance of women's massive and legitimate participation on the community

---

1 Urzúa, *Historia política electoral*, 124–26. Because several of the parties participated in these elections, it would have been very difficult for any one party to capture the majority of the votes. However, the PDC did remain the single largest political party in Chile.

2 Some of the major works on the Christian Democratic period are Burnett, *Political Groups;* Michael Fleet, *The Rise and Fall of Chilean Christian Democracy* (Princeton: Princeton University Press, 1985); Loveman, *Chile;* James F. Petras, *Chilean Christian Democracy: Politics and Social Forces* (Berkeley: Institute of International Studies, 1967); Scully, *Rethinking the Center;* and Smith, *Church and Politics.* For a woman's perspective, see Carmen Gloria Aguayo, *Des Chiliennes: Des femmes en luttes au Chile et Carmen Gloria Aguayo de Sota* (Paris: Des Femmes, 1982).

level."[3] The Mothers' Centers have given rise to a fair amount of debate. Did they serve to reinforce a patriarchal and traditional identity for women, or did they help break down women's isolation within the home, providing them with marketable skills and enhancing their sense of self-worth? This chapter engages the debate by discussing the PDC's goals for the Mothers' Centers, how the centers actually functioned, the context in which they developed, and the impact they had on the women who participated in them.

During the Popular Unity years, the Mothers' Centers were a focal point of political struggle between the government and the opposition. This chapter explores how women's experiences in the Mothers' Centers affected their political stance during the UP years. The PDC used the contacts and relationships it developed with poor and working-class women in the Mothers' Centers to organize a substantial sector of these women against the UP government.

The 1960s also witnessed significant changes in the right. The emergence of the Christian Democrats as the single most important political party transformed the political landscape in Chile—not only displacing the Radical Party as the traditional party of the center, but also exposing the weaknesses in the Liberal and Conservative parties, the two traditional parties of the right. Confronted by their decline in popularity and challenged by the strength of both the PDC and the left, these two parties merged to form a new one: the National Party. The Frei years also witnessed the beginnings of the *gremio* (guild) movement. From its origins in the Catholic University under the leadership of Jaime Guzmán, the *gremio* movement emerged as one of the principal ideological forces on the right. The *gremios* and the National Party played a critical role in the opposition to the UP government.

A Brief History of the Christian Democratic Party

The roots of the Christian Democratic Party lie in the Conservative Party of Chile. In 1934 a group of young Catholic intellectuals, many of them students at the Catholic University in Santiago, joined the youth branch of the Conservative Party. Two years later, while still members of the youth branch, they formed the National Falange, a Catholic-inspired movement. Conflict between the Falangists and the leadership of the Conservative Party intensified until the latter expelled the young rebels in 1938.[4]

3 Teresa Valdés, Marisa Weinstein, María Isabel Toledo, and Lilian Letelier, *Centros de Madres 1973–1989: ¿Solo disciplinamiento?* (Santiago: FLACSO, n.d.), 1.

4 For a detailed description of the origins and early years of the National Falange, see Fleet, *Rise and Fall*, 43–58.

Although both groups were anticommunist and elitist, they differed on the question of how best to oppose the heightened demands for social reform voiced by the left. The Conservative Party chose to ignore the calls for change in an effort to maintain its traditional economic position and political control. The Falangists, encouraged by recent papal encyclicals that urged the faithful to actively oppose communism, believed that the moral and viable solution to social unrest demanded reforms within a capitalist, hierarchical order. In opposition to the left, they stood against class struggle and believed that "corporatist economic institutions [were the best] means of overcoming the conflict between capital and labor."[5] During most of the 1940s and 1950s, the National Falange was a minor player in Chilean politics. However, in the late 1950s—at which time the National Falange changed its name to the Christian Democratic Party (PDC)—more people began to vote for it. In the 1953 congressional elections the National Falange received only 2.8 percent of the vote. By the 1957 congressional elections, that figure had increased to 9.4 percent. Most indicative of the PDC's increased popularity, however, were the 1958 presidential elections in which Eduardo Frei obtained 20.7 percent of the vote; with that, the PDC replaced the Radical Party as the most important party of the political center.[6]

The growing popularity of the PDC paralleled the political changes taking place in Chile and within the Catholic Church. During most of the twentieth century, the Conservative Party had projected itself as the political representative of the church. However, by the late 1950s and the early 1960s, the Chilean church began to shift its politics and alliances. Reflecting the more progressive international currents heralded by Vatican II and the emergence of a younger generation of Chilean clerics, many of whom had studied and formed friendships with the founders of the Christian Democratic Party, the Catholic Church began to distance itself from the Conservative Party and proclaim policies similar to those then being formulated by the PDC.[7]

For many women, the PDC was the party that best allowed them to combine their religiosity and political activism. As the Catholic Church became increasingly concerned with social justice in the late 1950s and the 1960s, membership in the PDC seemed, to many women, a natural extension of their church-related social and charitable activities; their

5 Fleet, *Rise and Fall*, 46.

6 Urzúa, *Historia política electoral*, 101, 102.

7 For a description of relations between the Conservative Party and the Catholic Church, see Smith, *Church and Politics*, 72, 82, 84, 94, and 112–16.

religious beliefs and politics became indistinguishable. Steven Neuse points out that because the Catholic Church "further[ed] women's interests" and "provid[ed] services for them," women's support for the PDC was based on "careful calculation rather than blind conservatism." He adds that "Frei's female oriented policies did much to rally women to the Christian Democratic cause."[8]

One of the many women who supported the PDC was Raquel Fernández, a middle-class woman and mid-level leader in the party who has dedicated much of her life to the organization. Although her father was a longtime member of the Conservative Party, she joined the National Falange in 1939, when she was only fifteen. Her religious faith led her to identify first with the Falange and later with the PDC. She explained the party's appeal by saying that "the Christian Democratic doctrine is just like the Christian doctrine. They both have the same principles. So, I couldn't be in any other party because that is how I live."[9]

Teresa Maillet de la Maza joined the Christian Democratic Party in 1964. Like many middle-class women of her generation, she only became politically active after her children were grown, when she had "some time to dedicate to politics." She began her political career in Valparaíso as provincial director of the party and rose through the ranks to become a national leader of the PDC's women's department in 1970.[10] From that position, she led party women to oppose the Allende government and helped organize the December 1971 March of the Empty Pots and Pans against the UP.

Her comfortable home displays mementos testifying to her profound engagement with the Catholic religion and her strong identification with the PDC. On her walls hang two huge portraits facing one another—one of the pope and the other of Eduardo Frei. Maillet reveres Frei: "I always wanted a man with his qualities to be president of Chile." When asked which qualities she values, she replies, "his intelligence, his capacity to understand the people. People went to him and they left feeling comforted." It was not only Frei who attracted her to the party, but the Christian Democratic ideology as well. According to Maillet, "The Christian Democratic doctrine brings together positions that any Christian woman

8 Steven M. Neuse, "Voting in Chile: The Feminine Response," in *Political Participation in Latin America*, vol. 1, *Citizen and State*, ed. John A. Booth and Mitchell A. Seligson (New York: Holmes and Meier, 1978), 138.

9 Raquel Fernández, interview by author, tape recording, Santiago, 18 May 1994.

10 Chile's political divisions included provinces, districts, and communes. In 1970, Chile was divided into twenty-five provinces (roughly equivalent to states in the United States).

can well understand: work for the common good, work for the good of others . . . the belief that others require compassion from us in order to be understood. . . . Our politics are not ambitious ones that only seek to gain power; however, we are ambitious of perfection."[11]

The PDC had long harbored different political tendencies within it. More conservative party members grudgingly acknowledged the need for some limited reforms, while more radical ones urged fundamental changes in Chile's economic and social structures. If Teresa Maillet de la Maza represents the former, then Carmen Gloria Aguayo, who was director of the women's department of the PDC in the 1960s, embodies the latter. She became a member of the National Falange in the 1950s.[12] Aguayo joined because she believed that "it was better to struggle to change the structures of society that engendered injustice than to try and individually help a small number of families. At that point in time, the means to do so was through political action, so I joined the National Falange." She defines the Falange as "a small party primarily composed of students and young Christian intellectuals who were in revolt against the conservative traditions of Catholicism."[13]

Christian Democratic Women and the 1964 Elections

One reason why such a large number of women voted for Frei is that prior to the 1964 elections, the PDC recognized the importance of women and made overtures to attract their support. In order to do so, the party developed an innovative strategy that took the specific realities of women, especially poor ones, into account. Carmen Gloria Aguayo helped fashion and implement this strategy.

Aguayo was born into a wealthy family in Santiago. As a teenager in the 1940s she accompanied her mother to church-sponsored discussion groups for poor women in the *poblaciones* (poor neighborhoods). These groups, called Centros de Madres Techo,[14] "taught women religion and how to be good wives and mothers," and Aguayo considers them the forerunners of the Mothers' Centers. In retrospect, she characterizes these efforts as "missionary works, . . . [undertaken] by upper- and middle-class women who went to the *poblaciones* in order to carry out, as they say, good works." By the end of the 1950s, the Catholic Church developed a new policy toward these discussion groups. As Aguayo recalls it, in that period,

11 Teresa Maillet de la Maza, interview by author, tape recording, Valparaíso, 14 June 1994.

12 She later joined MAPU and led the National Secretariat of Women under the Allende government.

13 Aguayo, *Des Chiliennes*, 58–65.

14 *Techo* literally means "ceiling." The name implied a welcoming, homelike center for mothers.

There was a spirit of reform and modernization within the Catholic Church. Above all, this came from the Jesuits. They were the most advanced group within the Catholic religion. They developed the idea that the Mothers' Centers should no longer depend on a Señora [upper- or upper-middle-class lady] who went and taught the women who just sat there passively. Instead, the centers should become a source of employment so that the women could learn to work and earn money. . . . [As a result], the Techos became workshops that taught women sewing skills and provided them with a minimum amount of materials to carry out their labor. [Through] the Techo organization the women first learned how to enter into active life. In our society, we only consider "active life" that activity which earns money.[15]

In 1962, Carmen Gloria Aguayo was appointed director of the women's department of the PDC. Her job was to maximize women's votes for Frei. Using her experience with poor women, the Catholic Church, and the Centros de Madres Techo, she developed the idea of working with and creating new PDC organizations: "I said, let's carry out the campaign by creating Mothers' Centers. . . . So we went into the *poblaciones* and they multiplied enormously." The Mothers' Centers expanded so rapidly that on some days, Aguayo inaugurated two or three centers in one afternoon.[16] The centers allowed the PDC's women's department to work with previously unorganized and isolated women and provided the party with a more secure base of electoral support.

Antonia Meyer was also instrumental in organizing women to support the party. In 1958, right after Frei lost the presidential elections, she joined the Christian Democrats. She had close ties with the Frei family. Meyer worked as a secretary to Irene Frei, Eduardo Frei's sister and an active leader in the Christian Democratic Party, until Irene Frei's death shortly before the 1964 elections.

In 1962 Meyer moved to Puente Alto, an industrial suburb south of Santiago that is home to La Papelera, the huge paper processing plant that belonged to the Alessandri family.[17] Although residents of Puente

15 Aguayo, interview. After the coup, Aguayo lived in political exile in France until 1986, at which time she returned to Chile. While in France she authored a pioneering history of the Mothers' Centers based primarily on her own recollections and those of other Chilean women in exile. The Jesuit to whom Aguayo refers is Father Del Corro, who had the idea to turn the Mothers' Centers into workshops so that the women would learn skills and earn some money. See Aguayo, *Des Chiliennes*, 58–65.

16 Ibid., 61.

17 Today, the urban sprawl of Santiago has extended to such a degree that the highway from Santiago to Puente Alto is one uninterrupted chain of houses and small businesses. During the UP years, Puente Alto was the site of a major political dispute between the UP government, which wanted to nationalize the plant, and the owners and some sectors of the workers, who resisted its attempts to do so (see Chapter 7).

Alto supported Alessandri in the 1958 elections (see Table 4.1)—most likely because his family was the single most important source of employment in the town—the PDC began to make inroads into the industrial community during the early 1960s, as did the left. Table 4.1 indicates, however, that the PDC obtained most of its success with female voters. The male vote in Puente Alto went to Allende. Since this gendered split reflected national trends, the example of Puente Alto can shed some light on what the PDC did to obtain such a high percentage of women's votes.

In many ways, Meyer was a typical PDC female activist. A middle-class woman whose political involvement began when she joined the party, Meyer dedicated enormous amounts of time and energy to building the PDC. In order to cultivate the notion that support for Frei extended beyond party affiliation, Irene Frei asked Meyer to conceal her party membership and to present herself as the independent president of Women for Frei in Puente Alto. She agreed to do so. Like Aguayo, Meyer understood that in order to succeed at the polls, the party needed to expand beyond its middle-class origins and membership and win over the poor and marginalized sectors of the Chilean population. In Puente Alto, Meyer worked very closely with the director of the Frei campaign, a woman of very "humble origins" who convinced Meyer that they should organize the *poblaciones*. To do so, the two women—accompanied by other female volunteers—went door-to-door in the poor neighborhoods, introducing the PDC to women in the *poblaciones* and Meyer to the realities of life for huge numbers of Chile's urban poor.[18]

Meyer, in turn, convinced Frei to make Puente Alto one of his campaign stops. Frei was reluctant to visit the city. Not only had people booed him when he campaigned there in 1958, but he had also received a lower percentage of the inhabitants' vote there than elsewhere (see Table 4.1).[19] Frei's 1964 tour of Puente Alto, organized by Meyer and the Women for Frei, reflected the candidate's growing popularity, however. When the group visited a maternity ward of the hospital, they heard no jeers; instead, Meyer noted that "all the women wanted him to be their baby's godfather."[20] According to Meyer, Frei left Puente Alto surprised and happy with the reception he had received and pleased with the accomplishments of his female supporters, particularly their work among women.

18 Antonia Meyer, interview by author, tape recording, Providencia, 26 May 1994.

19 Although Frei came in third nationally in the presidential elections, as he did in Puente Alto, he generally received a much higher percentage of the vote elsewhere than he did in Puente Alto. Thus, the votes he obtained in Puente Alto reflect a disproportionately low percentage of the vote when compared to his national figures.

20 Meyer, interview.

Table 4.1 A comparison of voting results from the 1958 and 1964 presidential elections in Puente Alto, by gender

Candidate and Election	Women's Vote #	Women's Vote %	Men's Vote #	Men's Vote %	Total
1958 elections					
Alessandri (PC & PL)	**1,371**	**45%**	2,111	39%	**3,482**
Allende (FRAP)	844	28	1,977	36	2,821
Frei (PDC)	398	13	563	10	961
1964 election					
Frei (PDC)	**6,261**	**60**	4,998	47	**11,259**
Allende (FRAP)	3,785	37	**5,217**	**49**	9,002

Note: Five candidates ran in the 1958 elections. However, for purposes of comparison, this table excludes two of the candidates (as well as the listings for null and blank votes). The totals, therefore, will not add up to 100 percent. However, the percentages do illustrate the proportion of votes obtained by the candidates discussed in this study. Similarly, the 1964 election results do not include the null and blank votes cast, so the percentages listed in the table will not add up to 100. Boldface type indicates the candidates who received the most votes.

Source: República de Chile, Servicio Electoral, "Elección presidencial de la República del 4 de septiembre de 1958" (Santiago: Servicio Electoral, n.d.), and República de Chile, Servicio Electoral, "Elección presidencial de la República del 4 de septiembre de 1964" (Santiago: Servicio Electoral, n.d.).

Frei won the 1964 elections in Puente Alto, as he did nationally, and his victory was largely due to women's votes. The high percentage of women who voted for Frei offset the large number of men who voted for Allende. What is most striking is the tremendous change in the women's vote from 1958 to 1964. Not only did many more women vote, but they also preferred Frei over Allende at a rate of almost two to one. After the elections, Meyer was thrilled to note that Frei "mentioned Puente Alto, since he was so surprised that the elections had reversed themselves and he had received a very high vote."[21] This turnaround in women's votes reflects the success that Meyer and other female activists achieved in winning women over to the PDC candidate.

The work of Aguayo and Meyer illustrates an aspect of Frei's 1964 campaign that has gone largely unnoticed: the active role played by women in encouraging and organizing other women to vote for Frei. Prior to the 1964 presidential elections, the Frei campaign—like Allende's—formed support committees made up of (supposedly) nonparty independents. Their function was "to involve all those sectors that were not members of any party. These sectors could increase a candidate's vote to the extent that they supported the candidate as a person, based on the

21 Ibid.

ideas he proposed, . . . [and] regardless of his party membership." Since the majority of women did not belong to any party, party workers created special women's committees, such as Women for Frei. The party also sponsored women's teas, which were held in supporters' homes and attended by a large number of women. During the teas, women listened attentively as the candidate—or a female member of his family—addressed them and answered their questions.[22]

The Scare Campaign convinced many women that they should not vote for Allende. The work of female PDC activists (along with that of male party supporters) gave them reasons to vote for Frei. Because more women voted in the 1964 elections than had ever voted before in Chile, their votes mattered. Neuse believes that such a high number of women voted for the PDC because it "invested the campaign with a sense of moral urgency, suggesting that women had a considerable stake in the choice between Eduardo Frei's 'revolution in liberty' (which would insure stability and maintain the family as the primary social unit) and Salvador Allende's 'communist revolution' (which would threaten stability and the home)."[23]

The Christian Democratic policies of working through or creating Mothers' Centers in the *poblaciones*, of establishing a women's department and Women's Committees for Frei, and of encouraging women to campaign actively for the PDC candidate help explain the astonishingly high number of women who voted for Frei. By going into the *poblaciones* of Santiago, the Christian Democrats scored a major success. Seventy-five percent of first-time female voters cast their ballots for Eduardo Frei.[24]

The Christian Democrats and the Mothers' Centers

A key tenet of Christian Democratic ideology was the belief that Catholics had a social responsibility to work for the common good of all Chileans. As astute politicians and as members of a relatively young party, Christian Democratic leaders also understood the need to carve a space for themselves in the crowded terrain of Chilean politics. To accomplish both goals, the Christian Democrats sought to develop a base among those sectors of the Chilean population that were the most marginalized and in need of help and organization: the urban poor and the peasantry.

Many of these people lacked both party affiliation and an established network to which they could turn for assistance. It was with these people

[22] For a description of these candidates' efforts to organize women, see Edda Gaviola, Lorella Lopresti, and Claudia Rojas, *Segundo informe de avance: La participación política de la mujer en Chile 1964–1973* (Santiago: n.p., n.d.), 5.

[23] Neuse, "Voting in Chile," 132.

[24] Fleet, *Rise and Fall*, 70.

in mind that the PDC designed and implemented the national Promoción Popular (Popular Promotion) program in 1964. Through this program, the PDC planned to organize "marginalized" sectors of Chilean society and incorporate them into the economic and political life of the nation.

Much of the theory and impetus for this program came from the church-affiliated Bellarmino Center under the charismatic leadership of Father Roger Vekemans. Vekemans, a Belgian Jesuit and sociologist, came to Chile in 1957 and established the Centro Para el Desarrollo Económico y Social de América Latina (DESAL, Center for the Economic and Social Development of Latin America), which later became the Centro Bellarmino.[25] Vekemans exercised a substantial intellectual and programmatic influence on the social philosophy and policies adopted by the Christian Democrats both before and after they came to power in 1964. According to Penny Lernoux, who has written extensively on the Catholic Church in Latin America, Vekemans also served as a conduit for CIA funds that flowed into Chile to ensure Frei's election and then to bankroll his development projects.[26]

Under the auspices of the Popular Promotion program, the Christian Democrats began a massive national campaign to organize the urban and rural poor in order to "integrate them into the development of the country."[27] According to Vekemans, the primary definition of marginality is "lack of participation." This "lack of participation" operates on two levels. First, those who are "marginal are defined, in this case, by a lack of participation with respect to the wealth that should be common to all." Second, those who are marginal suffer from "a lack of active participation in decision making." Vekemans believed that the Popular Promotion program would do away with marginality through the incorporation of the disenfranchised into society—a process that could only be effected through an "external agency."[28] To combat marginalization, the

---

25 Penny Lernoux, *Cry of the People* (New York: Penguin, 1982), 25–27. Lernoux writes that "the financial management of the fast-talking Jesuit left a good deal to be desired, judging by the hanky-panky uncovered in an AID audit. The free-spending Vekemans was saved from an AID criminal investigation only because the U.S. Embassy in Chile insisted that to mark him as a criminal would damage the Christian Democrats, whom the CIA had financed through various Vekemans projects" (290).

26 Ibid., 25–27, 289–93; Labarca Goddard, *Chile invadido*, 75–106. Father Vekemans also set up the School of Sociology at the Catholic University.

27 Valdés and Weinstein, *Mujeres que sueñan*, 54.

28 Roger Vekemans, *Marginalidad, incorporación e integratión* (Santiago: DESAL, 1968), 3–5, 11. In 1967, Vekemans estimated that 50 percent of Chileans were marginal. Of these, 32 percent were peasants, 17 percent urban poor, and 5 percent sub-proletariat.

Christian Democratic government set up two key organizations, the Junta de Vecinos (Neighborhood Committees) and the Centros de Madres (Mothers' Centers).[29] Hundreds of thousands of marginalized peasants and urban poor joined the Neighborhood Committees or the Mothers' Centers and, as a result of their participation, came to see themselves as people whose voices and votes mattered.[30] The Mothers' Centers both provided the PDC government with an entrée into the poor neighborhoods and brought the women who lived in these areas into direct contact with the government.

In 1964, First Lady María Ruiz-Tagle de Frei organized CEMA (Central Relacionadora de los Centros de Madres, Central Organization for the Mothers' Centers) in order to, as the name suggests, "integrate all the Mothers' Centers existing in the country."[31] Gabriela Varela, her private secretary, explained that "the Mothers' Centers exist in order to integrate that enormous nucleus of women, the 'housewives,' into the community by giving them the means to collaborate economically in their home. Since they are all part of this country, they can contribute their efforts toward the improvement of the financial and social situation that afflicts us."[32] To achieve this, the Mothers' Centers would provide women with the economic and technical means to produce items that their families needed and they could sell. Their production, in turn, would benefit their households and the nation at large.

In his campaign speeches, Frei promised that if he were elected, every Chilean woman would receive a sewing machine.[33] The fulfillment of this campaign pledge was one of the first and most important activities of CEMA. Aguayo believes that Frei's vow boosted his standing among women and helps explain the huge outpouring of female support for him. She noted that having a sewing machine

was like a dream for them. It's as if nowadays you would say to young people, each one of you will have your own computer. . . . The government . . . imported immense quantities of sewing machines and gave them to the women. . . . The women had to buy them, but they received a lot of help from the government to

29 *El Mercurio*, 30 June 1966.

30 Scully, *Rethinking the Center*, 161.

31 Valdés and Weinstein, *Mujeres que sueñan*, 56.

32 *El Mercurio*, 1 June 1966.

33 Veronica Oxman, *La participación de la mujer campesina en organizaciones: Los centros de madres rurales* (Santiago: Academia de Humanismo Cristiano, 1983), 34. Frei's campaign promise to women sounds much like the Chilean equivalent of the Republican Party's 1920s pledge to "put a chicken in every pot."

do so. Trucks loaded with sewing machines bearing the words CEMA *went from Arica [the northernmost city in Chile] to the south.*[34]

Blanca Peinenao, a Mapuche Indian who was born on a *reducción* (reservation) and grew up speaking no Spanish, was one of the hundreds of thousands of women who received a sewing machine. When she married her husband, Segundo, who is also a Mapuche, they moved to the small farm they inhabit today, located about one hour by bus from the southern city of Villarrica. Although they have put a great deal of effort into building their home, they still lack running water and electricity.

Today, as in the 1960s, Ñancul, the closest town, is a forty-minute walk over rolling hills and down dusty paths. Blanca helped start the first Mothers' Center in Ñancul. At first, Segundo did not like the idea of his wife joining a Mothers' Center, because the meetings would take her away from home and her domestic responsibilities. Her desire to belong, however—coupled with the concrete benefits membership offered—helped wrest grudging permission from her husband. A representative from the Frei government helped Blanca and thirty-nine other women start the center. She joined "so that we would get help. We all needed help." She believes that Frei sponsored the centers "in order to help poor people, those who were in need." She remembers the sewing machines very well. The sewing machine allowed her to make "school uniforms for the kids, *delantales* [a combination of apron and housecoat worn by Chilean housewives and schoolchildren], and pants for my husband." She paid off the sewing machine little by little, and she remembers that "it took us a year and a half to pay it off." Through the center, she could obtain material and yarn, which she also paid for over time. She would have been unable to purchase the goods in a store, since she lacked cash. Like many of the women in the Mothers' Centers, Blanca used the yarn both to make sweaters for her children to wear and to produce clothing to sell. Every year, the Mothers' Centers held an exposition in Villarrica, at which time the women offered their products for sale. The transactions served to integrate these women into the market economy, which was one of the government's goals.[35]

Irene Pilquinao Peinenao is Blanca's daughter. At age thirty-five, she still retained vivid memories of the Mothers' Center in Ñancul. As a child she often accompanied her mother to the weekly meetings. Her mother

[34] Aguayo, interview. To help women take advantage of Frei's pledge, the government allowed them to purchase the sewing machines on easy credit.

[35] Blanca Peinenao, interview by author, notes, Ñancul, 19 February 1994.

loved the meetings, although Pilquinao "got bored. They just talked about their things." Pilquinao remembered how important the sewing machine was to her mother and the entire family. "My mother was happy . . . to get the sewing machine for the kids. Without the Mothers' Center, she would never have gotten one. At that time, having a sewing machine was the one thing she most longed for. . . . Once she got it, we all learned how to sew, even my brother!"[36]

Over seventy thousand women received sewing machines, thanks to the Frei government.[37] The machines not only allowed women to make clothes and household items for their families, thus cutting down on costs, but also permitted them to produce items for sale on a larger scale than had been previously possible. Furthermore, the sewing machines introduced these women very directly to modern technology and led them to see themselves as the direct beneficiaries of a state-sponsored national program directed toward women.[38]

Rosa Elvira Durán, who lives in Renca, a poor area on the northwest side of Santiago, was a member of a local Mothers' Center from 1964 to 1990. She believed that the Mothers' Centers had a very positive impact on women's self-esteem and their identities as women.[39] In an interview, she recalled her own experiences in the center:

Thirty years ago, when I first joined a Mothers' Center, at a quarter to five everyone left because they had to get home to put on the teapot, take care of their kids, and serve once [afternoon tea] to their husbands. Now, if you go to a Mothers' Center, you'll hear the women saying, "el viejo [my husband] is about to get home. Well, he can serve himself tea." That's the difference. Women's personalities have changed. When women got together they shared things. . . . They learned to value themselves, to defend themselves. Above all, they learned to work. When you work and contribute economically to the household, then your status changes.[40]

Thousands of Chilean women had experiences similar to those recounted by Peinenao, Pilquinao, and Durán. Their stories indicate the

36 Irene Pilquinao, interview by author, tape recording, La Florida, 8 October 1993.

37 Valdés et al., *Centros de Madres*, 17–18.

38 Valdés and Weinstein point out that this program has been called "the revolution of the sewing machine" because of the enormous impact it had on women. See Valdés and Weinstein, *Mujeres que sueñan*, 57.

39 Rosa Elvira Durán, interview by author, tape recording, Renca, 26 November 1993.

40 Durán, interview. I first met Rosa when she was visiting a Mothers' Center in the neighborhood of Pedro Aguirre Cerda (her sister is president of the center). *Once* is a uniquely Chilean word that refers to afternoon tea, which is served between 5:00 and 7:00 P.M. It can be as simple as a cup of tea and bread or as elaborate as a four-course meal.

extent to which the Christian Democratic government penetrated hith-
erto ignored regions and sectors of Chilean society. By 1966, there were
3,000 Mothers' Centers in Santiago and 2,500 throughout the rest of the
country. According to one estimate, an average of 34 women were allied
with each Mothers' Center, which means that approximately 187,000
women were affiliated with the program at that time. The impact of the
Mothers' Centers was enormous. Each woman belonged to a household
estimated to average at least five people; thus, "the work of the Mothers'
Centers [reached] around one million people, most of them in poor or
deficient economic conditions."[41] By 1970, at the end of Frei's presidency, 450,000 women were involved in one of the 9,000 Mothers' Centers throughout Chile.[42]

These centers promoted the organization, social involvement, and political participation of women. For the first time, literally, hundreds of thousands of women had the state's (and eventually their husbands') approval to
leave their homes and to meet with other women in non-church-related
social activities. This experience gave women the opportunity to discuss
their lives and to listen to other women's stories on an ongoing, organized
basis. For both rural and urban women, membership broke the daily routine of household chores and the isolation of work within the home. The
women received different kinds of training. In 1967, 1,142—and in 1968,
2,127—women attended courses on leadership development. Women
could also learn some skills. The classes primarily taught women "manual
skills, . . . [such as] how to make certain products that were useful to the
family and, occasionally, could be sold."[43] In 1967 and 1968, 39,300 and
43,050 women, respectively, took such courses.

The importance that the Frei government gave to the Mothers' Centers, coupled with the substantial state resources budgeted for them, fostered their rapid growth and allowed them to spread throughout Chile.
The Frei government named 4 November 1969 as the "National Day of
the Mothers' Centers" and celebrated it with a ceremony in the National
Stadium in Santiago. During the event, President Frei planned to read
the "conclusions of the national meeting of leaders of the Mothers' Centers" that had taken place on 3–4 November and had involved "five hundred delegates from throughout the country."[44] One contemporary

41 *La Nación*, 10 October 1966, cited in Oxman, *La participación de la mujer campesina*, 35.

42 Aylwin et al., *Percepción del rol político de la mujer*, 38.

43 Valdés et al., *Centros de Madres*, 19–20. Through the centers' classes, women learned, for example, how to make stuffed animals that they could sell.

44 *El Mercurio*, 1 November 1969.

observer compared the Neighborhood Committees and the Mothers' Centers and concluded that "in terms of organizational effectiveness, the Mothers' Centers have been more successful. Most of their support has come from lower-class urban women."[45] The Mothers' Centers allowed the PDC to reach into the *poblaciones* and organize poor women in unprecedented numbers.

Debate on the Impact of the Mothers' Centers

Despite the success of the Mothers' Centers—or perhaps because of it—the organizations have provoked debate. Differences in opinion about the political usefulness of the centers emerged during the UP years. Some members of the UP believed that the centers were "paternalistic and traditional." They asked, "For how long are we going to teach women how to sew?" Others, whose arguments ultimately predominated, believed that the centers were "a school for women that allowed them to organize themselves, get out of the house, learn, and become leaders."[46] Backed by the government, the centers grew in number during the UP years. By 1973, roughly one million women were involved in the twenty thousand centers that existed throughout the country.[47]

Edda Gaviola, Lorella Lopresti, and Claudia Rojas, three Chilean scholars, have a relatively positive view of the centers. They argue that "the Mothers' Centers . . . constituted the first massive step that at least allowed women to criticize the isolation they were subjected to in the confines of their homes. . . . They were organizations that unconsciously offered women a minimal exercise of resistance to patriarchal ideology." They conclude that "the Mothers' Centers were, in one way or another, the seed of a massive, popular movement that could not be consolidated, due to the break with democracy that took place in 1973."[48]

Other scholars do not share this assessment. As one of Chile's leading feminists, Julieta Kirkwood contributed to a theoretical understanding of feminism and actively participated in the feminist and anti-Pinochet movement that developed in Chile in the late 1970s and early 1980s.[49] She points out that the roots of the Mothers' Centers can be found in the

45 Petras, *Political and Social Forces*, 230.

46 Aguayo, interview.

47 Edda Gaviola, Lorella Lopresti, and Claudia Rojas, "Chile Centro de Madres: ¿La mujer popular en movimiento?" in *Nuestra memoria, nuestro futuro: Mujeres e historia, América Latina y el Caribe* (Santiago: Isis Internacional, n.d.), 86.

48 Ibid., 87.

49 She died of cancer in 1985.

Asociación de Dueñas de Casa (Association of Housewives), the function of which was "to prepare poor women to better carry out their tasks as housewives." From her point of view, the Mothers' Centers neither transformed women's roles in society nor served as the seed for the beginnings of a progressive women's movement. Far from challenging women's position within the family, the Mothers' Centers "became the place where the most traditional family values, maternity, and the gender role of the housewife were reaffirmed." Kirkwood acknowledges that the PDC ushered in a new level of organization for women. However, far from producing any fundamental changes in women's relationship to power, the Christian Democrats' policy toward women was nothing more than "a revised religious-secularized ideology that allowed them to maintain a conservative [agenda] disguised as a progressive one." In fact, Kirkwood argues that during the UP years, the Mothers' Centers provided the opposition with a base from which to organize both the March of the Empty Pots and Pans and Poder Femenino; later, they served as a source of "unconditional support for the Pinochet dictatorship."[50]

Teresa Valdés, a Chilean sociologist who has extensively studied the Mothers' Centers, notes that they had a "dual character." On the one hand, they served to "incorporate women into the search for solutions to community problems and channeled their social demands to government structures." Thus, they helped "integrate the community." At the same time, though women learned different skills in the centers, the skills were all "related to the traditional role of women, [such as] how to make certain products that were useful to the family and, occasionally, could be sold . . . to increase the family's income. Women's position within society, in terms of their incorporation into the apparatus of production, was not substantially modified." Despite this drawback, she concludes that the Mothers' Centers were "powerful tools of the popular movement," because they increased women's political participation.[51]

These diverging assessments of the Mothers' Centers raise several theoretical questions. Can the process of collective participation effect changes in women's identities even when the parameters of this involvement are defined by a traditional interpretation of womanhood? To what extent can women's involvement alter the limits set by a conservative program? What, exactly, constitutes resistance to patriarchy? How can we, as

50 Kirkwood, *Ser política*, 144, 60. Also see "El voto femenino y la política," *¿Qué Pasa?* 17 November 1983.

51 Valdés et al., *Centros de Madres*, 19–20.

social scientists, judge the changes that take place in women's consciousness? What processes are likely to produce these transformations?

The experience of the Mothers' Centers does not provide any clear-cut answers to these questions. Some women see their participation in the Mothers' Centers as a transformative experience, while others recall primarily the concrete benefits they received from membership. For certain women, the Mothers' Centers provided an outlet from the monotony and isolation of their domestic routine. For Rosa Elvira Durán and women like her, the centers also offered the opportunity to earn a small amount of money—and enhanced their self-esteem. However, it does not appear that women's experiences in the Mothers' Centers led them to see any need for a social movement capable of questioning women's role within society and struggling for an alternative reality.

Of course, the Christian Democratic government did not set up the Mothers' Centers in order to create a movement that would fight to end women's oppression in Chile. Instead, they hoped to integrate women—one of the most "marginal" sectors of Chilean society—into the PDC's project. Just as the PDC's "Revolution in Liberty" reformed some of the more egregious aspects of capitalism in Chile but did not produce any revolutionary social change, the Mothers' Centers improved women's lives but did not radically transform them.

In fact, one reason why so many women joined the Mothers' Centers is that they did not fundamentally challenge gender roles in Chilean society. As their very name indicates, they were premised on the belief that a woman's role was to be a mother. This is not to say that membership in the centers did not produce changes in women's lives. Women had to disrupt their normal domestic routines in order to belong to a center. The Mothers' Centers encouraged women to realize that they had needs that could not be met solely within the walls of their homes. The experience of working and sharing with other women helped members assess their domestic situation from a different perspective, one informed by the awareness of other women's realities. As Durán's testimony reveals, it encouraged women to think more of their own needs (instead of ignoring them to satisfy those of their husbands). It also brought women into contact with other women in an organized and ongoing fashion. They developed or deepened friendships, and the experience of making plans, setting goals, and accomplishing projects together gave them greater self-confidence.

Although the Mothers' Centers achieved these results, there were several important things that they did not do. They did not undermine women's maternal identities. They did not train women in marketable skills that would have permitted them to find paying jobs outside the home.[52] They did not contribute to breaking women's economic dependence on male breadwinners. They did not sponsor the emergence of an independent women's movement. They did not encourage women to embrace leftist politics. They did, however, draw hundreds of thousands of previously unaffiliated and unorganized women into a closer relationship with both the Christian Democratic Party and the middle-class female PDC activists who directed the centers.

These networks and bonds of loyalty were very useful to the PDC during the UP years. The sheer number of women involved in the centers, many of whom retained their allegiance to the party even though Frei was no longer president, provided the PDC with a mass base. When the PDC took up active resistance against the UP government, the party turned to the Mothers' Centers to help recruit women to participate in its anti-Allende activities. For example, as we shall see in the next chapter, women from a Mothers' Center in the working-class neighborhood of Conchalí participated in the December 1971 March of the Empty Pots and Pans, and afterward, they wrote angry letters to Allende about the way the police had treated them during the demonstration.[53] On another occasion, women who claimed to represent seventy thousand members of two thousand Mothers' Centers— centers located in poor communities throughout the capital—protested in downtown Santiago because the government had taken over their food cooperative. The government accused the women and the store of hoarding food, a charge the demonstrators labeled "a lie."[54]

The fact that most of the members of the Mothers' Centers were poor and working-class women also meant that the PDC was able to recruit activists among those sectors of the population that were deemed the UP's key supporters. These women not only undercut the image that the working class allied solidly with Allende, but they also prevented the successful implementation of UP programs in the neighborhoods. A recent study pointed out that women from the Mothers' Centers "disrupted the UP's rationing programs by setting up alternate distribution networks and harassing workers in the rationing centers."[55]

52 As discussed in Chapter 2, only about 22 percent of Chilean women worked outside the home in 1970.

53 La Prensa, 5 December 1971.

54 Las Ultimas Noticias, 6 April 1973.

55 Joan Supplee, "Women and the Counterrevolution in Chile," in Women and Revolution in Africa, Asia, and the New World, ed. Mary Ann Tétreault (Columbia: University of South Carolina Press, 1994), 405.

This is not to say that the Mothers' Centers operated in a monolithic fashion. The hundreds of thousands of women who participated in the multitude of different centers did not constitute a unified force or even share the same political beliefs. They did not all side with the PDC against the UP. This diversity of responses, which is usually ignored by scholars who have written on the centers, explains why many of the centers were sites of political struggle between those women who supported the UP government and those who opposed it. Because the organizations represented a substantial bloc of votes, an organized (if not unified) sector of women, and a resource to be mobilized by each political tendency, both the UP and the Christian Democrats attempted to gain or maintain political control of the Mothers' Centers. While many Mothers' Centers retained their affiliation with the Christian Democratic Party, others gave their allegiance to the UP, and some, rent by internal differences, divided along political lines.[56]

Michèle Mattelart, a French sociologist, argues that the Mothers' Centers were "mechanisms of integration instituted by the [Christian Democrats]" that greatly facilitated the organizing of women's opposition to Allende. She acknowledges that during the UP years, the Mothers' Centers were sites of contention that, she claims, the left occasionally won. By and large, however, the politics upon which the centers developed "rested on norms of participation and ideological formulas that . . . revealed themselves more likely to channel women's mobilization toward the defense of the traditional system's interests."[57]

As both Kirkwood and Mattelart point out, during the UP years, the opposition to Allende exploited Chilean women's primary identity as wife and mother, and it took advantage of the ties that had been built between middle- and upper-class Christian Democratic activists and women in the *poblaciones* to mobilize women against the government. As the economic crisis deepened, the Mothers' Centers that had allied themselves with the Christian Democrats provided the anti-Allende movement with a direct entrée into the poor and working-class neighborhoods of Santiago. Gaviola's statement that the Mothers' Centers served as a seed of a massive popular (women's) movement is, therefore, only partially true. In fact, two

56 Aylwin et al., *Percepción del rol político de la mujer,* 38; Aguayo, interview. For an example of the kind of dispute that broke out in the Mothers' Centers between the Christian Democrats and the left over which tendency controlled them, see *La Prensa,* 11 December 1971 and 14 December 1971.

57 Michèle Mattelart, "La mujer y la linea de masa de la burguesía: El caso de Chile," in *La mujer en América Latina,* ed. María del Carmen Elu de Leñero (Mexico City: Secretaría de Educación Pública, 1975), 144.

very different women's mobilizations emerged from the Mothers' Centers—one in solidarity with the UP, and one in opposition to it.

The Modernization of the Right

The right reorganized and strengthened itself during the Frei years. In 1966, the Conservative and Liberal parties—the two traditional parties of the right—and the National Action Party, headed by far-rightist Jorge Prat, dissolved themselves and reemerged as the National Party.[58] Much of the leadership for the PN came from the National Action Party, a political force that "stamped [the PN] with an undeniable authoritarianism."[59]

Sofía Correa, a Chilean historian who studies the right, argues that the newly formed PN was born out of the 1964 *naranjazo* (see Chap. 3). Correa believes that the decision of the Conservative and Liberal parties to support Frei in the 1964 elections was "an act of suicide" that originated in "a loss of confidence" and, in the case of the Conservative Party, the belief that "the party had lost its *raison d'être*." The PN was "a politically confrontational force," very different from "the previous parliamentary elites, who had been experts in [the art of] negotiations and jointly-agreed-upon pacts."[60] Correa is quite accurate in asserting that the PN was more confrontational than its predecessors had been. However, it is worth noting that the PN's aggressive stance responded to the changed political conditions in Chile—conditions shaped in part by the PDC's policy of land reform, the growing strength of the left, and the UP's victory in the 1970 presidential elections.

Although the party was authoritarian and hierarchical, it demonstrated a willingness to adopt new policies to further its political interests. The right

58 Early in the 1964 presidential campaign, Jorge Prat had been a potential candidate. After the right's defeat in Curicó, however, he withdrew his candidacy in order to avoid dividing the anti-Allende forces (see Burnett, *Political Groups*, 249–50). Jorge Prat founded the National Action Party in 1963. As a young man, he had established Estanquero (Urzúa, *Historia política electoral*, 127), a nationalist group made up of "intellectuals inspired by corporatism and Hispanic integrationism. The group was characterized by its militant anti-communism and a declared support for the Franco and Oliveira Salazar dictatorships." It also published a magazine of the same name between 1946 and 1954. See Carlos Maldonado, "Grupos paramilitares de derecha en Chile, 1900–1950," (Santiago: unpublished, 1992), 15.

59 Urzúa, *Historia política electoral*, 127.

60 Sofía S. Correa, "La Derecha en Chile contemporáneo: La perdida del control estatal," *Revista de Ciencia Política* 11, no. 1 (1989): 16–19. Correa cites three additional factors to explain the confrontational nature of the National Party: the agrarian reform, which "destroyed an essential part of the elite's symbolic universe, . . . the National Congress' loss of powers, . . . [and] businessmen's loss of power within the Public Administration and the semi-federal institutions" (18–19).

realized that in order to survive the challenge posed by both the left and the Christian Democrats, it had to adapt to the new conditions in which it found itself. Thus, the party manifested a certain tactical flexibility—overlooked by many scholars—along with its belligerent attitude. One clear example of the party's ability to respond to the exigencies of the period was its emphasis on the mobilization of women. Victoria Armanet, a longtime political activist on the right, believes that the PN attempted to project a new image of the right, one more in tune with the air of modernization sweeping Chile in the latter half of the 1960s. When the PN formed after the "debacle of the 1965 congressional elections," she joined and led the women's section.[61] In that position, she helped organize the party throughout Chile. Armanet, who was a leader of Poder Femenino during the UP years, believes that the PN opened the door to the participation of women on the right. According to Armanet, "many women had wanted to become involved in politics," but they had not wanted to join the Liberal or Conservative parties, because "they felt put off by such antiquated organizations." In contrast, the PN "appeared to them to be a modern and flexible force" in which they felt welcomed and appreciated. As a result, Armanet concludes that "right-wing women's participation in politics began with the PN."[62]

The right used the PN to recover from its disastrous defeat in the 1965 elections. In the 1969 congressional elections, the PN came in second, with 20.9 percent of the vote. The right increased its number of senators from nine in 1965 to thirty-four in 1969.[63] Conversely, the Christian Democrats dropped from 42.3 percent of the votes in the 1965 congressional elections to 29.7 percent. Further foreshadowing the polarization of Chilean politics, the Communist Party and the Socialist Party both increased their percentages of votes as well. The Socialists went from 10.8 percent in 1965 to 14.5 percent in 1969; the Communists augmented their share from 11.4 percent in 1965 to 15.9 percent in 1969.[64] In her

61 The results of the 1965 parliamentary elections illustrated the strength of the PDC and the decline of the right. The PDC obtained 41.1 percent of the vote, while the Conservative Party received 5.4 percent, and the Liberal Party, 10.1 percent. In the 1961 parliamentary elections, the Conservative Party had received 14.7 percent—and the Liberal Party, 16.5 percent—of the vote. See Urzúa, *Historia política electoral,* 124.

62 Victoria Armanet, interview by author, tape recording, Santiago, 17 March 1994. Although Armanet does not define modern, I believe that she means a party no longer tied so closely to (and identified with) the landowners, one that is therefore more able to attract and incorporate new sectors.

63 Susanne Bodenheimer, "Stagnation in Liberty—The Frei Experiment in Chile, Part II," *NACLA Newsletter* 3, no. 1 (March 1969): 9.

64 Urzúa, *Historia política electoral,* 134.

insightful study of the Frei years, Susanne Bodenheimer analyzes the upsurge in support for the PN that the March 1969 elections reflected, and she concludes that "if the results of this month's parliamentary elections . . . are any indication of a trend in Chilean electoral politics, the main beneficiary of popular disillusion with the Frei government and of the PDC's electoral decline is not the Left but the rightist Partido Nacional (which . . . from 1964–68 had been at an all-time low)."[65]

Of equal portent for political developments in the next two decades, and largely ignored at the time, was the emergence of the *gremio* (guild) movement. According to David Cusack, the reforms engineered by the Christian Democrats "made the economic elite realize how extensive was the Chilean state's control of the economy and how fragile was their hold on the state." It is in this context that the "business elite and their political advisors initiated the gremio movement."[66] Much of the organizational impetus for the *gremio* movement came from professors and students of the Catholic University, the school that educated the sons and daughters of Chile's elite. During the mid-1960s, Jaime Guzmán was a law student at the Catholic University in Santiago. Like students throughout the world during the 1960s, many young Chileans demanded a greater democratization of the university and of society in general. When students (many but not all of them affiliated with political parties) shut down the university in October 1967 and demanded that a new rector be appointed, Jaime Guzmán was appalled. An ardent admirer of Jorge Alessandri, Guzmán believed that partisan politics had no role in government and that political parties had no place in the university. Repelled by the political ferment and polarization all around him, the reforms enacted during the Frei presidency (particularly the agrarian and educational reforms), and the growth in union membership, Guzmán looked to the medieval guild as a model for the kind of organization that would most effectively represent the needs of different social groups. Guzmán helped form the *gremio* movement in 1966 because he believed that the *gremios* offered the elite protection from the left (and other forces calling for change) and prevented conflict between various social sectors.[67]

According to Guzmán, *gremialismo* (the *gremio* movement) has its roots "in the most classical theoreticians of Christian philosophy. It incorporates the contributions that humanitarian doctrines have developed throughout

65 Bodenheimer, "Stagnation," 10.

66 Cusack, *Revolution and Reaction*, 25.

67 Jaime Guzmán, *Escritos personales* (Santiago: Editorial Universitaria, 1992), 31–45.

time." *Gremialismo* "neither rejects nor scorns political activity. . . . What *gremialismo* condemns is the political utilization of nonpolitical intermediate societies, because it is unnatural, distorts their end, and weakens the contribution that the national community requires from them. Politicization of the universities, the guilds, or any organization whose goal is not political, furthermore, is an attempt against their autonomy and thus a weakening of one of the pillars of a free society."[68]

Close links existed between the *gremio* movement and the conservative Catholic movement called Tradition, Family, and Property. During the 1950s and 1960s, the church in Latin America had shifted its alliances from more conservative parties to more moderate ones. In response, Dr. Plínio Corrêa de Oliveira, a Brazilian philosopher, founded TFP in Brazil in the early 1960s. Penny Lernoux characterizes the members of the Brazilian TFP as being "from the wealthy, propertied classes . . . [who] yearn for an earlier time when the Latin American Church upheld the right of a few patrones to rule a mass of peons."[69] In Brazil, as in Argentina and Chile, TFP mounted an increasingly virulent anticommunist campaign and clearly identified itself with the extreme right. Daniel Levine notes that "TFP members see themselves as part of a general counterrevolutionary offensive, and they explicitly attribute most of the ills of the modern world to the aftereffects of the French Revolution."[70]

The Chilean group maintained very close ties with its Brazilian counterpart. *Fiducia*, the publication of the Chilean TFP, frequently reprinted speeches and documents from the Brazilian organization. Following the electoral victory of Eduardo Frei, denunciations of agrarian reform filled the pages of *Fiducia*, and some of the articles were direct translations of writings by Corrêa de Oliveira.[71] Jaime Guzmán, who also published in *Fiducia*, defended the right of property as "a natural right, necessary for the formation of a Christian society, which allows those who form part of it to realize themselves as human beings."[72] Linking the defense of property to the protection of established social relations, one article in *Fiducia* warned that agrarian reform threatened property and would also destroy

---

68 Ibid., 46, 52–53.

69 Lernoux, *Cry of the People*, 294.

70 Daniel H. Levine, *Religion and Politics in Latin America: The Catholic Church in Venezuela and Colombia* (Princeton: Princeton University Press, 1986), 49. Levine adds that "TFP militants played a major role in organizing public opposition to the Goulart regime. Later, in Chile, TFP was active in the opposition to Allende, often forming the core of right-wing groups such as Patria y Libertad" (49).

71 For example, see *Fiducia*, November 1964, 6.

72 Ibid., 9.

the family and tradition.[73] Reflecting TFP's conservative perspective on social issues, *Fiducia* is replete with articles that argue against divorce, claiming that "divorce is corrupt. It offends both the natural order and the supernatural, God. We cannot allow it, especially here in Chile, because we constitute a nation of obvious Catholic traditions."[74]

Brian Smith illuminates the connections between the *gremio* movement and conservative Catholic groups. Tracing the 1960s *gremio* movement from the Catholic Integralist movement in the 1930s and 1940s, Smith points out that Jaime Guzmán studied with Jaime Eyzaguírre (as did Elena Larraín's father), "professor of the Catholic University and intellectual leader of the Chilean Catholic Integralism in the previous generation."[75] Jaime Eyzaguírre, along with other conservative Chilean thinkers, espoused social corporatist ideas "based on the teachings of *Quadragessimo Anno*."[76]

By the end of the 1960s, Jaime Guzmán had developed his antiparty, antipolitics tendency into the flourishing *gremio* movement. The movement brought together previously unmobilized students (especially those from the conservative Catholic University), small business owners, truck drivers, white-collar employees, and professionals, uniting them into supposedly apolitical groups whose stated goal was to ensure the corporate interests of their members.[77] Despite their claims of being apolitical, guilds became a formidable and united political force against the Allende government in the early 1970s. When one branch of the guild movement went out on strike against the UP government, the other *gremio* organizations followed suit. Since the *gremio* movement controlled much of Chile's transportation system, businesses, financial institutions (many bank unions had pro-*gremio* leaders), and private medical care (the president of the Santiago Regional Council on Medical Schools was a *gremialista*), a strike

73 See "La 'Reforma Agraria': Un ataque a la propiedad, la familia y la tradición," *Fiducia*, August 1964, 8–11.

74 "El divorcio y las tendencias románticas," *Fiducia*, August–September 1965, 4.

75 Smith, *Church and Politics*, 139–40 n. 26.

76 Renato Cristi and Carlos Ruiz, "Conservative Thought in Twentieth-Century Chile," *Canadian Journal of Latin American and Caribbean Studies*, no. 30 (1990): 40–41. This article provides an excellent overview of the ideas of five conservative intellectuals and ties those ideas to the military regime. In 1931, Pope Pius XI proclaimed the encyclical *Quadragessimo Anno* as part of the church's efforts to oppose secularization and to reassert papal and church authority. The encyclical encouraged Catholics to apply church teachings to their daily lives and to social issues.

77 Since many of these middle-class sectors—and even lower-middle-class ones—considered themselves superior to the working class, they had shunned the trade union movement and had failed to develop organizations of their own prior to joining the *gremio* movement.

called by its members could wreak havoc on the Chilean economy. For example, what initially began as a truckers' strike in October 1972 and August 1973 escalated into a massive shutdown of much of Chile's transportation, commercial, and professional system, causing massive shortages, widespread chaos, and personal discomfort. After the September 1973 military coup overthrew the Allende government, members of the *gremio* movement occupied key positions in the Pinochet regime, and Jaime Guzmán served as chief ideologue for the military government.

Reflections on the Christian Democratic Party and Women

Despite its shortcomings, the Christian Democratic government touched people deeply during its six years in power. For many of the women I interviewed, the memory of this period is inextricably linked to their feelings about Eduardo Frei. All of the Christian Democratic women interviewed retain fervent and fond memories of Eduardo Frei Sr. For many older women, he was the Chilean president who most perfectly approximated their idea of what a political figure and a Catholic gentleman should be. Others remember him as the president who kept his promises. Blanca Peinenao could not remember Salvador Allende's name, but she instantly recalled the name of the president who had established the Mothers' Center in her town.[78]

The Christian Democrats encouraged the active participation of women in the Frei campaign. Once Frei was elected, they organized hundreds of thousands of women into the Mothers' Centers. There is no evidence to suggest, however, that they had any intention of altering patriarchal relations of power within Chilean society, in the Christian Democratic Party, or between men and women.

Indeed, Aguayo evoked an image of Frei that stands in sharp contrast to the glowing recollections shared by many women still loyal to the first Christian Democratic president of Chile. Discussing her experiences in the 1964 campaign, she remarked that

working with Frei, as a candidate, was not easy. He really did not like women to participate in social struggles. He was, like so many others, one of those men who want to see their wives in the home. The traditional discourse that valued the mother and the family came to him easily because it sincerely reflected his thoughts.

78 It is important to note that these women's memories are shaped by the three years of the UP government and the seventeen years of military dictatorship. In contrast, the six years of the Frei government stand out in their minds as a period of calm, prosperity, and idealism. For many women, too, the Frei years represented the high point of their political involvement and youthful energy.

Women leaders [in the party] had a very difficult time in making ourselves heard, having our opinions respected, and really playing a role in the leadership of the party. They wanted us to be docile, what women are always asked to be.[79]

A 1964 interview with Eduardo Frei and his wife, María Ruiz-Tagle, confirms Aguayo's comments. The interviewer asked the couple how a wife could help in a presidential campaign. Frei responded,

In my case, the most important thing has been the knowledge that I have a safe refuge in my own home, that my children continue with their studies, and that at least in my house the torrents of politics don't enter. . . . My greatest comfort, when I leave on tour, is knowing that my children will arrive home and find their mother. I don't believe that both the husband and wife can be politically involved at the same time. Often I have arrived home to eat at eleven or twelve o'clock at night to find María awake and waiting to heat up the food for me.[80]

Ruiz-Tagle seconded his statements: "I don't get involved in politics, since I stay at home. My life revolves around the house, not around political campaigns." The interviewer then asked the couple, "What is the image that you feel Chilean women want the First Lady to have, and what are you doing to implement this image?" Frei answered, "I believe that Chileans want the wife of the president to be a Chilean lady. That is to say, one who is not inquisitive, fake, or exhibitionist, but rather one who has dignity and is calm. One who is a mother, a good wife and who is concerned with presenting a good image to the world of her country in humanistic and social terms rather than political ones. . . . María does not have her own bank account and has never signed a check in her life."[81]

In 1969, toward the end of Frei's term, the Christian Democratic government organized Chile's first National Women's Office. One year later, in May 1970, the office organized a seminar to study "How the Chilean Women Face the Process of Change." The degree to which the international women's liberation movement had made its presence felt in Chile—and just what kind of changes the seminar did *not* plan to address—were reflected in the opening words of Gabriela Merino, the director of the National Women's Office: "Women's attitudes must not be based on the absurd desire to establish a matriarchy in this country through feminist demands. Quite the contrary! By profoundly respecting ourselves, we will

79 See Aguayo, *Des Chiliennes*, 71–72.
80 *Ercilla*, "Con la familia Frei," 25 May 1964.
81 Ibid.

seek, together with men, happiness, the common good, and the establishment of a just society."[82]

In many ways, this seminar serves as a fitting summation of the Christian Democratic Party's policies toward women. It came at the end of Frei's six-year term as president, just as the campaign for the next presidency was swinging into full gear. The seminar itself recognized that Chilean women lived in a changing world, a world that was becoming more modern. Eduardo Frei addressed the seminar participants and cautioned the women with these words:

Please forgive me if I, a man, dare to give you a few words of advice at this time. I know this is a very bold thing to do. I beg of you that as you undertake this process of change you do not repeat the errors which we men have fallen into.

I believe that women are free of hate. Change can be undertaken in a realistic way. Your contributions can be great and concrete. Please don't imitate us. Be yourselves! Bring to it new values and this feeling of generosity and sacrifice that you possess.

Women are the sanest thing in Chile. You have demonstrated this in the past and the present.[83]

The opposition used precisely this view of women—that they are different from and morally superior to men, lack political experience, and act without self-interest—during the UP years to help mobilize women against the Allende government and in support of the military coup.

82 *La Nación*, 29 May 1970.
83 *La Nación*, 28 May 1970.

5

From the Scare Campaign to the March of the Empty Pots and Pans

The Beginnings of the Anti-Allende Women's Movement

ON 4 SEPTEMBER 1970, Salvador Allende, the candidate of the Popular Unity coalition, won the presidential election. Allende governed Chile until the military overthrew him on 11 September 1973. His election—and the politicization that characterized the UP years—infused Chileans' lives, attitudes, and behavior with new meanings and possibilities. The majority of Chilean women had not been very active in politics previously, and they became swept up in the maelstrom. Mobilized in unprecedented numbers, women saw themselves playing a central role in the political drama sweeping Chile and contributed to the dynamic unfolding of events. The women who had the greatest impact on politics during this period were those who most *resisted* the changes proposed by the UP government.[1] This chapter examines the development of the anti-Allende women's movement from the 1970 presidential elections through the famous—or perhaps infamous—March of the Empty Pots and Pans in December 1971.

The 1970 Presidential Campaign

Buoyed by its success in the 1969 parliamentary elections, the right felt an increased confidence in its ability to win the presidency in 1970.[2] At the same time, the right realized that in a period of democratic upsurge and growing demands for social justice, many Chileans associated the

---

[1] Women who supported the Popular Unity government also increased their political activity. Their involvement is the subject of another study.

[2] In the 1969 elections for deputies and senators, the National Party received 21 percent and 17 percent of the vote, respectively. See J. Biehl del Río and Gonzalo Fernández, "The Political Pre-requisites for a Chilean Way," in *Allende's Chile*, ed. Kenneth Medhurst (London: Hart-David, MacGibbon, 1972), 61–62. For an interesting political discussion of this period in Chilean history, see Moulian, "Desarrollo político," 105–58.

National Party with the elite who had ruled Chile for decades. As a result, they viewed the PN with suspicion and hostility.[3] Hoping to evoke nostalgic dreams of a stable and prosperous past, the right ran septuagenarian Jorge Alessandri, an independent and former president of Chile (1958–64), as its candidate. For the fourth time, the left nominated Salvador Allende. The Christian Democrats named Radomiro Tomic, a representative of the left wing of the party, as their presidential candidate.[4]

Despite having had their morale boosted by the 1969 parliamentary elections, the Alessandri forces knew that winning would be difficult. The 1969 results showed that support for the left had increased since the 1965 parliamentary elections. Although the percentage of votes given to the Christian Democrats in 1969 had dropped precipitously from the 1965 elections, the Christian Democratic Party was still the largest and most powerful party in Chile. In addition, a slate of three candidates meant that it would be difficult to get a majority in the first round. The Alessandri forces could not look to the Christian Democrats for support against the left, because Radomiro Tomic had promised publicly to support Salvador Allende, should the latter win—provided he did so by at least thirty thousand votes.[5]

Given this challenging electoral reality, the Alessandri forces relied on women to guarantee their candidate's victory, just as women had done in the 1958 presidential elections.[6] In order to ensure that the female vote went to Alessandri, his supporters developed a variety of programs that appealed directly to women. They held meetings and teas organized by and for women.[7] Using the abundant monies supplied by both the

3 Hermógenes Pérez de Arce, interview by author, tape recording, Providencia, 9 June 1994. Pérez de Arce is a journalist and a longtime member of the right. During the UP years, he successfully ran as a National Party deputy from Santiago.

4 Pushed by its own poor showing in the recent parliamentary elections, the growing strength of the left, the increased popular mobilizations, and the general political upheavals of the late 1960s, the PDC looked to its left wing as its only chance of winning. However, the choice of Tomic did not sit well with the large number of Christian Democrats who had favored the more conservative Frei. Their displeasure with Tomic was so great that some of them voted for Alessandri rather than support the program endorsed by Tomic, which contributed to the latter's defeat. The radical drop in votes for the PDC also reflected the increased polarization of Chilean politics and the PDC's marked decrease in popularity.

5 Allende made the same promise to Tomic. After Allende won the election, Radomiro Tomic went to Allende's house and said, "I have come to greet the President-elect . . . of Chile, my old friend Salvador Allende." Sigmund, *United States and Democracy*, 49.

6 Of course, Alessandri forces also counted on the votes of the wealthy in Chile. However, in Chile (as elsewhere), the wealthy made up the minority of the population, whereas women represented the majority.

7 Both the Tomic and Allende campaigns organized similar events. See Gaviola, Lopresti, and Rojas, *Segundo informe*, 5.

Chilean elite and the U.S. government, they designed massive publicity campaigns to convince Chileans that Alessandri was the best candidate for the job. One aspect of this publicity consisted of ads from the official Alessandri campaign. Acción Mujeres de Chile (Women's Action of Chile) and Chile Joven (Young Chile)—the latter a rather nebulous group that attempted to organize young men against Allende—sponsored another series of ads. Although both sets of ads conflated Allende with communism and stressed anticommunist themes, the tone of the official propaganda was measured, while alarmism permeated the latter. The official Alessandri campaign focused on projecting a positive image of the candidate, while those from Acción Mujeres de Chile and Chile Joven portrayed the horrors that a UP victory would, they claimed, inevitably entail.[8]

An analysis of the Alessandri campaign ads illustrates several important points. The Alessandri publicity reveals a sophisticated understanding of how to use gendered propaganda in a presidential campaign, and its materials were designed to appeal specifically and separately to women and men. The themes developed during the Alessandri campaign were similar to those used during the 1964 Scare Campaign and foreshadowed the language that the right would employ to attack the Popular Unity government once it came to power.

From May until September 1970, ads supporting Alessandri filled the conservative newspapers *El Mercurio* and *La Tercera*. These ads consistently projected Alessandri as the wise and caring patriarch who was above party politics, rejected violence, and would benevolently safeguard the well-being of all Chileans. Many of these ads asked women, as mothers, to vote for Alessandri in order to ensure their children's safety. For example, in one picture, a wide-eyed young girl about eight years old stares directly at the reader (see Fig. 1). The text below the ad reads:

These eyes look at the world without understanding the conflicts that convulse it. She is unaware of the violence and hate that are so close. She doesn't know how fragile freedom is, how little it takes to lose it. She doesn't know the meaning of a life without dignity and justice. Her mother is aware of the current dangers and wants to eradicate them forever. She knows that the future of her children will be decided today.

---

8 The right was not alone in using negative campaign ads. Sigmund points out that the left consistently insinuated that the unmarried Alessandri was gay. In the homophobic atmosphere of Chile, this was a heavily loaded charge. See Sigmund, *Overthrow*, 102–4. William Sater also noted that the left attempted to discredit Alessandri by calling him "a senescent homosexual" who was "the passive instrument of U.S. economic interests." See Sater's *Chile and the United States: Empires in Conflict* (Athens: University of Georgia Press, 1990), 160–61.

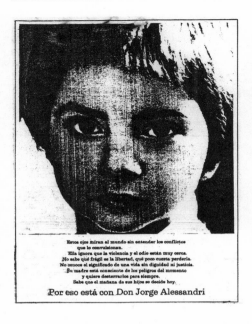

Fig. 1 An advertisement from Alessandri's 1970 presidential campaign featured an innocent, wide-eyed child. The ad tried to communicate a simple message to mothers: voting for Alessandri would guarantee the safety of their children.
La Tercera, 11 July 1970.

That is why she supports Don Jorge Alessandri.[9]

Other advertisements feature Alessandri dressed soberly in a long, dark coat, wearing a hat, walking alone. They portray "Don Jorge" as the father of the Chilean family, the one who will restore patriarchal order and governmental authority. The caption to one ad represents Alessandri as an independent man of the people, beholden to no political party (see Fig. 2). It reads:

Just by walking calmly through the streets of Santiago when he was a Deputy, a Senator, a Minister, a President, and as a sure-to-win candidate, Don Jorge has demonstrated, throughout his entire life, that he cannot conceive of violence either from those who support him or from his worst enemies.

Don Jorge Alessandri will govern Chile with the authority of his independence.[10]

The national leadership of Women for Alessandri encouraged women to become actively involved in the Alessandri campaign, because his victory would prevent the communists from taking over Chile. Stressing the urgency of the situation, Alessandri's female supporters argued that "now is the time of our most important decision." In probably unintentional irony,

9 *La Tercera de la Hora,* 11 July 1970. For more examples, see *La Tercera,* 15 July 1970 and 23 July 1970.
10 *El Mercurio,* 8 July 1970.

Con sólo caminar tranqui-
lamente por las calles de
San iago, cuando Diputado,
cuando Senador, cuando
Ministro, cuando Presidente
y cuando candidato a segura
reelección, Don Jorge ha de-
mostrado, con toda una vida,
que no concibe la violencia ni
en sus partidarios ni en sus
peores enemigos.

DON JORGE ALESSANDRI
GOBERNARA A CHILE
CON LA AUTORIDAD
DE SU INDEPENDENCIA

Fig. 2 In another advertisement from
Alessandri's 1970 presidential campaign,
the candidate was pictured as an independent "man of the people" and a
patriarch who could restore order to the
Chilean family.
El Mercurio, 8 July 1970.

the group's ad borrowed a slogan from the Spanish Republicans: "here in the free soil of Chile, [the communists] *no pasaran.*" The pro-Alessandri women also promised that their candidate would make women's lives better. Indeed, Alessandri's program pledged to "directly benefit women" by "modifying the legislation that deals with family abandonment, providing pensions for children, ensuring that women receive equal pay for equal work, that housewives get insurance, and that married women obtain full legal equality."[11]

The right attempted to demonize Allende through its 1970 version of the Scare Campaign. Agencia Andalién, a publicity agency connected to numerous right-wing individuals, publications, think tanks, and companies, developed the ad campaign. In hearings held in the Chilean Congress on the Scare Campaign, Christian Democratic Deputy Luis Maira stated that "Andalién is the center of a huge web, the central coordinating point which brings together numerous organizations and persons tied, some more and some less, to . . . the political and economic right in Chile." Through its links to the right, the agency received monies from wealthy Chilean families and some rather "shadowy North Americans."[12]

11 *La Tercera,* 27 July 1970.

12 The report provides no further explanation of who these men are, and I have been unable to determine their identities. See Congreso Chileno, Senado, legislatura extraordinaria, *Acusación*

Women from Acción Mujeres de Chile met with the staff of the ad agency to help develop the campaign, sharing the knowledge and experience they had gained from their work in the 1964 Scare Campaign. The staff at Agencia Andalién analyzed the work of Acción Mujeres de Chile and concluded that "in formal meetings they contributed valuable ideas concerning the feelings of women, young men, and the citizenry in general, which leads us to conclude that they are keenly in touch with the current political moment." The agency also considered class differences when it designed the campaign materials. It critiqued preliminary sketches of the radio announcements and pointed out that "even when the content is mature and concise, we believe that it must be more appealing and accessible to a public that is of a more modest social extraction." Agencia Andalién coordinated the posting of campaign literature all over Chile and made sure that many of the poor and working-class neighborhoods of Santiago were plastered with pro-Alessandri posters.[13]

As part of the campaign, Agencia Andalién developed numerous newspaper ads, radio spots, and publications that aimed to scare people into voting against Salvador Allende and, to a lesser extent, against Radomiro Tomic. The agency produced twenty thousand copies of a pamphlet titled "Women and Communism (For You and Your Best Friend)." Another pamphlet, *The Fatal Consequences*, chillingly predicted that rationing, shortages, a loss of freedom, and repression would result from an Allende victory. In a particularly creative initiative, Agencia Andalién sent people pretending to be members of the UP coalition into the poor neighborhoods of Santiago with a questionnaire called "Urban Reform." The document asked homeowners to list all their property, the number of rooms and inhabitants in their houses, and additional personal information. The directions instructed each recipient of the questionnaire to "fill it out and keep it until it is asked for by an official representative of the Urban Reform of the new Popular Government. This will demonstrate your loyalty to the revolutionary cause."[14] As part of their effort to instill fear and suspicion among Chileans, the pro-Alessandri forces hoped that this fake form would convince poor people that neither their homes nor their possessions would be secure if Allende won the elections.

---

constitucional en contra del Ministro del Interior Don José Tohá González, sesiones 49, 50, 52, 54, and 56, 18–22 January 1972, 2427–31, 2508, 2573, 2581.

13 Ibid., sesión 38, 2523, 2512, 2515. According to Agencia Andalién documents, Acción Mujeres de Chile had two thousand members in 1970 and existed throughout Chile.

14 Ibid., 2457, 2489; for a reproduction of *The Fatal Consequences*, see 2540–52.

Much of the agency's campaign consisted of ads that blared from radios and newspapers throughout Chile during the months of May, June, and July 1970. The publicity was massive, national in scope, sophisticated, and effective. During these three months, forty radio stations and twenty-two newspapers broadcast or published announcements that were strikingly similar in content and tone (see Appendixes B and C). The Chilean Congress subsequently investigated the ad campaign and reported that the combined time of all the radio ads added up to eighteen hours a day for three months. The radio announcements cost 7,680,000 escudos, and the total cost of newspaper ads came out to 8,400,000 escudos.[15] The U.S. government helped finance this publicity.

In 1970, as in 1964, the U.S. government opposed Allende's victory and worked to ensure his loss. President Richard Nixon and Secretary of State Henry Kissinger regarded the possibility of an Allende victory with concern.[16] In March 1970, the 40 Committee (part of the executive branch that reviewed proposed major covert actions) "decided that the United States should not support any single candidate in the election but should instead wage 'spoiling' operations against the UP coalition." In the months before the September elections, the United States spent somewhere between $800,000 and $1,000,000 on covert actions. Much of this money went directly into the anti-Allende Scare Campaign. Referring to the CIA's work, the Senate Committee that investigated U.S. covert action in Chile reported that

the CIA made use of half-a-dozen covert action projects. Those projects were focused into an intensive propaganda campaign which made use of virtually all media within Chile and which placed and replayed items in the international press as well. Propaganda placements were achieved through subsidizing right-wing women's and "civic action" groups. *A "scare campaign" using many of the same themes as the 1964 presidential election program, equated an Allende victory with violence and Stalinist repression [emphasis added].*[17]

15 Ibid., 2404, 2421, 2578–79. Paul Sigmund points out that the right referred to the investigating committee as "The Dracula Committee." See Sigmund, *Overthrow*, 103.

16 In his memoirs, then Secretary of State Henry Kissinger criticizes the State Department for its reluctance to support Alessandri's candidacy fully. According to Kissinger, the State Department disliked Alessandri "ostensibly for being too old, in reality because he was considered insufficiently progressive." Kissinger, however, believed that "if Allende was to be stopped, it would have to be by the conservative Jorge Alessandri." He openly asserts that the U.S. government sent money to Chile "in support of democratic candidates." In fact, he bemoans that this support was too little and too late. See Henry Kissinger, *White House Years* (Boston: Little, Brown, 1979), 663–65.

17 Senate Select Committee, *Covert Action: Report*, 2, 19, 20, 21 [quotation from 21]. The right-wing women's group is most likely Acción Mujeres de Chile; the civic action group may be Chile Joven.

The ad campaign, however, was short-lived. On 21 July 1970, members of the Communist Youth broke into the offices of Agencia Andalién.[18] They left a short time later, carrying with them all the papers they could lay their hands on, along with the briefcase of Salvador Fernández Zegers, general manager of Agencia Andalién. A few days later, several prominent journalists received packages with copies of the papers, as did members of the Chilean Congress. The documents contained evidence of the right's involvement with the Scare Campaign. These papers and the publicity surrounding the break-in convinced the Chilean Congress to carry out an investigation of the Scare Campaign and Agencia Andalién. Revelations from the investigation enraged—and temporarily united—the UP and the Christian Democrats and effectively put an end to the advertisements.[19]

Both the PDC and the UP coalition took the Scare Campaign very seriously. They believed that it not only hurt their candidates, but that it also undermined the Chilean polity in general. The Chilean Congress asked the psychology department of the University of Chile to conduct a study on how the Scare Campaign had affected certain sectors of the Chilean population. According to Luis Soto Becerra, director of the psychology department, "several of the messages appear designed to suggest the eventual instability of certain currently accepted social values, such as respect for nationalism, the integrity of the family, maternal-filial love, or the honesty of the justice system." In a revealing illustration of his attitudes toward women (and implicitly, those of the members of the Christian Democratic and UP parties that supported his study), Professor Soto added that

the massive use of stimuli of a threatening character contains the danger of affecting, in a special manner, certain sectors of the population that, due to their characteristics, are more vulnerable; in particular, broad sectors of the female population, students and adolescents, along with those of a low educational level, limited intelligence or psychopathic tendencies. These are the ones who are most notoriously affected by the threatening stimuli of this propaganda campaign.[20]

18 Although members of Agencia Andalién condemned the illegal seizure of their papers, they did not question their authenticity. See *El Mercurio*, 22 July 1970. Similarly, members of the National Party who opposed the congressional investigation of the Scare Campaign did so on the grounds that the Congress had no authority to investigate an advertising campaign. Since neither Agencia Andalién nor any members of the Chilean Congress challenged the legitimacy of the materials seized by the members of the Communist Youth, I have treated these papers as reliable sources.

19 For a recounting of what happened by the Communist Youth members who broke into Agencia Andalién, see "Sí, Nosotros Asaltamos Andalién," *Ramona*, 10 December 1971, 24. *El Mercurio*, 22 July 1970, offers the perspective of the police and the Agencia Andalién manager.

20 Cámara de Diputados, *Informe de la Comisión Especial Investigadora*, sesión 25, 2419–20.

Fig. 3 In the Acción Mujeres de Chile advertisement, the signature graphic reads, "Chilean woman, the fate of the fatherland is in your hands." *La Tercera,* 29 July 1970.

The Right's Use of Gender to Appeal to Women

One of the major themes of the ad campaign was that women, not men, controlled the destiny of Chile. Therefore, it was up to them to save their families and the nation from the communist menace that currently threatened them. To reinforce this view of the role played by women, the ads routinely ended with the signature graphic of Acción Mujeres de Chile— a pair of slim, white, well-cared-for hands holding up the letters C H I L E with the caption "Chilean woman, the fate of the fatherland is in your hands" (see Fig. 3).

A recurrent theme ran through these ads: Alessandri was not political . . . and neither were women.[21] In Chile, to be political meant membership and

21 As noted above, Acción Mujeres de Chile sponsored the ads. Since its inception in 1963, women in Acción Mujeres de Chile consciously defined themselves as independent from the political parties.

participation in a political party. Since the majority of women did not belong to any political party at that time, many Chileans inferred that women were neither involved nor interested in politics. The right used this belief to its advantage and applauded women's distance from party politics, which were dominated by incessant struggles for power. Instead, it appealed to women based on their supposedly natural and politically disinterested concern for their homes and their families.

Most of the ads assumed that the most effective way to reach women was by telling them what would happen to their children and husbands if Allende were elected. One ad warned women that a leftist victory guaranteed that their children would not be able to develop in a peaceful and secure environment (see Appendix B). Another one cautioned wives that their husbands' jobs (and, by extension, the family's livelihood) would be precarious under the UP government, unless the men toed the party line. Yet another ad, recognizing that some women worked outside the home, declared that "Chilean women don't want promises . . . we want secure work for ourselves and our husbands . . . [and] security for our children."[22] However, this acknowledgment that some Chilean women worked outside the home was the exception, not the rule. Believing that a woman's identity was subsumed under her role as wife and mother, the ads spoke to women almost exclusively in those terms and ignored any independent identity a woman might have had. The campaign overlooked unmarried women and single mothers and never questioned the idea that the home was a woman's sphere. Instead, it defined Chile as one big home, extending women's purview to encompass the entire nation. In this way, it called upon women to make a political choice but did not challenge their domestic identities.

The Right's Use of Gender to Appeal to Young Men

The second target of the Scare Campaign was Chilean men. Agencia Andalién also designed this campaign, and an organization called Chile Joven signed the ads (see Fig. 4 and Appendix C). Chile Joven, which materialized exclusively in connection with the 1970 presidential campaign and disappeared once it ended, appears to have been a much less substantial organization than Acción Mujeres de Chile. In response to the congressional investigation of its role in the "Anticommunist Truth Campaign," Chile Joven published a two-page ad in *El Mercurio* that proclaimed its anticommunist positions, denounced the Chilean Congress's investigation of Chile

---

22 Cámara de Diputados, *Informe de la Comisión Especial Investigadora*, sesión 25, 2466.

Fig. 4 The advertisements from
Chile Joven fused terror and
delinquency, portraying the horrors
that would follow a UP victory.
La Tercera, 1 July 1970.

Joven, and rejected any attempts to link the campaign to foreign (U.S.) sources or financing. Jovino Novoa, the president of Chile Joven, and hundreds of other young men signed the ad.[23] In congressional testimony, Christian Democrat Luis Maira derided the ad and questioned the existence of Chile Joven. Maira commented that "the people who appear in the list [of signatories] are not members of Chile Joven. Instead, they merely supported the campaign carried out by this body. They are twelve-, thirteen-, fourteen-year-old kids who study in private schools in Santiago. Most of them are 'pre-members' of the Chilean Society for the Defense of Tradition, Family, and Property, a movement commonly known as Fiducia."[24]

23 *El Mercurio*, 16 August 1970. In the 1990s, Jovino Novoa was president of Unión Demócrata Independiente (UDI, Independent Democratic Union), the extreme right, pro-Pinochet party; he was elected senator from 1998 to 2004.

24 Cámara de Diputados, *Informe de la Comisión Especial Investigadora*, sesión 25, 2576. For background on Defense of Tradition, Family, and Property, see Chapter 4.

The agency was clearly conscious of gender differences, just as it was aware of class distinctions. Ads directed at women and men targeted very different emotions and identities. Agencia Andalién defined women as mothers and men as fathers (or future fathers) who were financially and physically responsible for their families. Based on this assessment, the agency determined that Chile Joven ads should be "direct, brutal, essentially negative, [a campaign] of terror which, on some points, will also involve Tomic." Conversely, the campaign aimed at women should be "more positive, showing the terror [that would result from an Allende victory], positing ideas about the future of the homeland and what women can expect from this." The women's campaign should be "sensitive, more melodramatic" and feature images of "women overwhelmed and women triumphant, as the national symbol." Gender differences also determined the medium used to reach potential voters. Recognizing that far more men than women purchased and read newspapers, the campaign decided that "the newspapers will be reserved exclusively for Chile Joven, whereas women will be reached through radio announcements and leaflets." Communicating with women through ads on radio stations made sense, because 95 percent of Chilean homes had radios in 1970—and many of them were on during the day, when women were working at home.[25] (See Fig. 3; see also Appendix B.)

The Chile Joven ads echoed some of the themes developed in the Acción Mujeres de Chile publicity, such as the idea that politics and politicians serve their own interests rather than those of the Chilean people. These ads also referred to men's property rights and their financial responsibility to their families. They implied that communism meant the end of private property, that neither a man's house nor his salary would be safe if Allende won. Over and over again, the ads declared that if Allende were elected, then the "fruits of [a man's] labor" would be taken away from him. The message was that a leftist victory threatened a man's ability to earn money and support his family. Fusing terrorism and delinquency, the ads also stated that the UP supported terrorism and that the Christian Democrats had proven themselves incapable of stopping it (see Fig. 4; see also Appendix C). By way of contrast, they presented Alessandri as the candidate of law and order: he would restore security and end crime and terrorism.

The Results of the 1970 Campaign

Although a smaller percentage of both men and women voted for Allende in 1970 than had done so in 1964, he won the election because he ran

---

25 Ibid., 2576, 2521, 2484. The ads implied that Tomic—and the PDC in general—lacked the will to end leftist violence and the growth of crime.

Table 5.1 A comparison of voting results from the 1964 and 1970 presidential elections, by gender

Candidate and Election	Women's Vote		Men's Vote		Total	
	#	%	#	%	#	%
1964 elections						
Frei (PDC)	**756,117**	**63%**	**652,895**	**49%**	**1,409,012**	**56%**
Allende (UP)	384,132	32	593,770	45	977,902	39
Durán (Radical)	57,162	5	68,071	5	125,233	5
1970 elections						
Allende (UP)	438,846	31	**631,488**	**42**	**1,070,334**	**36**
Alessandri (PN)	**552,257**	**38**	478,902	32	1,031,159	35
Tomic (PDC)	429,082	30	392,719	26	821,801	28

Note: Boldface type indicates the candidates who received the most votes. This table does not include listings for null and blank votes; the totals, therefore, will not add up to 100 percent.
Source: República de Chile, Servicio Electoral (Santiago: Servicio Electoral, n.d.).

against two candidates (not one, as he had in 1964). Are we to conclude that the Scare Campaign was not successful? An examination of the voting results suggests that the campaign *did* have an impact. While my conclusions are somewhat speculative, the fact remains that nationally, women gave the largest percentage of their vote to the conservative candidate, Jorge Alessandri (see Table 5.1). Men gave Allende most of their votes—and the victory. By a margin of 10 percent, men favored Allende over his runner-up, Jorge Alessandri, and women preferred Alessandri by about 8 percent.

The most clear-cut support for Alessandri came from upper- and middle-class women. A comparison of women's vote in the upper-class neighborhoods of Providencia and Las Condes indicates that women not only gave their votes to Alessandri; they did so at a proportionally higher rate than men from the same neighborhoods did (see Table 5.2). Equally, the middle-class women from Ñuñoa and La Reina cast their votes for Alessandri over either Tomic or Allende at an almost two-to-one margin. Clearly, the votes from these women reflected their class interests. However, if class alone was the significant factor in determining voting tendencies, then upper- and middle-class men's voting patterns would have mirrored those of women—and they did not. The other factor that influenced women's vote had to do with gender and the particular appeals made to women through the Scare Campaign.

While any conclusions about the impact this propaganda had on Chilean women can only be tentative, it does appear that the Scare Campaign either reinforced or helped shape anticommunist fears in women that their male counterparts did not share. The Scare Campaign was particularly effective because it spoke to their fears so directly. It told them that if Allende were elected, then that which they most valued and upon which they based their hopes and aspirations—their families—would be taken from them. Because women had less experience with the left than men had, they were more willing to accept that an Allende victory posed a real danger to them and their families. Men, especially working-class men, worked directly with leftists at their jobs; many of them had struggled together for better working conditions. As a result, they could more easily reject the Scare Campaign's message and appreciate the benefits that socialism could potentially offer them.

Indeed, figures from the working-class neighborhoods reveal that both working-class women and men gave the largest percentage of their votes to Allende. However, gender differences still emerge among working-class voters, just as they do among middle- and upper-class ones: more working-class men than working-class women voted for Allende.

There are several ways to interpret women's voting patterns in the 1970 presidential elections. Mariana Aylwin and her colleagues argue that the women's vote in the 1970 elections should not be interpreted as a vote for conservatism and against change. Instead, these authors believe that women's votes for Allende or Tomic—which add up to 60 percent of the women's vote overall—represented a call for change, because Tomic's 1970 presidential program proposed many of the reforms that Allende's did.[26] However, it is equally likely (if not more so) that women's choice of Tomic represented a preference for continuity and loyalty to the party of Frei, a politician so many women adored. Thus, it is possible to reverse the argument. If, for example, we combine working-class women's votes for Alessandri and Tomic and categorize them as an anti-UP vote, then the majority of working-class women (and men, in most cases) voted against the UP. Furthermore, the number of votes received by Alessandri from working-class women and men is sizable. Alessandri came in second to Allende in several of the working-class neighborhoods, and he obtained more votes than his PDC rival. For example, in San Miguel—a neighborhood that was considered a bastion of the left—Jorge Alessandri came in second to Allende among both women and men. He did the same in the working-class neighborhoods of Conchalí and La Granja. This working-class vote for Alessandri indicates a surprising amount of support for conservative politics among those social sectors believed to have been the UP's

26 Aylwin et al., *Percepción del rol político de la mujer*, 66.

Table 5.2 Results of the 1970 presidential elections in selected Santiago districts, by gender

Neighborhood	Women's Vote						Men's Vote					
	Allende (UP)		Alessandri (PN)		Tomic (PDC)		Allende (UP)		Alessandri (PN)		Tomic (PDC)	
#	#	%	#	%	#	%	#	%	#	%	#	%
Working-class												
Barrancas	**7,503**	**42%**	4,467	25%	5,795	32%	**9,167**	**54%**	3,663	22%	4,482	29%
Conchalí	**11,673**	**35**	10,778	33	10,399	31	**14,624**	**46**	8,699	27	8,120	26
Renca	**4,828**	**36**	4,098	31	4,360	33	**5,922**	**48**	3,071	25	3,294	27
Quinta Normal	**11,539**	**35**	11,248	34	9,849	30	**15,003**	**47**	8,890	28	7,854	25
San Miguel	**23,325**	**40**	18,913	32	15,591	27	**28,403**	**49**	13,686	25	11,930	22
La Cisterna	10,831	34	**11,011**	**35**	9,503	30	**13,329**	**46**	8,142	28	7,098	25
La Granja	**7,345**	**44**	4,632	28	4,134	25	**8,829**	**54**	3,380	22	3,189	20
Middle-class												
Ñuñoa	12,370	24	**24,991**	**48**	13,900	27	14,379	28	**16,814**	**40**	10,105	24
La Reina	2,062	25	**3,586**	**43**	2,550	31	2,332	28	**2,362**	**36**	1,769	27
Upper-class												
Providencia	3,427	12	**17,814**	**63**	6,520	23	3,217	18	**10,410**	**59**	3,901	22
Las Condes	4,514	16	**16,577**	**57**	7,509	26	4,706	24	**10,011**	**51**	4,544	23

Note: Boldface type indicates the candidates who received the most votes. This table does not include listings for null and blank votes; the totals, therefore, will not add up to 100 percent.

Source: República de Chile, Dirección del Registro Electoral (Santiago: Servicio Electoral, n.d.).

popular base. The votes also reveal that the elite sector was more unified as a class in Chile than the working class was.

Allende's Female Opponents Take to the Streets

Once it was clear that Allende had won the plurality of the votes, right-wing women mobilized to oppose his confirmation by Congress. In Chile, a candidate needed to garner more than half of all votes to be directly elected. If no candidate received this majority, then the Chilean Congress would select the president. Typically, as had happened with Alessandri in 1958, Congress confirmed the candidate who received the most votes. According to Thomas Powers, the CIA worked feverishly to prevent Allende being named president. In order to oversee its efforts, the CIA brought officer David Phillips "back from Brazil to head a special Chile Task Force for the duration of the operation."[27] The PN and the U.S. government hoped to break Chile's tradition of declaring the candidate with the most votes president—thus averting the confirmation of a socialist as president of Chile.[28] Both the PN and the U.S. government knew that in order to achieve their goal, they had to convince members of the PDC not to vote for Allende. Although wracked by internal debate on whether to support Allende, ultimately the PDC rejected this underhanded scheme and gave its congressional votes to Allende.[29]

In the six weeks between the presidential vote and Allende's confirmation, upper-class women from the PN took to the streets of Santiago to protest Allende's election. Impatient with what they perceived to be passivity on the part of PN men, these women decided to take matters into their own hands. Beginning on 5 September, the day after the elections, they began a campaign to pressure the Christian Democrats to vote against Allende. That afternoon—and every afternoon, until Congress confirmed

[27] Thomas Powers, *The Man Who Kept the Secrets: Richard Helms and the CIA* (New York: Knopf, 1979), 235.

[28] For a more detailed description of U.S. government plots and actions designed to prevent Allende's ascension to power, see Senate Select Committee, *Covert Action: Report*, 12–13, 23–26. U.S. government attempts to prevent an Allende presidency involved both a constitutional and a military solution. Track I, the legal solution, "consisted of inducing enough congressional votes to elect Alessandri over Allende with the understanding that Alessandri would immediately resign, thus paving the way for a special election in which Frei would legally become a candidate." This tactic failed because the PDC refused to go along with it. Track II, the military option, "was initiated by President Nixon on September 15 when he instructed the CIA to play a direct role in organizing a military *coup d'état* in Chile." For a description of one agent's involvement in this episode, see the memoirs of David Atlee Phillips, *The Night Watch* (New York: Ballantine, 1977), 282–87.

[29] My thanks to Ivonne Szasz for noting that the PDC's decision to reject this plan only came after prolonged internal debate.

Allende as president—women marched in front of La Moneda, the presidential palace. Dressed in black to symbolize their state of mourning for the imminent death of democracy in Chile, these women called upon President Frei not to "surrender the country to communism."[30]

On 19 September, Armed Forces Day in Chile, anti-Allende women joined the masses of Chileans who lined the Alameda (Santiago's main street) to cheer the military parade and the presidential carriage. Unlike most of the people assembled that day, these women—who numbered three thousand, according to one witness—came to protest Frei's willingness to respect Chilean political customs and the popular vote by voting for Allende. Allende's election had horrified them, and so did the jeers and attacks they received during their protest—a new experience for these upper-class ladies. According to María Correa Morandé, young people from the Ramona Parra and Elmo Catalán Brigades (youth groups tied to the Communist and Socialist parties, respectively) met the women with "obscene insults, threatening gestures, and insolent shouts." As time went by, the "extremists" became more aggressive. One participant claimed that "they began to surround us and throw stones and money at us." Shocked by such treatment, one woman remarked to a friend, "Communists are not Chileans." Her friend responded, in unintentional irony, that "the only thing I know is I would like to see them dead . . . they are causing hatred."[31]

Allende's election, the PN's response to his election, and the treatment meted out to them by UP supporters convinced these women of two disagreeable probabilities. First, under the UP, their privileged position as female members of Chile's elite—a reality that had always offered them an invisible but impenetrable shield of protection from the lower classes—would be battered, if not shattered. Second, they could not count on the male political leaders of their party to respond effectively to the danger that confronted them and their families.[32]

Fortified by their belief that Allende posed a threat to them, undeterred by the insults and attacks, and convinced that the future of Chile was in their hands, these women worked up until the last minute to prevent Allende's confirmation. Braving the streets of downtown Santiago,

---

30 Correa Morandé, *La guerra*, 11. These women targeted Frei because his leading role in the PDC gave him a great deal of power to determine how members of the PDC congressional delegation would vote on the question of Allende's confirmation.

31 Ibid., 14–15.

32 See ibid., 9–10, and Teresa Donoso Loero, *La epopeya de las ollas vacías* (Santiago: Editora Nacional Gabriela Mistral, 1974), 45–50.

they gathered twenty thousand names on a petition that called on Frei "not to surrender the country to communism." When their drive was complete, the women placed the white petitions in a blue envelope, tied with a red ribbon (evoking the colors of the Chilean flag), and presented the package to President Frei.[33] Despite their efforts, and those of other anti-Allende forces, the Chilean Congress confirmed Allende as president of Chile on 24 October.

Once in power, the UP government took immediate steps to implement its agenda. It increased wages and lowered unemployment. During Allende's first year, "real wages increased an estimated 30 percent . . . [and] this, together with increases in employment and a clamp-down on prices, meant that the share of national income going to labor increased from 55.0 percent in 1970 to 65.7 percent in 1971."[34] Chileans' heightened purchasing power led to a growing consumer demand that, in turn, encouraged factories to increase production. Unemployment in greater Santiago dropped from 8.3 percent in 1970 to 3.5 percent in 1971.[35] However, toward the end of 1971, shortages of basic necessities (such as food and clothing) and of more durable consumer items, such as televisions and refrigerators, began to occur. These shortages can be attributed to the inability of the Chilean system of production to increase its output sufficiently in a short period of time; they can also be attributed, though, to the attitude of the factory owners and landowners. Most of them opposed the UP government, and they were unwilling to adopt policies that favored the government. Moreover, wealthy Chileans sabotaged production and decapitalized their own industries in order to undermine the UP government.

The opposition, which consisted of the PN, the PDC, and the *gremio* movement, was divided and in disarray. For much of 1971, the PN, shaken by Allende's victory, was not able to rally its forces sufficiently nor adequately plan a strategy to damage the UP government. Nor could the PDC overcome its own internal divisions between those sectors willing to work with the UP and those, led by former president Frei, against it. This lack of internal and intra-party unity weakened the opposition's ability to develop a coherent alternative to the UP.

The women who opposed Allende were not visibly active during his first year as president. Most PN women, like the rest of their party, had

33 Correa Morandé, *La guerra*, 17.

34 Barbara Stallings and Andy Zimbalist, "The Political Economy of the Unidad Popular," *Latin American Perspectives* 2, no. 1 (Spring 1975): 72.

35 "The Blockade Takes Effect," NACLA 7, no. 1 (January 1973): 24.

been unprepared for Allende's victory. When they failed to convince the PDC to vote against Allende's confirmation, they were unsure of their next move. The shock left them temporarily paralyzed. They distrusted and were hostile to the PDC, both as a result of the Frei presidency and because they believed that the PDC had allowed Allende to become president. For their part, many PDC women shared the party's initial willingness to give Allende a chance. They showed little inclination to form an anti-Allende women's bloc with PN women. The 1971 by-election in Valparaíso provided an opportunity for the opposition parties to ally around a specific issue. The PN backed the PDC's candidate, Oscar Marín, who won the election. As in so many other elections, women's votes were decisive, securing Marin's election. The effect of their unified vote encouraged opposition women to seek other areas in which they could work together.[36]

The opposition's yearlong period of disunity and defensiveness came to an end on 1 December 1971. On that day, thousands of anti-Allende women strode through Santiago's streets to protest UP government policies and the presence of Fidel Castro in Chile. The women's march, known as the March of the Empty Pots and Pans, was a pivotal event in the anti-Allende struggle. The conservative women who participated in the march effectively overcame the confusion, lethargy, and indecisiveness into which opposition politicians had sunk during the previous year. The march revitalized the opposition and convinced conservative women that they were a dynamic force in Chilean politics.

The march has provoked tremendous controversy. To what extent did women spontaneously organize the march, and to what degree did the opposition parties manipulate the marchers for their own ends? Were the participants in the march predominantly wealthy women who, in defense of their class interests, protested government policies? Or did women from all classes join in the march? What role did the U.S. government play in organizing the march and in encouraging the development of an anti-Allende women's movement? Did the example of the anti-Goulart women's marches in Brazil inspire their Chilean counterparts?

Many of these questions lack definitive answers. Opposition women leaders claim that they organized the march independently of men and, some profess, of the parties. Yet most of the principal organizers of the march were upper- or middle-class leaders in the opposition parties. Their memories of the march's origin and how the protest was organized tend to be either vague, contradictory, or self-serving.

36 Correa Morandé, *La guerra*, 27–40.

Carmen Saenz, a member of Chile's landowning aristocracy and a leader of the PN during the UP years, was a main organizer of the March of the Empty Pots and Pans. In an interview years later, Saenz offered three different explanations for the origin of the march. She reported that the first discussion of the march took place in a Mothers' Center, where she met with a *pobladora* (poor urban woman) who had worked in Jorge Alessandri's electoral campaign. Saenz recalled the woman as "a short, fat woman, very much of the people, [who] said, 'why don't we go out in the streets with an empty pot and hit it over and over again.'" She attributed the idea of the March of the Empty Pots and Pans—the watershed event in the building of an activist, conservative women's movement—to a poor woman in order to convey the idea that all women, rich and poor alike, opposed Allende. To do so, she evoked a very stereotypical image of a poor woman. To be a short, fat woman in Chile not only implies a lower-class origin, but it also marks one as being at least partially indigenous. Saenz's attempts to assign credit for the march to a poor woman serve to obscure the reality that elite women organized the march—and that these women mainly related to short, fat women as employers. Ironically, Saenz's efforts to prove the classless nature of the anti-Allende women's movement illustrate how deeply entrenched class relations, stereotypes, and differences in fact were.

Saenz offered two other possible sources for the march. Perhaps, she said, "the idea had come from Brazil, where women in a small town had used pots and pans to demonstrate"—thus making it clear that she was very familiar with the anti-Goulart movement in Brazil. Saenz also recalled that she had been meeting with political women from the PDC, PN, and Radical Left Party, and they jointly decided to go out in the streets beating the pots and pans. In order to stress the "apolitical" aspect of the march, she added that many "independent" women, such as members of Acción Mujeres de Chile, joined them.[37]

Other women claimed that the march was spontaneous and had apparently organized itself based on its mass appeal to women. María Correa Morandé, also a leader of the PN, said that "a relative called me . . . and asked me about the march. I told her I didn't know anything yet. She was really, really mad, furious [about the UP]. [I thought] if this woman, who has never liked politics, now believes that it is necessary to act, then something must be in the air."[38] In 1971, Teresa Maillet de la Maza was

(margin note: copied Brazilian movement?)

---

37 Carmen Saenz, interviews by author, tape recordings, La Reina, 4 December and 27 December 1993.

38 María Correa Morandé, interview by author, tape recording, Santiago, 4 January 1994.

national director of the Christian Democratic women's department. According to her, the idea for the march came from "all the departments of the women's organizations. We talked with each other and went door-to-door, and everywhere we went we got a very positive reception. So we decided to tell Allende that we were sick and tired of the lines, the threats of violence, and all those things."[39]

In order to determine the degree of accuracy of these women's statements, several factors must be considered. One is that the women spoke of the march more than two decades after it took place. After so many years, participants' memories of the protest depended less on the actual events surrounding the march and more on how they defined and shaped its meanings. Compounding the difficulty of retaining a clear memory of events more than twenty years after they occurred was the reality that the women's march achieved almost mythical stature within the opposition. The telling and retelling of the story of the march, first by the opposition during the Allende years and then by the military and its supporters during the dictatorship, helped construct and define memories of that event, making remembrances of it more uniform. For example, Saenz's insistence that the idea for the march came from a poor woman probably does not reflect reality. Instead, her comments illustrate the right's attempts to convince people that the demonstration, like all of the anti-Allende activities carried out by women, reflected a multi-class, female-based opposition.[40] Correa Morandé's example of her apolitical cousin informing her of the march is probably not very likely, given Correa Morandé's close relationship to the PN and that party's involvement in planning the activity. Instead, the comment reflects her deliberate attempt to disassociate the PN from the organization of the march and to emphasize its spontaneous nature.

It is likely that many women confused their memories of the march with other activities and feelings they experienced during the Allende years. For example, Maillet de la Maza remembered that the demonstration was called to protest having to wait in lines. In fact, in December 1971, very few women waited in lines. Although there were some shortages, and possibly some lines, it was only in 1972 that shortages and lines

---

39 Maillet de la Maza, interview.

40 It is interesting to note that the left also mythologizes the march. When I spoke with UP supporters about it, several of them informed me that the anti-Allende women marched in fur coats. The idea of wearing fur coats to a march suggests both the abundant lifestyle the marchers enjoyed and the frivolous nature of their protest. However, it should be pointed out that the march took place during the Chilean summer and that 1 December 1971 was a particularly hot day. It is extremely unlikely that women wore fur coats to the march.

became a daily reality for the average Chilean woman. Neither the media coverage of the march nor the statements of the marchers mentioned lines in 1971.

It is also disingenuous to claim that the parties did not sponsor the march. Many of the women who organized the march were members or leaders of the opposition parties, and it is unlikely that they would have planned the march without the approval of their parties. The coverage given to the march by opposition newspapers—all of them connected to a political party—indicates the high level of party support. Also, the presence of the male youth brigades from the PDC, the PN, and Patria y Libertad (Fatherland and Liberty, an extreme right paramilitary organization that accompanied the female marchers to offer them protection) suggests that the party leadership strongly backed the march.

However, the women's efforts truly made the march a success. Women publicly called for and organized the march. Given that most Chilean women did not participate in political parties, the established (male) patterns of political organizing could not be used to build a woman's march. In addition to the more standard practices of public announcements and press conferences, women also called their personal networks of friends on the phone and urged them to join in the event. They knocked on the doors of their neighbors and encouraged them to attend. They announced the demonstration in church-related activities.[41] It took the women's dedication, energy, and knowledge of how to reach their female compatriots to make the march the surprising success that it was.

The March of the Empty Pots and Pans

The March of the Empty Pots and Pans came at the end of a three-week visit by Fidel Castro to Chile. When Castro arrived in Chile, hundreds of thousands of Chileans poured into the streets of Santiago to welcome him as "a Latin American leader who defied the power of the United States."[42] But for the PN and the conservative sector of the PDC, Castro's visit represented the unwelcome intrusion of a foreign communist into Chile's internal affairs.[43] It heightened the opposition's fears of a communist takeover: it signified increased unity among the leftist parties, a radicalization of the UP's politics, and a strengthening of ties between the UP

41 Maruja Navarro, interview by author, tape recording, Las Condes, 15 December 1998.

42 Ivonne Szasz, personal communication, 8 September 1996.

43 For an editorial in *El Mercurio* that expresses this perspective, see *El Mercurio*, 10 November 1971. For a collection of many of Fidel Castro's speeches in Chile, see The National Education Department of the Socialist Workers Party, *Fidel Castro on Chile* (New York: Pathfinder, 1982).

government, Cuba, and the Soviet Union. As a result, the visit increased tensions between the UP government and the opposition parties.

The march was the opposition's response to Fidel Castro. Of particular significance is the fact that the opposition parties viewed a women's march as the most appropriate response to Castro's visit. In Chilean politics, nationalism was a contested issue. Both the right and the left claimed that their political tendency represented the true spirit and interests of the Chilean nation, while their opponents answered to foreign forces. The left decried the right's alliance with foreign economic and political interests, principally those of the United States, while the right critiqued the left's allegiance to communism (which rightists defined as a foreign political doctrine), to Cuba, and to the Soviet Union.[44]

The opposition chose to demonstrate its rejection of Castro and the UP government by reaffirming the role that Chilean women have historically played in defending the nation. The women who organized the march publicly identified themselves with the national symbols of Chilean womanhood—Inés de Suárez, Javiera Carrera, and Paula Jaraquemada.[45] Because the organizers believed that women's fundamental role in society was a maternal one, it followed that they would portray women's primary identity as one that transcended class, regional, and ethnic differences. Furthermore, because the majority of Chilean women did not belong to any political party, they operated independently of the political divisiveness that defined much political struggle in Chile. As a result, women supposedly represented the nation: lacking foreign or political allegiances, they were purely driven by the well-being of their families—and, by extension, of Chile. When the Christian Democrat Josefina Larraín de Zaldívar called on women to attend the March of the Empty Pots and Pans, she did so as a "woman and Chilean mother" who was horrified at "the violence and lack of security in the University of Chile and the shortages that the Chilean

44 Although the right lumped the Communist Party and the Socialist Party together, the Communist Party in Chile—like most communist parties around the world—had a very close relationship to the USSR, while the Socialist Party had always defined itself as independent of the Soviet Union.

45 Inés de Suárez was a Spanish woman who led the successful defense of Santiago against the Mapuche Indians in the sixteenth century. See Donoso Loero, *La epopeya*, 10. Javiera Carrera fought in the Chilean war for independence from Spain. Elsa Chaney, citing Chilean author Francisco Encina, defines her as "Chile's formidable 'woman of iron.'" See Chaney, *Supermadre*, 51. Paula Jaraquemada is another Chilean heroine who gained prominence for her actions during the anticolonial struggle. See "El nuevo poder," *Ercilla*, 29 August–4 September 1973, 10. Chapter 6 discusses the relationship between these national heroines of Chile and the women who opposed Allende.

home is suffering."[46] Combining family security with the protection of the nation, Larraín urged women to remember that "you are the light and the defense of your children, [and] you must defend your home, physical and spiritual liberty. Remember that you descend from Guacolda and Javiera Carrera, indomitable women who defended the integrity of Chile."[47]

On 26 November 1971, a group of women led by Silvia Alessandri, a PN deputy, sought and received permission from the provincial governor of Santiago to hold a march and rally on 1 December 1971.[48] Three days later, a small article appeared in *El Mercurio* and *La Tribuna* (a PN-supported newspaper whose *raison d'être* was to attack the Allende government). It called on women to come out to the "March of Chilean Women." The call stressed certain themes: the independent and spontaneous nature of the march, its independence from any political party, and its popular, classless base of support (see Appendix D). The title given to the event—the March of Chilean Women—exemplified the attempt to project the march as one that would involve all Chilean women, was neither sponsored by nor limited to any political tendency, and neither represented nor excluded any class.[49]

Several poor women formed part of the march committee. Because they were not particularly well known and made no future public appearances, their inclusion hints at the efforts of PN and PDC women to convey the appearance that a cross-class group of women organized the march. One of the women, Olga Salinas, was identified as a peasant leader from Pomaire; another, Dina Méndez, as a housewife; another, Otilia Contreras, as a national leader of *pobladores*. These women directed the call to

---

46 *La Prensa*, 1 December 1971. During October and November 1971, the University of Chile was the scene of intense struggle between UP supporters and their PDC, PN, and independent right opponents. Edgardo Boeninger, a Christian Democrat, was rector of the university and stood at the center of a fierce battle between these opposing forces for control of the institution. For both the right and the PDC, the fighting at the University of Chile (which included student takeovers both of buildings and of Boeninger's own office) represented the politicization of education and the chaotic state of affairs they abhorred. For a fuller description of events, see Kaufman, *Crisis*, 83–90.

47 *La Prensa*, 1 December 1971. Guacolda is a Mapuche woman whom the chronicler Alonso de Ercilla mentions in his famous poem, "Araucana." She, too, represents courage and valor, a woman who "demonstrated more courage than men, one of the many Chilean women who, like Joan of Arc, was a guide to lead her people." *Ercilla*, 29 August–4 September 1973, 10.

48 Congreso Chileno, Senado, *Acusación constitucional*, 52a sess., 20 January 1972, 2756.

49 *El Mercurio*, 29 November 1971, and *La Tribuna*, 29 November 1971. On 1 December 1971, banner headlines in the PDC newspaper, *La Prensa*, announced the demonstration later that day: "Women Against Violence and the Scarcity of Food." A smaller headline stated that "housewives take to the streets today to protest."

"all the women of Chile": "We, more than anyone, are living the profound drama that our country has suffered for the past year." The call established the right of women to organize the demonstration, because they were the ones most directly affected by the crisis. Unused to participating in public protests (and, perhaps, not planning to do so on an ongoing basis), they claimed that they were organizing the demonstration "so that once and for all, we can have our say [on the issue of] the future of Chile and our children."[50]

These women were compelled to act, they wrote, by "the abuses [being committed] in the University of Chile, where the rector, Edgardo Boeninger, is the victim of an infamous campaign of insults" (students had taken over the university and his office and demanded Boeninger's replacement). Moreover, they held that Allende was not living up to the established norms of a Chilean president. According to them, during Allende's presidency, "hate has been sown, [along with] the lack of respect for authority and those values that for us are fundamental: personal honor and physical integrity." Clearly, the elite women who issued the call felt threatened by the "subversion of the hierarchical order" that the UP government and the mobilization of non-elite sectors represented.[51] They feared that the change would bring an end to the ordered world they enjoyed (and to which they were accustomed). For them, this social upheaval represented chaos.[52] The call also indicated these women's concerns with the increasingly higher prices and the scarcity of food. It read, "we are not inventing false campaigns to attack the government. Daily we see that there is no meat, chicken, milk, noodles, and other essential items, and when we do find these products, we have to pay prices that are far beyond our resources."[53]

The article called on women to bring pots and pans with them in order to highlight the lack of food. *La Tribuna* added—either in genuine anticipation of violence, in the hope of generating a climate of fear, or as part of the PN's overall portrayal of the UP government as the sponsors of violence—that the women could use the pots and pans as helmets, "if it should be necessary."[54]

50 *El Mercurio*, 29 November 1971. Pomaire is a small rural community about eighty-three kilometers west of Santiago. It is best known for its pottery and *chicha* (Chilean cider made from grapes or apples).

51 My thanks to Ivonne Szasz for emphasizing this point to me.

52 I would like to thank Temma Kaplan for pointing this out to me.

53 *El Mercurio*, 29 November 1971.

54 *La Tribuna*, 29 November 1971.

On 29 November, representatives from the women's departments of the National, Christian Democratic, and Radical Democracy[55] parties held a joint press conference, along with the independent organizers of the march, in the Chamber of Deputies. Together, they called on women to attend the march—now called the March of the Empty Pots and Pans—and to bring an empty pot and a Chilean flag. The press conference showcased both the independent nature of the march as well as the political backing of it by the key opposition parties. Nina Donoso, described as "an independent who leads a sector of apolitical women," said that "although party militants will participate in the march, politics will not be key." Instead, she said, women will demonstrate because "we have no formula to feed our babies and they get sick with diarrhea . . . our husbands are forced to attend political meetings in order to keep their jobs."[56]

During the press conference, the women took pains to point out that they had not received political or financial support from anyone. They stated that the leaders of the movement had used their own resources, time, and energy to organize the march. In order to raise money for ads, for example, they put cans in beauty salons, a site clearly associated with women. They communicated news of the march by "phone, messages in beauty salons, stores, Mothers' Centers, and through friends."[57] Not only were all these places clearly associated with women and women's networks, but the inclusion of the Mothers' Centers (which primarily existed in poor neighborhoods) also established the cross-class nature of the organizing effort.

The fundamental appeal to women as mothers proved especially effective and flexible. During the Scare Campaign, the right hoped to scare women into voting against Allende by telling them that the victory of the UP would mean that their children would be taken from them and turned into their enemies. The call to the March of the Empty Pots and Pans echoed this definition of women as mothers, but adapted it to new circumstances. According to the call for women to participate, the UP government meant that women could no longer feed their children. In both cases, the definition of women as mothers had a corollary: as mothers, women were portrayed as being largely disinterested in politics as well as

---

55 The newly formed Radical Democracy Party was made up of former members of the Radical Party who had rejected its alliance with the UP.

56 *El Mercurio*, 30 November 1971.

57 Ibid.

formally uninvolved in the parties. Reflecting the perceptual division of the world into women's private sphere and men's public sphere, the call assumed that a woman's world was circumscribed by the home and by her role within it. The march, then, was not a political demonstration but an extension of women's domestic roles. It came as a response to the need for mothers to feed their children. In the organizers' lexicography, "feeding children" was not political; it was the natural duty and indeed the definition of womanhood. Thus, although women left the private world of the home behind and went out into the streets, they did so as mothers, not as political actors.

Continuing the schematic division of the world between female (private) and male (public), the call to march portrayed a husband as the member of the family who worked outside the home and was part of the political world. Since the UP had infused work with politics and politics with force, intimidation, and threats (just as the ads of Acción Mujeres de Chile predicted), men had to participate in the political rallies of the UP government and support its policies or risk losing their jobs. Given men's inability to act—caught, as they were, in a web of work and political responsibilities from which women were excluded—it was up to women to protest and to save their husbands, protect their children, and preserve their own roles within the family.

Even as the women stressed the apolitical nature of the march, the opposition political parties did not hesitate to evince their support for it. They gave the march their approval and encouraged female members and supporters of their parties to attend. The march served the opposition parties well, and they did not want to lose the opportunity to reap political benefits from it. In an article in *El Mercurio*, PN member Carmen Saenz wove together the multiple strands of patriotism, gender, and the purported apolitical and independent nature of the march by declaring that "PN women, as Chileans and mothers, cannot remain impassive given the anguished moments facing Chile. Conscious of our responsibility to the fatherland and its children, we lend our unconditional support to the march organized by independent women."[58]

---

58 Ibid. UP supporters did not plan to let the march proceed unchallenged. *El Siglo*, the paper of the Communist Party of Chile, published an announcement from student leaders calling for a demonstration in front of the University of Chile on 1 December. See *El Siglo*, 29 November 1971. The next day, Radio Portales denounced the women's march as "a group of *señoras*" who would "parade with their Marmicoc pots and pans," and it announced the demonstration of a group of "*pobladores* from the popular sectors" who would "meet at 6:00 P.M. [the same time as the women's march] in front of the University of Chile." Marmicoc is the brand name of one of the more expensive lines of Chilean kitchen utensils. By identifying the brand, the radio

Fig. 5 The March of the Empty Pots and Pans was a crucial moment in the struggle against Allende. It bolstered the opposition and proved that women were an undeniable political force in Chile. *El Mercurio,* 2 December 1971.

On 1 December 1971, thousands of Chilean women gathered in downtown Santiago's Plaza Italia in the evening after a hot, sunny day (see Fig. 5).[59] Most of the marchers were women. However, men from the opposition parties' youth groups and from Patria y Libertad accompanied the march in order to provide security for the women. Carrying pots and pans, waving banners and Chilean flags, these women rallied against the UP government. They marched, they claimed, to protest Fidel Castro's prolonged visit to Chile, the violence and sectarianism of the UP government, the increased politicization of life in Chile, and the scarcity of food. As they marched, the women chanted a number of slogans.

"Allende, listen, we women are many!"
"Chile *si!* Cuba *no!*"
"Dungeon, dungeon, Fidel go home!"
"There's no meat—smoke a Havana!"
"The left has left *us* without food!"
"There's no meat in the pot, and the government looks
    the other way!"[60]

---

announcer was also defining the class of the women he expected to attend the march, because only the upper or middle class could afford these pots. My thanks to Patricio Mason for this information.

59 Estimates of the number of women who attended the march range from several thousand to one hundred thousand. Five thousand is the most commonly accepted number.

60 *La Prensa,* 2 December 1971; *El Mercurio,* 2 December 1971.

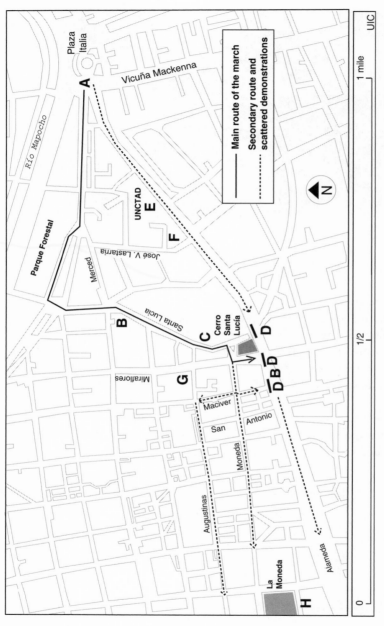

Map 3 Route of the March of the Empty Pots and Pans, 1 December 1971

A. The main body of the march starts here at 6:00 P.M.   B. UP supporters protest the march   C. Fighting breaks out between the marchers and UP supporters   D. Police set up barricades to prevent the female marchers from reaching La Moneda (H); marchers push past the police and proceed down the Alameda at 8:00 P.M.   E. Construction workers throw building materials at the marchers from the UNCTAD (UN Commission on Trade and Development)   F. Three hundred marchers attack the offices of the Radical Party at 7:30 P.M. G. Four hundred demonstrators attack the headquarters of the Radical Party at 8:30 P.M.   H. Planned destination of the march

Violence broke out as the march proceeded through the main streets of Santiago. There are conflicting reports about who started the violence; each side stated that the other was responsible. The women who participated in the march claim that young male supporters of the UP government pelted them with bricks and other objects as they marched. The left asserts that violence broke out when the men who accompanied the march attacked UP supporters jeering the protest. In any case, minor skirmishes took place along the route (see Map 3). Construction workers building the new UNCTAD (UN Conference on Trade and Development) building on the Alameda threw bricks at the women as they passed below.[61] However, the main scene of violence was Cerro Santa Lucía, a hilly park near the center of Santiago. The police stood nearby with orders to prevent the demonstration from going past the park—and effectively stop it from reaching La Moneda, the presidential palace. When the protesters attempted to push past Cerro Santa Lucía and head downtown, the police began spraying them with tear gas and water. The female marchers and the men who accompanied them clashed with the supporters of the UP government and the police.[62] In the melee that followed, 99 people (60 men and 39 women) were injured. Of the injured, 54 were classified as slightly wounded, 35 as moderately hurt, and 10 as seriously injured.[63]

The bulk of the marchers disbanded by 9:00 P.M., although scattered groups of protesters roamed the downtown until at least 10:00 P.M. Earlier, approximately 300 anti-Allende demonstrators from the march had attacked a nearby office belonging to the Radical Party, one of the parties that formed the UP coalition. They tore down the front door, destroyed furniture, and broke windows (see Map 3).[64] Other men accompanying the march attacked a downtown office of the Communist Youth.

The protests lasted until the early hours of the morning. At dawn the following day, police sprayed tear gas on a group of women and young people

61 Congreso Chileno, Senado, *Acusación constitucional*, 54a sess., 21 January 1972, 2848. For further description of the march and the violence, see *El Siglo*, 2 December 1971.

62 For reports that convey the marchers' point of view, see the Chilean newspapers *El Mercurio, La Prensa*, and *La Tribuna* for the first weeks of December 1971. Also see Correa Morandé, *La guerra*, 32–40, and Donoso Loero, *La epopeya*, 57–63. During the same period, pro-government newspapers *El Siglo, El Clarín*, and *La Nación* detailed acts of aggression and violence committed by the marchers.

63 Congreso Chileno, Senado, *Acusación constitucional*, 52a sess., 2756, and Congreso Chileno, Cámara de Diputados, legislatura extraordinaria, *Acusación constitucional en contra del Ministro del Interior Don José Tohá González*, sesión 38, 6 January 1972, 2847.

64 Congreso Chileno, Senado, *Acusación constitucional*, 49a sess., 18 January 1972, 2621, and Congreso Chileno, Senado, *Acusación constitucional*, 52a sess., 2787.

in Providencia (an upper-class neighborhood of Santiago) who were beating pots and pans in support of the marchers.[65] By the time the demonstrations ended, a total of 187 people—at least 140 of them men—had been arrested.[66]

On 2 December, the government declared Santiago an emergency zone.[67] General Augusto Pinochet, then chief of the military garrison of Santiago and the newly appointed head of the emergency zone for the entire province of Santiago, prohibited all public demonstrations and news reports that could "incite public disturbances" and forbade the carrying of weapons.[68] Later, critics argued that the military, not just the police, should have been deployed to maintain order. Pinochet responded prophetically: "I always turn over control of the streets and the maintenance of order to the police. When the army comes out, it comes out to kill."[69]

Protests involving pots and pans outside the capital were first reported three days later in Valparaíso, a port city located about two hours west of Santiago. There, the PDC called for a march to protest attacks against the Catholic University and the PDC headquarters in Valparaíso as well as "the aggression to which the women of Santiago were subjected by extremist groups and the police." Some of the female marchers struck pots and pans as they walked.[70] La Tribuna reported that the pots and pans protests had spread south from Santiago to Rancagua, the principal city of the huge El Teniente copper mine.[71] Banging empty pots, upholding their role as mothers and wives, and demonstrating against the UP government, anti-Allende women made their dramatic appearance on the complex stage of Chilean politics.[72]

Popular Unity's Response to the March

The left viewed the female marchers as neither courageous heroines nor defenseless victims. Despite the magnitude of the women's protest, the UP

65 *La Prensa*, 3 December 1971.

66 *El Mercurio*, 3 December 1971.

67 Congreso Chileno, Senado, *Acusación constitucional*, 52a sess., 2760.

68 *El Siglo*, 3 December 1971.

69 *La Tribuna*, 4 December 1971.

70 *La Prensa*, 5 December 1971.

71 *La Tribuna*, 13 December 1971.

72 Anti-Allende women throughout Chile took up the beating of pots and pans to protest the UP government. For example, on 31 August 1972, "more than seven thousand women from all social groups participated in an impressive demonstration banging pots and pans" in the northern city of Arica. See *El Mercurio*, 1 September 1972. A few days later, on 3 September, women marched in San Fernando, beating their pots and echoing the chants that women had yelled during the Santiago march on 1 December 1971. See *El Mercurio*, 4 September 1972.

either dismissed the marchers as wealthy women or disregarded them, emphasizing instead the involvement of the opposition parties and the presence of men in the march. Much of the left's media coverage focused on the violence perpetrated by the men who accompanied the female demonstrators. The left press generally viewed the March of the Empty Pots and Pans as "part of a fascist plan organized against the government," in the words of *El Siglo*. Responding to the right's portrayal of the marchers as peaceful protesters, pictures in *El Siglo* illustrated the "fascist violence" employed by the men "protecting" them. A typical caption on the newspaper's front page offered this description: "a young boy who protested against the farce carried out yesterday by the *momias* [mummies] of Patria y Libertad, the PN, and *Freismo* [the conservative wing of the PDC that supported Frei] is violently attacked by a horde of fascists armed to the teeth." Under a picture of a large young man holding a chain, *El Siglo* sardonically observed, "Pots with chains. This 'malnourished' and hairy demonstrator is trying to convince the public, with a huge metal chain, that in Chile we don't have anything to eat. Without a doubt, this is a very nourishing argument!"[73]

Deeply influenced by the Marxist conception of revolution, which privileges the working class, the UP considered the working class and the peasantry as the primary beneficiaries of its government. It understood that the upper class, along with some sectors of the middle class, opposed its goals of agrarian reform, higher wages for workers, redistribution of wealth, and improved social services for the poor. As José Tohá, minister of the interior and member of the Socialist Party, explained, "the revolutionary content of the government is born from the fact that its coming to power signified what we can call a class transfer of power. With the UP, the working class, along with other middle sectors, became the direct protagonist of the administration of the state."[74] Therefore, when the left spoke of

---

73 *El Siglo*, 2 December 1971. On 5 December 1971, *El Siglo* published a special supplement entitled "The Face of Fascism," which featured many pictures of armed men—purported to be anti-Allende demonstrators—in the march. During the march, fighting broke out between the youth brigades from the PN, PDC, and Patria y Libertad and young supporters (mainly male) of the UP. Each side attempted to portray itself as having engaged in violence only to protect itself in the face of a brutal attack from the other.

In the *El Siglo* caption, the word *momia* means mummy. It was originally used by the left during the UP years to refer to the dead and dying bourgeoisie. Later, it was applied to all those sectors or individuals who opposed the UP government. The Communist Party referred to *Freismo* instead of to the Christian Democrats because they hoped to work with the more leftist sectors of the party. Thus, their use of the term *Freismo* both identified those members of the PDC who attended the march as the right wing of the party and attempted to drive a wedge between the different sectors of the PDC.

74 Congreso Chileno, Senado, *Acusación constitucional*, 54a sess., 2869.

those who opposed it, they defined—and dismissed—them exclusively in terms of class, portraying them as members of Chile's elite. To counter the criticisms made by women during the march, the UP defended its policies by citing the benefits that the government had brought to the working class. Moreover, it ridiculed the demands made by the female marchers as expressions of bourgeois women's fears of losing their wealth and power.

For example, *El Siglo* noted that the women who attended the march were from the wealthy Santiago neighborhoods of Las Condes, Providencia, La Reina, and Ñuñoa. In order to establish the women's class identity, the newspaper commented that they wore "Spring Dior," while the young girls in the march wore "the latest in hot pants from the exclusive shops." Under a picture of women waving pots and pans, *El Siglo* wrote, "These were the housewives . . . wearing the latest innovations in hairstyles, pants, tops and new pots which they had, possibly for the first time, in their hands." One editorial in *El Siglo* scornfully dismissed the marchers as women who "have undertaken the supreme sacrifice of giving up their afternoon teas or their appointments at the beauty parlor to protest in the name of their class."[75]

In his farewell speech to Fidel Castro at the National Stadium on 2 December, Allende echoed the theme that all the women at the march were rich. First he decried the "fascist upsurge" that the demonstration represented, attributing it to reactionaries and the right. He concluded that the women who had attended the march were "women from upper-class neighborhoods who had come to downtown Santiago." After having dismissed these women because of their class, Allende then went on to what, for him, was more important—the presence of men in the march. Allende stated that "people need to know that this large group of women was preceded by a group of young men well armed with helmets, masks, and sticks with pieces of metal embedded in them. Similar groups of men flanked the column and brought up the rear of it as well." Allende saw the protest as a case of "the utilization of women by the reactionaries." In response, Allende urged the workers and progressive sectors to unite. He did not call on the UP parties to redouble their efforts to organize women.[76]

Luis Corvalán, secretary general of the Communist Party of Chile, echoed Allende's perceptions of the march. Denying any validity to the women's protest against food shortages, Corvalán pointed out that

75 *El Siglo*, 2 December 1971.

76 *El Siglo*, 3 December 1971. If, indeed, the women were only from the upper class, then it is not clear why Allende considered them to have been used by the reactionary forces. He could also have interpreted their marching as a demonstration of their own class interests.

[t]hroughout the years, the bourgeoisie has organized the best commercial network precisely in its own neighborhoods. Department stores, supermarkets—they have it all in Providencia, Las Condes, Vitacura. Most of the women who went to the march have virgin hands. They have never worked for anyone for even one day. They have no idea what it's like to cook and wash pots. In addition, it has been proven that shortages only served as a pretext, because once they were downtown, all they did was chant against the government and insult and use offensive language against Fidel Castro and the President of the Republic.[77]

Like Allende, Corvalán looked to the working class to oppose the fascist attacks represented by the march: as he saw it, "the working class and the Chilean workers constitute a bulwark in this country, a bulwark that is impossible to move." Furthermore, like Allende, Corvalán saw the struggle between the left and the right in male terms, a struggle carried out by men. He noted that "the Communist Party has one hundred and fifty thousand members, fifty thousand of them strapping young [male] communists who are willing to duke it out with the right." As he said colloquially, "Let's see how tough your cock is in the [cock] pit."[78]

The pro-government newspaper *El Clarín*, known for its use of slang and popular language, wrote about the march in the following way:

The rightist upsurge of Patria y Libertad, the PN, and the Christian Democratic Party has been set into motion. Yesterday, groups of scoundrels from the upper-class neighborhoods, who attend the most high-class and expensive schools, came to downtown Santiago to yell against the people of Chile. Against President Allende and Fidel Castro. They protested because Compañero *President is governing for the poor and will not allow the rich owners of the industries to keep on robbing the people. That's why those street bums who smoke marijuana, the really foxy . . . girls, and the old women with wrinkles went out to protest the shortages.*[79]

And Oscar Weiss, director of the pro-government *La Nación*, described the marchers as "the most stinking reactionary . . . parade of old women who can barely move and who brayed hysterically against the *rotos* [the poor]. . . . The women gave signs of a great deal of hysteria." Weiss reported that the women came to the march "in their station wagons or Impalas, picking up any idiot who was walking around the upper-class neighborhood." He added, "their standards were low, since they even accepted servants." Weiss concluded that the government should "send

77 *El Siglo*, 4 December 1971.
78 Ibid. My thanks to Patricio Mason for his help with these translations.
79 *El Clarín*, 3 December 1971.

the old ladies with the pots and pans back to their houses with their tails between their legs."[80] His commentary included the standard insults that some men employ when they wish to belittle women. He labeled the women as old—in other words, not sexually appealing to men; he categorized their chanting as the noises of animals, adding that all-too-familiar qualifier, hysterical; and he assumed that many of the women who participated in the march had only the vaguest idea why they were marching.

The left press in Chile also argued that the concept of and financing for the march came from abroad. *El Siglo* immediately targeted Brazil and the CIA as the culprits. The newspaper claimed that the CIA was attempting to revitalize "Plan Goulart," setting it into motion in Chile. In a joint press conference, Gladys Marín (secretary general of the Communist Youth), Carlos Lorca (leader of the Socialist Youth), and José Miguel Gacitúa (a leader of MAPU) stated that "imperialism is putting 'Plan Goulart' into action, since our country is experiencing the same demonstrations that preceded the overthrow of the constitutional presidency of Brazil."[81]

Close to twenty years after the 1973 coup, two female activists who had designed and implemented much of the UP's program for women looked back at the March of the Empty Pots and Pans and the right-wing mobilization of women against Allende. One, Inés Cornejo, had been a member of the central committee of the Communist Party. She recalls that "the *cacerolazo* [March of the Empty Pots and Pans] caught us completely by surprise." In retrospect, she believes that "we [the Communist Party] never carried out any serious or profound studies of the right's capacity to organize women, since we considered all its work paternalistic."[82]

The other, Carmen Gloria Aguayo, left the PDC and joined MAPU. Along with several other women, she headed up the National Secretariat of Women created by the UP government in September 1972 to work with women. Aguayo remembered the day of the March of the Empty Pots and Pans very well.

We didn't know how to react. . . . Fidel Castro had arrived and there was a reception for him. All the leaders of the UP were invited. I remember we worried about what to wear, how to fix our hair. On that very same day the right organized a demonstration in the streets. Fidel Castro was outraged. He asked us what we were doing here [at the embassy]. Why weren't we in the streets yelling at those women? . . . We weren't in the streets, I think, because we were overwhelmed by their power.[83]

80 Ibid.
81 *El Siglo*, 3 December 1971.
82 Inés Cornejo, interview by author, tape recording, Santiago, 21 June 1994.
83 Aguayo, interview.

International Ties to the March of the Empty Pots and Pans

Are the Chilean left's accusations of U.S. government involvement in attempts to implement of "Plan Goulart" accurate? Although there is much evidence indicating that they are, any conclusion must remain somewhat tentative until the CIA and the State Department release all the relevant documents relating to Washington's efforts to destabilize the UP government. The U.S. government understood that the success of its strategy to remove Allende from power required the mobilization of a sizable portion of Chilean society in opposition to the UP government. One key element of this strategy most likely included support for a women's movement that would first oppose and then call for the removal of Salvador Allende. Though the anti-Allende women's movement was a Chilean creation, the U.S. government provided it with financial and political aid.

It is also highly probable that Brazilian women's anti-Goulart activities served as a model for both the U.S. government and the Chilean right. Marlise Simons, then a reporter for the *Washington Post*, documented a very direct connection between the women's anti-Goulart activities in Brazil and those against Allende in Chile. Chileans who left the country once Allende was elected and lived in Brazil came into contact with the Institute of Research and Social Studies (IPES), which, Simons notes, was founded in 1961 to help unseat "Brazil's 'communist-infiltrated' civilian government." Simons quotes Dr. De Paiva, a founder and key member of IPES: "[We] taught the Chileans how to use their [*sic*] women against the Marxists. . . . Women are the most effective weapon you have in politics. . . . They have time and they have a great capacity to display emotion and to mobilize quickly. For example, if you want to spread a rumor like 'The President has a drinking problem,' or 'he had a slight heart attack,' you use women. The next day it is around the country."[84]

David Cusack studied the *gremio* movement in Chile and confirmed Simons's statements. Elite members of the Chilean business community established a new organization, the Center for Public Opinion Studies, which was a Chilean parallel to IPES. According to Cusack, the Center "was set up to coordinate the strikes and attacks on the Allende government." Cusack wrote that IPES gave "important assistance to [its] Chilean counterparts after the election of Allende."[85]

U.S. government officials have steadfastly denied any connection to the march. Only one day before it took place, however, Herbert Klein, the White House director of communications, told reporters that the UP

84 *Washington Post*, 6 January 1974.

85 Cusack, *Revolution and Reaction*, 108.

government "won't last long."[86] Nathaniel Davis, U.S. ambassador to Chile in 1971, witnessed the March of the Empty Pots and Pans, but disclaimed any U.S. involvement in it or any of the subsequent women's marches against Allende. Davis wrote in his memoirs that "so far as I know, the CIA did not conceive of or foment the march of the empty pots. In fact, at the time the station chief expressed chagrin to me that his organization had not had better and earlier intelligence about the initial planning of it."[87]

One factor to keep in mind is that the U.S. government used different channels to support the opposition in Chile. It sent funds to *El Mercurio* and other opposition newspapers, for instance. In the days leading up to the protest, these newspapers carried a significant number of articles that advertised the march and called on women to attend it. In addition, the U.S. government sent money to both the PDC and the PN. As the Church Committee report, *Covert Action*, noted, "money provided to political parties not only supported opposition candidates in the various elections, but also enabled the parties to maintain an anti-government campaign throughout the year, urging citizens to demonstrate their opposition in a variety of ways."[88] Some of this money probably helped cover the expenses of the demonstration, or, over the next two years, went to Poder Femenino. In an interview, María Correa Morandé stated that the PN did support Poder Femenino and gave it money to sustain its work.[89]

Edy Kaufman writes that "support for the women was probably channeled through other groups, such as the opposition parties and the press, who maintained contacts with U.S. sources and who were probably actively involved in organizing the women's movement." In terms of the march, Kaufman points out that "while official U.S. sources do not point to a direct connection, the CIA is known to have organized street demonstrations during the same period."[90] Additionally, two North American scholars who have studied the role of the CIA in Chile during the UP years believe that "the most important effort made by the CIA and the Chilean

---

86 In response, *New York Times* journalist Tad Szulc dryly commented that "it is unusual for senior Administration officials to discuss publicly the possibility of the overthrow of a foreign government with which the United States maintains correct relations." *New York Times*, 1 December 1971.

87 Nathaniel Davis, *The Last Two Years of Salvador Allende* (Ithaca: Cornell University Press, 1985), 47, 323–25.

88 Senate Select Committee, *Covert Action: Report*, 29.

89 Correa Morandé, interview.

90 Kaufman, *Crisis*, 69.

right to show mass popular opposition to the government focused on women. The campaign to create a seemingly broad women's movement was modeled on a similar campaign in Brazil in 1963–64. . . . The campaign to mobilize women began when the economic boom was still going strong. That December [1971] the right organized the march of the empty pots and pans."[91] However, until more documentation is made available to the public, a definitive assessment of the nature and extent of U.S. involvement in the March of the Empty Pots and Pans does not appear possible.[92]

The Significance of the March of the Empty Pots and Pans

For most historians of the UP, the March of the Empty Pots and Pans represents little more than a footnote, a sideline to the main struggles that were taking place during the tumultuous years of 1970–73. They miss the significance of the march. It heralded the public appearance of a women's opposition movement, one that grew and played an increasingly important role during the next two years of the Allende government. This movement mobilized previously unorganized women against the UP and helped create a climate that would encourage the military coup that overthrew the UP government on 11 September 1973.

The size of the march surprised its organizers. Lucía Maturana, who later became active in SOL (an anti-Allende, family-based organization), remarked that "we never thought it would be such a success! The idea of ladies beating pots and marching seemed a little ridiculous, no?" Maturana, like many others, measured the success of the march in terms of the number of women who turned out, the impact it had, and the response of the women who attended it. What struck her was the courage and fighting spirit demonstrated by many of the women when the "Marxist brigades" attacked them. Maturana proudly commented that the women marchers "defended themselves with the very same pots. One woman hit a man who was attacking her with her pot. His head got stuck in the pot and they had to take him to the public health center. They could only get it off with a can opener!"[93]

91 Adam Schesch and Patricia Garrett, "The Case of Chile," in *Uncloaking the CIA*, ed. Howard Frazier (New York: Free Press, 1975), 45.

92 To date, all of my attempts to determine to whom the money was sent in Chile have met with failure. Senators who served on the Church Committee claim that they cannot remember details from the hearings. Staff members who prepared the final report have made similar statements. The CIA has refused to honor my FOIA requests for information.

93 Lucía Maturana, interview by author, tape recording, Santiago, 26 October 1993.

The class composition of the marchers is difficult to determine. While most of the women who organized the march were middle- and upper-class, poor and working-class women also attended. Some were domestic servants, employees of the wealthy women who organized and attended the march.[94] Whether they came voluntarily or came at their employers' command has not been ascertained. Women active in the Mothers' Centers also attended. Following the march, 150 women from the poor neighborhood of Conchalí wrote an open letter to President Allende to protest the violence and insults that they had suffered during the march. They defined themselves as "women of the people who have a clear understanding of morality and are interested in building a better future; apart from being eminently Chileans and patriots, we are not subject to any of the political parties, since we represent all the tendencies." They ended their letter to Allende by saying, "don't forget that our ancestors were Inés de Suárez, Javiera Carrera, and Paula Jaraquemada."[95]

Certainly the opposition tried to get working-class women to attend the march. In December 1971, Beatrice Campos worked in a Santiago factory that produced textiles. The owners of the factory told several of the female workers that if they went to the demonstration, they would receive taxi fare and would not have the time they spent at the demonstration deducted from their pay. Campos, who had voted for Jorge Alessandri in the 1970 election, was only too happy to go to the march; four other women and two men from the factory joined her. Because they were poor, they pocketed the money meant for the taxi and went to the march by bus.[96]

The March of the Empty Pots and Pans was the first major foray of the anti-Allende women into the public limelight. As a result, those who went to the march were likely to be connected already to party structures or some other affiliated organization such as the Mothers' Centers, or to have personal ties to the women and men organizing the demonstration. As the movement expanded, however, it drew in other sectors of the

94 Of the forty women injured at the march, eight identified themselves as servants, one as a worker, one as a seamstress, one as a journalist, one as a nurse's aide, one as a businesswoman, and ten as students. Two were children, and fourteen did not identify themselves. *El Mercurio*, 3 December 1971.

95 *La Prensa*, 5 December 1971.

96 Beatrice Campos [pseud.], interview by author, tape recording, Puente Alto, 3 February 1994. Beatrice Campos is not her real name; she requested anonymity. Although she had opposed Allende during the Popular Unity years, Campos was horrified at the violence and abuse of the military government. She switched her loyalties, joined the resistance, and worked against the military government. Her son, who encouraged her opposition to Pinochet, was in political exile in Europe at the time of the interview.

Chilean population and developed a mass strategy that made women's participation on a cross-class basis more workable.

The opposition used the march to its maximum advantage. Employing the various media resources at its disposal, it projected the event as a quasi-epic: Chilean women, en masse, had rejected socialism. More immediately, the march certainly met one of the opposition's goals. It completely overshadowed Fidel Castro's departure. News of the march, not of Castro's final speech in the National Stadium, spread throughout Chile and around the world.

The march had a substantial impact on the women who attended it as well as on those women who did not protest that day but were sympathetic to the marchers. Many women who had previously seen themselves as negligible or minor political actors now viewed themselves as heroic figures who led the struggle to save Chile from communism. The vast amount of commentary that the march elicited from all sides (and from international sources) encouraged the female participants to see themselves as courageous women who were willing to brave the Marxist hordes in order to defend their families and their nation.[97] Furthermore, the March of the Empty Pots and Pans was the first large march against the Allende government. This fact confirmed the perception of many women that they, not the men, were at the forefront of the struggle against the UP. Many women stated that the march helped them overcome their fears of demonstrating in public and of being attacked by opponents. In order to explain this feeling, women frequently referred to themselves as "mother lions defending their cubs."[98] Like lionesses, they were willing to brave their opponents' attacks to defend their dens and cubs. To do so, the women turned their pots and pans into weapons that they used against their opponents—both figuratively and literally.

Pots and pans became much-touted symbols of women's opposition to Allende. For the rest of the month of December, *La Tribuna* featured a

97 For international coverage of the march, see *New York Times*, 1–4 December 1971, *Christian Science Monitor*, 3–4 December 1971, *Wall Street Journal*, 2–3 December 1971, *Washington Post*, 2–3 December 1971, and *The Times* (London), 3–4 December 1971.

98 "She was like a mother lion, who smells a threat from afar." See, for one example, Donoso Loero, *La epopeya*, 19. A white working-class mother in Boston—one who opposed the enforced busing of her children to desegregated schools—described herself using the same language. Explaining why "mothers had been more active in the movement than fathers," she said, "'I always say it's like a lioness in her den. You know, these are my children.'" See Julia Wrigley, "From Housewives to Activists," in *No Middle Ground: Women and Radical Protest*, ed. Kathleen Blee (New York: New York University Press, 1998), 261. It is not clear to what extent other women who link their activism to motherhood use this analogy or whether it has particular appeal for conservative women.

Fig. 6 The March of the Empty Pots and Pans took place on 1 December 1971. For the rest of the month, an illustration of an empty pot graced the front cover of *La Tribuna,* as in this issue from 3 December 1971.

drawing of a pot on its front cover (see Fig. 6). Henceforth, whenever women demonstrated against Allende, they brought with them empty pots and pans. Women proudly sported tiny pins of pots and pans on their blouses as the symbol of their opposition to Allende. Wealthy women purchased gold pins in the shape of pots and pans (designed for them by Cartier).[99] Poorer women had theirs made of copper.

As a direct result of the march, the opposition forces mustered enough votes in Congress to impeach José Tohá, minister of the interior, when, in January 1972, ten members of the PDC brought charges against him for repressing the march. They accused him of violating the Constitution, breaking the law, and having "seriously compromised the security of the nation."[100] Specifically, they accused Tohá of tolerating the existence of armed groups in Chile (they referred exclusively to armed groups on the left, not those on the right), not allowing groups to protest publicly or not offering them protection when they did, illegally closing radio stations, and arbitrarily and illegally arresting individuals.[101] All of these charges stemmed from the march and its aftermath. The Chamber of Deputies upheld the charges, and from 18 January to 22 January, the Chilean Senate held impeachment hearings. On 22 January, the Senate found José Tohá guilty of the charges listed above.[102] The vote allowed

99 Saenz, interview, 27 December 1993.

100 *El Mercurio,* 18 January 1972.

101 The opposition routinely accused the UP government of supporting or tolerating—or, minimally, not clamping down on—violence from the left. These charges echoed the accusations Chile Joven made during the 1970 presidential campaign. To support these accusations, the opposition pointed out that Andrés Pascal Allende, a leader of the MIR, was Salvador Allende's nephew. The opposition considered the MIR a violent group.

102 The UP controlled neither the Senate nor the Chamber of Deputies. The PDC had the largest bloc of votes, followed by the UP. The combined votes of the PDC and the PN could easily

the PN and the PDC to remove one of the UP's more popular and skilled ministers.[103]

Because of its success, the march also heralded a significant shift in the tactics of the opposition.[104] Instead of focusing all its energies on Parliament and negotiations between the parties in smoke-filled rooms, the opposition, led by the right, increasingly engaged in street demonstrations and direct actions to challenge the UP government. The opposition saw these activities as more confrontational, more challenging, and, in the end, more likely to build a movement that called for and supported the overthrow of Salvador Allende and the UP government.

The march changed the way the opposition parties considered—and represented—women. Prior to the march, the parties had mainly looked to women as a source of votes. In the aftermath of the demonstration, they regarded women as an essential source of support, determination, and militancy against the UP government. However, a certain ambiguity is evident in the male politicians' descriptions of the female marchers. They portray the women both as courageous heroines who fought back against the Marxist brigades and as defenseless victims of these vicious forces. Victor García,[105] a senator from the PN, articulated these ideas in an interview with *El Mercurio*.

And the crowning glory of this blind violence was the attack against the women who were marching to express their opposition. This attack has converted the women into the most courageous, self-sacrificing, and determined enemies of the UP.

More than a despicable thing to do, attacking defenseless women, allowing extremists to pelt them with stones and insults and the police to spray them with tear gas, was the idiocy of the century.[106]

---

defeat the UP in any voting that took place in Congress. The UP senators requested that the voting be held in secret, because they believed that the PDC senators were under orders to vote for Tohá's impeachment. If the voting was public, then the PDC senators would have to follow party orders and vote to impeach Tohá. If it was done secretly, the UP hoped that enough PDC senators would vote according to their own beliefs, not by order of the party. When the Senate refused to allow a secret ballot, the UP senators rose, withdrew en masse from the chambers, and did not participate in the vote. See Congreso Chileno, Senado, *Acusación constitucional*, 54a sess., 2889–91.

103 After the September 1973 coup, the military arrested Tohá. He died in a military hospital weighing only 110 pounds (he had previously weighed 170). Mary Helen Spooner, *Soldiers in a Narrow Land: The Pinochet Regime in Chile* (Berkeley and Los Angeles: University of California Press, 1994), 79–82.

104 Cusack, *Revolution and Reaction*, 43.

105 He was the husband of Victoria Armanet, who headed the women's section of the National Party and was one of the founders of Poder Femenino.

106 *El Mercurio*, 5 December 1971.

Propelled forward by their victorious excursion into Chilean politics and anti-Allende activities, many of the women who had organized the march decided that it was essential to form a group that would consolidate their efforts. A few months after the march, some of the women who had led the protest joined with others to form Poder Femenino, the dynamic organization that galvanized women to act against Allende and the UP government.

6

Poder Femenino and the
Anti-Allende Women's Movement

THE SUCCESS OF the March of the Empty Pots and Pans encouraged anti-Allende women to intensify their work against the Popular Unity government. Following the march, they—along with the opposition parties—hailed women as the heroines of the fatherland, calling on them to unite across class lines to save Chile and their families from communism. Early in 1972, these women formed Poder Femenino (PF, Feminine Power) in order to advance their struggle against the Popular Unity government. For the next year and a half, PF spearheaded women's opposition to the UP government.

This chapter argues that PF was able to organize large numbers of women against the socialist government because it focused on gender, not class (which the UP emphasized). Moreover, PF members projected themselves as the representatives of *all* Chilean women. In the face of the economic crisis and the shortages that hit Chile from 1972 onward, PF defined itself as the defender of Chilean women. To explain PF's success with women, this chapter examines the leadership, formation, activities, and beliefs of PF and the group's use of ideas about gender to organize a multi-class movement of women against Allende. This chapter also discusses how opposition men understood the anti-Allende women's movement.

The Formation, Structure, and Organization of Poder Femenino

Early in 1972, prominent women from the opposition parties and the *gremio* movement, along with independents, met and formed Poder Femenino. From then until the September 1973 coup, PF functioned as a coordinating committee that planned antigovernment activities for women. PF also provided much-needed support to and resources for the wide array of forces that protested the Allende government.[1]

Two of the group's founders and leaders, Maria Correa Morandé and Elena Larraín, claim that the group started among a circle of friends who wanted to make women's resistance to the government more visible and effective.[2] Larraín, who had led Acción Mujeres de Chile, explains that PF started "in order to recuperate lost values, home life, and tranquility, to extinguish the tensions that destroy families, and so that the struggle for subsistence would not be so harsh and bitter. A group of friends spontaneously united. . . . Later the idea spread around."[3]

Larraín was well equipped to start the group. Her years of work in Acción Mujeres de Chile had provided her with experience in political organization and confidence in her own abilities as an organizer. The fact that she had always remained an independent conservative allowed her to work with a variety of opposition political parties and increased PF's ability to portray itself as apolitical.[4]

Despite its apolitical appearance, PF enjoyed close ties to the opposition parties. In order to form PF, Larraín recalled, "I spoke personally with the presidents of each [opposition] party to ask them to name two delegates [to PF] so that it would be official. Then I went to talk to the *gremios* so that they, too, would send delegates to the meeting. As a result, we formed an enormous coordinating council of, perhaps, twenty women."[5] Each opposition political party—the National Party, the Christian Democratic Party, Padena (Partido Democrático Nacional, National Democratic Party), Izquierda Radical (Left Radical Party), and Democracia Radical (Radical Democracy)—sent two delegates to the weekly meetings of PF. The coordinating council also included representatives from the *gremios*, the women's section of SOL (Solidaridad, Orden y Libertad, Solidarity, Order, and Liberty), Patria y Libertad, Javiera Carrera, UNAFE

[handwritten in left margin: formed from all parties]

---

1 For articles on Poder Femenino, see Crummett, "El Poder Femenino"; Pat Garrett-Schesch, "The Mobilization of Women During the Popular Unity Government," *Latin American Perspectives* 2, no. 1 (Spring 1975); Michèle Mattelart, "Feminine Side"; Supplee, "Women and the Counterrevolution"; Townsend, "Refusing to Travel *La Vía Chilena*"; and Waylen, "Rethinking Women's Political Participation."

2 Correa Morandé, interview; Larraín, interview by author, 16 March 1994. Elena Larraín, who had led Acción Mujeres de Chile from 1964 to 1970, was an independent. María Correa Morandé was one of three National Party representatives to Feminine Power. The other two representatives were Victoria Armanet and Carmen Saenz.

3 "El nuevo poder," *Ercilla*, 29 August–4 September 1973.

4 Larraín, interviews by author, 16 March and 8 July 1994.

5 Ibid.

(Unidad Nacional Femenina, National Feminine Unity), Unión Cívica Democrática (Democratic Civic Union), Unión Mujeres Libres (Union of Free Women), and unaffiliated business- and professional women.[6]

The representatives from the PN, the PDC, and the *gremio* movement exercised significant influence in PF. These women and the groups to which they belonged each contributed certain elements that enhanced PF's ability to organize a militant, broad-based, anti-Allende women's movement. The PN's representatives to PF brought with them an unwavering determination to remove Allende. Over the next year and a half, their clarity of vision allowed them to argue for increasingly militant actions against the government. In addition, their membership in the PN afforded them access to money, the media, the elite, and the military. For example, Silvia Alessandri, who had obtained the permit for the March of the Empty Pots and Pans and worked with PF, was a PN deputy and member of the Defense Commission in the Chilean Congress. As such, she frequently met with military officers and discussed the political situation with them.[7]

The Christian Democratic representatives greatly aided PF's attempts to mobilize beyond its middle- and upper-class base. Through their influence over many of the Mothers' Centers, they impelled large numbers of poor and working-class women to participate in the anti-Allende movement. Despite the efforts of UP women to gain control of the centers, the Christian Democrats managed to maintain political dominance over a large number of them. The party encouraged these women to both attend the anti-Allende marches and oppose UP efforts on the community level.

6 *El Mercurio*, 17 October 1972. Feminine Power took out an ad and listed these groups as members of the coordinating council. Padena was a very small party made up of the "residue of Carlos Ibáñez's followers who fused together in 1960." During the early 1960s, some sectors of Padena joined with the Christian Democrats, while others supported the FRAP coalition. However, by the late 1960s, Padena supported the Christian Democrats and opposed Allende. See Burnett, *Political Groups*, 178, 215–16, 277. The Radical Democracy party formed prior to the 1970 elections. Its members did not support Allende and had rejected Radical Party support for Popular Unity. See Biehl del Río and Fernández, "Political Pre-requisites," 62. The Left Radical Party quit the Radical Party and the Popular Unity coalition two months after the Popular Unity came to power. *La Tercera*, 16 April 1972. No further explanation was given as to who or what the Javiera Carrera Organization, the Democratic Civic Union, or the Union of Free Women (UNAFE) were. Nina Donoso was Secretary General of UNAFE. The group played an active role in organizing the March of the Empty Pots and Pans and published an article extolling the female marchers. See *El Mercurio*, 5 December 1971. SOL was a "family organization" that started when several couples, none of them members of any political party, decided to "convert our concerns into a civic family movement that would struggle for the ideals and rights that we Chileans were losing." *La Patria*, 19 May 1975.

7 Silvia Alessandri, interview by author, tape recording, Santiago, 23 March 1994. Alessandri is the niece of former president Jorge Alessandri. She was a PN deputy during the Popular Unity years.

Carmen Gloria Aguayo, who helped establish the Mothers' Centers during the Frei years, confirmed the extent of PDC influence in the centers during the UP years.[8] Aguayo noted that "[t]he opposition, although defeated, maintained a great deal of its power over the organizations that it had created. It used them skillfully, cleverly using them to serve its interests and to transmit its discourse. In order to maintain its base among women and its influence over the Mothers' Centers, the opposition tirelessly repeated the slogan: 'The Mothers' Centers do not engage in politics.'"[9]

In addition, the Christian Democrats provided PF with important ties to the working class as a result of their efforts within the trade union movement. When labor conflicts broke out in La Papelera and El Teniente (see Chap. 7), PDC influence in the respective unions helped generate working-class opposition to Allende and greatly facilitated the participation of PF women in these struggles. PF women, in turn, used these connections to make contact with the wives of workers and with female employees—thus broadening their movement. They put these conflicts to use, projecting an image of Chilean womanhood that, they claimed, transcended class and served to unify a divided country. They represented themselves as the force capable of restoring peace and order to the nation, which, they declared, was wracked by strife created by the UP government.

Representatives from the *gremio* movement extended PF's ties even further and facilitated PF's connections with many of Chile's professional unions (representing doctors, lawyers, engineers, agronomists, and journalists) and small business owners, especially the combative truck drivers and white-collar employees, became involved with the group. These relationships allowed PF to expand its network beyond the upper class and provided PF members with a broader range of issues around which to mobilize. For example, when the truckers went out on strike in October 1972 and August 1973, PF organized women to go door-to-door to collect food to feed the strikers.

During the UP years, PF leader Elena Larraín met with prominent representatives of the independent right on a weekly basis to analyze the political situation and to plan upcoming activities. Over lunch, she discussed opposition tactics and strategy with Jorge Alessandri, the former

8 During the last year of UP rule, Aguayo (who had joined MAPU, part of the UP coalition) helped direct the government-sponsored National Secretariat of Women Aguayo, interview. To date, a study of how the different Mothers' Centers responded politically during the Popular Unity years has not been undertaken. As a result, it is not yet possible to pinpoint which centers maintained their loyalty to the PDC, which aligned themselves with the UP, and which ones split over political differences.

9 Aguayo, *Des Chiliennes*, 88–89.

president (1958–64) and unsuccessful presidential candidate; Eduardo Boetsch, the former leader of Chile Libre; and Jaime Guzmán, the theoretical leader of the *gremio* movement.[10] Larraín served as a conduit between PF and this important sector of the opposition for information and planning.

PF representatives met once each week to discuss politics and to organize anti-Allende events. The meetings were held in the organization's office, a luxurious house located in the upper-class neighborhood of Providencia.[11] Many women have described the office of PF as the scene of feverish activity. Women frequently put in ten- or twelve-hour days at the office, abandoning their domestic responsibilities in order to advance the anti-UP cause. Victoria Armanet, one of the PN's representatives to PF, remembers that "every day there was something [to do]. We got together [in the office of PF] at ten in the morning and we never stopped doing things."[12]

PF organized women, emboldened them to undertake aggressive actions, and reassured them that their efforts were both necessary and respectable. When the coordinating council decided that the women should pursue a particular course of action, they initiated a series of phone calls that reached hundreds of women within a matter of hours. Through this organized phone tree, they could rapidly communicate with a large number of women who generally had the leisure time and the commitment to respond immediately to the call.

Although the PF women consistently denied their upper- and middle-class status, that class background greatly facilitated their organizing efforts. Unlike the vast majority of lower-middle-class or poor women, the PF women had phones, which enabled them to get the word out quickly to group members and others sympathetic to their cause. They owned cars or could afford taxis, so they could easily get to meetings or

10 Larraín, interview by author, 8 July 1994; Boetsch, interview.

11 Larraín saw an ad for the house and decided that it was the ideal space and location for the group. However, she recounted, the owner of the house did not want to rent to the group because she was worried about having her home used for political purposes. In order to convince the landlady to rent her the house, Larraín drove there and brought with her the entire year's rent in cash. She asked the landlady to hold the money for her while she ran an errand, explaining that she felt insecure carrying all that cash with her. By the time she returned to collect the money, the landlady's reluctance to part with it overrode her concern for the safety of the house, and as a result, Feminine Power acquired its new office. Larraín informed me that she had obtained the large sum of money from her brother, who lived in the United States. She vehemently denies that the group ever received any support from the CIA. Larraín, interview by author, 8 July 1994.

12 Armanet, interview.

to actions. Furthermore, they had maids. The maids prepared the food, watched the children, and ran the house, thus relieving the activist women of any concern about meals or the need to be home when their children returned from school. Many of the women in PF did not have jobs. Thus, they had disposable time and critical resources needed to oppose the UP government.

Carmen Saenz, another PN representative to PF, remembers that the group kept up a steady stream of activities until the time of the coup. Sometimes, PF members went to "the tall buildings downtown and hid on the roofs until noon. At noon we threw leaflets to protest the government."[13] PF organized boycotts of stores that they believed were owned by members of the Communist Party, such as the Caffarena chain.[14] When the truck drivers went out on strike in October 1972 and again in August 1973, the women of PF "brought them food so that they would keep on resisting."[15]

Choosing a Name

The debate that erupted among the female activists over what to name their group indicates that many of them felt a certain ambiguity over their identity and role. Their choice, Poder Femenino, simultaneously sustained this ambiguity and reflected a definite sense of who they were. While "Femenino" projected an essentialist vision of women as dependent, weak, and submissive, "Poder" inverted that meaning to affirm women's strength. The women understood that they needed a name that would accurately define who they were—but would not offend the men with whom they worked. The need to choose the right name was so intense that the women consulted a psychologist who helped them come up with the name Poder Femenino. Some of the women worried that the inclusion of the word "power" in the name was "too strong."[16] Elena

---

13 Saenz, interview, 7 December 1993. Every day, a cannon shot from Cerro Santa Lucía in Santiago signals the noon hour. This loud noise, which is heard throughout downtown Santiago, allowed the women to coordinate their throwing of leaflets.

14 Alessandri, interview.

15 Armanet, interview.

16 Nellie Gallo, interview by María de los Angeles Crummett, notes, Santiago, 19 July 1974. Nellie Gallo was one of the *gremio* movement's representatives to Poder Femenino. I am very grateful to María de los Angeles Crummett, who generously allowed me to use her notes from interviews with Chilean women and men. In 1974, Crummett traveled to Chile and interviewed leaders of PF and SOL. Twenty years later, I spoke with some (but not all) of the women and men she interviewed. Nellie Gallo died before I did my research, so I am particularly thankful that Crummett managed to interview her. Crummett based her article, "El Poder Femenino," on these interviews.

Larraín remembered that at first most women opposed the name; they found it "too harsh and fierce." However, she felt that the group needed a name "men would respect." Over time, she added, the women "grew to enjoy the word 'power.'"[17]

In *La guerra de las mujeres*, María Correa Morandé, the PN representative to PF, reproduced the discussion that she claimed took place among the coordinating council as the members determined the group's name.

Feminine Power. What do you think?

A sudden silence followed these words. . . .

Then [the room] overflowed with different voices, opinions for and against.

No, asserted Emilia, I think it's pretentious. We will create a lot of enemies for ourselves. The men will see it as a challenge.

Good, that's what it is, a challenge. We have to be straightforward or we won't achieve anything, Barbara argued firmly. Furthermore, Feminine Power is not anything new that should frighten anyone, it exists and has always existed . . . exercised one way or another. . . .

Before proposing it . . . we spoke with a psychologist and it seemed like a good idea to him. Power currents exert an influence on humanity. . . .

The name was approved. The success was overwhelming.

It seemed as if the name contained a magic interpretation of ancient hidden inhibitions, suppressed for millennia, forced to contain anxieties: of acting, speaking, showing the truth, propelled from the street level of the theater and onto the stage in order to be heard, in order to deliver our distinct and complementary message that continued to be missing in the place where decisions are made.[18]

The debate, in which Correa Morandé claims that neither men nor the parties participated, suggests that PF enjoyed a certain degree of autonomy from them. In reality, it is likely that the organization had a more complex relationship with the parties. Many of the women in PF belonged to the opposition parties. Although they routinely denied it to me, it is likely that they often discussed their activities and coordinated their plans with the party leadership. At the same time, I believe that the women in PF developed their own dynamic and frequently transcended and occasionally challenged the (male) party leadership. Their deliberations about which name to choose reflect the dual character of their relationship to the parties. The women's initial, fearful response to the use of the word "power" indicates that they felt that their declaration of strength could provoke hostility and rejection from men and, perhaps, scare other

17 Elena Larraín, interview by María de los Angeles Crummett, notes, Santiago, 18 July 1974.
18 Correa Morandé, *La guerra*, 56–57.

women. Yet their decision to adopt it illustrates their faith in themselves and their willingness to question—and conceivably even defy—male power. Even though the opposition press touted them as courageous heroines, the members of PF knew that they had to tread carefully on the political terrain that most Chileans considered masculine territory. It is probable that they did not want to be mistakenly identified as a feminist group, one that might therefore be considered antagonistic to men. At the same time, these women recognized their exclusion from the centers of power and struggled to have their voices heard within them.

During the early 1970s, news of the U.S.-based women's liberation movement penetrated the Chilean media. The image presented to the Chilean people of women's liberation was usually one depicting women who burned their bras, hated men, and rejected the roles of wife and mother.[19] During this period, Aurora Posada was a UP supporter and activist. She remembers that many Chilean women thought that feminists were "*putas*" (prostitutes) because they were sexually free women who would sleep with any men they desired, including other women's husbands and boyfriends.[20] Partially as a result of this distorted idea of women's liberation, most Chilean women—from all sides of the political spectrum—rejected North American feminism. At the same time, it is possible that the women's movement did influence Chilean women, if only subconsciously. It is significant that the group chose to call itself PF, a name that both accepts a restricted definition of womanhood and challenges the limitations that such a description implies.

Poder Femenino, Anti-Allende Women, and Gender

In representing themselves publicly, the women of PF consistently downplayed or ignored the extent to which their own political careers and experiences and their access to group resources facilitated their efforts to organize women against the UP. Instead, they attributed their organizational strengths and successful activities to the fact that they were women. They embraced an essentialist and mystical definition of womanhood that transcended class, geography, time, and ethnicity. In the face of divisions caused by politics and class, PF presented a vision of eternal womanhood, changeless, unmarked by time, historical developments, or material realities.

One way to assess how these women defined themselves is to examine how they chose to portray themselves in their writings. Two books that

19 In fact, feminists never did burn their bras, and many had children. These images are merely media creations.

20 Aurora Posada, personal communication, Chicago, 24 February 2001.

illustrate this are *La guerra de las mujeres (Women's War)*, by ?
Morandé, and *La epopeya de las ollas vacías (The Epic of the Empty* ^
Teresa Donoso Loero. Both authors were rightist women who partͰ
pated in the anti-Allende movement.[21] A recurrent theme that ran
through both books is that the women who resisted Allende could be
compared to—even directly linked to—the national heroines of Chile.
Just as the organizers of the March of the Empty Pots and Pans called on
women to follow in the spirit of Inés de Suárez, Guacolda, Javiera Carrera, or Paula Jaraquemada, these writers explained women's courage and
resistance as a legacy passed on to them by the heroines who preceded
them.

Teresa Donoso began her book by retelling the story of Inés de Suárez.
Donoso's portrayal of de Suárez provided Chilean women with a historical prototype to explain and justify their political activities against the UP
government. Inés de Suárez was a Spanish woman who accompanied her
husband to Peru in the 1500s. While in Peru she met Pedro de Valdivia,
the would-be conqueror of the Mapuche people, and fell in love with him.
Abandoning her husband, de Suárez accompanied Valdivia to Chile and
participated in the wars against the indigenous population. The action for
which she is best known was her defense of Santiago and the Spanish
presence in Chile against the attacking Mapuche people. At the time,
seven Mapuche chiefs were imprisoned in Spanish jails in Santiago. The
captive chiefs sent word to their fellow Mapuches to attack the Spanish
and rescue them. In order to prevent such a rescue, de Suárez "seiz[ed] a
sword" and "told the two men guarding the chiefs . . . to kill them
instantly." One of the terrified guards asked her, "How should I kill
them?" She immediately responded, "Like this." She "unsheathed her
sword" and killed them all. She then "ordered [the guards] to throw the
heads on the attackers," an action that so horrified the Mapuches that
they turned and fled. Apocryphally, Donoso notes that this event took
place on 11 September 1541.[22]

De Suárez's lack of fidelity to her husband, and her obvious lack of
respect for the institution of marriage and the family, were not among the
qualities that Donoso highlighted when she proffered de Suárez as an

---

21 Teresa Donoso was both an author and a journalist with *El Mercurio*. In 1973, she won the
prestigious Helena Rubinstein award for journalist of the year. She was also president of the
Asociación de Mujeres Periodistas (Association of Women Journalists) that year. See *¿Qué
Pasa?* 28 December 1973. In 1975, she published a conservative critique of the progressive
Catholic movement, Christians for Socialism. See Teresa Donoso Loero, *Historia de los cris-
tianos por el socialismo en Chile* (Santiago: Editorial Vaitea, 1975).

22 Donoso Loero, *La epopeya*, 9–10.

example of a national heroine.[23] Nor did she waste any sympathy on the seven Mapuche chiefs who so summarily lost their heads and their lives. Instead, what made de Suárez a heroine in Donoso's eyes—and those of countless other Chilean women—was her willingness to do what was needed to defend Chile. When the men hesitated at her orders to kill the Mapuche chiefs, she fearlessly stepped forward, sword in hand, and did the bloody deed. Thus, she served as a role model for the women who, clutching their empty pots and pans, went out into the streets and braved the tear gas thrown at them by the police and the attacks meted out to them by the supporters of the UP in order to save Chile from the communists.

Furthermore, Donoso believes that many men (like the soldiers in her book) refused to act against the threat of a communist takeover, thus jeopardizing their families. Men's passivity in the face of such an "imminent danger" forced women to take to the streets of Santiago, just as centuries before, the indecision of men had prompted de Suárez to decapitate the Mapuche chiefs.

The idea that women's political activity stemmed from men's passivity and from women's domestic responsibilities permeated the thinking of PF women. PF leader and author María Correa Morandé believes that women were the first to organize against the UP government only because the men refused to do so. She observed that "we desperately wanted people to react. The men didn't react but we wanted them to. So, we women began to join together."[24] Repeating the familiar metaphor, another PF leader, Carmen Saenz, remarked that "women are lionesses when we have to defend jobs, our children, education, everything that is family."[25]

Elsa Chaney notes that gender defined much of Chilean women's political activity. From her research among female politicians and activists in the late 1960s, Chaney argues that women's political involvement does not challenge their position as mothers, since this work is seen as part of their domestic role: women "almost invariably appear to consider their intervention as an extension of their family role to the arena of public affairs." In fact, Chaney concludes, Chilean women become more politically active in times of crisis. She notes that "women's active political

---

23 It appears that most of the Chilean heroines left home and family behind to carry out their noble deeds. For example, one article extolled the heroine Javiera Carrera because "she changed herself into a *caudillo* with her own hands. At a given moment she abandoned her husband, small children, elderly father, and all her comforts to accompany her brothers through the mountain passes and the Argentine pampa, led by her ideals." See "El nuevo poder," *Ercilla,* 29 August–4 September 1973, 10.

24 Correa Morandé, interview.

25 Saenz, interview, 4 December 1993.

intervention in Latin America (as elsewhere) in any numbers has always occurred at the crisis point in their nations' histories."[26] For many women, the UP government represented such a crisis.

Underlying the belief that women respond politically only in times of crisis was the notion that men and women have separate and distinct roles in life. Men's duties demanded an active participation in the public world, the world of jobs and politics. Women, in turn, were responsible for their families and their homes. Men's failure to do what was required of them forced women to abandon the physical sphere of their duties in order to defend its spiritual and material core.

Many of the PF women believed that motherhood explained their political activity. Despite the fact that PF leaders had years of political experience, they routinely claimed that they did not understand politics (which they defined as a male activity) and that they acted solely to protect their children. Being mothers gave them special insights that men lacked. María Correa Morandé attributed the more conservative nature of Chilean women to motherhood.

Being a mother makes a woman more conservative, more responsible. She attaches a great deal of importance to this reality. Men, well, I believe that a father's love is an acquired one, conscious, responsible, a rational love but not an instinctive one. There is nothing instinctual in a father's love. . . . He did not carry the child inside him as the mother did. He didn't feel it live. He didn't feel it being born. Women have a much greater responsibility for the human race. That's why I believe women are more cautious, more responsible. That's the only reason why I think more women support the right. The right is more ordered, more respectful.[27]

PF women often criticized male passivity and praised women's courage. Although they did not make any specific suggestions about what men should do, members of PF frequently expressed disappointment and anger at what they perceived to be men's acceptance of the UP government and their refusal or unwillingness to act against it. However, despite their criticisms, these women did not call for a fundamental restructuring of gender roles. In fact, one of the reasons the women complained so vehemently was that men's failure to fulfill their gender-defined duties forced women to take them on. Their struggle was not to replace men, but to convince men to take up their biologically and socially assigned duties.

26 Chaney, *Supermadre*, 20, 23.
27 Correa Morandé, interview.

Although these anti-Allende women routinely transgressed accepted norms of correct female behavior, then, they did not do so in order to challenge ideas of proper gender roles. They did so because of their profound identification with and acceptance of their role as wives and mothers. When feminists carry out bold and nontraditional actions, they do so as part of their pursuit of a new definition of womanhood; they mean to challenge the belief that there is an essentialist or biologically based definition of womanhood.[28] Conversely, these conservative women carried out their activities in order to ensure their safe return to traditional female roles and practices. These women seldom questioned patriarchal relations or structures within the home or within society. Far from attempting to construct a more inclusive politics, these women struggled to strip their activist role of any overt political meaning by identifying themselves as women and mothers—not as politicians.

Donoso Loero, for example, concludes the introduction to her book by affirming traditional gender roles and the proper position of women within Chilean society. According to her, women were not the sole protagonists of the anti-Allende struggle; rather, they acted as the stalwart and intuitive companions of men. Their courage forced men to fulfill their duty, just as the women had carried out their own. Donoso writes that "without supplanting the men, much less the soldiers, they [the women] were the torch in the night and the clarion call to battle. Until the dawn arrived."[29]

Opposition Men's Perspective on Anti-Allende Women

Far from feeling threatened by women's active role in the anti-Allende movement, most men in the opposition applauded it. They supported it because it reflected their own ideas about gender and, as a result, did not challenge them or their dominant position in society. In addition, they understood how important women's participation was in the struggle against the UP and valued women's contribution to that struggle. Even as they heaped praise on the women who opposed Allende, however, they asserted the ultimate importance of the male-dominated political parties and of that most masculine of institutions, the armed forces, in Allende's overthrow.

Opposition men, like opposition women, had precise ideas about gender. According to Eduardo Boetsch, the founder of Chile Libre who attended the weekly strategy sessions with Elena Larraín, Jorge Alessandri,

---

28 My thanks to Steve Volk for this observation.

29 Donoso Loero, *La epopeya*, 51.

and Jaime Guzmán, "women are much more courageous than men. Men tend to be irresponsible, have vices, are drunks, and play around. Women are much more serious."[30] Like the female activists, many conservative men attributed women's activism first and foremost to the fact that women were mothers. In order to explain what impact this has on women's politics, Francisco Prat, a landowner, senator from Renovación Nacional (National Renewal) during most of the 1990s, and proud father of nine children, pointed out that as mothers, "women have always had to be the responsible one in the family. [As a result], women are much more realistic than men." Because they are mothers, Prat believes, "women have had a greater appreciation for security [than men have had] and security has always been more closely associated with the right than with the left." Women are more conservative because "women are more in tune with historic and religious values; therefore, they protect them better than men do."[31]

Hermógenes Pérez de Arce was a journalist and PN deputy in the early 1970s. According to him, women "are more resolute than men, more courageous and they demonstrated this politically. Men [who opposed the UP] did not dare go into the streets because the UP had armed groups that would attack us. They scared us. Women, however, were not scared. They went into the streets and when they hit them they just got madder and went back out again."[32] Sergio Onofre Jarpa, who was president of the PN during that time, also ascribes women's activism to the fact that they were mothers. As mothers, they opposed the UP's plans to reform the educational system through ENU because "the government was going to take charge of the children and obviously the mothers opposed that." They were also motivated by "the lack of food. That's why they organized the March of the Empty Pots and Pans."[33]

Former president Gabriel González Videla was asked, "Why did so many women join this [anti-UP] movement?" He explained that "the protests flow from the very roots of the home. Women are the mothers and wives and as such are constantly watching out for their loved ones. . . . They want this government to ensure the peace and security of their homes."[34]

30 Boetsch, interview.

31 Francisco Prat, interview by author, tape recording, Valparaíso, 12 April 1994.

32 Pérez de Arce, interview.

33 Sergio Onofre Jarpa, interview by author, tape recording, Providencia, 4 August 1999.

34 La Prensa, 25 October 1972. In the same interview, González Videla stated that he was "proud of having given women the vote because they are now the firmest pillar upon which rests the defense of our nation's democratic regime, which is being threatened by international communism."

José de Gregorio Aroca was manager of Radio Balmaceda and a leader of the Christian Democratic Party during the Allende years. Like Onofre Jarpa, he asserted that motherhood led women to protest the government. Many women feared ENU because they did not want their children "to be educated according to Marxist ideology." Unlike Pérez de Arce, he believes that women were "more dangerous [to the UP] than men were, because you can attack a man in the street, but it is more difficult to attack a woman."[35]

These men categorically deny that they helped organize the March of the Empty Pots and Pans or any of the women's other activities. They stress that they were autonomous events, planned by the women themselves, and that there was no connection between them and the parties. Onofre Jarpa first commented, "I thought only a few people would go to the march." He then added that he only knew about the march "because I saw it go by me. Men were not invited. The women carried out the march without the help of the parties. It was their idea."[36] Not only are these statements contradictory, but the fact that the youth section of the PN accompanied the march—and that Carmen Saenz, a vice president of the PN, helped organize it—could also lead one to question their accuracy.

The emphasis on autonomy reflected the desire of these men to disassociate the anti-Allende women's movement from the parties. To acknowledge the involvement of the parties would be to recognize that the women's activities were politically motivated, which they did not want to do. Despite the fact that some women played important roles in the parties, the men clearly viewed the parties as their own domain and differentiated them from the "apolitical" activity of the women. Distinguishing the women's protests from the parties allowed the men to exalt women's role in the movement and maintain their own positions within the parties simultaneously.

Although opposition men heaped praise upon the women who demonstrated against the UP, they emphasized that it was the organizations dominated by men that made the overthrow of Allende possible. When I asked de Gregorio about the opposition to Allende, he listed all the organizations that mobilized against him. He only mentioned women when I directly asked him about them. He rejected the idea that men were passive and explained that "women are more passionate" and therefore were more visible in the movement.[37] Onofre Jarpa granted that what women

35 José de Gregorio Aroca, interview by author, tape recording, Santiago, 4 August 1999.
36 Onofre Jarpa, interview.
37 de Gregorio Aroca, interview.

did was very important, "especially in terms of publicity," but asserted that "men's actions made the change in government possible."[38]

Since the anti-Allende women did not challenge either gender roles or men's position in society, they did not threaten opposition men, who accepted women's activism because they understood it as part of their function as mothers. The women did not want to supplant the men—and the men did not feel displaced by them. Had the women called for an essential restructuring of gender roles or demanded greater social equality, then it is likely that the men would have responded negatively to them.

Poder Femenino: The Midwives of Oppositional Unity

The women of PF believed that they had a mission—to save Chile from communism—and that in order to achieve it, they needed to unify the opposition. As women, and as members of PF, they felt that they were ideally suited for the job. Reflecting the perspective that had dominated in both Acción Mujeres de Chile and the March of the Empty Pots and Pans, the women of PF believed that men's and women's relationships to politics were fundamentally different, defined by their distinct biological makeup. Although many of the women in PF represented political parties and were leaders in those parties, they consciously and strategically chose to characterize themselves as women first and as members of political parties second—if at all. When the PF women spoke, they referred to themselves primarily as representatives of Chilean women. In contrast, they viewed the men as politicians and used men's party membership to explain their actions and beliefs. This gendered definition of the Chilean population allowed women in PF, even those active in parties, to project (and perhaps see) themselves as responsive to the needs of Chile, while men principally answered to the demands of their parties.

In order to advance the idea that women and men engaged in politics differently, the women of PF built an organization that contrasted markedly with those of the political parties. In sharp distinction from the male-dominated political parties (and strangely reminiscent of organizational politics among feminist groups in the sixties and seventies in the United States), the female members of the coordinating council did not promote themselves as individuals or even publicly take credit for their work.[39] PF members rotated the chairing of the meetings to ensure that

38 Onofre Jarpa, interview.

39 A central distinction between PF and feminist groups in the United States is that PF did not believe that women were oppressed. They did not join together as women to fight for women's liberation; rather, they united to end the Allende government.

all women would have the opportunity to direct them.[40] To guarantee the participation of all the women, regardless of organizational affiliation, the leadership of the group passed from member to member.[41]

From the March of the Empty Pots and Pans onward, most of the women (and many of the men) in the opposition heralded the example of the anti-Allende women. They saw them as a model of unity worth emulating among the political parties. Why was unity so critical to the anti-Allende opposition? The PDC and the PN knew that their united front had prevented the election of Allende in 1964, and their disunity had allowed it in 1970. Counterbalancing this recognition was the bitter enmity that had developed between the two parties during the Frei years and the 1970 electoral campaign—not to mention the party chauvinism that permeated Chilean political parties.

PF brought together representatives from the opposition political parties and encouraged dialogue between them. It facilitated open interchanges between female members of the different parties, invited speakers from both the PDC and PN to their weekly meetings, and inspired a greater amount of unity among them. For example, PF invited Senator Víctor García from the PN and Senator Rafael Moreno from the PDC to a meeting early in 1972. Senator García spoke first and "answered their questions, [and] informed them . . . about his feelings that UNITY had been achieved between the two parties that were, without a doubt, the pillars of the opposition." Then Senator Moreno spoke. According to Correa Morandé, he "managed to weaken this impression [that unity had been achieved]." In fact, "he tried to make us see that it was impossible to achieve this goal." In response, Diana (no last name given), the Christian Democratic representative to PF, spoke out frankly: "Rafael, I have already said this in the party. We women will not allow the leadership to expose the country in this fashion. It is also our nation and that of our children. We women are the majority. Either you achieve the unity we need to save us from Marxism or we will never vote for you again."[42]

40 Donoso Loero, *La epopeya*, 71.

41 Saenz, interview, 4 December 1993.

42 Correa Morandé, *La guerra*, 80–81. María Correa Morandé, a leading member of the PN, wrote this account of the meeting. As a result, she emphasized the affability and charm of Senator García and the role that the PN played in engineering unity between itself and the Christian Democrats. Equally, she emphasized the Christian Democrats' willingness to seek dialogue with the UP parties and reluctance to unite with the National Party. While this characterization reflects political realities, it ignores any positive aspects of the attempt by the Christian Democrats (or at least by a segment of the party) to work with the UP government and to avoid a military coup.

Following her remarks, other women spoke and also urged unity. Their words appeared to have had the desired effect. Shortly before leaving, "Rafael Moreno responded with a new and different cordiality. . . . He tried to establish certain points of departure for possible joint actions and displayed all his political charm." Silvia Pinto, a PN deputy and journalist, attended that particular meeting of PF. After the meeting, she commented, "looked at from the outside, it seems incredible how much you can achieve in meetings like this one."[43] Author Teresa Donoso Loero was even more explicit in her estimate of the role played by PF, writing that in the weekly PF meetings, "there, right there, the unity of the opposition was born."[44] That Sunday in Rancagua, while campaigning for the upcoming senatorial elections, "Rafael Moreno championed unity among the opposition."[45] This unity served the opposition well. In a special election held on 16 January 1972, in the agricultural provinces of O'Higgins and Colchagua, the combined support of the PDC and the PN allowed Rafael Moreno to defeat Hector Olivares, the UP candidate for deputy.[46]

Not only did the women of PF see themselves as the force capable of achieving unity among the opposition, but they also saw themselves as the group to bring together all Chilean women—except for the Marxists, whom they dismissed out of hand as their enemies. Their newspaper ads consciously reflected this perception of themselves. In March 1972, PF published an ad that identified its members as women who, despite "our ideological differences, are united by our common condition as women and by our unbreakable vow to struggle for the homeland, for the integrity of our homes, and for the freedom of our children."[47] Their newspaper ads routinely called on all women to join with them, irrespective of class or politics. A typical headline read, "Chilean Woman: There Is Still Time to Save Your Fatherland. All [Women] United, March Today for Democracy!"[48]

"The Empty Pot Is Now the Symbol of the Government's Failure"

PF women understood that in order to make the image of themselves as the true representatives of Chilean womanhood real, they needed to

43 Ibid., 82.

44 Donoso Loero, *La epopeya*, 71.

45 Correa Morandé, *La guerra*, 82.

46 "Elección extraordinaria de un senador," Dirección del Registro Electoral, Santiago, n.d.

47 *El Mercurio*, 22 March 1972.

48 *El Mercurio*, 12 April 1972.

involve larger numbers of women from different classes in the anti-Allende struggle. The factor that most effectively helped anti-Allende women broaden their movement to include poor and working-class women was the economic crisis that beset Chile from late 1971 onward. They brilliantly exploited this situation to their advantage by developing an instantly recognizable symbol, the pot, and an easily adoptable tactic, beating it, to incorporate large numbers of women into their movement.

Several elements explain the economic crisis. Briefly, they include Popular Unity's mismanagement of the economy; the efforts by the elite to sabotage production and distribution, decapitalize the country, and block government attempts to increase production; and the actions taken by Washington to undermine the economy. The U.S. government cut aid to the UP government (but not the military), stopped shipment of spare parts to Chile, and pressured international financial institutions not to make needed loans to Chile.

As the economic crisis deepened, broad sectors of Chilean society adopted a more critical stance toward the Allende government. Women felt the impact of the crisis very directly through shortages in food and other household items. These shortages favored the growth of a black market, caused women to wait in long lines for food at all hours of the day and night, and frequently made it difficult for them to find the goods they needed. Poor women—those in the sector of society promised the most by the UP government—were frequently the most hurt. Despite the increase in their husbands' salaries, they could not afford the skyrocketing prices charged on the black market. Unlike the upper- and middle-class women, they could not send their maids to stand in long lines to wait for food. They *were* the maids. Nor could they jump in a car and travel to country estates for needed food, as the wealthy could and did, since they lacked both.

To understand how the right exploited this issue, it is first necessary to understand the economic situation of 1972 and 1973. During 1972, Chile's economy worsened. The number of shortages (which had first appeared toward the end of 1971) increased. The UP had promised to redistribute Chile's wealth, improve the living standards of the poor, and maintain or better those of the middle class. Late in 1970, then, the Allende government raised wages, froze prices, and decreased unemployment. As a result, the purchasing power of large sectors of the Chilean population increased. More Chileans than ever before now had the income to buy products that previously had been beyond their means. In order for their increased demands to be met, production also had to expand. But it did not, by and large—at least not in sufficient quantity or with enough speed to satisfy the demands of the newly emerging consumer market.[49] Food production grew by only 3 or 4 percent during late 1971 and early 1972, but people's increased access to money meant that they were buying more food than ever before. In order to meet this demand, the UP government imported food. While this tactic worked in the short term, it also led to a drastic decline in Chile's foreign reserves: these dropped from $334 million in December 1970 (shortly after Allende assumed office) to $30 million in December 1971. Compounding the problem, industrial production dropped while inflation rose.[50]

The credit blockade and economic warfare that the United States engineered against Chile exacerbated the nation's economic woes. U.S. banks sharply reduced the amount of money they were willing to lend to Chile from about $220 million prior to 1970 to about $35 million after the UP came to power. International lending agencies such as the World Bank and the Inter-American Development Bank (both of which were dominated by the United States) cut back on their loans to Chile, as did the Eximbank.[51]

The UP attempted to overcome the problem of shortages in a variety of ways. The government and the trade unions encouraged workers and peasants to produce more. Additionally, government officials tried to destroy the black market and counter industrialists' and landowners' efforts to sabotage and decapitalize their enterprises. To involve people in this campaign, the government set up the JAPs in neighborhoods throughout Chile. *El Siglo* defined the JAPs as "popular instruments of struggle [whose goal is] to achieve a normalization of supplies, to fight the speculation and false shortages, and to impede hoarding and price speculation."[52] The JAPs functioned as neighborhood organizations whose primary duty was to ensure that supplies reached the people in the local community. Women were the most active members of the JAPs, and women from the pro-UP Mothers' Centers frequently led them.[53] In June 1972, there were 1,000 JAPs in Chile, 635 of them in Santiago.[54] By January 1973, roughly a year

49 Stefan de Vylder, *Allende's Chile: The Political Economy of the Rise and Fall of the Unidad Popular* (Cambridge: Cambridge University Press, 1976), 202.

50 Stallings and Zimbalist, "Political Economy," 74–76.

51 NACLA, "Chile: The Story Behind the Coup," *North American Congress on Latin America* 7, no. 8 (October 1973): 25.

52 *El Siglo*, 13 January 1972.

53 For a discussion of women's participation in the JAPs and interviews with women active in them, see *Chile Hoy*, 30 October and 16 October 1972.

54 *El Mercurio*, 5 June 1972.

after they were first organized, there were 2,500 JAPs in Chile, of which 1,500 were in Santiago.[55]

The opposition treated the JAPs as nothing less than a government attempt to establish local organizations to spy on people and to extend communist control into the neighborhood and family. One PN ad showed a mousetrap with a piece of cheese on it and a succinct caption: "JAP, [a] Communist trick."[56] An editorial in *El Mercurio* defined the JAPs as "a tool of the Communist Party to gain control of the flow of food and other essential articles of consumption."[57]

The opposition helped create the shortages and then skillfully manipulated the difficult situation to its advantage. In order to foment a sense of crisis and chaos among the population, the Chilean elite encouraged speculation, hoarding, and the sabotage of both agricultural and industrial production, and it discouraged investment.[58] The elite then blamed the shortages on UP mismanagement, charging that the JAPs were rife with corruption and served only those who supported the UP government. The opposition's extensive media outlets facilitated its efforts to define the JAPs as sectarian and ineffective institutions. They skillfully and repeatedly published or broadcast that the UP was responsible for the shortages and the black market. In addition, the right had a long and successful history of convincing women that the left could not be trusted and was responsible for their problems. As Norma Stoltz Chinchilla writes, "the issues directly affecting most women's daily lives (housework, childcare, education, morality and family life) were not considered political issues by any of the parties, including the socialists and communists. They became political issues, however, at the instigation of the bourgeoisie who saw in them the possibility of appealing to 'universal feminine concerns,' ignoring their class links."[59] Finally (and most important) was the basic, inescapable fact that despite the UP's blaming of the U.S. government and the opposition for the shortages, the establishment of the JAPs, and its own attempts to improve the situation, economic conditions worsened. Shortages were exacerbated. Lines of women hoping to purchase products grew longer and more common. Inflation and the black market drove prices upward. As a result, women's ability to obtain the goods they

55 *Ramona*, 23 January 1973.

56 *El Mercurio*, 14 January 1972.

57 *El Mercurio*, 4 August 1972.

58 NACLA, "Story Behind the Coup," 20–21; Winn, *Weavers*, 231.

59 Norma Stoltz Chinchilla, "Mobilizing Women: Revolution in the Revolution," *Latin American Perspectives* 4, no. 15 (Fall 1977): 89.

needed decreased. Their level of exhaustion intensified, and their patience shortened. When they got out of bed at three, four, or five o'clock in the morning to stand in a line for bread or for a kilo of rice, they cursed the situation; in many cases, they cursed the government.

The opposition devised a perfect tactic that allowed women to express their feelings of anger against the government. Beginning shortly after the March of the Empty Pots and Pans, women began banging empty pots and pans nightly from the gardens, balconies, or front steps of their houses. Without even leaving the confines of their homes, ordinary Chilean women participated in a national movement of outraged house-wives who criticized the government, assigning it responsibility for their economic woes.[60]

Although the nightly banging of the pots and pans was most prevalent in upper- and middle-class neighborhoods, articles in newspapers and interviews with participants indicate that poor and working-class women also joined in the protest. During the UP years, María Eugenia Díaz lived in the working-class neighborhood of San Miguel. According to her, "everyone, all my neighbors, hit the pots and pans here because we were all hungry. We all needed to eat. We all needed to have food daily and to stop waiting in lines."[61]

Paloma Rodríguez, another San Miguel resident during the UP years, confirmed Díaz's statement. Unlike Díaz, Rodríguez supported the UP government and was a leader in the UP's women's organization, the National Secretariat of Women. Rodríguez agrees with Díaz that poor women in the *poblaciones* banged pots and pans in response to the short-ages of food. The right's success in organizing women stemmed in part, she believes, from the tendency of women to retreat when faced with the unknown—and the left's failure to take the factor of fear into account. The right exploited these feelings and channeled them into an anti-Allende movement. Rodríguez added that women are not biologically more fearful than men. Their response results from women's upbringing in a patriarchal culture that "permeates everything. It's internalized from the time we are little children and we are told, 'you can't do that because you are a girl.'"[62]

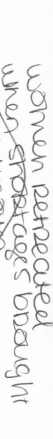

women retreated when shortages brought the unknown

---

60 Although the interviews cited below are drawn from women in Santiago, the banging of the pots and pans took on the character of a national movement. For example, on the night of 31 August 1972, women and men "in all parts [i.e. all classes] of the northern city of Antofagasta opened their windows and wildly beat on their pots for one hour to repudiate the critical short-age of food." See *El Mercurio*, 1 September 1972.

61 María Eugenia Díaz, interview by author, tape recording, Pedro A. Cerda, 16 March 1994.

62 Rodríguez [pseud.], interview.

The banging of the pots and pans was an ideal form of protest for many women. The utensils were both familiar and accessible to them. The action took place in their homes, where the majority of women spent a huge portion of their lives. Women did not have to leave their homes to participate in this activity. They did not have to worry about what to do with their children. The activity did not challenge their identity as mothers whose primary responsibility was to their children; in fact, it confirmed it. No one could accuse them of abandoning their domestic duties or of being loose women for leaving the home, since they stayed right there. At the same time, banging the pots and pans allowed women to participate in political activity and to feel themselves part of a larger movement. Exemplifying this reality, a photo in *La Tribuna* showed an entire family in Viña del Mar (a coastal resort town) banging pots together, converting the protest into a family affair.[63] The tactic was so successful that *La Tribuna* could justifiably proclaim, "The Empty Pot Is Now the Symbol of the Government's Failure."[64]

Beginning in December 1971, *La Tribuna* strongly encouraged women to keep on banging their empty pots and pans. One article in *La Tribuna* advised Chileans that "at ten o'clock you have to keep on beating them [the pots and pans]. The housewives are continuing to hit the pots at ten o'clock to demonstrate that the shortages continue. They don't want to take up any more of the UP's time . . . the government can leave whenever it wishes."[65] Headlines in *La Tribuna* proclaimed that "the noise of empty pots and pans is heard from the north to the south of Chile." An article in the same newspaper boasted that "the banging of pots and pans that began in Santiago has spread throughout the entire city of Rancagua." The newspaper even injected humor into the situation by counseling women to "hit the pot as if it were your husband."[66]

Once the idea was generated, it took fairly little effort to keep going. The opposition radio stations simply announced that women should bang their pots and pans, usually between eight o'clock and ten o'clock at night, and many of them did. As with other activities planned by opposition women,

---

63 *La Tribuna*, 10 December 1971.

64 *La Tribuna*, 3 December 1971.

65 *La Tribuna*, 8 December 1971. The article explains that according to the Municipal Code it was illegal to make noise in public after 11:00 P.M. However, the newspaper pointed out that the Municipal Code refers to people talking, music, radios, and so on, "but not to pots and pans." Therefore, the article concluded, "if your neighbor denounces you, it means that he [or she] supports the UP and deserves the neighborhood's complete repudiation."

66 *La Tribuna*, 13 December 1971.

much of the work of communicating news was done woman to woman. Middle- and upper-class women with phones called their networks of friends to inform them that they should bang the pots. Hilda Hernández, a social worker from the middle-class neighborhood of Ñuñoa, remembers that neighbors would walk around her area and tell the inhabitants to bang the pots that evening. Women waiting in the food lines would also tell each other which night to bang the pots. Hernández recalls, "I have a neighbor who went to stand in the lines and she knew all the news. She would say to me, 'Hildita, we are going to bang the pots today at eight.' So we would bang the pots and let me tell you, the entire neighborhood did it."[67]

Conclusion

Inspired by the impact of the March of the Empty Pots and Pans, Poder Femenino brought together women from the different political parties, female independents, and women who had been previously inactive in politics—most of whom had never worked with each other before—and made their anti-Allende activity a priority. PF encouraged cooperation among the women despite their varied organizational affiliations. In the process, the group helped build a political identity that, if it did not transcend party differences, certainly helped weaken them. PF created an image and reality of conservative women's political activism and resistance, independent of the parties, which encouraged greater participation by larger numbers of women. It provided a vehicle for dissatisfied women (many of them upper- and middle-class, but also some who were poor and working-class) who had never been active in politics and had never conceived of themselves as political to act on their opposition to the UP government.

PF did not work in isolation from the larger anti-Allende movement. Its relationship to the opposition was fluid, flowing in both directions; it both took leaders from and provided leadership for the parties. PF consistently encouraged the opposition parties to unite, and it criticized the male leaders who refused to do so. It also coordinated its work with that of the opposition and followed the political strategy designed by these parties. Yet even as it worked in concert with other anti-Allende forces, PF established and maintained its own identity, role, and agenda. PF promoted anti-Allende political activity among women and allowed them to work as a united and powerful force.

PF facilitated the organizing of women against Allende. Women provided the opposition with a symbol of resistance that appeared to be apolitical—

67 Hilda Hernández, interview by author, tape recording, Santiago, 5 October 1993.

and therefore highly legitimate. Since many of these women did not work (inside or outside the home), they had plenty of time, money, other resources, and valuable networks to devote to the cause. They unstintingly contributed all of this to help build the anti-Allende movement.

7

Poder Femenino and the Working Class

Elite Women and Workers' Struggles

THE WOMEN OF Poder Femenino understood that in order to build a
national movement against Allende, they needed to obtain the support of
working-class sectors. They, along with the rest of the opposition, knew
that working-class resistance to Popular Unity would both enhance their
ability to thwart government policies and undermine the government's
pro-worker image. This chapter analyzes PF's effort to broaden the
movement to include working-class women. It begins by looking at working-class women's reaction to the economic crisis and the shortages discussed in Chapter 6. It then analyzes two examples of anti-Allende
women's attempts to mobilize workers against the UP government: the
drive to prevent the nationalization of the huge paper company, La Papelera, and the strike by the El Teniente copper mine workers. In both
instances, members of PF—along with other anti-Allende women—built
multi-class alliances with female employees and the wives of workers.

In order to build these cross-class relations, the anti-Allende women
denied the reality of class privilege and exploitation and held the UP government responsible for the class conflict that increasingly dominated
Chile between 1970 and 1973. These elite women accused the UP of
fomenting national disunity and class hatred, by which they meant poor
people's anger and resentment toward the wealthy (not the disdain and
antipathy the elite felt toward the working class and peasants). To support
their position, they pointed out that in one of his first speeches after
assuming office, Allende had identified himself as the president of the
workers, the peasants, and the poor, not of all Chileans.[1] Long accustomed

---

[1] In his recent critical study of the Latin American left, Mexican Jorge Castañeda wrote that "just
after he took office as president of Chile, in November of 1970, Allende ventured a statement

to defining the nation based on their interests and in their image, elite members of the opposition believed that because the UP's policies hurt them, they therefore damaged the Chilean nation as a whole. In contrast, they claimed, the opposition represented the needs of all Chileans, because it made no distinction based on class or party affiliation. During the UP years, the opposition consistently attempted to portray itself as being "above party politics" or "class interests" and as favoring national unity.

To promote this goal, the middle- and upper-class founders of PF worked to shed their public image as wealthy women who opposed Allende in order to defend their position and wealth. They, along with other anti-Allende women and the opposition in general, intervened in different labor struggles to form temporary alliances with workers against the UP government.

Shortages and Working-Class Women

Like many working-class women, Beatrice Campos (the working-class woman whose boss paid her to attend the March of the Empty Pots and Pans) hated the shortages, lines, and chaos prevalent during the Popular Unity years. She was a trusted worker who had risen from the factory floor to become an employee in a textile factory's main office. Even though she witnessed her own bosses' attempts to create shortages and charge exorbitantly high prices, Campos blamed the government and her fellow workers for her own difficult situation. "The disorder [of the UP years] bothered me. I arrived home and there was nothing to eat. The owners [of the textile factory] gave me oil and sugar. I looked around the factory and I saw *compañeros* who were supposed to be working more to increase production. . . . Instead they asked permission to go to a demonstration and went to the movies. . . . So all this disorder made me detest the government."[2]

Beatrice Campos lived in Renca, a poor community on the northwest side of Santiago. The UP set up a JAP in her neighborhood. Like many working-class women, Campos perceived the JAPs as one more example of government corruption and party favoritism.

---

that seemed to confirm his opponents' worst apprehensions. . . . Allende declared that while he would of course respect the rights and opinions of all Chileans during his mandate, he was not the president of all Chileans, but of the workers and peasants, of Chile's poor." Castañeda concludes that this statement was "perhaps one of the master politician's least prudent or thoughtful reflections." See Jorge G. Castañeda, *Utopia Unarmed: The Latin American Left After the Cold War* (New York: Vintage, 1994), 394.

2 Campos, interview.

The leadership of the JAP was in the hands of the different political parties who made up the UP, especially the Communists. . . . When ten liters of oil arrived and there were, let's say, twenty families who belonged to the JAP, then each family should have received one half-liter of oil. But, that's where they weren't consistent with their politics. . . . For example, if I was the leader of the JAP and I was supposed to get one half-liter, well, I took one liter for my family, one liter for my friend, and I sold one. I saw that with my own eyes.

Take meat for example. I went to the butcher, Victor, he was called. I gave him a list for one kilo each of beef, steak, fat, bones, hamburger meat, all the things you buy. You always bought more than you could eat because you never knew if you could find anything next week. . . . It was a psychosis. If oil arrived, you put your brother, your friend, your kids in the line to buy oil. I only needed one liter of oil a week, but I bought five. . . . If you went to the leadership's houses, you could buy things, but only under the table, as they said. The disorder was disgraceful. I thought that the government was responsible for it all. I never said, these people are a disgrace, the party should get rid of them. I always blamed the government.[3]

María Eugenia Díaz is another example of a working-class woman who suffered as a result of the economic crisis and blamed the UP for her problems. During the UP years, she was in her twenties, recently married, with three children. Her parents adored Eduardo Frei because, among other things, the PDC government had given them a house. Her favorite president was Augusto Pinochet, whom she refers to as "Mi General." Like many working-class women, she remembers the UP years as a time of shortages and endless waits in lines.

During the Allende government I had my three small children. I always had to leave my kids with my mother because I lived in the lines. I got up at around four o'clock in the morning . . . and walked for blocks just to buy a kilo and a half of bread. That's all they would sell a person. To buy meat I had to go out at around nine or ten at night, spend all night in line, in order to buy two kilos of meat. It was like the system they have now in Cuba, where they ration everything. . . . The meat, the bread, the milk, the diapers, everything was rationed.

For Christmas 1972, the family wanted to prepare a special dinner. Díaz remembered the purchase of meat for the dinner as an ordeal. "On December 23rd, my mother went to a big butcher shop on Blanca Encalada Street. She went at four o'clock in the afternoon. At eight o'clock I went to relieve her, so she could come home. I stayed the rest of the night

3 Ibid.

until six o'clock the next afternoon in order to buy two chickens and two kilos of beef. I took a thermos of tea with me."[4]

Even working-class women who supported the UP recall those years as a time of particular hardship for them as housewives and mothers. According to Rosa Elvira Durán, a poor woman who had long been active in the Mothers' Centers, the first year of the Popular Unity government "was a honeymoon. Wages rose, things were good. But the second! Never, never again would I want to go through what I went through! It was total anarchy! Do you know that in order to buy a skinny chicken for New Year's 1972, I waited in line from eight o'clock at night until ten the next morning? And all they sold me was a skinny, malnourished chicken."[5]

The shortages, combined with the high prices charged on the black market, provided the opposition with an organizing bridge into the poor and working-class communities of Santiago. Until late 1971 and early 1972, much of the organized opposition to Allende came from the members of upper-class (and, to a lesser extent, middle-class) sectors of Chilean society who feared that the UP government meant a loss of their class privileges. The widespread reality of shortages, coupled with the fact that they particularly affected poor and working-class women, enabled the opposition to challenge the UP's claims to be the government of the working class, demonstrate that UP policies hurt the poor and the working class, and broaden its own appeal beyond those sectors and classes that had traditionally supported it.

Opposition Women and the Fight Against the Nationalization of La Papelera

It is highly significant that one of the first public pronouncements PF made was its declaration of support for the "women workers and the wives of workers of La Papelera" on 22 March 1972. The group urged other women to show solidarity with the workers of La Papelera by demonstrating with them on 24 March in a "March for the Fatherland."[6] The struggle over control of La Papelera, of which the march was one of the first public demonstrations, became a major battle between the UP government and the opposition. Women from La Papelera, along with conservative women from the opposition in general and PF in particular, played a key role in this conflict—and, ultimately, helped defeat the UP's plans to nationalize the paper company.

4 Díaz, interview.

5 Durán, interview.

6 *El Mercurio*, 22 March 1972. The march was also called the March of Freedom.

La Papelera, whose complete name was Compañía Manufacturera de Papeles y Cartones (Manufacturing Company of Papers and Cartons), was a massive company located in Puente Alto that "supplied 90 percent of Chile's paper needs."[7] Jorge Alessandri was president and owner of La Papelera, which was "the only private source of newsprint in Chile."[8] The UP hoped to nationalize the huge paper company as part of its general program to break up monopolies.[9] Forces opposed to Allende claimed that the government's efforts to nationalize La Papelera were nothing less than an attempt to cut off the opposition newspapers' access to newsprint, part of the UP government's strategy to control the media and limit freedom of the press.[10]

In order to gain control of the paper company, the government offered to purchase shares of the company's stock for 2 escudos at a time when the shares were valued at 0.3 escudos.[11] The management of La Papelera, businessmen, journalists affiliated with the *gremio* movement, politicians, and other figures on the right sprang into action to oppose the sale of La Papelera stock.[12] They set up a National Fund for Defense of Freedom of the Press and urged shareholders not to sell their shares to the government.[13]

Women joined the antinationalization struggle even before the formation of PF. On 14 November 1971, shortly after the UP announced its plans to purchase stock in the company, a group of women who called themselves the "wives, mothers, and daughters of the workers of La Papelera" formed the "Committee of Ladies of the *Población* La Papelera." They took out an ad in *El Mercurio* to publicize their "reject[ion of] the nationalization of the company." The ad, which included the names of the officers of the newly formed group, was signed by nearly seven

7 Jerry W. Knudson, *The Chilean Press During the Allende Years* (Buffalo: State University of New York, 1986), 17.

8 Moss, *Chile's Marxist Experiment*, 134–35.

9 The government also claimed that La Papelera did not reforest. Moreover, it did not "reinvest in plant development, . . . [or] meet [the] shortages of paper, . . . [and it] abandoned exports and neglected industrial safety." See "Secretos de la 'Operación Papelera,'" *¿Qué Pasa?* 21 October 1971.

10 One ad in *El Mercurio* that opposed government plans on this basis was entitled "We Defend the Freedom of the Press." It was signed by Silvia Alessandri (PN deputy), Eduardo Boetsch (the founder of Chile Libre), Gisela Silva (Patria y Libertad), Sergio Diez (National Party), and Jaime Guzmán (founder of the *gremio* movement), among others. See *El Mercurio*, 14 November 1971.

11 At the time, 15 escudos equaled $1.20 in U.S. dollars. *¿Qué Pasa?* 21 October 1971.

12 For a statement from journalists who opposed the sale, see *El Mercurio*, 14 November 1971.

13 Knudson, *The Chilean Press*, 17–18. Paul Sigmund notes that this organization was set up "with CIA financing." See Sigmund, *Overthrow*, 157.

hundred women. Their arguments against nationalization reflected both their own political outlook and a gendered perspective on female and male social roles. They dismissed the government's assertion that the workers of La Papelera suffered difficult working conditions. In fact, they stated that the workers "enjoy a highly satisfactory economic and social situation." The women feared that if the government took over the plant, then "the business would go under, political persecution would begin, and the workers' conditions would rapidly decline."[14]

Members of the "Ladies Committee" also opposed government control because of the impact it would have on them. As female workers and as the wives of workers, they wrote that "one thing is clear: the maintenance of our homes cannot be threatened by political decisions that the immense majority of workers and their families reject." They added that "the women who sign this ad are conscious of our rights as mothers, wives, and daughters of La Papelera workers. We defend the non-nationalization of the industry, the source of work, well-being, and progress not only for our families but also for the people of Puente Alto."[15]

The ad defined all the women who signed it as the female relatives of male La Papelera workers. It is likely that the women used the term "worker" to include both the white-collar employees and the blue-collar workers, because they did not distinguish between the two groups. Economic status and political differences existed, though, between the employees and the workers in the company; they belonged to separate unions. Of the fourteen unions that operated in La Papelera, five belonged to the workers and nine to the employees. Four of the five workers' unions had pro-UP leaders and supported nationalization. The white-collar unions held their own plebiscite and voted, by a majority of 80 percent, against nationalization.[16] Subsequently, the professional unions joined the conservative anti-Allende *gremio* movement.[17] It is unclear, then, just how many of the women who identified themselves as the "mothers, wives, and daughters of La Papelera workers" were actually related to blue-collar workers. Most of them may very well have been family members of the white-collar employees. On the other hand, the signers probably included some working-class women whose husbands opposed nationalization and held a minority opinion within their unions, or women who disagreed with the men in their family and followed their

14 *El Mercurio,* 14 November 1971.
15 Ibid.
16 *¿Qué Pasa?* 21 October 1971.
17 Moss, *Chile's Marxist Experiment,* 139.

own political beliefs. Unfortunately, documents from the time do not allow a more precise identification of which La Papelera women signed the ad and opposed nationalization.

Daniel, who (like his father before him) worked in La Papelera, knew that many workers and their wives wanted the company to remain in private hands. Although he supported the government's plans to nationalize the company, he was aware that many workers did not. The paternalistic policies practiced by the owners of La Papelera muted the workers' awareness of their exploitation and inculcated a sense of loyalty and trust toward the Alessandri family. Over the years, the company had built homes and schools and developed neighborhoods for the workers, making Puente Alto a company town headed by a benign patriarch. As a result, Daniel believes, "the average La Papelera worker thinks with his stomach and not with his head. If anyone spoke against the factory or urged others to stand up for their rights, they accused him of being an *upeliento*." He believes that "women played an important role" in the anti-nationalization drive. "They met a lot, although I don't know what they decided in their meetings, since I never went to them! They believed that if the company was nationalized, then their husbands would lose their jobs. They were so obsessive! All they thought about was their husband's job!"[18]

The opposition consistently proffered the Ladies Committee as evidence to support its claim that members of the working class opposed the UP. Once PF formed, it eagerly embraced the La Papelera struggle, because it offered the group an excellent opportunity to accomplish two goals: to project itself as the forgers of unity among all classes (just as it worked to bring the different parties of the opposition together), and to build an alliance with working-class women.

Middle- and upper-class female stockholders, some of whom were members of PF, formed a "Provisional Committee of Stockholders" to oppose nationalization.[19] Family connections and political ties linked some of the women of PF with key actors in the drive to oppose La Papelera's nationalization. One of the leaders of the Provisional Committee of Stockholders, for instance, was Irene Larraín, a relative of Elena Larraín—the co-founder of PF who met weekly with Jorge Alessandri. It is

18 Daniel [last name withheld], interview by author, tape recording, Puente Alto, 16 December 1998. Although he is now retired, Daniel still lives in the housing community established by Luis Matte Larraín, the founder of La Papelera. For his own security and that of his family, he preferred not to give his full name. *Upeliento* was a negative term used by the opposition to disparage those who supported the UP.

19 Crummett, "El Poder Femenino," 107.

likely that these strategy sessions included a discussion of how to involve
PF in the struggle to ensure Alessandri's continued ownership of the company. The female stockholders' campaign, which was part of a large, well-
financed, highly public drive to discourage the sale of La Papelera stock,
complemented the efforts of La Papelera women: in one of its first
actions, the Provisional Committee mailed or hand-delivered fourteen
thousand letters to all of the stockholders of the company, urging them
not to sell their stock.[20] This direct appeal required tremendous amounts
of money and time, resources that the female stockholders had in abun-
dance. Furthermore, it was a strategic effort. If the stockholders refused
to sell their stock to the government, then—according to its own conditions—the government could not expropriate the industry.

This alliance between the wives, mothers, and daughters of La Papelera workers and employees and the female stockholders helped project an
image of cross-class unity to women's opposition to the UP government.
The combination of these distinct groups of women also served to
strengthen each group's demands, credibility, and capabilities. La Papelera women who publicly claimed that they opposed the UP's plans to
nationalize the industry because it would hurt the workers and their families thus weakened the government's arguments that UP policies would
benefit them; they also legitimized the stockholders' arguments against
nationalization. Middle- and upper-class women referred to the worries
of working-class women to argue against nationalization. They further
claimed that nationalization would give the UP control over the production of paper and therefore weaken the freedom of the press.

La Papelera women denied any connection between their concerns and
politics. Instead, they argued that nationalization would have a negative
impact on them as wives and mothers. The female stockholders also
rejected the idea that politics inspired their actions and explained their
opposition as a result of "their obligation to defend higher interests, indis-
pensable in any democracy," not as part of a generalized anti-UP politics.[21]

The priority that the women of PF and the opposition in general gave
to the struggle of La Papelera workers is illustrated by the fact that the
first women's march to be called following the December 1971 March of
the Empty Pots and Pans was the March 1972 demonstration in support
of "female paper workers." Emboldened by the success of the March of

---

20 *El Mercurio*, 13 January 1972. Precisely 14,952 people owned stock in Papelera. Of this number, 400 people and corporations controlled 70 percent of the stock. Knudson, *The Chilean
Press*, 17.

21 *El Mercurio*, 13 January 1972.

the Empty Pots and Pans, opposition women felt confidence in their ability to organize public demonstrations and marches. This is particularly significant because, prior to that march, most of these women had never publicly demonstrated in their lives. On 13 March 1972, the La Papelera women's committee—which had changed its name to the "Feminine Committee of Family Members of the Free Workers' *Gremios* of the Manufacturing Company of Papers and Cartons"—sought permission to march through Santiago on 24 March as the final act in a national meeting of "female paper workers." Jaime Concha, the provincial governor of Santiago, granted the women permission to march.[22] PF issued a call to women to join in the March for the Fatherland in support of the "women workers and wives of workers of La Papelera." However, that same night, the national government revoked permission for the women to march. Hernán del Canto, minister of the interior, justified his withdrawal of authorization by charging that "they are trying to use this demonstration to repeat the disorders that occurred last December [during the March of the Empty Pots and Pans]." Del Canto added that the government was studying a possible lawsuit against the coordinating council of PF "for an infraction of the Law of Internal State Security."[23] He pointed out that the government's cancellation of the march in no way "changes the permanent and unbreakable will of the government to facilitate the right to meet, as long as the activities are sponsored or supported by responsible people or entities and not by anonymous *poderes femeninos.*"[24] The opposition seized upon the government's refusal to allow the women's march to take place and ridiculed the UP for its unmanly behavior. In a huge banner headline, *La Tribuna* mocked the government with the words, "The Government Was Afraid of the Women."[25]

Both the timing of the government's retraction of permission (the same day as the PF ad) and del Canto's references to PF strongly suggest that the government's decision to oppose the march stemmed from its concerns about this group's involvement in planning the event. The March of the Empty Pots and Pans and the disorders that broke out during and after it—activities the government clearly associated with PF, even though they predated the group's existence—were still fresh in the minds of officials. The government did not want to risk a repeat of the

22 *El Mercurio,* 23 March 1972.

23 *La Tercera,* 23 March 1972.

24 *El Mercurio,* 23 March 1972. The Popular Unity consistently denied PF's existence and legitimacy. Allende referred to PF as *"El Poder Fantasme* [The Phantom Power]."

25 *La Tribuna,* 23 March 1972.

embarrassing spectacle of police attacking women, a response that out-raged many in Chile and around the world. Furthermore, the government feared (correctly) that the participation of PF would entail the involve-ment of the opposition political parties, especially their youth brigades and Patria y Libertad, a volatile coalition of forces that the government wanted to keep off the streets of Santiago.

Carmen Saenz, who in addition to being a leader of PF was also vice president of the PN and president of its women's department, took the opportunity offered by the government's decision to lambaste the UP gov-ernment's stance toward women and to applaud the civic spirit of opposi-tion women. "The fact is that the government has demonstrated that it fears women. [We] were going to defend, once again, a group of coura-geous women, the wives of La Papelera workers. It was an act of solidar-ity. This [government action] is an attempt against the freedom to meet which is guaranteed in the Constitution. It's the beginning of the end of the right to meet."[26]

In order to answer these criticisms, Hernán del Canto called a press conference. In his statement, del Canto made it clear that the UP retained proper respect for women and that, far from being scared of women, the government adored them. He explained, "we are not afraid of women. Quite the contrary, we have a great deal of affection for them. We love them very much." Despite these sentiments, del Canto announced, "we will take all the necessary steps to ensure that the march does not take place."[27]

PF used the UP government's rejection to urge the opposition to work together and to intensify anti-UP actions. Reflecting their image of them-selves as forgers of unity, PF members challenged the government's deci-sion and called on "all the opposition parties and the *gremios* to work together . . . to organize a huge protest march."[28] The opposition parties took up PF's call and organized the March for Democracy for 12 April. The march protested that the government "frequent[ly] [went] beyond the legal limits" and either caused or tolerated "the unemployment, shortages, and armed groups."[29] Unlike the demonstration planned for 24 March, a march that had been called by women (and primarily sup-ported by the PN), the opposition parties jointly sponsored the march on 12 April.

26 *La Tercera*, 24 March 1972.
27 *El Mercurio*, 24 March 1972.
28 Correa Morandé, *La guerra*, 70.
29 *La Tercera*, 16 April 1972.

The march attracted massive support. One conservative newspaper declared it "the largest [demonstration] that has ever taken place in Chilean political history" and claimed that "close to one-third of the population of Santiago" turned out.[30] Opposition estimates of the number of people who attended the march ranged from five hundred thousand to one million.[31]

The choice of speakers was significant—Patricio Aylwin, a middle-class leader of the PDC and president of the Senate, and Eliana Vásquez de Rivera, "a *pobladora*" and member of the PN, who spoke "in the name of women."[32] Eliana Vásquez identified herself as an inhabitant of Las Barrancas, a poor neighborhood of Santiago, and as the mother of seventeen children. She had demonstrated at the December March of the Empty Pots and Pans, along with other women, in order to defend "the tranquility of our homes and the security of our husbands and children." In April 1972, she marched because "the fatherland called her . . . to defend the future of Chile. To defend the future of our children . . . freedom, [and] democracy." Vásquez believed that women had a certain role to play "in the face of the threat to our country." They had to "participate in the Mothers' Centers, the neighborhood committees, [and] the parents' centers in order to help defend our homes." Vásquez's ideas about women's relationships to men and politics paralleled those expressed by many other anti-Allende women. Like them, Vásquez believed that women had to "energize [their] husbands and [their] children so that they won't be marginalized from the struggle and the political responsibilities that they need to assume today."[33]

The opposition newspapers' coverage of the march exemplified the rightist media's skillful use of resources to bolster the political vision endorsed by those forces that opposed Allende. The pages of all the opposition papers ran huge pictures of women who had attended the rally. The caption under one of these pictures read, "women were in the front ranks of the historic demonstration yesterday. Government and media threats did not frighten them. At an early hour, they left their domestic duties to keep their appointment of honor with democracy." *La Segunda* offered a

---

30 *La Segunda*, 13 April 1972.

31 *La Prensa*, 13 April 1972, cited 1 million; *La Segunda*, 13 April 1972, cited five hundred thousand to seven hundred thousand.

32 *La Prensa*, 13 April 1972. In 1989, Patricio Aylwin was elected president of Chile in the first free elections since the 1973 coup. *Pobladora* refers to a female inhabitant of a *población*. I attempted to locate Eliana Vásquez several times in order to interview her, but I was unable to do so.

33 For her complete speech, see *El Mercurio*, 13 April 1972.

large picture of Eliana Vásquez and the words, "she is yet another demonstration of the courage of our country's women." *La Prensa*, the PDC's paper, featured an exuberant woman, smiling and waving, with the caption, "the Chilean woman gives yet one more example of her elevated civic consciousness—not like those in the government and the UP who say that women have no political capacity—by attending the huge March for Democracy."[34] The coverage faithfully reflected the opposition's efforts to present these women as the symbol of legitimate resistance to the UP government. In order to counter the UP's charges that only "wealthy *viejas* [old women]" opposed the government, the organizers of the rally projected Eliana Vásquez as a worthy spokesperson for all anti-Allende women and as the embodiment of poor women's rejection of the workers' government. To highlight her importance, the anti-Allende forces made her one of only two speakers at the rally in support of "democracy."

The opposition won the fight to prevent the UP from nationalizing La Papelera. This struggle was the first significant attempt made by the opposition in general and women in particular to build a cross-class alliance against the "government of the workers and peasants." The campaign's effectiveness lay in its ability to combine appeals to stockholders not to sell their holdings with the public opposition of La Papelera workers and employees who resisted the UP's plans for the company. Their joint efforts allowed the opposition to create a force capable of resisting government plans to nationalize the giant paper manufacturing company. This campaign united the disparate realities and resources of the middle- and upper-class stockholders, anti-UP politicians, and PF with those of the employees and workers of La Papelera. Over the next year and a half the opposition repeated, under different conditions and in different circumstances, their strategy to undermine the UP by organizing workers—the social grouping most likely to be loyal to the government—against it. Without a doubt, the most visible demonstration of this strategy took place in 1973 during the struggles of the workers of the El Teniente mine.[35]

34 Ibid.; *La Segunda*, 13 April 1972; *La Prensa*, 13 April 1972.

35 In their book on the El Teniente strike, Sergio Bitar, the minister of mines during the strike, and Crisóstomo Pizarro, a sociologist, point out that "the conflict in El Teniente highlighted [the opposition's] use of a new strategy to fight the UP government. The work stoppage of October 1972, initiated by truck drivers and businessmen, taught the opposition that the government was able to ensure the partial functioning of the country and that the overthrow of Allende would not be a simple task. [In order to overthrow Allende] it was necessary to break the government's social front. Toward this end, the opposition tried to incorporate workers on its side." Sergio Bitar and Crisóstomo Pizarro, *La caída de Allende y la huelga de El Teniente: Lecciones de la historia* (Santiago: Las Ediciones del Ornitorrinco, 1986), 58–59. As the minister of

El Teniente Workers and Anti-Allende Women

El Teniente is located near the Chilean town of Rancagua, south of Santiago. In 1970 El Teniente was one of the three largest copper mines in Chile. For much of the twentieth century, copper exports accounted for a huge percentage of Chile's foreign earnings; by 1970, copper sales generated 80 percent of Chile's total sales abroad.[36] From 1904 until July 1971, the Braden Copper Company (a subsidiary of the U.S.-based Kennecott Company) owned and operated El Teniente.[37] In July 1971, the Chilean Congress voted unanimously to nationalize Chile's copper.[38]

Chilean copper miners received higher salaries than any other industrial workers.[39] Their high wages stemmed from three related factors. First, copper production was crucial to Chile's national budget; it provided the Chilean economy with the largest percentage of its income. Second, Chilean copper miners had a long and successful history of combative struggle for higher wages and better work conditions. Finally, since copper production generally reaped a large profit, the companies could afford to pay mine workers a higher salary.[40] Chilean copper workers, then, found themselves in a strategic position from which to demand increased wages and benefits.

In April 1972, workers at El Teniente signed a contract that contained a clause known as *"la escala móvil"*—the "escalator clause." According to the contract, whenever the basic cost of living increased more than 5 percent, due to inflation (which was then running rampant), the workers' salaries would increase one-half of whatever the inflation rate was. Although they had already won the escalator clause, in October 1972

---

mines, Sergio Bitar was integrally involved in the El Teniente conflict. During the months of the strike and in the two months that followed its resolution, Bitar and Pizarro wrote their analysis of the strike. Following the coup, the military imprisoned Bitar on Dawson Island and in other prison camps. His imprisonment and subsequent exile effectively put an end to their plans to publish the study in Chile. In the early 1980s, Bitar and Pizarro met up again and decided to publish the work. The book is unique in that it contains both the results of the study undertaken in 1973 and an interview with Bitar from the mid-1980s. The interview is a self-reflective analysis of the El Teniente strike and the politics of the UP.

36 See de Vylder, *Allende's Chile*, 116.

37 Moss, *Chile's Marxist Experiment*, 73.

38 For U.S. government and corporate perspectives on the Chilean government's nationalization of Chilean copper, see Congress, House, Committee on Foreign Affairs, Subcommittee on Inter-American Affairs, *United States and Chile During the Allende Years, 1970–1973*.

39 For a history of El Teniente miners, see Thomas Miller Klubock, *Contested Communities: Class, Gender, and Politics in Chile's El Teniente Copper Mine, 1904–1951* (Durham: Duke University Press, 1998).

40 Gary MacEoin, *No Peaceful Way: Chile's Struggle for Dignity* (New York: Sheed and Ward, 1974), 147.

union leaders at El Teniente stated that the workers wanted to adopt Labor Law 17,713, starting that month. According to this law, all workers' salaries and benefits would be automatically readjusted to keep pace with inflation.[41] The UP government rejected this demand because it believed that such an arrangement unfairly privileged the workers of El Teniente. The government argued that by implementing both the escalator clause *and* Law 17,713, the workers received, in effect, a double readjustment of their salaries. Furthermore, the salaries of El Teniente workers were already much higher than those of other Chilean workers.

Like La Papelera, El Teniente contained a diverse labor force. Of the nine unions, five belonged to the employees and four to the workers. Leftists had traditionally led the workers' unions and Christian Democrats headed those of the employees.[42] However, in October 1972, the UP candidates suffered a reversal when "the PDC captured three out of five leadership positions in . . . the copper-miners' syndicate."[43] One possible explanation for this shift to the PDC lies in the politics of struggle that had historically dominated the El Teniente mine workers. James Petras, who examined El Teniente workers' responses to the July 1972 nationalization of Chile's mines, found that the majority of workers supported nationalization because they believed that it would "substantially improv[e] their income levels," not because it would enhance the national economy.[44] Given their political history, it is not surprising that many workers who had originally voted for the UP shifted their allegiances to the PDC when the party's labor leaders appeared willing to fight the UP for an increased salary. In response to the government's refusal to accept their new demands, seven thousand out of twelve thousand workers voted to go out on strike on 18 April 1973.[45] Over the next two months, the UP made four different proposals to end the strike. Workers' responses to the strike and government efforts to settle it varied. Many miners participated in the strike, a sizable number refused to strike at all, and still others rejoined the workforce at varying times during the two-month walkout.[46]

41 See Bitar and Pizarro, *La caída de Allende*, 58–59.

42 See de Vylder, *Allende's Chile*, 131.

43 Cusack, *Revolution and Reaction*, 61. Cusack adds that "throughout 1972, Christian Democratic strength in labor unions and community organizations had been growing."

44 James F. Petras, "Nationalization, Socioeconomic Change, and Popular Participation," in *Chile: Politics and Society*, ed. Arturo Valenzuela and J. Samuel Valenzuela (New Brunswick, N.J.: Transaction, 1976), 178–79.

45 Kaufman, *Crisis*, 78.

46 Attempts to ascertain the number of workers who supported the strike and those who opposed it have proved difficult. Accounts of the strike tend to be partisan and often contradictory. For

Women publicly joined the struggle for higher wages on 13 May 1973. On that day, one thousand women met in the offices of the Sewell and Minas Professional Union (an employees' union) and formed the Women's Committee to Support the Striking Workers. They identified themselves as the wives of El Teniente workers and as striking workers. The women who spoke at the meeting adopted the language of working-class struggle to define their role in the strike. They stated that "the wives of the miners . . . wish to tell those who betray and want to divide the cause of the workers that we will support our husbands to the end."[47] Personal and political connections linked the women of El Teniente to the women of La Papelera. Teresa Vargas de Ramos, vice president of the women's committee of La Papelera, attended the meeting and spoke. In her speech, Vargas de Ramos described how her colleagues had "spent many anguished months witnessing the problems suffered by their husbands due to the government's attempts to nationalize La Papelera." She stressed how much "women's support for their husbands in these [difficult] circumstances mattered."[48]

On 15 May, the twenty-seventh day of the strike, the Women's Committee to Support the Striking Workers issued a public declaration. They questioned the UP's definition of itself as the government of the working class, given that it had refused to accede to El Teniente workers' demands. Referring to the women's history of struggle, the statement read:

This is not the first time that the wives of workers have supported a strike. On many occasions, we have joined with our husbands to fight for social justice. Nevertheless, we never expected that the government of the workers would be deaf to the pleas of miners.

---

example, Bitar and Pizarro point out that three of the four workers' unions opposed the strike. Yet they write that on 7 May, only 60 percent of the miners had returned to work. Their statement indicates that prior to 7 May, a larger number of workers did not work and that a sizable minority, roughly 40 percent, were still absent from work. One possible explanation for this discrepancy is that pro-government union leaders influenced the voting process; the votes cast, therefore, would not truly reflect the sentiments of the workers. It is equally possible that pressures brought to bear on the miners by those in favor of the strike made it difficult for the miners to work.

47 It is unclear what percentage of miners' wives—as opposed to the wives of white-collar employees and female employees—supported the strike. There is no question that some did. Sociologist and UP supporter Michèle Mattelart lived in Chile during the UP years. In an article discussing the Chilean bourgeoisie's successful efforts to organize women, Mattelart observes that the "right had the support of working-class and petit-bourgeois women" and confirms that "the wives of the striking mine workers" did indeed participate in anti-UP activity. See Michèle Mattelart, "La mujer y la linea de masa," 137.

48 *El Rancagüiño*, 15 May 1973.

We and our children are willing to suffer hunger, cold, deprivation. However, we say to the workers of El Teniente, don't give up; you are waging a just struggle, and the entire country has recognized this.

Although they opposed the left, the women adopted leftist slogans and discourse for their own ends. They called on women to operate with class and gender solidarity. Appropriating and modifying for their own use the slogan most associated with the UP, the women chanted, "Mujeres unidas, jamás serán vencidas" ("the women, united, will never be defeated").[49]

In the face of the divisive and difficult conflict, Edith González, the wife of a miner, urged women to take action and to work together. She called on the wives and mothers of workers "to be friends, to struggle together. We won't be held back by the few who are working. We all have to struggle . . . along with our husbands until we get a just and precise solution to their struggle. If we are hungry, we will all be hungry together."[50]

In response to her call, on 17 May, the Women's Committee organized two hundred women to stone and vandalize buses carrying workers ("strikebreakers") to the mine for their evening shift. They broke the windshields of two buses and let the air out of the tires of two others, thus making it impossible for the buses to transport the assembled workers to the mine.[51] Carmen Miranda, the wife and daughter of copper miners, participated in this action. Miranda recalls that by mid-May 1973, "things were getting really bad for our husbands." So the women talked to each other and they "all agreed . . . that we had to go into the streets." The women decided to go "beat up" the "scabs." They went to the spot where the buses picked up the "scab" workers to transport them up to the mine, and they began "beating the shit" out of any "scab" they came across. Their husbands did not participate; instead, "they stood on the sidewalk and watched."[52] Although the police chief in Rancagua asked the women "not to be so impulsive" and begged them to be calm, the women ignored his pleas.[53] The women met the next day "and decided to do the same thing again."[54]

49 *El Rancagüiño,* 16 May 1973. The women refer to "cold" because the Chilean winter begins in May. Rancagua is located higher up in the *cordillera* (mountains) and therefore is colder than Santiago. The UP chant was "el pueblo unido, jamás será vencido" ("the people, united, will never be defeated").

50 Ibid.

51 *El Rancagüiño,* 18 May 1973.

52 Carmen Miranda, interview by author, tape recording, Rancagua, 8 June 1994. Miranda's father died of silicosis at age fifty-eight. No one in her family had ever joined a political party. However, they had all voted for Jorge Alessandri in 1970.

53 *La Prensa,* 20 May 1973.

54 Miranda, interview.

On 22 May, members of the Women's Committee "spontaneously" took over Radio Rancagua in order to broadcast the reality of the striking miners to all of Chile.[55] Once they had convinced the radio staff to show them how the radio functioned, the women hooked Radio Rancagua up with Radio Agricultura in Santiago.[56] Radio Agricultura was the voice of the National Society of Agriculturists, the conservative landowners organization, and it represented the politics of the PN. Furthermore, it had the capacity to broadcast—or link up with radio stations—throughout Chile. In a statement published the next day, the Women's Committee criticized the UP authorities who had failed to grant the workers' demands. They singled out Luis Baeza, a communist and the governor of O'Higgins province (in which Rancagua is located), who "had been a labor leader in 1943, imprisoned and sent to Pisagua for having fought for the *escala móvil*. Now, he's lashing out against the workers when the government is trying to take back their gains, gains won at the cost of blood, sweat, and tears, as he very well knows."[57]

The women did not mince words. They wrote that "we hereby notify the traitors and divisive elements within the Chilean workers' movement that your days are numbered. We are sure that by supporting our husbands, we will win this struggle." Recognizing their ties to the national *gremio* movement, the statement further declared, accurately, that "we have the solidarity of all the *gremios* of the country."[58] According to David Cusack, "members of the small merchants, farmers, and truckers associations were instructed to cooperate in every way possible with the striking miners. . . . The committed opposition was united in a clear consciousness that a successful miners' strike could break the stalemate of October and the March election."[59]

The women occupied the radio station for forty-one days. Their occupation illustrated the critical difference that women's participation in the anti-Allende struggle made. According to one editorial in *El Rancagüino*, the local conservative newspaper, "at a time when many thought that after thirty-five days the strike initiated by the workers of El Teniente would die a natural death, the spirit and initiative of a handful of women managed to

55 *El Rancagüino*, 23 May 1973. The tactic was subsequently used by other women throughout Chile in August and September 1973.

56 Miranda, interview.

57 *El Rancagüino*, 23 May 1973, 13. Pisagua was a small fishing village in northern Chile. Both the González Videla (1946–52) government and the Pinochet regime (1973–90) imprisoned leftists in prison camps there.

58 Ibid.

59 See Cusack, *Revolution and Reaction*, 64.

bring it back to life." *El Rancagüiño* was directed by Gilda González, a woman who defended the striking workers and participated in actions in support of them; the paper applauded the efforts of the "courageous women." One article cited the examples of heroic Chilean women who "struggle indefatigably to obtain the daily food for their children and family," as well as those who "went into the streets to prevent the 'strike-breakers' from working." Indicating that women in Chile knew about the activities of women in Brazil, the article devoted most of its space to detailing and lauding the Brazilian women who took action in 1964, a time when "Brazil was on the point of falling under the power of a voracious communism." After listing the various activities of the anti-Goulart women, the article concluded by asking its readers, "isn't it true that that is completely applicable to our country?"[60]

Although the women took over the radio station in order to support the men, they asserted that they acted on their own, without their husbands' knowledge. Hilda Zarate, the daughter of miners and a member of a local Mothers' Center, stated firmly that "none of the husbands knew anything about it. We women decided to do it, without anyone pressuring us."[61]

Despite the women's bold actions, it does not appear that their participation in the struggle seriously challenged their identities as wives and mothers. Whenever the women spoke, they always stressed that they joined the struggle to support their husbands. Even while they occupied the radio station, the women still felt responsible for the well-being of their children and husbands. They organized teams to make sure that their houses were cleaned, the cooking was done, and their children were supervised.

At the same time, the experience of being away from their homes and in the company of other women produced some changes and offered at least some of the women a new perspective on domestic responsibilities. One female journalist, having talked with several of the women who occupied the radio station, noted that "the return to normality won't be so easy: the women have already seen their husbands cook, wash plates, and take care of the children." As one of the women interviewed remarked, "they [the men] aren't going to be able to slip out of it [childcare and housework] so easily anymore."[62]

60 *El Rancagüiño*, 24 May 1973.

61 *El Rancagüiño*, 7 June 1973. Zarate joined her local Mothers' Center in 1965, during the Frei government. Her lengthy participation in the Mothers' Centers probably indicates some level of affiliation with the PDC. The women allowed one man to accompany them in the takeover and occupation—Don Baltasar Castro, an elderly poet and former senator.

62 *Ercilla*, 6 June 1973.

The women struggled to ensure that even though they engaged in militant and unladylike actions, they were still accorded the respect to which they were accustomed as women in a patriarchal society. Carmen Miranda objected when "UP supporters treated her in an insulting fashion." She saw that when women from the radio station went outside to give coffee and sandwiches to their male supporters, "groups that had infiltrated the gathering insulted us and made rude comments. We believe that as ladies, we deserve respect. The fact that they don't agree with us doesn't give them the right to treat us that way."[63] In order to ensure their safety, the women who occupied Radio Rancagua called on their men to surround the station to protect them in case they should be attacked.

Nationally and locally, PF actively supported the striking miners and employees and the activist wives. Members of the local PF chapter worked with the miners and the miners' wives, and they participated in the takeover of Radio Rancagua. PF members from Santiago provided them material and logistical support and joined with them when they marched to Santiago.

A PF chapter had started in Rancagua in February or March of 1972, shortly after it had formed in Santiago. Initially, it "brought together women from different opposition parties as well as a good number of independents." The group saw itself as part of the "civil resistance." However, PF had some problems in Rancagua. Unable to agree on local candidates, the group apparently suspended its work until after the crucial March 1973 election.[64] Either in response to public criticism of this decision, or simply because its internal differences ended, PF came back to life in Rancagua shortly after the March elections. On 23 March, the group held a public forum to denounce ENU, the UP government's proposed educational reforms; a week later, PF took out an ad in the local Rancagua newspaper to protest what it labeled "the undignified campaign unleashed against the Catholic University's Channel 13 and its executive director, Raúl Hasbún."[65] The group actively aided the striking miners, and Ana Marcuello, a member of the Rancagua chapter of PF, joined other women in the occupation of Radio Rancagua.[66]

The PF chapter in Santiago also supported the striking workers and the women involved in the struggle. Toward the end of May, members of the

---

63 *El Rancagüiño*, 8 June 1973.

64 *El Rancagüiño*, 9 March 1973.

65 *El Rancagüiño*, 26 March 1973; *El Rancagüiño*, 31 March 1973.

66 Ana Eugenia Marcuello, interview by author, tape recording, Rancagua, 8 June 1994.

group drove down from Santiago to deliver supplies and food to the striking workers. According to one participant, they came to "link hands with the courageous women quartered in Radio Rancagua to defend the rights acquired by their husbands, fathers, and sons."[67]

Realizing the need to bring national attention to their struggle, the striking miners and employees decided to march from Rancagua to Santiago, a distance of eighty-two kilometers. Opposition politicians—including three female Christian Democratic deputies who had earlier visited occupied Radio Rancagua—led the march. In response, the government announced that it would not permit the march to take place. However, on 15 June, between four and five thousand marchers (including hundreds of women) set off for Santiago. In order to prevent them from entering Santiago, the Allende government sent tanks equipped with tear gas and hundreds of police to stop the march at the bridge over the Maipo River (see Map 4). Once the marchers reached the bridge, pandemonium ensued, and the chaos continued for several hours. Although the opposition media made much of the fact that the UP government used tear gas and police against the miners and female demonstrators, it is not clear whether anyone was actually injured. Undeterred by police efforts to stop them, and aided by the opposition, the marchers retreated to Buin from the bridge and then slipped into Santiago in privately owned cars.[68] Members of PF joined the efforts to transport the miners into the city. Elena Larraín reported that PF members drove down to Buin prepared for police repression. As on other occasions, they carried lemons to counteract the effects of the tear gas, since "during those years we didn't carry lipstick or powder in our purses, we had handkerchiefs, lemon, salt, those types of things."[69]

Once the workers arrived in Santiago, they went to the PDC headquarters. The offices could not hold all the demonstrators, so students at the Catholic University, now controlled by the *gremio* movement, offered them housing and food at the school. Once again, members of PF provided transportation to the El Teniente workers. Larraín recalled that

a top official of the PDC came to the PF office and asked us to help transport the miners. At the time we were meeting with businessmen, so a lot of women were there. We took off right away in about twenty or thirty cars. I went in my car

67 *El Rancagüiño*, 30 May 1973.

68 For opposing accounts of the march, see *El Mercurio*, 15 June 1973, and Bitar and Pizarro, *La caída de Allende*, 38–41.

69 Larraín, interview by author, 16 March 1994.

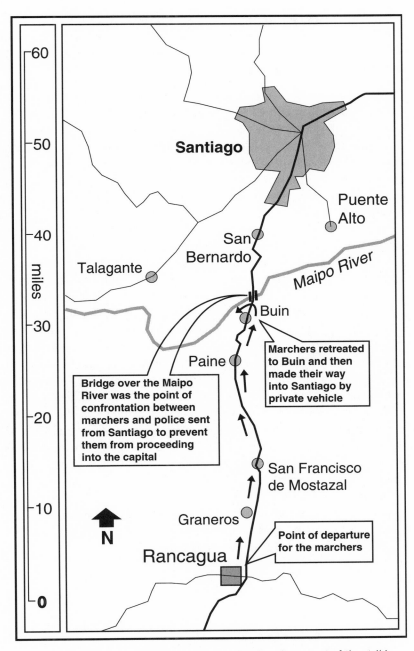

Santiago

Puente
Alto

San
Bernardo

Talagante

Maipo River

Buin

**Marchers retreated
to Buin and then
made their way
into Santiago by
private vehicle**

Paine

**Bridge over the Maipo
River was the point of
confrontation between
marchers and police sent
from Santiago to prevent
them from proceeding
into the capital**

San Francisco
de Mostazal

N

Graneros

**Point of departure
for the marchers**

Rancagua

miles

60

50

40

30

20

10

0

Map 4 Route of the march from Rancagua to Santiago in support of the striking
El Teniente miners and employees

alone so I could pick up four miners. All the miners here are fat. They hadn't bathed in three days and tear gas had been thrown at them, so they really smelled bad. We took them to the Catholic University where Jaime Guzmán welcomed them. I made three or four trips back and forth transporting miners.[70]

The opposition took full advantage of the presence of the El Teniente workers in Santiago to attack the UP government for its failure to support the miners and other employees. On 19 June, the anti-Allende forces held a large rally across from La Moneda, the presidential palace, to "give their support and solidarity to the struggle of the El Teniente workers."[71] Exploiting the contradiction of a workers' government that did not support striking workers, the protesters chanted, "El Teniente unido, jamás será vencido" ("El Teniente, united, will never be defeated") and "traición, no es revolución" ("betrayal is not revolution").[72] In one of the more ironic moments of this rather bizarre episode, young people from the National Party and Patria y Libertad—groups not heretofore particularly distinguished by their support for the working class—collected funds in the upper-class neighborhoods of Santiago to support El Teniente strikers.[73]

Despite the enormous pressure placed on it, the UP government continued to reject many of the strikers' demands. In order to heighten the conflict, women in Rancagua who supported the strike marched to Santiago on 23 June.[74] Once in Santiago, representatives from the women's march met with Allende, who promised that he would send them a new proposal on how to settle the conflict. Then on 29 June, sectors of the Chilean military (working closely with Patria y Libertad) unsuccessfully attempted to overthrow the government. Due to the decisive opposition of General Prats, the army commander in chief, the joint military-paramilitary uprising was put down (see Chap. 8). This failed coup intensified pressure on the UP government to settle the strike. As a result, on that same day, Allende sent his final proposal to the El Teniente women with whom he had met, and to Armando Garrido, president of the El Teniente regional workers' organization. On 30 June, the workers met and voted to accept his proposal.[75] By 4 July, most of the workers had returned to the mine.[76]

70 Ibid.
71 *El Mercurio*, 19 June 1973.
72 *El Mercurio*, 20 June 1973.
73 Bitar and Pizarro, *La caída de Allende*, 41, 70.
74 *El Rancagüiño*, 23 June 1973.
75 Bitar and Pizarro, *La caída de Allende*, 43, 72.
76 *El Mercurio*, 5 July 1973.

Although the struggle in El Teniente was finally over, the damage caused to the UP was tremendous. The prolonged nature of the strike had cost the government millions of dollars. Sergio Bitar, Allende's minister of mines, estimated that the El Teniente strike cost the UP government thirty-five million dollars.[77] Pictures of government tanks spraying tear gas on striking workers had undermined UP declarations that it was the government of the workers. The struggle united the anti-Allende forces and "helped swing the balance of power in the 'struggle for the bases' to the opposition."[78] As Bitar commented, "this was the first strike of the workers against the government of the workers. It dealt us a psychological blow, because no one could imagine that workers would oppose Allende. In this sense, it represented a tremendous psychological victory for the opposition."[79]

Conclusion

Many people erroneously assume that only wealthy and middle-class women composed the anti-Allende women's movement. The original activists did indeed hail from the middle and upper classes. However, from December 1971 to September 1973, these women worked very hard to incorporate poor and working-class women into their movement. The shortages facilitated their efforts to generate anti-Allende sentiments among working-class women: the testimony of the working-class women whose voices opened this chapter emphasized that shortages and the need to stand in lines were heavy burdens for these overtaxed women to bear and fueled their resentment of the UP government.

The struggles in La Papelera and El Teniente illustrate the role that anti-Allende women played in the opposition's attempts to tarnish the UP's image as a government of the workers. In both cases, PF successfully built ties between working-class women and itself. Its work with the women's groups of La Papelera and El Teniente allowed the organization to project itself as the force capable of representing and uniting all Chileans. The knowledge of the critical part they played in both conflicts did not escape the anti-Allende women. They stressed that their participation provided the workers and employees with the impetus needed to keep on struggling at difficult moments. Their approach, which eschewed traditional political and social affiliations, encouraged unity among diverse classes and political tendencies within the opposition movement.

77 Bitar and Pizarro, *La caída de Allende*, 57.

78 Cusack, *Revolution and Reaction*, 63.

79 Sergio Bitar, interview by author, tape recording, Santiago, 10 December 1998.

In place of class struggle and party membership, they proffered themselves as women whose function in life—to support their husbands and ensure the well-being of their children—positioned them above political divisions and made cross-class alliances possible. The working-class women who participated brought a history of struggle and an economic urgency to the battle that infused their fight with determination and legitimacy. The elite women generously contributed their time, contacts, and resources. Their combined efforts helped guarantee the victory of the opposition and the defeat of the UP in these two critical labor struggles.

8

Allende Must Go!

*Anti-Allende Women and the Drive
to Overthrow the UP Government*

THE MARCH 1973 parliamentary elections were decisive for both Popular Unity and the opposition. The National Party and the Christian Democratic Party had formed the Democratic Confederation for the express purpose of winning a two-thirds majority in the March 1973 elections and thereby obtaining sufficient votes to impeach Allende.[1] The opposition did not achieve its goal; CODE received 54.6 percent of the vote, and the UP obtained 43.5 percent.[2] The failure of its electoral strategy did not deter the opposition. Instead of abandoning its hopes to remove Allende, it turned to its alternative strategy: military intervention.

This chapter examines the significant contributions opposition women made to the drive to oust Allende. They created the image of a civilian population that begged the military to overthrow him. They urged the armed forces to act against the UP government. Their attacks against General Prats caused him to resign—and led to the promotion of General Augusto Pinochet to the commander in chief of the Chilean military. Since the March 1973 elections were so pivotal, this chapter begins by discussing how women voted in them.

Women and the March 1973 Elections

How did the more than two years of UP rule affect women's votes? In the 1970 presidential elections, 31 percent of women had voted for Allende. In March 1973, even more women—39 percent—voted for UP candidates. The combined PDC and PN vote from women in 1970 was 68 percent, while in 1973, CODE received only 60 percent of their votes.

1 See Moss, *Chile's Marxist Experiment*, 176–77; see also Sigmund, *Overthrow*, 197.

2 "Elección ordinario de Congreso Nacional," Dirección del Registro Electoral, Santiago, n.d.

Given the enormity of the economic crisis that plagued Chile, it is remarkable that the UP managed to win more votes from women in 1973 than it had in 1970. UP supporters have accurately interpreted the increase in women's votes for the government as a sign that the left was gaining support among women.[3] However, this conclusion obscures the fact that 60 percent—almost two-thirds—of Chilean women voted against the UP government. It also ignores the fact that women continued to vote against Allende and for the opposition to a much higher degree than men did.[4] In 1970, women who did not vote for Allende had been divided between Radomiro Tomic, who represented reform and the more progressive wing of the PDC, and Jorge Alessandri, who stood squarely for conservatism. In 1973, though, 60 percent of Chilean women united around a reactionary project dominated by the PN. Analyzed from this perspective, the vote illustrates the strength of the right and its ability to win over the majority of Chilean women. In 1970, few of the women who voted against Allende had much organizing experience, and sharp divisions separated the supporters of the PDC from those in the PN. Three years later, many of these women had gained political experience from their anti-Allende work. Women from the PN and the PDC joined together to forge a solid, conservative bloc increasingly unified against the UP government. Thus, although the 8 percent increase among women for the UP is notable, the fact that 60 percent of women voted for CODE is more significant.

PDC women's vote for CODE reflected the political shifts that had taken place since the 1970 presidential elections and the concerted efforts undertaken by Poder Femenino, in conjunction with the opposition parties, to unite women against Allende. Fortified by its determination to remove Allende, the PN successfully established itself as one of two pillars (the other one being the UP) of an increasingly polarized political situation. From this position, the PN was able to dominate the opposition and use its power to solidify an anti-Allende front with the PDC. Facilitating this alliance was the fact that the conservative sector of the PDC, led by Eduardo Frei, had assumed control of the party by 1973. Only a minority of the party's leadership favored discussions with the UP; the majority chose confrontation with the left and an alliance with the PN. In addition, the results of the March 1973 elections revealed that the PDC's electoral

---

3 See Sigmund, *Overthrow*, 200.

4 The figures are as follows. In the March 1973 parliamentary elections, 1,074,602 women (60 percent) voted for CODE, while 699,561 (39 percent) voted for the UP coalition; 938,990 men (50 percent) voted for CODE, while 905,609 (48 percent) voted for the UP. "Elección ordinario de Congreso Nacional," Dirección del Registro Electoral, Santiago, n.d.

strategy against Allende could not succeed, making the PN's strategy for military intervention the only viable one to overthrow Allende. The increased tensions and hostility that permeated Chilean politics brought these two former political rivals together in opposition to Allende, so that in 1973, the right gained strength, the center moved to the right, and the left confronted a more powerful and determined opposition.

Anti-Allende women both influenced and responded to the increasingly combative and conservative politics of the PN and the PDC. Encouraged by their success in working together in PF, women from the different parties had long urged male party members to join forces as well. According to one member of PF, CODE came into existence as a result of pressure exerted by anti-Allende women. As the PF member recalled, "women pressured the Christian Democrats to join with the parties of the right by threatening to campaign against them in future elections if they refused [to work together]."[5] Although her comment may overstate the influence that PF had on the male-dominated parties, it does reflect a truth: the success of the women's work against Allende served as a model that encouraged the parties to work together in pursuit of a similar project. The growing alliance between the PDC and the PN, in turn, affected women members of the PDC. Party loyalty might explain why many PDC women were willing to cast their votes for CODE, but this ignores the stark transformation in the PDC's politics. During the previous two and a half years, the party had consolidated to the right—an unfortunate reality that made the survival of democracy in Chile doubtful.

Men's and women's votes continued to show a gender gap. As Paul Sigmund points out, "the opposition received majority support from women voters in all but two of Santiago's twenty-seven communes (Barrancas and La Granja)."[6] (See Table 8.1.) Conversely, a majority of men in all the working-class neighborhoods voted for the UP. Once again, middle- and upper-class women from Ñuñoa, La Reina, Providencia, and Las Condes voted overwhelmingly against the UP. Upper-class women were the most united force of the Chilean electorate. In Providencia, 84 percent (and in Las Condes, 78 percent) of women voted against Allende, while 80 percent and 72 percent of men did, respectively. Also worth noting is that in both the middle- and upper-class neighborhoods more women voted than men, a fact that illustrates the growing interest in politics and increased electoral importance of conservative women during the Allende years.

5 Crummett, "El Poder Femenino," 107.
6 Sigmund, *Overthrow*, 201.

The results of the March 1973 parliamentary elections radically altered both the tenor and the agenda of the anti-Allende opposition. Dismayed by their failure to gain a two-thirds majority in the parliamentary elections and unwilling to wait for the 1976 presidential elections, the parties of the opposition decided that their goal of removing Allende could only be achieved through direct action, confrontation, and military intervention. Illustrative of this new strategy was the comment of the PN president, Sergio Onofre Jarpa, who said, "the struggle now is not in the ballot box but in the streets."[7] CODE's unsuccessful efforts to defeat Allende peacefully convinced the PN and conservative sectors of the PDC that the military was the only force capable of removing Allende from power.[8] From this point on, planning for the coup received a green light from the opposition parties and anti-Allende forces within the military.

However, a major obstacle confronted the coup planners: the armed forces were not yet united behind this solution. General Prats headed the army, the most powerful branch of the Chilean military, and he, along with several other high-ranking officers, was firmly committed to supporting the democratically elected government. The political sectors that favored a coup, then, had to remove Prats and to convince the majority of the officer corps that a coup was necessary and legitimate and that they had the civilian backing for it. This was essential because, as David Cusack writes, "the military needed the active support of significant sectors of the civilian middle class and probably the assurance of crucial international backing. These factors could help sway hesitant military leaders and undermine those who supported Allende."[9]

Women played a critical role in building and demonstrating this active support. While opposition men participated in behind-the-scenes schemes and discussions with the military, anti-Allende women presented the public face of support for the military option. As Sandra McGee Deutsch notes, "the rightist women left the actual counterrevolution to men, but as Gen. Augusto Pinochet recognized, they had summoned the men to action."[10] Instead of continuing to protest UP policies, opposition

---

7 MacEoin, *No Peaceful Way*, 192.

8 See Supplee, "Women and the Counterrevolution." Joan Jara noted in her memoirs that when CODE failed to achieve its desired election results, "the decision was taken to overthrow Allende by a military coup." See Joan Jara, *An Unfinished Song: The Life of Victor Jara* (New York: Ticknor & Fields, 1984), 209–10. For a description of post–March 1973 elections coup planning, see MacEoin, *No Peaceful Way*, 192–95; Kaufman, *Crisis*, 75–76, 153; Phil O'Brien and Jackie Roddick, *Chile: The Pinochet Decade* (London: Latin American Bureau, 1983), 30–41.

9 Cusack, *Revolution and Reaction*, 82.

10 Sandra McGee Deutsch, "Gender and Sociopolitical Change in Twentieth-Century Latin America," *Hispanic American Historical Review* 71, no.2 (1991): 303.

Table 8.1 Results of the March 1973 parliamentary elections in selected Santiago districts, by gender

Neighborhood	Women's Vote				Men's Vote			
	CODE #	%	UP #	%	CODE #	%	UP #	%
Working-class								
Barrancas	10,598	44%	**12,840**	**54%**	8,499	37%	**14,231**	**62%**
Conchalí	**21,470**	**54**	17,728	44	16,629	46	**19,171**	**53**
Renca	**8,854**	**54**	7,305	44	6,625	46	**7,681**	**53**
Quinta Normal	**20,373**	**56**	15,513	43	16,115	46	**18,034**	**52**
San Miguel	**34,442**	**52**	31,455	47	25,915	42	**34,940**	**52**
La Cisterna	**21,375**	**57**	15,564	41	16,113	48	**17,117**	**51**
La Granja	9,535	43	**11,967**	**54**	7,611	36	**13,219**	**62**
Middle-class								
Ñuñoa	**44,799**	**70**	18,987	29	**30,374**	**60**	19,375	39
La Reina	**8,753**	**69**	3,750	30	**5,933**	**61**	3,728	38
Upper-class								
Providencia	**26,987**	**84**	4,982	16	**15,913**	**80**	3,884	20
Las Condes	**29,748**	**78**	8,164	21	**18,325**	**72**	7,141	28

Note: Boldface type indicates the candidates who received the most votes. This table does not include listings for null and blank votes; the totals, therefore, will not add up to 100 percent.
Source: República de Chile, Dirección del Registro Electoral (Santiago: Servicio Electoral, n.d.).

221

women began to call actively for Allende's removal. In the months between the March 1973 elections and the September coup, these women had five goals: to remove General Prats, the constitutionalist commander of the Chilean armed forces; to convince the military that the civilian population supported a coup; to create a climate among the general public that made military intervention acceptable, and even desirable; to mobilize women against Allende and for military intervention; and to encourage the military to stage a coup.

The Women's Campaign Against General Prats and for Military Intervention

General Prats was a career officer in the Chilean army who became commander in chief of the military following the kidnapping and murder, by right-wing extremists, of Army General and Commander in Chief René Schneider in October 1970.[11] As the top military commander under President Allende, General Prats had repeatedly demonstrated his determination to respect and defend the elected government. In order to settle the difficult October 1972 truckers' strike, General Prats, along with several other military officers, joined Allende's cabinet. As minister of the interior, Prats worked to ensure that the March 1973 elections took place without incident. And on 29 June 1973, after several army officers had led their troops in an unsuccessful attempt to capture the Defense Ministry and the presidential palace, General Prats rushed to the scene and personally convinced the officers to surrender. His intervention foiled the coup attempt and achieved a speedy resolution that upheld the UP government.[12] Such decisive intervention in support of the elected government angered the opposition and convinced sectors of the opposition in favor of the coup that Prats must be removed. Anti-Allende women were pivotal in achieving his resignation.

The first attack against Prats took place on 27 June, and it has raised a certain amount of debate. Alejandrina Cox, the woman who initiated the event, claims that her actions were nothing more than a spontaneous response to an accidental encounter with General Prats. She adds that the right, with whom she was not affiliated, exploited the incident to its

---

11 Schneider was a "constitutionalist": he believed that the military's duty was to uphold the Chilean Constitution and support the elected government. For a discussion of his position, see Kaufman, *Crisis*, 125. His view, which supported military neutrality, became known as the Schneider Doctrine.

12 *El Mercurio*, Edición Internacional, 25 June–1 July 1973.

advantage.[13] Supporters of the UP, on the other hand, have claimed that Cox's attack was the opening salvo in an increasingly intense and ultimately successful campaign to force Prats to resign. The incident in question happened shortly after Prats left an arduous meeting with his fellow generals and headed to the Defense Ministry, which was located in downtown Santiago. During the meeting, Prats had experienced "a vague feeling of anxiety . . . like the dark portent of some sordid event."[14] In addition, Prats had just learned that the military had arrested seven of its members, all with close links to Patria y Libertad, for carrying out anti-UP plans within the armed forces.[15] As he drove down a main street in an upper-class neighborhood, Alejandrina Cox, a middle-aged woman from Chile's landowning aristocracy, stuck out her tongue at him.[16] Because Cox sported a short haircut and no makeup, Prats mistook her for a man and, outraged at the insult, drew his pistol and fired at her car, all the while demanding that she get out of the vehicle (see Fig. 7). When she did, he realized that she was a woman, a fact that deeply affected him: shooting at an unarmed woman broke his code of honor as an officer and as a gentleman whose duty was to protect women. Compounding his disgrace was the fact that while his car was stopped, a large crowd of people gathered to jeer him and cheer Cox. They punctured his tires and painted "General Prats, Murderer" on his car.[17] Angered and humiliated by the growing crowd that had gathered in support of Cox, Prats jumped in a taxi and

13 Alejandrina Cox, interview by author, tape recording, Vitacura, 24 June 1994. In my interview with her—the only one that she has ever granted—Cox stresses that her action was unplanned and unconnected to any group. She claims that she was a Christian Democrat who did not support the coup and who opposed Pinochet. She granted me the interview because a mutual acquaintance (Paloma, the former leader of the UP's National Secretariat of Women) asked her to do so. Despite my initial skepticism, the fact that Paloma believes her, Cox's insistence that her action was spontaneous, her apparently sincere remorse for Prats's murder, and her stated opposition to Pinochet convinced me that she was telling the truth. Cox is also a very religious woman who feels that she is in some way responsible for Prats's murder. Her sense of guilt for this crime might lead her to emphasize the spontaneity of her action in order to minimize its implications. Nevertheless, I offer her version of events as she told them to me. The reader may make her or his own decision as to its truthfulness.

14 Carlos Prats González, *Memorias: Testimonio de un soldado* (Santiago: Pehuén Editores., 1985), 414.

15 *¿Qué Pasa?* 5 July 1973.

16 According to Prats, "I was driving in military uniform in a military car . . . when people traveling in four or five cars repeatedly made disgusting gestures at me and yelled obscene epithets at me." Prats believed that he was the victim of a coordinated public attack. He later said, by way of explanation, that he had thought that all those who did this were men and that he feared a repeat of the Schneider kidnapping and murder. See *El Mercurio*, 29 June 1973. For Prats's full account of the incident, see Prats González, *Memorias*, 414–17.

17 *El Mercurio*, 29 June 1973.

Fig. 7 Alejandrina Cox
and General Prats. Their
encounter led the general to
offer his resignation—and
the opposition to claim Cox
as one of their own.
El Mercurio,
29 June 1973.

sped away. He drove to La Moneda and offered Allende his resignation, which the president refused.[18] Because the incident involved the commander in chief of the Chilean military, local police took Cox to jail, where she was held until late in the night.

It was a small event, but one that immediately acquired enormous significance in the tense atmosphere reigning in Santiago. Not only did it provoke Prats into offering his resignation, but it also indicated the depth of the opposition's hatred for him. The right seized the opportunity to castigate Prats and the UP government and to present its chosen symbol of patriotic womanhood (in this case, Cox) as both a heroine and a victim of the UP. Opposition women enthusiastically hailed Cox's "courageous" action and claimed her as one of their own. When she was still in jail, PF women gathered outside the police station to cheer her by singing the national anthem and demanding her release.[19] Opposition men from all over Chile sent her flowers to thank her for her bravery and women sent her letters comparing her to Joan of Arc. Her upper-class neighbors changed the name of the street she lived on to Calle Alejandrina Cox.[20] Teresa Donoso Loero—whose book, *La epopeya de las ollas vacías,* credits PF and other "valiant" women with creating an atmosphere conducive to the coup—writes that "even General Carlos Prats fell prisoner to the fear that Poder Femenino inspired: he had an incident with Alejandrina Cox, a citizen who stuck out her tongue at him."[21]

18 For contemporary media coverage of the incident from the opposition's point of view, see "La aventura fracasada," *Ercilla,* 4 July 1973; "Tercer Round," *¿Qué Pasa?* 5 July 1973; *El Mercurio,* 28 June 1973.

19 *El Mercurio,* 28 June 1973.

20 Cox, interview.

21 Donoso Loero, *La epopeya,* 75.

Since the incident took place only two days before the attempted coup of 29 June, UP supporters concluded that there was a link between the two. They vilified Alejandrina Cox as a reactionary and credited her with further poisoning the already venomous atmosphere in Santiago.[22] The North American Congress on Latin America (NACLA), which favored the UP, claimed that "Fatherland and Liberty [the paramilitary organization that actively participated in the 29 June coup attempt] sent one of its women to harass General Prats."[23]

What lay behind Cox's confrontation with Prats, and why did it engender such controversy? In my interview with her, Alejandrina Cox claimed (despite allegations to the contrary) that she had no connection with any group and that her action had nothing to do with the abortive coup of 29 June. In 1970 she had voted for Tomic, not Alessandri, and had accompanied her pro-UP daughter to the victory celebration the night of the election. She was initially willing to give Allende a chance; Cox stated, "I began by accepting him." She did not participate in the March of the Empty Pots and Pans or in any of the anti-Allende marches. However, she gradually lost her openness to the UP and became increasingly dissatisfied with it. According to Cox, her alienation resulted from her perception that "poverty was increasing, [and the UP] was an economic disaster for the country." She remembers the incident in this way:

I came to a red light and I found myself next to General Prats. Just as I had always stuck out my tongue at the nuns who bothered me [at school], I stuck out my tongue at General Prats. I didn't think anything more of it. [When the light changed] we drove on. All of a sudden my nephew, who was with me, said "Aunt, General Prats is taking out his revolver." I thought, he's going to shoot at my license plate and I didn't think any more about it. Just then I heard a shot. . . . He pulled up and ordered me to get out of the car, so I got out. . . . Poor General Prats, when he saw that I was a woman—I had short hair like always, no makeup and dark glasses—he nearly died. He realized that he had really blown it.[24]

Far from boasting about her role in Prats's demise, Cox seems to regret it deeply. She now defines her actions as "stupid" and was pained by the

22 In July 1973, the UP published its account of the failed coup attempt, which explicitly linked Patria y Libertad to the uprising. The UP publication also claims that the Prats-Cox incident was jointly instigated by Poder Femenino and the CIA. See Documentos Especiales, *El tancazo de ese 29 de junio* (Santiago: Quimantú, 1973).

23 This quotation is the editor's explanatory comment in the article by Michèle Mattelart. See Michèle Mattelart, "Feminine Side," 17.

24 Cox, interview.

murders of Prats and Sofía de Prats, his wife, in September 1974.[25] Nonetheless, Cox's actions wounded Prats and weakened his standing within the military. The impact had as much to do with the context in which the Cox-Prats incident took place as it did with what it meant to be a Chilean man and a military officer at that time.

By June, the political situation in Chile had worsened. The PN declared that the Allende government "was no longer legitimate."[26] Prats knew that he did not have the full support of his officers. Subjected to a high degree of pressure, the incident with Cox overwhelmed him. What troubled Prats the most was the fact that he had fired on a woman. (In fact, as a military officer, he should not have shot at any unarmed civilian.) As he stated in a public letter regarding the incident, "I would not have shot if I had known she was a woman. . . . I publicly repeat my apologies to Señora Cox, in her condition as a woman."[27] As a gentleman and an officer in the Chilean military, Prats was required to control his emotions and to defend women. In this situation, he had done neither. Publicly humiliated, lacking the support of his officers, he believed that resigning was the only course left open to him. Only Allende's refusal to accept his resignation prevented the loss of one of the president's few remaining military allies.[28]

By August, the political situation in Chile had deteriorated even further. On 25 July, the *gremio* movement called on its members to strike in an effort to weaken the Allende government to the point of exhaustion. In response, the National Truck Owners' Association urged its members to protest the lack of spare parts (which was, in fact, the result of the U.S. embargo against Chile), low wages, and the UP's efforts to establish a government-run transportation company and form a pro-government transportation workers' union. Underlying these demands, and in contrast to the October 1972 transportation strike, this strike "was explicitly aimed at the overthrow of the UP regime."[29] From one end of Chile to the other, truck drivers refused to transport goods, shopkeepers closed their shops, and the professional *gremios* ceased working—including many medical

---

25 Following the coup, the military forced General Prats to resign. He subsequently sought refuge in Argentina. There, on 30 September 1974, forces from the Chilean DINA blew up the car that Prats was driving, killing him and his wife Sofía. The DINA was the army's intelligence service. It was responsible for the much of the torture, disappearances, and killings during the dictatorship. See the *New York Times*, 17 February 1996.

26 MacEoin, *No Peaceful Way*, 160.

27 *El Mercurio*, 29 June 1973.

28 Prats González, *Memorias*, 416–17.

29 Kaufman, *Crisis*, 266–67.

personnel, who denied treatment to their patients. A group of female doctors issued a statement in support of the work stoppage, declaring that "[a]s women, mothers, wives, and professionals, we feel compelled to declare that we cannot work as we should as long as there is no spiritual peace; as long as we lack even the minimum of professional equipment needed to fulfill our work. We know that our mission as women doctors is doubly delicate and in the current work conditions, we can only offer words, and they are not enough to heal our patients."[30]

Heating fuel, on which many in Santiago depended for warmth during the Chilean winter, was difficult—if not impossible—to obtain.[31] Street fighting between pro- and anti-UP youth escalated in downtown Santiago. Dialogue between the PDC and the UP broke down, and future possibilities to reopen it seemed unlikely. On 22 August, in an effort to establish the illegality of the UP government and the "moral basis for military intervention," the Chamber of Deputies voted eighty-one to forty-seven to declare the UP government unconstitutional. The UP retorted that PN and PDC deputies had "attempted to seize total power, with the evident purpose of subjecting everyone to the most rigorous economic and political controls" and, as a result, had "violated the Constitution."[32]

In conjunction with the increasingly polarized political situation, anti-Allende women stepped up their activities. By the end of August, the coordinating council of PF met every day.[33] On 8 August, wives of military officers publicly demonstrated their antipathy toward Allende for the first time. They gathered in front of the Ministry of Defense in downtown Santiago to show their support for Air Force General César Ruíz, one of Allende's foes within the high command, and their anger at Allende's attempt to force him to resign.[34] At their second demonstration, hundreds of women (estimates of numbers range from three hundred to fifteen hundred), mainly military wives and members of PF, went to General Prats's home on 21 August.[35] They attempted to deliver a letter to Sofía de Prats, the general's wife, that demanded Prats's resignation. Initially, Sofía de Prats refused to meet with them, but upon recognizing certain generals' wives in

---

30 *El Mercurio*, 9 September 1973.

31 Sigmund, *Overthrow*, 228.

32 Moss, *Chile's Marxist Experiment*, 197.

33 Correa Morandé, *La guerra*, 185.

34 Crummett, "El Poder Femenino," 107, and Kaufman, *Crisis*, 273–74.

35 Prats writes that "very quickly it was not just women yelling in front of my house: [the numbers had grown to] 1,500 people—women, men and children—who uttered all sorts of gross insults against me. Out of respect for my reader, I prefer not to include them." Prats González, *Memorias*, 477.

the crowd, several of whom she considered her "friends," she told the door-man to receive the letter.[36] Their actions, which represented the domestic sector of the population invading the private space of the top military commander, proved to be the last straw for Prats. On 24 August, General Prats resigned, and General Augusto Pinochet succeeded him as military commander. Prats's resignation and Pinochet's promotion removed the last remaining obstacle between the military and a coup. Prats linked his resignation to the women's demonstration. In a phone conversation with the press, he stated that "the wives of several generals participated in the demonstration [which took place] in front of my house. They [the generals] have not acted as they should. I could not divide the army. The president has accepted my resignation."[37] Banner headlines in *La Tribuna* triumphantly proclaimed, "Women Throw Out Prats."[38] Planning for the coup was now unhampered by the presence of the military commander who had maintained his loyalty to the Constitution he was sworn to uphold.

Be a Man, Overthrow Allende

They said that we were chickens. They left corn at the doors of our houses.
They said we were cowards. Anyone in my position would have acted.
There was no other way out.
—GENERAL GUSTAVO LEIGH
Air Force commander and member of the September 1973 Junta

In addition to their efforts to remove Prats, conservative women also worked to shame military men, troops and officers alike, into action by questioning their masculinity. Between March and September 1973, conservative women went to military barracks and threw corn and feathers at the troops, thereby insinuating that the men were "chickens" and "sissies."[39] According to Ernesto Torres, a noncommissioned officer in the Chilean air force during this time, they did this to tell the men that "they were not capable of defending their mothers, their wives, their daughters, or their families. They lacked the courage and intellectual capacity to defend them. They were chicken." In a homophobic society such as Chile's, to call a man a coward was highly offensive. As Torres

---

36 Ibid., 476–77. For a copy of their letter, see *La Prensa*, 25 August 1973.

37 *El Mercurio*, 24 August 1973.

38 *La Tribuna*, 24 August 1973.

39 In February 2001, a group of Pinochet supporters threw corn at the military. This time they were protesting the armed forces' lack of support for Pinochet, who was facing trial on charges of murder and abuse of human rights. *Santiago Times*, 7 February 2001.

explains, "the men believed that they were macho, so it was insulting to call them chickens, or fags, or not real men."[40] Army General Medina Loes confirms Torres's observations. "From the point of view of a military man, nothing is more offensive than to be called a coward! The military hated it!"[41] When the troops marched in public, or as their officers "stood at attention in their resplendent uniforms," these women threw chicken feed and feathers at them and urged them to be real men.[42] By "real men," these women meant men who would fulfill their prescribed role as defenders of women and of the nation. They wanted to convince the armed forces to overthrow the UP government, which, these women claimed, had caused so much hardship, chaos, and disorder in their lives. The military men would thus be faithful to their roles and, in the process, allow the women to return to theirs.

PF, along with women from SOL and Patria y Libertad, participated in this activity.[43] Elena Larraín says that women went to the barracks because "we wanted them to carry out a coup. The women divided all the barracks up throughout Chile and went to them."[44] María Correa Morandé, one of the leaders of PF, recalls that women sent the military envelopes full of feathers: "no letter, just chicken feathers. We did it to incite them. We also sent the generals a piece of paper on which we wrote 'Djakarta.'"[45] ("Djakarta" referred to the capital of Indonesia, where, following the 1965 coup, the military murdered somewhere between three hundred thousand and four hundred thousand members of the Indonesian Communist Party.) In order to drive home the point, opponents of Allende also spray-painted "Djakarta" on the walls of Santiago to urge the Chilean military "to liquidate the communists" as their Indonesian counterparts had previously done.[46] Nora Pulido, a middle-class woman from

40 Ernesto Torres, interview by author, tape recording, 29 December 1998.

41 General Medina Loes, interview by author, tape recording, Santiago, 24 December 1998. During the UP years, Medina Loes was commander of an army unit stationed close to Santiago. After the coup, he served as translator for Pinochet. In 1998 he worked in the Academia Nacional de Estudios Estratégicos (National Academy for Strategic Studies).

42 Samuel Chavkin, *Storm Over Chile: The Junta Under Siege* (Chicago: Lawrence Hill, 1989), 206.

43 In her autobiographical novel, *Paula*, Isabel Allende writes that elite men in the opposition encouraged their wives to participate in this action. According to her, "my father-in-law, like many other men, sent Granny [her mother-in-law] to the Military Academy to throw corn at the cadets, to see if they could stop behaving like hens and go out and defend the nation as they were sworn to do." Isabel Allende, *Paula*, 186.

44 Larraín, interview by author, 8 July 1994.

45 Correa Morandé, interview.

46 See MacEoin, *No Peaceful Way*, 164.

Ñuñoa (and not a PF member), went to the military barracks to throw corn at the troops and "to call them chickens." She claimed that she did this "out of desperation. The chaos [in the country] was savage. I did it when I didn't have any food to cook." Pulido believed that far from being angry with the women, the troops understood the symbolism of the corn and sympathized with the women's goals. After all, she pointed out, "they had families too. Their wives had to go stand in line. The troops were just waiting for their officers to make the pronouncement [to overthrow the government]."[47] It is notable that these women were not scared of how the military would respond to them. Women who opposed the Pinochet dictatorship did not dare to defy the armed forces in such a fashion following the 1973 coup for fear of what the armed forces would have done to them![48]

Although the campaign was both intensive and extensive, it required very few resources, except the determination of these conservative women to get rid of Allende. Some women incorporated pro-coup activity into their daily lives. Whenever her car pulled alongside an officer, Lucía Maturana, an upper-class member of SOL, would roll down her window and sing the children's song, "los pollitos dicen 'pío pío pío'" ("the little chicks sing 'cheep, cheep, cheep'").[49] Gabriela Basaez, a middle-class woman active in both SOL and Patria y Libertad, always carried corn and chicken feathers in her purse. Whenever she came across a police officer, she positioned herself in front of him and "dropped some wheat, corn, or feathers [to let him know that] the military were cowards because they wouldn't defend us." Unlike Pulido, Basaez believes that the police and the guards in the barracks, where she also went, got angry. But "they never responded, they just remained silent."[50]

This campaign demonstrates conservative women's ability to influence political events through their combined appeals to proper gender codes

47 Nora Pulido, interview by author, tape recording, Santiago, 29 November 1993. Many conservative, pro-military women and men in Chile refer to the coup as a *"pronunciamiento militar"* (military pronouncement) because they refuse to recognize that a military coup ever took place. They base this belief on their perception that "the entire population" begged the military to intervene and throw out the Allende government. Therefore, they argue, the military merely responded to the popular demand to get rid of Allende.

48 My thanks to Temma Kaplan for this comparison. For a discussion of how the armed forces treated women who opposed them, see Ximena Bunster, "Surviving Beyond Fear: Women and Torture in Latin America," in *Women and Change in Latin America*, ed. June Nash and Helen Safa (South Hadley, Mass.: Bergin & Garvey, 1986).

49 Maturana, interview, 26 October 1993.

50 Gabriela Basaez, interview by author, tape recording, Santiago, 3 March 1994.

and nationalism. A poem by PF member Nina Donoso, titled "Golpeando las puertas de los cuarteles" ("Beating on the Barracks Doors"), expresses these sentiments clearly (see Appendix E). Donoso's emotion-laden poem projects a female identity common in rightist women's discourse: woman as apolitical mother, as patriot, as symbol of the nation. She evokes a vision of the noble, courageous, and suffering mother who, inspired by love for the fatherland and her children, has grieved for three years, and now turns to the military—where "lies the conscience of the Father-land"—to save the nation.[51] Donoso ignores women's role as political actors and the connections that exist between the armed forces and the opposition. She represents women in terms of their maternal qualities and presents the troops as a group of individual Chilean men. "We are not coming to talk with the uniforms, . . . / we are looking for the man, for the Chilean, to ask him about Chile and his flag!" Stripped of their polit-ical realities and institutional affiliations, both women and the military symbolize disinterested and self-sacrificing Chilean patriotism and love for the fatherland.

The poem praises the military, the embodiment of Chilean manhood, and calls on the armed forces to "redeem the Fatherland we once had." The women in the poem appeal to the armed forces, "cry[ing] on our knees," to act against Allende. When they overthrow Allende, they will redeem the nation from the "ten thousand mercenaries," the "foreign jackals" who have attacked it. By reclaiming the nation, they will also restore proper gender roles. Although the women in the poem offer to be the "vanguard, your deputies and nurses . . . / . . . the first to die," they clearly know that their task is to encourage the military to overthrow Allende. The women call upon the armed forces to act, to fulfill their duty as men to their "sweethearts," "wives," and "grandmothers," and to save the homeland, so that the women can return to their homes and continue their lives as wives and mothers.[52]

Although the campaign probably angered some, even many, of its tar-gets, military discipline prevented them from responding in any visible fashion to the taunts and jeers. It is unclear to what extent the campaign effectively built support among the military for intervention. According to Medina Loes, the women's actions "added more internal pressure to the commanding officers."[53] Gustavo Leigh (whose remarks open this

---

51 Correa Morandé, *La guerra*, 144–45.

52 Ibid.

53 Medina Loes, interview.

section) suggests that he overthrew Allende because he could no longer tolerate being called a chicken.[54] However, while he may have found this treatment personally annoying, it is unlikely that he, or any officer, would stage a coup solely in response to women's irritating behavior. In fact, plans for the coup had started long before the women went to the barracks and threw corn at the military. Although the answer must remain speculative until more research is done, is it not more likely that these women's actions were part of a coordinated campaign—one endorsed by the opposition parties and the pro-coup sectors of the military—to provide legitimacy to military intervention? Is it not equally possible, given the contacts and conversations that existed between pro-coup civilian politicians and the military, that the military either suggested, approved of, or at least did not oppose women throwing corn?

In any case, the women's actions did serve several key purposes. They mobilized and solidified an increasingly virulent core of women in support of military intervention. The women also provided a public and supposedly apolitical face to the call for military intervention. Finally, these women's activities allowed the armed forces to claim legitimacy for their illegal seizure of power. As Temma Kaplan has noted, after the coup, the Chilean military continuously referred to women's calls for intervention to justify it, as if to say, "our mothers made us do it."[55]

Carmen Frei, a PDC senator and the daughter of President Eduardo Frei (1964–70), believes that these women's actions "created an atmosphere that made it seem like women wanted the military to intervene. In this sense, I believe that the military felt that there was a sizable group of important women who wanted an armed outcome. These women helped influence public opinion into believing that women wanted the military to act."[56]

54 Thomas G. Sanders, "Military Government in Chile," in *The Politics of Anti-Politics*, ed. Brian Loveman and Thomas M. Davies Jr. (Lincoln: University of Nebraska Press, 1978), 272. Leigh made this statement in September 1973, after the military seized power. One factor to consider in analyzing Leigh's statement is whether it accurately reflects his feelings or whether he said it as part of the military's attempts to legitimize the coup by referring to civilian demands that it intervene in Chilean politics.

55 See Temma Kaplan "Rethinking Identity in Latin America" (paper presented at the Latin American Studies Seminar on Rethinking Identity in Latin America, Yale University, 1994), 32. Cited with permission of the author. A new version of this material will appear in Kaplan's forthcoming book, *Taking Back the Streets: Women, Popular Democracy, and Collective Memory* (Berkeley and Los Angeles: University of California Press).

56 Carmen Frei, interview by author, tape recording, Santiago, 4 May 1994. Although Frei disavows her past actions today, during the UP years she, too, encouraged the military to intervene. At the time, Frei was a PDC *regidora* (alderperson) from Santiago. When the wives and daughters of military officers demonstrated against Allende's efforts to force Air Force General Ruíz to resign, Carmen Frei joined the protest. See *La Prensa*, 21 August 1973.

¡Allende, Proceda, Imite a Balmaceda!

Harassing the military was not the only tactic of the anti-Allende women. In order to present the image of a population united in its desire to remove Allende, opposition women knew that they had to both popularize this demand and obtain visible support for it. To achieve these ends, they once again took their campaign to the streets, demonstrating against UP policies and asking people to join with them in calling on Allende to resign. Led by PF, women throughout Chile asked passersby to sign petitions demanding that Allende step down. According to *El Mercurio*, the petition campaign was so successful that it "became a national crusade."[57] On 27 August, the Rancagua chapter of PF displayed a huge sign that read, "Señora, Señor, if you want 'him' to go, sign this petition." According to one local newspaper, hundreds of people formed lines to sign the petition, and in only two hours, PF women collected more than a thousand signatures.[58] In downtown Santiago, anti-Allende women organized by both PF and the *gremio* movement gathered names of citizens who supported an end to Allende's presidency.[59] Raquel Hurtado, vice president of the PDC women's department, urged all members and supporters of the party to sign petitions asking Allende to resign.[60]

In a similarly coordinated fashion, during the month of August, PF encouraged women to take over radio stations in cities throughout Chile to intensify the media campaign against the UP and to call for support for the striking transportation workers. Between 15 and 17 August, hundreds of women, many of them the wives of the striking transportation workers, occupied at least fourteen radio stations (see Map 5). Organizations on the extreme right, such as Patria y Libertad, also supported this activity. According to the wife of a truck driver who participated in the takeover, "Patria y Libertad women helped us seize and maintain control of the stations."[61] Once they gained control of the stations, the women sang the national anthem, called on the listeners to support the striking truck and

---

57 *El Mercurio*, 5 September 1973.

58 *El Rancagüiño*, 28 August and 29 August 1973.

59 *La Prensa*, 5 September 1973.

60 *El Mercurio*, 5 September 1966. Hurtado's actions reflect the Chamber of Deputies' declaration on 22 August that the Allende government was unconstitutional. Although the majority of the PDC supported this strategy, a small sector of the party rejected the alliance with the PN and the call for Allende's resignation and urged the party and Congress to make concessions to the UP. However, the conservative sector of the PDC, led by former president Eduardo Frei, rejected this appeal. See MacEoin, *No Peaceful Way*, 166.

61 Crummett, "El Poder Femenino," 106.

Map 5 Cities with radio stations seized by anti-Allende women,
August–September 1973

bus drivers, and invited other women to join them.[62] As in the case of the takeover of Radio Rancagua in support of the El Teniente strike, which probably inspired this wave of takeovers, many women remained in the occupied radio stations for extended periods of time. For example, a group of *gremialista* women took over Radio Lautaro in Talca on 15 August and were still inside the station on 11 September, when the coup took place.[63]

As part of its final push to undermine the Allende government, the strikes unleashed by the opposition at the end of July brought much of the Chilean economy to a halt. To increase the pressure on the government to meet the transportation workers' demands, on 21 August, the wives of the truck drivers took over the grounds of the National Congress and continued to occupy them until the day of the coup.[64] Members of PF, who had probably helped plan the takeover, carried "huge pots of tasty and warm food" to the women as a gesture of "solidarity," an act that they claimed "built a new and different link for the future of the country."[65] By September, the success of the transportation strike—then nearly three months old—meant that food and other necessary items, already in short supply, had all but disappeared from the shelves of the few shops that remained open. Despite these hardships and tensions, or perhaps because of them, however, hundreds of thousands of supporters of the UP (UP activists place the number of participants at one million) marched through Santiago on 4 September to celebrate the third anniversary of Allende's electoral victory. It was the largest demonstration ever held in Chile.[66]

Partially in response to the 4 September demonstration, and partially following their own agenda, women of PF and the *gremio* movement called for a demonstration on 5 September to demand Allende's resignation. A few days before the demonstration, ads addressed to "Chilean Women" appeared in *El Mercurio*. Signed by Poder Femenino and the Mujeres Gremialistas de Chile (Women *Gremialistas* of Chile), among others, the ads reminded the reader that Allende had promised to "resign if the working people asked him to."[67] Even though the majority of working-class

62 Donoso Loero, *La epopeya*, 130–32.

63 *El Mercurio*, 11 September 1973.

64 Donoso Loero, *La epopeya*, 116–17.

65 Correa Morandé, *La guerra*, 168.

66 Sigmund, *Overthrow*, 238.

67 On 28 August, Allende said that he "would not hesitate to resign in a moment if the workers, peasants, technicians, professionals, and the UP would so demand or suggest." See *El Mercurio*, 5 September 1973, and Kaufman, *Crisis*, 318.

men supported Allende, these women arrogated to themselves the right to speak in the name of the nation. They claimed to represent the majority of the population ("we are the people") because they were mothers who "gave birth to every child of this land." They used these dual aspects of their identity to imbue their demand "that Allende fulfill his promise [to resign]" with moral legitimacy. In order to buttress their claim, their ad listed the names of other "groups," such as Mujeres Dueñas de Casa (Housewives), Mujeres Campesinas (Peasant Women), and Mujeres Pobladoras (Neighborhood Women), who supposedly backed the demand for Allende's resignation. Since the list included almost all possible sectors of women in the Chilean population, it is probable that PF and the *gremialistas* who ran the ad created the names of these "groups" to indicate the breadth of opposition to Allende. In fact, it is unlikely that these groups actually existed; the absence of real names suggests that they are nothing more than fictitious creations of the right.[68]

Although the women's departments of the opposition parties supported the demonstration and turned out a sizable percentage of the marchers, the conservative news coverage stressed the marchers' lack of political ties. The opposition media continued to highlight women's actions against Allende because they conveyed the consciously constructed image of a massive, apolitical, and cross-class grouping of Chileans, untainted by ties to the political parties, that wanted to remove Allende from power. One newspaper credited PF with the organization of the protest and commented that "the women who participated in the event lacked any sense of party politics and made no distinction between the parties."[69] In fact, of the three public organizers of the march, only one, Elena Larraín (PF), was an independent; the other two, Raquel Hurtado (PDC) and Carmen Saenz (PN), were leaders in their respective parties. Nevertheless, as had happened so frequently during the previous few years, the protesters claimed that their condition as women elevated them above sectarianism and politics. To exemplify this view, the media quoted one of the participants as saying that "the fatherland is in danger, as is our children's future. The defense of these values has no boundaries."[70]

68 *El Mercurio*, 2 September 1973. The other "groups" that signed the ads were Mujeres Transportistas (female transportation workers or the wives of transportation workers), Mujeres de la Papelera (La Papelera women), Estudiantes (students), Mujeres Comerciantes (businesswomen), Mujeres Secretarías (female secretaries), Mujeres Enfermeras (women nurses), Mujeres Asistentes Sociales (female social workers), and Mujeres Profesionales (professional women).

69 *Ultimas Notícias*, 6 September 1973.

70 Ibid.

Thousands of women turned out for the 5 September march.[71] Stretching for blocks down the main street of Santiago, by most accounts, this anti-Allende women's demonstration was much larger than the March of the Empty Pots and Pans had been. Waving white handkerchiefs—defined as the "symbol of democratic women"—and banging pots and pans, the women chanted, "adiós, que te vaya bien" ("good-bye and farewell"), "que se vaya, que se vaya" ("leave, leave"), and "la única solución, que tome el avion" ("the only solution is for him to take a plane").[72]

An ominous note appeared in at least one of the speeches at the rally. Eduviges Zamora, the wife of a striking truck driver, called on Allende to "return to the path of honesty." If Allende felt himself "incapable . . . because the problems are beyond his authority," Zamora proclaimed, "there is another way. More difficult, perhaps, but more dignified. Don't talk about O'Higgins [Bernardo O'Higgins, the first president of Chile from 1818 until his resignation in 1823] and Balmaceda [president of Chile from 1887 until his suicide in 1891] if you are not morally capable of knowing how to imitate their actions and sacrifices for Chile."[73] When she finished, the crowd began to chant, "Allende, proceda, imite a Balmaceda" ("Allende, go ahead, imitate Balmaceda").[74] Because Balmaceda had committed suicide while he was president of Chile, Zamora's reference and the crowd's enthusiastic chanting had one obvious implication— for these women, Allende's death would be an acceptable outcome to the political impasse then confronting Chile.

In conjunction with the Santiago demonstration, opposition women in the Chilean provinces also expressed their repudiation of the Allende government (see Map 6). These nationwide demonstrations indicate the existence of networks of anti-Allende women throughout Chile. Although the center of the anti-Allende women's movement was in Santiago, members of PF claim that chapters of the group developed throughout the country. María Correa Morandé recalls that women from all parts of Chile contacted them, seeking information about how to form a local branch of PF; others just started them on their own.[75] Although it is not clear how many PF chapters existed in Chile, it is safe to say that the leadership and example provided

71 As always, estimates of attendance varied. The rightist *La Segunda* announced that "hundreds of thousands of women interpreting the national sentiment" attended the event. See *La Segunda*, 6 September 1973.

72 *El Mercurio*, 6 September 1973.

73 *Ultimas Notícias*, 6 September 1973.

74 *El Mercurio*, 6 September 1973.

75 Correa Morandé, interview.

by PF women in Santiago, the kinship ties that existed among conservative women, and the resources of the *gremio* movement and the political parties facilitated the emergence of women's oppositional activity and allowed it to be coordinated nationally.[76] In the southern city of Temuco, thousands of women formed a large chain made of white handkerchiefs and marched through the busy downtown area. Men who "wanted to express the same feeling as the women" joined the procession as a "rearguard" to offer the women protection. In San Felipe, a small agricultural town north of Santiago, three thousand women, "the largest women's demonstration [in San Felipe] on record," marched through the streets. In a comment designed to highlight the violent nature of the UP government, the women claimed that because they were protected by men, "no incidents occurred." In Los Angeles, six hundred women dressed in mourning marched to express their sorrow at "the trampled freedom and the murdered democracy" caused by the UP. PN women in Concepción demonstrated to show their "support for the striking transportation workers and to ask President Salvador Allende to resign."[77] Women in Puerto Montt gathered to protest the UP government and to show their solidarity with the women who had taken over Radio Cooperativa. Echoing the language of the female protesters in Santiago, the women in Puerto Montt identified themselves as "housewives who signed a declaration asking for President Salvador Allende's resignation."[78] In addition, thousands of women in Talca gathered in the Plaza de Armas to express "their support for the striking *gremios* and to repudiate the government's economic policies."[79]

Just as women in Brazil had done prior to the overthrow of Goulart, thousands of Chilean women demonstrated in the days leading up to the coup. They called for an end to the UP government and for military intervention. On 10 September, women from PF, along with wives of military officers, gathered in front of the Ministry of Defense in Santiago and implored the military to overthrow the government. For over two hours they chanted "Fuerzas Armadas al poder" ("Armed Forces, take power") and "Ejército, Marina y Aviación, salva la nación" ("Army, Navy, Air Force, save the nation").[80] In fewer than twenty-four hours, the armed forces fulfilled their wishes.

76 Outside of Santiago, the only PF chapter I have been able to locate was in Rancagua. More research in the provinces could, however, reveal the existence of PF chapters in other cities.

77 *El Mercurio*, 7 September 1973.

78 *La Prensa*, 7 September 1973.

79 *El Mercurio*, 11 September 1973.

80 Ibid.

Map 6 Cities in which anti-Allende women held demonstrations on 5 September 1973

The Coup and Its Aftermath

On the morning of 11 September, naval units in the coastal city of Valparaíso began the revolt. From Valparaíso, the uprising spread to Santiago and, in the next few hours and days, to all of Chile. By the end of the day, Allende was dead and La Moneda bombed. The military had overthrown the UP government, begun the mass arrests of UP supporters (to be followed by widespread torture and killing), and installed itself in power, ushering in seventeen years of a regime based on brutality and death.[81] A wealth of information details this bloody event in Chilean history.[82] This section discusses the response of the anti-Allende women to the coup and the subsequent years of military dictatorship.

The women who had struggled against Allende for the previous three years welcomed the coup with joy and celebration. Grateful women, inhabitants of the upper- and middle-class neighborhoods, applauded the military's overthrow of the UP government, hung the Chilean flag from their windows in a display of patriotism, drank champagne, and ignored or supported the military's systematic use of repression against UP supporters. In their eyes, the armed forces saved Chile from communism and fulfilled their duty to the nation. Nothing else mattered. Far from disassociating themselves from the coup and the abuse of human rights that followed, many anti-Allende women boastfully recount their role in bringing about military intervention.

Elena Larraín claims that she knew "something" was going to happen on 11 September, but she acted as if everything was normal. Early in the morning she went to the PF office and, along with ten other women, joyfully listened to the air force planes flying overhead on their way to bomb La Moneda.[83] Hilda Hernández, a middle-class opponent of Allende, remembers going into the street outside her house in Ñuñoa and drinking champagne with her neighbors. As she remembers it, "everyone was happy. I went out with my sons and flags were flying all over Santiago."

81 My thanks to Camilla Townsend for this formulation.

82 See Samuel Chavkin, *The Murder of Chile: Eyewitness Accounts of the Coup, the Terror, and the Resistance Today* (New York: Everest House, 1982); Davis, *Last Two Years;* John Dinges and Saul Landau, *Assassination on Embassy Row* (New York: Pantheon, 1980); Garreton and Moulian, *Análisis coyuntural;* Federico G. Gil, Ricardo Lagos, Henry A. Landsberger, *Chile 1970–1973: Lecciones de una experiencia* (Madrid: Editorial Tecnos, 1977); MacEoin, *No Peaceful Way;* Moss, *Chile's Marxist Experiment;* Moulian, *La forja;* Dick Parker, *La nueva cara del fascismo* (Santiago: Empresa Editora Nacional Quimantú, 1972), Ian Roxborough, Philip O'Brien, and Jackie Roddick, *Chile: The State and Revolution* (New York: Holmes and Meier, 1977); Arturo Valenzuela, *Breakdown;* Winn, *Weavers.* Two scholars who do discuss women's opposition to the UP government are Kaufman, *Crisis,* and Sigmund, *Overthrow.*

83 Larraín, interview by author, 8 July 1994.

Hernández participated in the March of the Empty Pots and Pans and spent many nights beating an empty pot in her backyard. She insists that "women played the decisive role in encouraging the military to stage the coup. . . . I do not think it was a dicta*dura*, it was a dicta*blanda*."[84] (*Dura* means "hard," and *blanda* means "soft"; Hernández thought that the dictatorship was not as brutal as so many people believe it was.)

Anabela Poblete is married to a high-ranking officer in the Chilean army. A fervent supporter of Pinochet, she believes that women's actions "caused the military to act more rapidly; [however,] in the long term, they would have acted the same way." She makes no apologies for the coup. In fact, she claims that it was "the best thing that could have happened to this country." Like many pro-Pinochet women, she believes that the left was planning a "civil war" and that the military's actions spared Chile the destruction and death that this would have caused. She fervently concludes that "the coup was well worth it, because now we are free."[85]

Silvia Jara, a member of the PDC, also welcomed the coup. She remembers the UP years as a period of chaos and shortages. On repeated occasions she had to walk blocks to find milk and diapers for her infant daughter. Whenever she heard that a certain item was on sale, even one she did not necessarily want or need, she dropped whatever she was doing and ran to stand in line to purchase it. She wanted a coup, she recalls, because she longed for "tranquility, so I could spend more time with my daughter." In 1973, she added, "everyone thought highly of the military. Everyone respected them." Like so many members of the PDC who supported the coup, Jara fully expected the military to rule for a short period of time, restore "order," and then hand power over to Eduardo Frei. According to Jara, "I thought they would only govern six months or so and then there would be a plebiscite and a new government."[86]

84 Hernández, interview.

85 Anabela Poblete Corfo, interview by author, tape recording, Iquique, 5 May 1994. In an attempt to prove such a patently false claim and terrorize those who had opposed the UP, the Junta filled the newspapers with details of the so-called Plan Zeta, which it defined as the left's plans to stage its own coup. Each day the list of people the UP purportedly had planned to kill filled the media. For a description of this farce, see Chavkin, *Storm*, 106–7. For the Junta's version of Plan Zeta, see Fuerzas Armadas de Chile, *Libro blanco del cambio de gobierno en Chile* (Santiago: Editorial Lord Cochrane, 1973). In fact, since the military coup met practically no resistance, the military's actions could more accurately be labeled a massacre than a war. On 30 January 1996, the Chilean Supreme Court formally rejected the military's claims that Chile was on the brink of a civil war in 1973, stating that "it is not possible to maintain that there were dissident armed forces or organized military groups with enough control over part of the national territory so as to allow them to carry out sustained and organized military operations." *La Epoca*, Santiago, 31 January 1996.

86 Silvia Jara, interview by author, tape recording, Santiago, 18 May 1994.

Gabriela Basaez, the middle-class member of both SOL and Patria y Libertad, is "happy to have lived at the time of the coup and to have experienced the events close-up." She is proud to have "asked the military to intervene" and believes that they did so because "we begged them to . . . we demanded that they do it." Far from regretting the military coup (to which she refers as a "military pronouncement"), she praises it because it gave her "security" and "tranquility."[87]

Olga Bran, one of the women who started SOL and was active in it in the 1990s, said the military acted "because we asked them to." Nora Blas, another member, added that "women's participation was very important. We acted with such daring that the men had to support us." She then asked the other SOL women present at the interview, "do you think the men would have acted without us?" Bran and Lucía Maturana, another longtime member of SOL, both emphatically said "No."[88]

The Fate of Poder Femenino After the Coup

Members of PF greeted the coup with joy. In an interview published shortly after the coup, women from the group extolled their work against Allende and praised the military regime, saying, "we have faith in the Junta because it guarantees order, respect, and patriotism. We will collaborate every way we can in the task of reconstruction."[89] Elena Larraín, the leader of Poder Femenino, announced the organization's plans to hold a rally for women on 11 September 1974 to "demonstrate our joy" one year after "the military pronouncement."[90] On the day of the rally, PF published a letter indicating the group's strong support for the military coup. Using language that conveys both the group's vision of women's role and its gratitude for the military's actions, the letter stated that

the Chilean woman, whose suffering, humiliation, and heroism kept Chile's hope for liberty alive during three years of Marxist government, emotionally thanks the Armed Forces who, on the anniversary of our national independence, returned freedom to the fatherland.

The Chilean woman understands that the reconstruction of Chile will require an effort worthy of a disciplined and patriotic people.

87 Basaez, interview.

88 Nora Blas, Olga Bran, and Lucía Maturana, interviews by author, tape recordings, Las Condes, 11 April 1994.

89 *Ultimas Notícias,* 24 September 1973. An anti-Allende journalist, Patricia Guzmán, wrote the article.

90 *El Mercurio,* 25 August 1974.

For this reason, Poder Femenino calls on all Chilean women to demonstrate, once again, their unquenchable spirit of sacrifice and to collaborate with the Armed Forces.[91]

Shortly after this demonstration, PF ceased to exist. According to María Correa Morandé, who is loath to criticize any aspect of the military, the organization "began to fall apart, little by little, all by itself, because [once the military took power] it was no longer necessary. Necessity creates the organization."[92] Elena Larraín remembers PF's end differently, perhaps because the organization was her brainchild. She recollects that the military asked PF to disband, a demand that saddened Larraín and depressed many PF members. Larraín knows that "there was no longer much reason for us to exist, but we would have liked to dissolve the group ourselves. . . . [One day] we were going ahead at two hundred kilometers an hour, [and] then, all of a sudden, we hit a brick wall and we felt like we didn't have anything to do."[93]

Why did the military dissolve Poder Femenino? It could not have doubted the women's support for the coup nor their willingness to participate in the project of national reconstruction. However, PF challenged many of the basic precepts the military held about gender and the role of women in society. It was not a feminist organization, but it operated with a level of independence that the military found unacceptable. Participation in the organization had opened new horizons for women. They undertook bold (and in their minds, even dangerous) activities that were a far cry from their previously sheltered lifestyles.[94]

Involvement in the women's organization changed how women thought of themselves. The women of PF appreciated the role they played in building a civic movement against Allende. In a conversation with María de los Angeles Crummett in 1974, Nellie Gallo, who had been the *gremio* movement's representative to the organization, commented that participation in PF helped her realize her importance as a person. She pointed out that many PF women experienced their work in the group as a kind of liberation. They saw themselves as people with vital roles who no longer needed to be treated like children.[95] The long hours spent at

91 *El Mercurio*, 14 September 1974.

92 Correa Morandé, interview.

93 Larraín, interview by author, 8 July 1994.

94 Armanet, interview.

95 Crummett interviewed Nellie Gallo in Santiago on 19 July 1974.

the PF headquarters discussing politics and debating their plans to carry out anti-Allende actions meant that they spent much less time at home attending to the needs of their husbands and children. Political responsibilities superseded domestic duties, a reality made possible because most of them had maids who could prepare the meals, clean the house, and be there when their children returned home from school.

Victoria Armanet was one of the PN's representatives to Poder Femenino. Although she had been active in the Liberal Party and then the PN, she believes that "my political life began with Allende's victory." Like many other members of Poder Femenino, she spent much of her time at the group's headquarters, completely caught up in PF's activities.

There was always something to do. We got together in the Poder Femenino office at ten in the morning and we never stopped. One day, after September 11th, I came home and I tried to turn on the light. I said to my maid, "Why, there's no light bulb." She said, "There hasn't been one for two years." And all the faucets were leaking! I will confess something to you. [During the Allende years] I was extremely happy. I had a great time. Many people say they suffered. I didn't suffer at all![96]

Whatever the intentions of the parties who supported the development of Poder Femenino or the expectations of the women who participated in it, women's real experiences of public political activity and the power that resulted from successfully organizing against the Allende government provided them with a sense of themselves as political actors that ran counter to the military's understanding of what women's roles should be. According to a member of SOL (which the military did not disband), "SOL still exists because it had nothing to do with power, while Poder Femenino was forced to disband because of the word *power*."[97] Or, as Larraín succinctly stated, "[the idea of] Poder Femenino was just too strong for the military."[98] The military demanded that Poder Femenino cease to exist because it offered women an independent political alternative that clashed with both the armed forces' plans for women and their ideas about gender.

The Military Dictatorship and Women

In an attempt to justify its illegal and brutal seizure of power, the Chilean military repeatedly asserted that it acted because civil society demanded that it overthrow Allende. To give weight to this contention, the armed

96 Armanet, interview, 17 March 1994.

97 Silvia Ripamonte, interview by María de los Angeles Crummett, notes, Santiago, 7 June 1974.

98 Larraín, interview by author, 8 July 1994.

forces continually highlighted the activities conservative women had carried out against the UP government. For example, in his first presidential message following the coup, General Augusto Pinochet extolled Chilean women who "exposed their lives and abandoned the tranquility of their homes to implore the intervention of the uniformed institutions."[99] However, even though the armed forces lauded the courageous actions of the women who fought against the "Marxist government," they made it clear that they had other plans for those women.

The military replaced women's political activity with membership in volunteer organizations headed by wives of military officers.[100] The two most important volunteer organizations—of which there were at least fifty-two in the early 1980s—were CEMA Chile (Mothers' Centers) and the Secretaría Nacional de la Mujer (SNM, National Secretariat of Women).[101] Lucía Hiriart de Pinochet, Pinochet's wife, headed both of these organizations. The volunteer movement served a dual purpose. It provided the military with an unpaid army of women whose charity work would cushion the severity of the military's economic policies, albeit minimally.[102] It harnessed women's energy and activism and used them to promote the military regime and its policies. Reflecting their ties with the military, members of the volunteer movement (the vast majority of whom were middle- and upper-class) wore differently colored uniforms as they spread throughout Chile to bring charity and propaganda to poor women. CEMA set up classes for poor women that taught them hygiene, how to prepare meals in a nutritional and cost-effective way, and how to educate their children to be patriotic and to support the military regime. CEMA offered women some basic artisanal skills, but not the kind of training that would have allowed these women to augment their income significantly. SNM held educational programs in which various officials from

---

99 Augusto Pinochet, "Un año de construcción," *Mensaje presidencial 11 septiembre 1973–11 septiembre 1974* (Santiago: n.p., 1974), 2.

100 See María Elena Valenzuela, *La mujer en el Chile militar: Todas ibamos a ser reinas* (Santiago: CESOC-ACHIP, 1987).

101 For a listing of the fifty-two volunteer organizations and a description of the work they performed, see Lucía Hiriart de Pinochet, *La mujer chilena y su compromiso histórico* (Santiago: Editorial Renacimiento, n.d.).

102 After it seized power, the military privatized the economy, cut subsidies to national industry, and opened the door to foreign imports. These policies resulted in unemployment and underemployment, lower salaries, and a vastly decreased availability of health care, social services, and education for many Chileans. Between 1970 and 1974, wages fell to less than half their value, and unemployment rose as high as 23.9 percent in 1982. For a concise description of the military's economic policies and the impact they had on the Chilean people, see O'Brien and Roddick, *Chile: The Pinochet Decade*, 38–41.

the military regime instructed the women about the policies and ideology of the government.[103]

The military supported a rigid gender hierarchy that reflected its views of social relations in general.[104] It believed that a woman's fundamental duty was to be a mother and homemaker. Women were central to the plans of the military government, because "the formation of the generations of tomorrow is in the hands of the mothers of today."[105] Although this vision of womanhood paralleled that proclaimed by the women who opposed Allende, the armed forces put it to use for a different end. The anti-Allende women used motherhood to leave their homes and to protest publicly against the UP government. The military used motherhood to push women back into their houses and to remove them from politics.

Conclusion

The March 1973 election proved that Allende could not be voted out of power. The pro-coup forces within the opposition knew that they had to convince the military to intervene and "save the nation," to remove or neutralize those sectors of the military that opposed a coup, and to build a public climate that favored Allende's overthrow. Women helped achieve these goals by humiliating and insulting General Prats in public and invading the privacy of his home. Lacking the support of most of his generals—many of whose wives joined the 21 August demonstration outside his home—Prats resigned as commander in chief of the military. With Prats gone, and Pinochet as his replacement, no officer in the army had the power or the will to put an end to the anti-Allende conspiracy that by then had permeated the officer corps.

In order to encourage the military to take action, the anti-Allende women questioned their masculinity. They threw corn and feathers at them to suggest that they were chickens, and therefore "sissies," not real men. The women wanted to humiliate them in their own eyes and in those of the men who surrounded them. And how could the soldiers reassert their gender identity and prove that they were men? The opposition

103 For a discussion of these organizations and their work among poor women, see Valdés and Weinstein, *Mujeres que sueñan*. Also see Margaret Power, "Defending Dictatorship: Conservative Women in Pinochet's Chile and the 1988 Plebiscite," in *Radical Women in Latin America*, ed. González and Kampwirth.

104 For an excellent analysis of the armed forces' attitude toward society as expressed through the language they used, see Giselle Munizaga, *El discurso público de Pinochet: Un análisis semiológico* (Buenos Aires: CLACSO, 1983).

105 Augusto Pinochet, "La Junta de Gobierno se dirige a las mujeres de Chile," in *Las mujeres y la dictadura militar en Chile*, by Teresa Valdés, Appendix I (Santiago: FLACSO, 1987), 22–23.

women offered a single answer: they could do so by resorting to violence, by overthrowing the elected president.

The anti-Allende women convinced a number of civilians that military intervention was the only solution to the economic crisis and political chaos in Chile. Some women, many of them Christian Democrats like Silvia Jara, naively believed that the military would take power, put things in order, and then call for elections in six months or a year.[106] Others, such as those from the PN, the *gremio* movement, and PF, cherished no such illusions or desires. Democracy had not provided them with the security and stability they longed for, and they were more than ready to embrace a military government on a long-term basis.

Above all, the anti-Allende women offered the military a facade of legitimacy. Unlike the other military dictatorships that came to power in the 1970s in the Southern Cone, only the Chilean one ever attempted to justify its rule with references to mass support. The military celebrated National Women's Day annually on 2 December in remembrance of the 1971 March of the Empty Pots and Pans against the Allende government. According to an editorial in the pro-government daily, *La Nación*, the military instituted *National* Women's Day (not *International* Women's Day) in 1976 because "women fought with strength against the Marxist government and demanded that the Armed Forces intervene in order to regain Chile's freedom."[107]

Despite his effusive praise for the conservative women who helped smooth the military's path to power, Pinochet disbanded Poder Femenino. He had no intention of allowing any independent organization to exist that could challenge his plans—and certainly not a women's group with the word "power" in its name. Instead, the military mobilized tens of thousands of women to participate in the massive volunteer movement under the leadership of the wives of military officers. To this day, most of these women retain a profound loyalty and sense of gratitude to the armed forces. When Pinochet was arrested in London, England, in October 1998, women were his most ardent supporters, the most visible sign of the fervent admiration that he continues to evoke in so many conservative women in Chile.

106 Most leaders of the PDC, including Eduardo Frei, held this view. In fact, except for a handful of PDC leaders, most of the top officials of the PDC welcomed the coup. See Pamela Constable and Arturo Valenzuela, *A Nation of Enemies: Chile Under Pinochet* (New York: W. W. Norton, 1991), 281.

107 *La Nación*, Santiago, 5 December 1984. The military and conservative women also wanted to supplant the traditional celebration of International Women's Day on 8 March because of the strong links that existed between it and the left.

Conclusion

CLOSE TO TWENTY-SEVEN years have passed since the Chilean military overthrew the democratically elected government of Salvador Allende. As I write these words, a picture in the *Chicago Tribune* shows "supporters of former Chilean strongman Augusto Pinochet demonstrat[ing] outside the Supreme Court in Santiago."[1] In the picture, five women are yelling and holding multiple posters of Pinochet, one with the title, "The Liberator of Chile." Two of them have their left arms extended to emphasize their anger that Pinochet may have to stand trial for crimes committed during his seventeen-year rule. Conservative women have rallied around Pinochet and the armed forces for nearly three decades. Despite the wrenching testimony about the human rights abuses committed by the military under Pinochet's command, these rightist women continue to adore the man who, in their eyes, saved Chile from the communists.

This book examines why a significant number of Chilean women opposed the UP government and actively implored the armed forces to overthrow it. It explores how and why rightist women, in conjunction with Christian Democratic and *gremio* women, built Poder Femenino and the anti-Allende women's movement. Using motherhood and nationalism as their *leitmotiv*, they mobilized large numbers of previously inactive women to participate in antigovernment street protests and to cast their ballots for the opposition. They convinced many women that only the violent overthrow of the elected government and the installation of a military regime could guarantee them the stability and security they needed to fulfill their roles as wives and mothers. Most rightist women applauded the establishment of the brutal Pinochet dictatorship and subsequently rallied around it as it arrested, tortured, and killed tens of thousands of their compatriots for over seventeen years.

Part of the explanation for why so many women opposed the Allende government lies in the historical relationship that developed between women and the right during the twentieth century. Many women, particularly but not exclusively elite ones, identified strongly with the principles and programs of the rightist parties. Because Christianity was the fundamental

1 *Chicago Tribune*, 26 July 2000.

spiritual force that guided many women's lives, they allied themselves with the Conservative Party, which embodied many of the beliefs and teachings of the Catholic Church. The Conservative Party, cognizant of the fact that female suffrage meant increased votes for it, was also the first party to propose a law granting women the right to vote.

Another reason why many women identified with the right is because it appealed to women as wives and mothers. Instead of minimizing women's role within society, the right exalted women's position within the family and pledged to pursue policies that would enhance it. Rightist women, in turn, embraced the Conservative and Liberal parties and became ardent spokeswomen and campaigners for them. The visibility of right-wing female activists both offered women role models with whom they could identify and encouraged the parties to develop programs that met the specific needs of women.

Political expediency played a large part in the development of the right's sensitivity toward women. The right understood that it needed to develop a base beyond the elite (a minority) and accurately deduced that women (the majority) represented their most likely source of support. The 1958 presidential elections provided the right with clear evidence of the importance of women's votes. The plurality of women voted for Jorge Alessandri, the most conservative candidate, and made his victory possible.

The decade of the 1960s was a transformative one in Chile—as indeed it was in much of the world. The push to democratize society, combined with the growing strength of the left, threatened the right and the political elite whose interests it represented. In response, the right first abandoned its candidate in the 1964 elections (endorsing Christian Democrat Eduardo Frei) and then, in 1966, dissolved the Liberal and Conservative parties, forming the National Party. While the first choice reflected the right's defensive recognition of its own weakness, the second corresponded to the right's willingness to take the offensive. Although these two actions constitute different tactical choices, they are consistent with the right's strategic goal: to prevent the left, "the communists," from coming to power in Chile. Despite these changes, the right continued to prioritize women, because it recognized that they offered a sure, substantial, and necessary foundation upon which it could rely.

In 1964, Salvador Allende stood a very good chance of winning the presidential elections. The Scare Campaign was central to the Frei campaign's plans to defeat him. This crusade, designed in part by members of U.S. ad agencies, funded by the CIA, and implemented by Chileans, used established ideas about gender to attack the increasingly popular left. It represented the first concerted effort by the right and the Christian Democrats to scare women and men into voting against Salvador Allende through an appeal to their gendered identities. The campaign relied on a direct, visceral message. It said to women that if Allende won, the government would take and indoctrinate their children, destroy their families, and deprive them of the opportunity to be mothers. It told men that a socialist government threatened their jobs and their capacity to maintain and protect their families. Although it has been impossible to calculate the precise impact the campaign had on people's consciousness, activists across the political spectrum agree that it generated increased support for the Christian Democrats in the presidential elections. By associating the left with the destruction of the family and women's and men's primary social functions within it, it also personalized and engendered anticommunism in an intimate fashion.

The Scare Campaign also reveals that the U.S. government understood the importance of using gendered propaganda to influence people's political beliefs. It shows that Washington specifically attempted to convince women that if Allende won, his government would destroy their families. The U.S. government had been involved in two previous operations that associated communism with attacks on the family and motherhood: Operation Pedro Pan in Cuba and the mobilization of women against President João Goulart in Brazil. This book argues that U.S. foreign policy experts learned significant lessons from both projects and applied them to Chile during the 1964 and 1970 presidential campaigns and against the UP government as well.

Acción Mujeres de Chile promoted anticommunism among women and contributed to Allende's defeat in 1964. Founded in 1963, it encouraged women to become active in the struggle against communism and offered them a vehicle to express their fear and hatred of it. It was in Acción Mujeres de Chile that Elena Larraín began her career as a superb promoter of anticommunism among women. She participated in the Scare Campaign, made sure that three radio stations played the damaging tape of Juana Castro denouncing communism, sustained Acción Mujeres de Chile through the 1970 presidential elections, and founded PF in 1972. As a leader of these anticommunist women's groups, she embodies the continuity that existed between the two organizations.

The Frei presidency capitalized on the massive outpouring of enthusiasm with which women greeted his candidacy by developing the Mothers' Centers in poor neighborhoods throughout Chile. The centers organized women and drew them closer to the party; they were so successful that at the end of Frei's term, roughly 450,000 women belonged to them, more women than had previously joined any secular organization.[2] They reinforced the idea that motherhood defined women's social and political activity, and by allowing women to develop a sense of themselves and of other women independent of their families, the Mothers' Centers developed a network of women with ties to the Christian Democratic Party and created political links between middle-class women who were party members and poor women in the sprawling urban neighborhoods or neglected rural corners of Chile. Because many women involved in the centers viewed themselves as social actors and developed a political identity, the Mothers' Centers became sites of intense political conflicts between the opposition and pro-UP forces during the Allende government. UP supporters attempted to gain leadership in them, but the PDC retained control of many of the centers. When the PDC joined the movement against Allende, a significant number of women adopted its antigovernment politics and participated in its activities.

Allende's victory on 4 September 1970 confused and disoriented the right and the Christian Democrats. It took the united efforts of women from the PN, the PDC, and independents to overcome this paralysis through their organization of the December 1971 March of the Empty Pots and Pans. The unexpected success of the march encouraged the women who participated in it—and the opposition parties that supported it—to prioritize the organization of women against the UP government. Poder Femenino formed early in 1972 in order to coordinate this work.

PF greatly facilitated the mobilization of women against the UP government. PF was important not because of its size (no more than twenty to forty activists were members of the coordinating council during its existence, which was less than a year and a half), but because of the impact it had on a significant number of women. The organization encouraged women to be active without linking them to any party. The group's self-definition as a nonpartisan women's organization allowed its members to define themselves simply as Chilean women. This identity enabled the group to issue inclusive appeals to all women to join it in saving their families and the nation as a whole from "communism." The upper- and middle-class women of PF, who had rarely thought of poor women except as objects of charity or as maids, now (rhetorically) embraced them as partners in the struggle.

From the March of the Empty Pots and Pans onward, Chilean women became the opposition's preferred symbol of protest against the UP government. The choice was cleverly strategic, as it allowed the right to

2 Aylwin et al., *Percepción del rol político de la mujer*, 38.

simultaneously declare that Allende's female opponents were apolitical, therefore pure; spontaneous, therefore genuine; victims, therefore innocent; and courageous, therefore heroines. Since politics in Chile was considered a masculine affair, the women who protested the UP government could define their activity as "apolitical" and identify themselves as "independents" or as "housewives." Even as they marched in the streets to protest the UP government, they refused to recognize, at least publicly, that they were carrying out political activity. Instead, they defined themselves as mothers and wives who protested because the UP government jeopardized their ability to take care of their families. This refusal to admit that they were being political permitted them to define their involvement as a natural extension of their role as mothers and wives, categories that embraced almost all women. This, in turn, allowed the right-wing women to appeal to all Chilean women, regardless of class, to reject the Allende government and to join what they claimed was *the* appropriate feminine response to the UP.

Even as these women denied the importance of class, they actively sought to organize a cross-class movement. They supported workers' struggles in La Papelera and El Teniente against the "government of the working class," and they took advantage of the shortages that increasingly hit the Chilean consumer to organize poor women against the UP. The shortages affected women most seriously, because they threatened or denied them the ability to fulfill their primary roles as mothers and wives. Anti-Allende female activists played on women's anger at the shortages, their frustration with standing in lines, and their growing desperation with the overall situation to foment antigovernment feelings.

The March 1973 elections exposed two significant facts: 60 percent of women, the majority, opposed the UP government, and the opposition did not obtain sufficient votes to impeach Allende. As a result, anti-Allende women accelerated their efforts to create pro-coup sentiments among the population, and the opposition realized that only military intervention would secure Allende's removal from office. In order to accomplish both goals, many opposition women petitioned, demonstrated, and took over radio stations between March and September 1973 to demand an end to the Allende government. They harassed General Carlos Prats until he resigned as commander in chief, thus clearing the way for the appointment of General Augusto Pinochet to this pivotal position. They ridiculed and shamed the military, telling them that it was their duty as men and members of the armed forces to overthrow Allende. (Their reluctance to do so, according to the opposition women, revealed that they were not real men, since real men serve and protect women.) These women welcomed the coup, praised the military for its courage, and celebrated the death of democracy and of thousands of their fellow Chileans.

Political activism radicalized the women who opposed the UP government. In 1970, only a few women, mainly from the PN, believed that Allende's victory indicated the need to violate Chilean electoral traditions. By 1973, tens of thousands of women marched in the streets and demonstrated, calling on the armed forces to overthrow the government. Much of the literature on women and political activism has focused on how activism affects progressive or leftist women. This study illustrates that political involvement—demonstrations, confrontations with the police, group membership, and the sense of belonging to a larger movement—also affects conservative women.[3] Prior to launching their anti-Allende crusade, few (if any) of these women had been teargassed, fought with the police, or shouted profanities at people with whom they disagreed politically. Such experiences changed these women's relationship to the state. The upper- and middle-class women ceased to see themselves as members of protected classes and no longer felt allegiance to a system that failed to sustain their privileged position in society. They ceased to support democracy, because it allowed anticapitalist forces to come to power. Women of all classes lost respect for the government that they held responsible for the disorder, shortages, and insecurity they faced. As a result, they engaged in ever more radical actions against it. Once their adherence to democracy waned, it was but a short step to calling on the military to intervene and overthrow Allende.

Although political activity affected these women's relationship to the state, it did not seem to have changed their ideas about gender substantially. These women did not struggle to alter either their condition or identity as women; they fought to maintain both. Their rhetoric reinforced fundamental assumptions about their roles as mothers and wives. They viewed their political work as both a reaffirmation of motherhood and a temporary aberration, one demanded by the conditions that existed during the Allende years. Although these women engaged in radical political activity and defied strictures on proper female behavior to do so, they

3 The literature on women and progressive struggles is vast. For some examples of it, see Sara Evans, *Personal Politics: The Roots of Women's Liberation in the Civil Rights Movement and the New Left* (New York: Knopf, 1979); Jo Fisher, *Out of the Shadows: Women, Resistance, and Politics in South America* (London: Latin American Bureau, 1993); Jane S. Jaquette, ed., *The Women's Movement in Latin America: Feminism and the Transition to Democracy* (Boston: Unwin Hyman, 1989); Peteet, "Icons and Militants"; Amy Swerdlow, *Women Strike for Peace: Traditional Motherhood and Radical Politics in the 1960s* (Chicago: University of Chicago Press, 1993).

were not feminists. They did not define male domination as a problem, and indeed, they fought to preserve gender relations.

The women who led or participated in the anti-Allende women's movement were not dupes of men or the political parties; they were not unwilling activists. In fact, many of them were self-confident women who participated in political action in pursuit of their own interests. If one ignores their ideology and examines their forms of organization, their willingness to engage in radical activity, and their championing of women's role in the struggle, then one will find many similarities between these right-wing women and groups of women who engage in feminist politics.[4] PF had a rotating chair to make sure that all women participated equally in running meetings. *Eva*, the women's magazine, counseled women to be physically fit and to learn self-defense—not in order to attract a man but to contribute to the struggle more effectively.[5] Many of the women spoke of how their determination to get rid of Allende gave them courage and allowed them to confront his supporters (even physically, on occasion). Still, these women rejected feminism, and they defined the socialist government—not men or patriarchal structures—as their oppressor.

They rejected feminism because they did not see the need for it. The right confirmed their beliefs about gender: for them, motherhood was the defining aspect of their identity, and they drew affirmation, self-respect, satisfaction, and joy from it. They wanted men to provide for them and their children, protect them, and take care of them.

Fernanda Otero, a member of the more moderate right party Renovación Nacional (National Renewal), articulates many right-wing women's attitudes toward feminism and femininity. As a teenager during the Allende years, Otero went door-to-door to collect cups of sugar for the striking truckers in October 1972 and August 1973. When I interviewed her in 1993, she was a journalist, wife, and mother of five children.[6] Otero vehemently rejected feminism and charged that the "feminist movements that struggle behind this utopian banner [that men and women are the same and equal] cause great damage first to women and then to society in general." She believed that women were essentially

4 For an analysis of one such group in the United States, see Margaret Strobel, "Consciousness and Action: Historical Agency in the Chicago Women's Liberation Union," in *Provoking Agents: Gender and Agency in Theory and Practice*, ed. Judith Kegan Gardiner (Urbana: University of Illinois Press, 1995).

5 *Eva*, 1 December 1972.

6 Fernanda Otero, interview by author, tape recording, Las Condes, 15 October 1993.

feminine and that it was both pointless and dangerous to deny their true nature. As she noted, "observing the physiological characteristics [of a woman] allows us to conclude that maternity is a woman's most out-standing trait. Her body is designed to give life, to protect it, to feed it, to take care of it." Far from questioning such an essentialist view about women, Otero embraced it and criticized feminist movements that have "not respected feminine dignity."[7]

Although Otero's ideas about gender were her own, seventeen years of life under a military dictatorship certainly influenced them. The military regime worked very hard to reinforce a patriarchal view of gender rela-tions.[8] After the coup, the armed forces said to their conservative female supporters (and I paraphrase), "We have taken control. You are safe. You can go back home now. The Chilean cavalry has come to your rescue." The military dissolved PF and channeled what had been women's semi-independent political activity into volunteer organizations controlled by the military and led by Lucía Hiriart, the wife of dictator Augusto Pinochet.[9] With ideological guidance from Jaime Guzmán and other con-servative forces, the dictatorship preached that the patriarchal family was the essential element of social organization.[10] Combining defense of the family with its overall efforts to restore law and order, the Chilean mili-tary equated feminism with an attack on Western Christian civilization and pledged to defeat the former and uphold the latter. Most of the con-servative anti-Allende women accepted these declarations and complied with this policy either because they agreed with them or because they realized that opposition to the armed forces was counterproductive. Although some of these women probably resented the armed forces' pri-mary reliance on male politicians and officers to direct the government (and the exclusion of women from positions of political power), to have raised criticisms of gender relations would have signified a rejection of the military's social policies. This was not something these women were will-ing to do.

7 Fernanda Otero, "Tras los pasos de la identidad femenina," *Veintiuno* 2, no. 6 (June 1992). For the expression of similar ideas by a conservative American woman, see Katherine Kersten, "What Do Women Want? A Conservative Feminist Manifesto," *Policy Review* (March 1991).

8 On women and the military, see María Elena Valenzuela, *La mujer en el Chile militar*, and Munizaga, *El discurso público*.

9 On the volunteer movement, see Margaret Power, "Defending Dictatorship."

10 Jaime Guzmán contributed many of the ideas contained in the 1980 Constitution, a document that also reflects the military's thinking on these matters. Article 1 of the Constitution reads, "The family is the fundamental cell of society." See *Constitución política de la República de Chile 1980* (Santiago: Editorial Andrés Bello, 1993), 10.

Rightist women's acceptance of conservative ideas about gender relations did not prevent them, however, from criticizing male behavior, which they had characterized as passive. Men's passivity, which the rightist women connected to men's immersion in the political system, justified their own activity. Their criticism did more than legitimize women's unprecedented involvement in politics; it also prepared the way for the military's seizure of power. Because politics and political parties were so closely associated with men, rightist women's repeated critique of men and of male political leaders actually served to undermine the entire political system. It bolstered the idea that forces outside the parties needed to rescue Chile from the morass into which their self-interested struggles for power had plunged it. Far from altering male-female relations, women's critique of men during the UP years served to justify the military's usurpation of power, legitimize its suspension of the political parties, and support its enforcement of patriarchal social relations.

The elite women who led the movement lived in a world structured by class. Even though they used women's identities as mothers and wives to build a cross-class movement of women in opposition to the government, they never shed their class-based reality (not that they wanted to!). After the March of the Empty Pots and Pans, several of the wealthy marchers remarked that they could not wait to get home and take a hot bath—a luxury not available to the majority of the population, many of whom lacked indoor plumbing, let alone hot water. They organized their demonstrations by telephone, at a time when most poor and working-class houses lacked phones. When I questioned them as to how they communicated with the poor women without telephones, several of the elite activists blithely replied that they sent their maids into the *poblaciones* (poor neighborhoods) with messages and concealed leaflets. To mobilize themselves, the elite women had cars or could afford taxis. Poor women had to depend on public transportation. While the upper-class female informants easily remembered the names of the upper- and middle-class women with whom they had organized, and supplied me with their phone numbers following a quick glance at their address books, none of them could ever recall the names of any of the poor women with whom they had worked.

When I interviewed these women and men, the knowledge that the armed forces had abused their fellow citizens during the military regime was widespread and public. In 1991, the National Commission of Truth and Reconciliation released the Rettig Report, which documented the military government's imprisonment, torture, and murder of 2,279

Chileans during its seventeen years of dictatorial rule.[11] Yet, with one exception, none of the right-wing women I interviewed expressed any remorse whatsoever for the flagrant abuse of human rights committed by the Chilean military.[12] Some of them denied that it ever took place. In fact, they claimed, the stories of imprisonment, torture, executions, and disappearances were lies invented by the international communist-run media to undermine the military government. The women who did acknowledge that people died during the dictatorship resolutely affirmed that they were killed in battles with the military in a vain attempt to uphold the myth that there had been a civil war in Chile. A few women justified the killings and disappearances and treated them as a military necessity, demanded by the severity of the "communist threat." Maruja Navarro, an upper-middle-class woman and member of the Independent Democratic Union, worked with Poder Femenino during the Allende years. She both denies that the military killed people and regrets that it did not kill more. After the coup, she remembers, "I went out in the streets and looked. There were not any dead people. They arrested a few people and held them in the Estadio Nacional, but it was only to determine which parties they had been involved in." She thinks that "Pinochet was too soft. Many of us think he should have killed more people. If he had, we would not have to go through what we are suffering today."[13] Another woman, a working-class member of Renovación Nacional, commented to me that Pinochet's one mistake was that he did not follow the example of General Ibáñez, the military ruler who governed Chile in the 1920s and 1930s and again in the 1950s. According to her, Ibáñez rounded up all the "homosexuals" and dropped them from planes deep into the ocean, thus removing both the "problem" and the "evidence."[14] "Unfortunately," she added, "Pinochet, *mi general*, did not do that and now people are uncovering the mass graves where the military had buried

11 See Ministerio Secretaría General de Gobierno, *Informe Rettig* (Santiago: 1991). These are conservative numbers. Other estimates place the number of Chileans imprisoned, tortured, disappeared, and killed at close to 100,000.

12 The sole dissenter prefers to remain anonymous.

13 Maruja Navarro, interview. I interviewed her two months after Pinochet was arrested in London on charges of terrorism, genocide, and murder. She refers to the anguish many women felt at seeing their adored leader held under house arrest.

14 A play about Ibáñez's persecution of homosexuals opened in Santiago in February 2001. Andres Pérez wrote the play in 1976. He waited twenty-five years to debut it until the climate was "more propitious for plays with gay themes" and because he believed that "it would evoke a more thoughtful and broader response in light of the current dialogue about the disappeared." *Santiago Times*, 7 February 2001.

the disappeared." She bemoaned this discovery only because it revealed the incontrovertible truth that the Chilean armed forces did indeed torture and murder their opponents.[15]

Testimony like theirs reveals a tragic truth: a large number of Chilean women mobilized to support the violent repression of democracy by the armed forces. Far from being dupes of men, these women willingly embraced ideas and movements that resulted in the overthrow of the UP government, sustained the military dictatorship, and reinforced women's subordination.

15 Sara Geraldo, interview by author, notes, Valparaíso, 2 December 1993.

Epilogue

ON 16 OCTOBER 1998, Scotland Yard arrested General Augusto Pinochet in London as he was recuperating from back surgery. They acted in response to an extradition request from Spanish judge Baltasar Garzón, who sought to try Pinochet in Spain on the charges of murder, terrorism, and genocide. The unanticipated arrest startled and thrilled many people around the world who had believed that impunity would prevail and that the dictator who had ruled Chile for seventeen years would go to his grave untried and unpunished. Pinochet's supporters, on the other hand, responded with outrage and anger and worked fervently to secure his release. The general's admirers, including members of two rightist parties—the Independent Democratic Union and Renovación Nacional (RN, National Renewal)—as well as the Pinochet Foundation and independents, attributed Pinochet's detention to the machinations of the "international socialist conspiracy," which, they claimed, was determined to seek vengeance on the man who had saved Chile from the "communists."

Certainly, blaming the international socialist movement for the detention of Pinochet reflected the right's recognition that cries of "international communist conspiracy" would ring fairly hollow following the demise of the Soviet Union. But in addition, the charge that the international socialist movement was responsible for Pinochet's arrest was key to the right's defense of the general. The right attempted to seize the moral and patriotic high ground and build opposition to Pinochet's detention on the grounds that his arrest in England violated Chile's national sovereignty. In addition, the right hoped to undermine the candidacy of Ricardo Lagos, a Socialist, in the upcoming 1999 presidential elections by linking him with foreign intervention in Chile's domestic affairs.

The Chilean right mobilized its vast array of resources and personalities to secure Pinochet's release and to create the image of a nation that rallied around its beloved leader. It pressured the Concertación government to prevent Pinochet's extradition to Spain. Leaders and members of Congress from the rightist parties, along with other supporters, traveled to London to demonstrate publicly their loyalty to the general. As it had done during the Allende years, the right also mobilized its rank and file to take to the streets of Santiago. The British and Spanish embassies, located in the wealthy neighborhood of Las Condes, became a favorite target of their protests.

Right-wing women sprang into action in defense of the general they cherished. María Angelica Cristi, an RN deputy, traveled to London to extend her support to Pinochet. Women dominated the street demonstrations that took place in Santiago. They congregated frequently at the metro stop located near the Spanish and British embassies and exhorted Chileans to protest Pinochet's arrest. Women who attended these demonstrations frequently wore T-shirts or buttons that said, "Yo amo Pinochet" ("I love Pinochet"). They compared him to Bernardo O'Higgins, Chile's nineteenth-century hero of the struggle for independence.

Many women wore yellow ribbons to convey the idea that Pinochet was an "illegally seized hostage."[1] In the 1970s, Maruja Navarro had organized against the Popular Unity government. During the Pinochet dictatorship, she worked in the volunteer movement directed by Lucía Hiriart, Pinochet's wife. When I spoke with her in 1998, she asked, "Haven't you noticed that our women are wearing this yellow ribbon? When he [Pinochet] returns, we will all welcome him back with our yellow ribbons."[2] Resurrecting the central symbol of the anti-Allende struggle, women in the upper-class neighborhoods also began beating pots and pans again, as they had done when Popular Unity was in power.

The years have not dampened Elena Larraín's hatred for the left or her belief in the need for organization. Following Pinochet's arrest, she formed, along with her old friend Eduardo Boetsch (the founder of Chile Libre) the Comité por el Honor y la Dignidad de Chile (Committee for the Honor and Dignity of Chile). The group's goal was to "bring [back] our General, our hero, Senator Pinochet, and to begin a second 11 September."[3] Their wish was only partially granted. Pinochet did not stand trial in Spain. On 2 March 2000, Jack Straw announced that extradition proceedings against Pinochet had been dropped "because he is medically unfit to stand trial."[4] However, the military did not seize power and the electoral process continued to function.

1 In the 1980s, many North Americans used yellow ribbons in a similar fashion after Iranians had seized the U.S. embassy in Tehran and held the North Americans they captured there as hostages.

2 Maruja Navarro, interview. When Pinochet returned to Chile in March 2000, women did not welcome him with yellow ribbons.

3 *La Nación*, 30 December 1998. The date refers to the coup on 11 September 1973 that overthrew the Popular Unity government.

4 *Santiago Times*, 2 March 2000.

The 1999/2000 Presidential Elections

On 16 January 2000, the Chilean people elected Ricardo Lagos as their president.[5] He owed his victory to the votes of men, not those of women. The majority of women voted for Joaquín Lavín, the candidate of the right.

In this election, as in previous ones, the rightist candidate appealed to women because he spoke directly to their primary concerns and promised that he would solve their most urgent problems. Although Lavín was a member of both the UDI and the conservative and elitist Catholic organization, Opus Dei, he projected himself as a "down-home kind of guy" who understood the conditions of poor people and cared about women. He adopted a folksy style that included spending the night in the homes of poor people throughout Chile and wearing informal clothing. He pledged to create a million new jobs and protect the rights of workers. He spoke directly to the fear that many women felt at the growing incidence of crime and personal assault. Making an end to "delinquency" his second programmatic point, he proclaimed that his government would "end the delinquent's party."[6]

Recognizing the importance of the female vote, Lavín dedicated one section of his program to women. He stressed the need to make it easier for women to work and maintain a family. To do so, he said, his administration would set up a program to help "lower-income women leave their children in the care of a neighbor." (He did not support the establishment of government-financed or sponsored day-care centers.) He encouraged women to work part-time, out of their homes. Instead of critiquing men's physical abuse of women, he said that his government would initiate educational programs "to prevent intrafamily violence."[7]

5 In order to be elected president in Chile, a candidate has to receive the majority of the votes. Six candidates ran in the December 1999 elections, and none of them received the majority. As a result, a second round of voting was held on 16 January 2000 in which the two candidates were Joaquín Lavín and Ricardo Lagos.

6 This demand harkens back to the 1970 Scare Campaign, which accused both Allende and the Christian Democrats of not being tough enough with criminals and unable to defend either the safety of the individual or private property. Lavín blamed the rise in crime on the Concertación governments, which, he said, had "been soft on crime for the last ten years." He further claimed that "delinquency is the root cause of unequal opportunity, since it affects the poorest people most strongly." In order to combat this problem, the government must use both hands: "a firm hand to sanction effectively the delinquents and a soft hand to prevent and rehabilitate [criminals], especially young ones." See Lavín, *Programa del cambio: El programa del gobierno* (Santiago: n.p., 1999), 5–10, 12–13.

7 Ibid., 43–46.

Lavín consistently projected himself as a family man, a loving husband, and a good father. He frequently campaigned with his wife, María Estela León. Many of his campaign materials featured pictures of him surrounded by his smiling wife and seven children. Both graphically and programmatically, Lavín strove to portray himself both as a responsible man whom heterosexual men could emulate and heterosexual women would appreciate.

His strategy paid off. In both the first and second round of voting, more women voted for Lavín than for Lagos. In December 1999, 50.6 percent of women voted for Lavín, while only 45.5 percent did for Lagos. By way of contrast, 50.9 percent of men voted for Lagos and only 44.1 percent chose Lavín.[8] Although Lagos managed to improve his standing among women for the second round (he received 48.7 percent of their vote), 51.4 percent still voted for Lavín. As had been true in December, the majority of men, 54.3 percent, voted for Lagos, while 45.7 percent cast their ballots for Lavín.

I asked girls and women why they supported Lavín. One enthusiastic thirteen-year-old who actively campaigned for Lavín said, "he is the ideal man, the ideal husband, a good father and a good man." She added, "he will bring the changes to Chile that we need."[9] A sixty-four-year-old woman who remembers the Allende government as a time of lines and shortages voted for Lavín because "he is a young man [and] he has new ideas." She believed that women vote for him because "women are more open than men. Women talk with each other, we discuss ideas; men do not. They are closed. They decide something and that's it." She added that Lavín "will raise salaries, [improve] the schools, and help old people as well."[10] One forty-five-year-old housewife voted for Lavín because he will "improve medical care. [To get into a clinic] we have to wait in line starting at six in the morning. [He will also] raise the salaries and make sure people have work. Everyone here is unemployed."[11]

Just as in the 1960s and 1970s, the right invested more heavily in developing a program that spoke to women than the left did. The fact that the majority of women voted for Lavín in the first round jolted the Lagos campaign, which then had to scramble to catch up with the right and try to win women's vote. To do so, it adopted a mixed message that both relied on traditional ideas of gender and took into account the changing

8 *New York Times*, 12 January 2000.

9 Pamela Olivares, interview by author, tape recording, Las Condes, 15 January 2000.

10 Anonymous, interview by author, La Florida, 16 January 2000.

11 Anonymous, interview by author, La Florida, 16 January 2000.

reality and expectations of women. Lagos appointed the popular Soledad Alvear, a Christian Democrat with close ties to the Catholic Church, as his campaign manager. New campaign posters featured the normally outspoken Luisa Durán, Lagos's wife, leaning her head on her husband's shoulder, indicating dependency and, perhaps, submission.

The campaign materials that purportedly spoke to women's specific needs and demands appear to have been assembled hastily and reveal a limited awareness of women's gendered reality. For example, one handbill was distributed widely in the Santiago metropolitan area a few days prior to the elections. One side of the leaflet reads, "Woman, Do Not Forget," and lists the accomplishments of the Concertación government. The other side reads, "Woman, Demand," and lists six demands for women. Of the seven accomplishments, only one relates exclusively to women. It refers to the legislation passed by the Concertación government that "eliminates the pregnancy test in work and [supports] the protection and training of female workers." Another one mentions the passage of a law "against intrafamily violence and sexual crimes." The other five accomplishments are equally applicable to both women and men. One, for example, testifies to the government's "support for artistic creation," while another points out that the government has "prohibited arrest on [charges] of suspicion alone." Of the six demands, again, only one— "equal pay for equal work"—appears specifically relevant to women. The other demands include "dignified work for young people" and "opportunities for young people; children without drugs."[12] Of course, the latter two speak to women as mothers concerned with the well-being and future of their children. This material reveals insufficient attention, though, to the development of a thoughtful program for women. It is sadly reminiscent of the practice of the Popular Unity coalition, which failed to devise a strategy that successfully dealt with the realities and aspirations of Chilean women.

---

12 The quotations are taken from a quarter-page-sized handbill that I found on 14 January 2000 on the streets of Puente Alto.

Appendix A

List of Informants

NAME	CLASS	AFFILIATION	POSITION IN MOVEMENT OR PARTY	OCCUPATION
Carmen Gloria Aguayo	Upper	MAPU	Leader	UP activist; leader, National Secretariat of Women
Silvia Alessandri	Upper	PN/ independent	Member	PN deputy
Rubi Alvarez	Lower	RN	Neighborhood leader	Housewife
Victoria Armanet	Upper	PN; Poder Femenino	Leader; leader	Housewife; political activist
Cristina Arraya	Upper	RN	Sympathizer	Administrator
Fresia Aymans	Lower/ middle	RN	Member	Social worker
Mireya Baltra	Lower/ middle	PC	Leader	Political activist
Juanita Barrientos	Lower	Independent right	None	Housewife
Gabriela Basaez	Lower/ middle	UDI	Neighborhood leader	Housewife
Soñia Becerra	Lower	PS	Sympathizer	Housewife
Sergio Bitar	Upper/ middle	PPD [Partido por la Democracia, Party for Democracy]	Leader	Minister of Mines; politician
Nora Blas	Upper	SOL	Leader	Housewife
Eduardo Boetsch	Upper	Chile Libre	Leader	Engineer
Olga Bran	Upper	SOL	Leader	Housewife
José Cademartori	Middle	PC	Leader	Minister of Economy; economist
Beatrice Campos [pseud.]	Lower	PN; MIR	None; sympathizer	Factory worker
Enrique Campos Menendez	Upper	SOL	Leader	Writer
Jacques Chonchol	Upper/ middle	PDC; MAPU; IC [Izquierda Cristiana, Christian Left]	Leader	Political activist

NAME	CLASS	AFFILIATION	POSITION IN MOVEMENT OR PARTY	OCCUPATION
Victoria Cofré	Lower	Independent right	None	Housewife
Inés Cornejo	Lower/ middle	PC	Leader	Political activist
María Correa Morandé	Upper	PN; Poder Femenino	Leader; leader	PN deputy; housewife
Consuelo Correo	Upper	National Secretariat of Women; RN	Leader; none	Housewife [UP years]; social worker
Marta Cousiño	Middle	UDI	Mid-level leader	Businesswoman
Alejandrina Cox	Upper	PDC	Sympathizer	Housewife
Virginia Cox Balmaceda	Upper	PL [Partido Liberal, Liberal Party]	Leader, Women's Secretariat	Writer; housewife
Daniel [last name withheld]	Lower	Independent	None	Worker
María Eugenia Díaz	Lower	Independent right	None	Housewife
Mirta Dubost	Upper	UDI	Local leader	Mayor/council member; businesswoman
Rosa Elvira Durán	Lower	Independent; CEMA	None; local CEMA leader	Housewife
Carmen Errázuriz de Guzmán	Upper	Independent [son, Jaime Guzmán, founded UDI]	None	Housewife
Eva [last name withheld]	Lower	Independent	None	Housewife
Olga Felíu	Upper	Independent; designated senator*	None	Lawyer
Raquel Fernández	Middle	PDC	Mid-level leader	Housewife; political activist
Juanita Flores	Lower	UDI	Local-level leader	Housewife; political activist
Carmen Frei	Upper/ middle	PDC	Leader	Politician
Fidelina Fuentes	Lower/ peasant	Independent	None	Housewife; servant
María Olivia Gazmuri	Upper	Patria y Libertad; RN	Member; neighborhood-level leader	Council member, La Reina

* According to the 1980 Constitution, which was designed during military rule, Pinochet had the power to appoint nine senators to the Chilean Senate. Olga Felíu was one of them.

NAME	CLASS	AFFILIATION	POSITION IN MOVEMENT OR PARTY	OCCUPATION
Sara Geraldo	Lower	RN	Neighborhood leader	Housewife
José de Gregorio Aroca	Upper/middle	PDC	Leader	Politician
Carmen Grez	Upper	Poder Femenino	Member	Housewife; mayor, Providencia
María Pía Guzmán	Upper	RN	Member	Director, Fundación Paz Ciudadana
Myrna Henriquez	Middle	Independent right	None	Housewife
Hilda Hernández	Middle	Independent right	None	Social worker
Magaly Huerta	Middle	PDC	None	Lawyer
María Teresa Infante	Upper	Gremialista	None	Technocrat during Pinochet regime
Silvia Jara	Middle	PDC	None	Administrator in Ministry of Public Works; housewife
Elena Larraín	Upper	Chile Libre; Poder Femenino	Member; leader	Housewife
Laura Leon	Middle	PN	Sympathizer	CEMA administrator
Bianca Lombardi	Lower/middle	Independent right	None	Housewife
Lydia [last name withheld]	Lower	Independent	None	Housewife
Liliana Mahn	Upper/middle	PDC	None	Minister of Tourism during Pinochet years
Teresa Maillet de la Maza	Middle	PDC	Leader of Women's Secretariat	Housewife
Ana Eugenia Marcuello	Middle	PN	Member	Journalist
Rosa Markmann de González Videla	Upper	PR	Member	First Lady (1946–52); housewife
Evelyn Matthei	Upper	UDI	Leader	Congressional deputy
Lucía Maturana	Upper	SOL; RN	Leader; member	Social worker; housewife
General Medina Loes	Upper/middle	Army	General	General
Antonia Meyer	Middle	PDC	Member	Housewife
Carmen Miranda	Lower	PN	Sympathizer	Housewife
María Muñoz	Lower	PDC	Sympathizer	Housewife

NAME	CLASS	AFFILIATION	POSITION IN MOVEMENT OR PARTY	OCCUPATION
Maruja Navarro	Upper/ middle	UDI	Member	Housewife
Sara Navas	Upper	Unknown	Unknown	Lawyer
Pamela Olivares	Middle	UDI	None	Student
Sergio Onofre Jarpa	Upper	PN	President	Landowner
Fernanda Otero	Upper	RN	Leader	Journalist; housewife
Nydia Otey	Middle	Independent right	None	Housewife
María Eugenia Oyarzún	Upper/ middle	Unknown	Unknown	Journalist
Blanca Peinenao	Lower	PDC	None	Housewife
Lily Pérez	Upper	RN	Mid-level leader	Municipal council member
Hermógenes Pérez de Arce	Upper	PN; UDI	Member; member	Deputy; journalist
Irene Pilquinao	Lower	Independent left	None	Domestic worker
Anabela Poblete Corfo	Middle	Independent right	None	Housewife
Miguel Angel Poduje	Upper	UDI	None	Minister of Housing; businessman
Hilda Porras	Lower/ middle	UDI	Mid-level leader	Municipal council
Aurora Posada	Middle	PS	Member	Student
Francisco Prat	Upper	RN	Leader	Congressional deputy
Nora Pulido	Middle	RN	None	Housewife
Paloma Rodríguez [pseud.]	Lower	MAPU	Leader	Leader, National Secretariat of Women
Alicia Romo	Upper	Poder Femenino; unknown	Leader	Academic
Ximena Rubio	Lower/ middle	PDC	None	Secretary
Carmen Saenz	Upper	Poder Femenino; RN	Leader; member	Housewife
Beatrice San Martín	Lower	Independent right	None	Housewife
Olga Sazo	Lower	PS	Member	Seamstress
Edith Senler-Berz	Middle	Unknown	None	Administrator
Graciela Soto	Lower	Independent right	None	Domestic servant

NAME	CLASS	AFFILIATION	POSITION IN MOVEMENT OR PARTY	OCCUPATION
Carlos Telep Quezada	Middle	Independent right	None	Landowner
Ernesto Torres	Lower	MIR	Member	NCO, Air Force
Ruperto Vargas	Middle	RN	Local-level leader	Anthropologist
María Vicuña	Upper	Partido Liberal	Member	Housewife
Virginia Vidal	Middle	PC [formerly]	Leader	Writer
Ana Zelaya Leiva	Lower	PN	None	Housewife

The interviews consist of taped discussions with ninety-one Chilean women and men between November 1993 and July 1994, in December 1998, in May, July, and August 1999, and in January 2000. Seventy-six of my informants were women, and fifteen were men. Fifty-eight of the people I interviewed identified themselves as being on the right, twelve as Christian Democrats, thirteen as leftists, and five as independents; one woman switched from the right (National Party) to the left (MIR). Three informants' political sympathies were unclear.

Determining the class status of the interviewees was not as clear-cut as defining their political leanings. While it was fairly easy to situate the wealthy and the poor according to class, a certain number of people I interviewed belonged in the upper portions of the middle class, while others were part of the lower middle class. When such a distinction appeared necessary, I have indicated it in Appendix A.

Since I conducted most of the interviews in the informants' homes, I could observe the economic conditions in which they lived. These insights, along with other factors—such as an awareness of the neighborhoods they lived in, where or if they worked, their educational backgrounds, and the extent or lack of foreign travel—created impressions of class position that I used to categorize the interviewees. Thirty-three of the informants were from the upper class, eight from the upper middle class, twenty from the middle class, seven from the lower middle class, twenty-two from the lower class, and one peasant. It was easier to obtain interviews with upper- and middle-class women, because many of them had been the public spokespersons for the movement and their names were known. They had telephones and permanent places of residence. Many of them knew each other. The middle- and upper-class women were educated, articulate, and self-confident.

On the other hand, many of the poor women were not famous, lacked phones, and were much harder to locate. I was able to find the lower-class women through the Mothers' Centers, the right-wing parties, and personal contacts. Though the upper- and middle-class women readily gave me the phone numbers of their peers, none of them could provide phone numbers or addresses for the poor women.

Appendix B

Radio Advertisements Sponsored by Acción Mujeres de Chile

Radio Advertisement 1

Announcer (male):	Political passions divide Chile and endanger our homes . . .
	Only a government free of commitments to the political parties will be able to assure respect for everyone's ideas and allow our children to develop in a climate of peace and security . . .
Announcer (female):	Chilean woman, the fate of the Fatherland is in your hands.
	¡Acción Mujeres de Chile!

Radio Advertisement 2

Announcer (female):	A political idea should not bring political repression down on our husbands . . .
Announcer (male):	Only an independent government can assure freedom of work, without persecution or threats . . . because we all deserve progress . . .
Announcer (female):	Chilean woman, the fate of the Fatherland is in your hands.
	¡Acción Mujeres de Chile!

Radio Advertisement 3

Announcer (female):	What constitutes the basic common sense of the Chilean woman?
	Her ability to reject the dangers that threaten Chile. Down with those systems that destroy freedom! Down with all this politicking, which can only lead us to disaster! Chile needs an independent government.

I would like to thank Luis Maira, who pointed out the existence of these documents to me. In 1970, he was a deputy from the PDC who participated in the investigation of the Scare Campaign. His own papers relating to the investigation were destroyed following the 11 September 1973 military coup. For a description of the Scare Campaign, see Mariana Aylwin et al., *Percepción del rol político,* 50. The first three radio advertisements reproduced here can be found in El Congreso Chileno, Cámara de Diputados, 25th Sess., 19 August 1970, 2465–66; the fourth is located in El Congreso Chileno, Cámara de Diputados, 25th Sess., 19 August 1970, 2483.

Chilean woman, the fate of the Fatherland is in your hands.

¡Acción Mujeres de Chile!

Radio Advertisement 4

Announcer (male):	The future of the Fatherland is the future of the home.
	Once again the judgment and courage of the Chilean woman will reject demagoguery.
Announcer (female):	Chilean woman, the fate of the Fatherland is in your hands.
	¡Acción Mujeres de Chile!

Appendix C

Radio Advertisements Sponsored by Chile Joven

Radio Advertisement 1

Announcer (male):   Demagoguery and politicking only favor those who strive to strip you of the fruits of your labor.

That's why the number of attacks, murders, and robberies is increasing.

That's why the terrorists continue to unleash violence.

We reject those who preach violence and those who are incapable of preventing it!

This was a message from Chile Joven.

Radio Advertisement 2

Announcer (male):   They rob banks and sow terror and violence.

They are heroes to those who prefer violence to work.

Only an authority free of any political strings can give us back the security our homes need.

We reject those who preach violence as well as those who are incapable of preventing it.

This was a message from Chile Joven!

These advertisements can be found in El Congreso Chileno, Cámara de Diputados, 25th Sess., 19 August 1970, 2484.

Appendix D

The Call to the March of the Empty Pots and Pans

La situación que vive el país nos hace dirigirnos a todas las mujeres de Chile. Nosotras, mejor que nadie, vivimos el drama hondo que desde hace un año está viviendo el país.

Cuando asumió el presidente Allende, analizadas las circunstancias que hicieron posible su ascenso a la Presidencia de la República, confiamos en que él sería el aval de la convivencia democrática, el respeto a todos los derechos y la seguridad que aquellos principios inalterables—que nos garantiza la Constitución—serían resguardado con celo por quien asumía el mando de la nación.

El tiempo nos ha señalado que esa seguridad es ficticia. Hemos sido testigos de cómo se ha ido sembrando el odio, la falta de respeto a la autoridad y a aquellos valores que para nosotras son fundamentales: el honor de las personas y su integridad física.

El sectarismo, la prepotencia de los funcionarios del gobierno, nos llena de inquietud frente al futuro de nuestra patria y el porvenir de nuestros hijos.

Hasta los valores más importantes se ven amenazados; se incendia una iglesia evangélica y se ataca a un pastor, nada más que por oponerse a ideas y actitudes totalitarias.

Es grave el intento del gobierno de controlar todos los órganos de expresión, sean radios, televisión, revistas, diarios. En estos últimos, la maniobra está dirigida a controlar el papel mediante la estatización de la Compañía Manufacturera de Papeles y Cartones. Sabemos que si eso ocurre, sólo tendrán papel las publicaciones adictas al gobierno.

Prometieron la tierra para el que la trabaja y la participación de los trabajadores en las industrias. Han hecho todo lo contrario; los campesinos no tienen tierra y el Estado se está adueñando de las industrias.

El colmo de los atropellos se produjo en la Universidad de Chile, donde el rector Edgardo Boeninger está siendo víctima de una campaña de infamias y vilezas sólo por exigir el respeto a los valores más sagrados del hombre.

Todas estamos viviendo el drama de la falta de alimentos. No se trata de campañas falsas para atacar al gobierno. A diario vemos que no hay carne, pollos, leche, fideos y otros alimentos esenciales, y cuando se encuentran, hay que pagar precios que están muy lejos de nuestros recursos. Por eso es que hacemos un

This call to the march appeared in *La Tribuna*, 29 November 1971. An English translation follows.

273

fervoroso llamado a todas las mujeres chilenas, para que de una vez por todas digamos nuestra palabra por el provenir de Chile y de nuestros hijos.

Unámosnos el miércoles 1° de diciembre, a las 18 horas, en la plaza Italia, en La Marcha de la Mujer Chilena.

The gravity of the situation facing our country has forced us to call upon all the women of Chile. We, more than anyone, are living the profound drama that our country has suffered for the past year.

When Allende assumed the presidency, we analyzed the conditions that made it possible for him to become the president of Chile. We were confident that he would secure our democratic lifestyle, respect our rights, and [that] the security of those unalterable principles—guaranteed by the Constitution— would be jealously guarded by he who assumed control of the nation.

Time has shown us that this security is illusory. We have witnessed how hate has been sown, [along with] the lack of respect for authority and those values that for us are fundamental: personal honor and physical safety.

Sectarianism and the arrogance of government officials have filled us with concern for the future of the fatherland and of our children.

Even our most important values are threatened; an evangelical church was burned, and a pastor was attacked simply because he opposed totalitarian ideas and attitudes.

The government's attempts to control all the media, the radio, television, magazines, newspapers, is serious. As part of this, [we see] the [government's] maneuvers to control the supply of paper through the nationalization of the Compañía Manufacturera de Papeles y Cartones. We know that if this were to happen, only those who support the government will receive paper.

They promised land to those who work it and workers' participation in the factories. The opposite has happened: the peasants do not have land and the state has taken over the factories.

The worst abuses have taken place in the University of Chile, where the rector, Edgardo Boeninger, is the victim of an infamous campaign of insults simply because he demands respect for man's most sacred values.

We all live the drama caused by the lack of food. We are not inventing false campaigns to attack the government. Daily we see that there is no meat, chicken, milk, noodles, and other essential items, and when we do find these products, we have to pay prices that are far beyond our resources. For these reasons we make this fervent call to all Chilean women, so that once and for all, we can have our say [on the issue of] the future of Chile and our children.

We will gather on Wednesday, December 1st, 6:00 P.M., Plaza Italia, in the March of Chilean Women.

Appendix E

"Golpeando las puertas de los cuarteles"

Hemos llorado tanto de rodillas
junto a la cuna y en las catedrales,
hemos llorado, por amor llorando,
quien llora por amor nunca se humilla!
Son tres años de llanto, mucho llanto,
de un llorar silencioso y sin destino,
lloramos por la estrella mancillada,
lloramos por los muertos y los vivos!
De miedo hemos llorado noche a noche
sin saber donde estaban nuestros hijos!
Ha sido necesario mucho llanto
para llegar aquí, hasta los límites
donde el honor de Chile sigue intacto!
Venimos de golpear todas las puertas,
hoy estamos golpeando en los cuarteles,
porque tras de estos muros poderosos
la conciencia de Patria permanece . . .
No venimos a hablar con uniformes,
ignoramos galón y charreteras,
venimos hasta el hombre, hasta el chileno,
a preguntar por Chile y su bandera!
Ustedes nos conocen, somos ellas,
las de las verdes fiestas septembrinas,
las novias, las esposas, las abuelas,
las que os dimos el beso más hermoso
en la cuna, en la fiesta o en la pena . . .
Las que lloramos por amor llorando
cuando os vimos jurar por la bandera!
Tenemos que deciros muchas cosas . . .
y decirlas llorando, de rodillas,
cuando lloran las madres por la Patria
llorando están la muerte de la vida.

This poem, "Beating on the Barracks Doors," is by Nina Donoso. An English translation follows.

Oidnos, es la historia la que llora
la tierra la que clama por sus crías,
es la mesa sin pan, la madre herida,
la que suplica aquí, la que solloza,
¡Quién ruega por la Patria no se humilla!
venimos a pedir, no por nosotras,
por el niño que encumbra volantines,
por la niña que reza una plegaria,
por las palomas y por los copihues.
Golpeamos llorando los cuarteles,
llamando a los azules marineros,
rogando a los soldados, aviadores,
a los aquí nacidos, por Dios de esta ignominia!
que rescatéis la Patria que tuvimos,
que solo son diez mil los mercenarios,
diez mil asesinando a la bandera,
abriéndole a la Patria en el costado
una herida más ancha que una guerra . . .
y cada uno de vosotros vale
más de cien mil chacales extranjeros!
Tenemos que deciros muchas cosas,
y decirlas llorando de rodillas:
Seremos si queréis en la vanguardia
vuestras lugartenientes y enfermeras,
que por vendar la herida de la Patria
en la muerte queremos ser primeras . . .
Y decimos también a los ajenos,
cara a cara, con rabia, con desprecio,
que aquí esta la mujer, en los cuarteles,
junto al hijo soldado y marinero,
para lavar el tricolor sagrado
con llanto de mujer que no se humilla
si llora por la Patria de rodillas!

We have cried so much on our knees
next to the cradle and in the cathedrals,
we have cried, cried for love,
crying for love is no disgrace!
Three years of sorrow, so much sorrow,
of silent and boundless grief,
we have cried for the sullied star,
we have cried for the dead and the living!
Fear has caused us to cry night after night
not knowing where our children are!

It has taken us much suffering
to bring us here, to our limits,
where the honor of Chile is still intact!
We have beaten on all the doors,
today we beat on the barracks doors,
because behind these powerful walls
lies the conscience of the Fatherland . . .
We are not coming to talk with the uniforms,
we do not care about the stripes and the epaulets,
we are looking for the man, for the Chilean,
to ask him about Chile and his flag!
You know us, we are with you
in the fiestas of September,
we are your sweethearts, your wives, your grandmothers,
the ones who bestowed on you the most beautiful kiss
in the world when you were in the cradle, joyful or sad . . .
Those who cried for love,
crying when we saw you swear on the flag!
We have much to say to you . . .
and we will say it crying, on our knees,
when the mothers cry for the Fatherland
they are crying for the death of life.
Listen, history is crying
the land that clamors for its offspring
the table without bread, the wounded mother,
the one who begs here, the one who weeps.
To pray for the Fatherland is no disgrace!
We come to ask you, not for ourselves,
but for the little boy flying a kite,
for the little girl saying a prayer,
for the doves, and for the *copihues*.
We beat on the barracks doors weeping,
we call on the sailors,
we beg the soldiers, the Air Force,
all those born here, God! enough of this disgrace!
Redeem the Fatherland we once had,
there are only ten thousand mercenaries,
ten thousand assassinating the flag,
inflicting a wound on the Fatherland
more serious than a war. . . .
Each one of you is worth
more than one hundred thousand foreign jackals!
We have much to say to you,
and we will say it on our knees, crying:

If you wish, we will be the vanguard,
your deputies and nurses,
in order to bind the wounds of the Fatherland,
we want to be the first to die . . .
We also say to the indifferent people,
face to face, with fury, with scorn,
the women are here, in the barracks,
together with their sons in the army and the navy,
to wash the sacred tricolor
with the sorrow of a woman who is not ashamed
to cry on her knees for the Fatherland!

Bibliography

Government Documents

CHILE

Congreso Chileno. Cámara de Diputados. Legislatura Ordinaria. *Informe de la Comisión Especial Investigadora encargada de conocer de la legalidad, financiamiento y responsabilidad de las actividades de las organizaciones denominadas "Chile Joven" y "Acción Mujeres de Chile" y la determinación de una encuesta política realizada en el Gran Santiago, atribuida a un organismo dependiente del Mercado Comun Europeo.* Sesión 25, 19 August 1970.

Congreso Chileno. Cámara de Diputados. Legislatura Extraordinaria. *Acusación constitucional en contra del Ministro del Interior Don José Tohá González.* Sesión 38, 6 January 1972.

Congreso Chileno. Senado. Legislatura Extraordinaria. *Acusación constitucional en contra del Ministro del Interior Don José Tohá González.* Sesiones 49, 50, 52, 54, and 56, 18–22 January 1972.

República de Chile. Servicio Electoral. [Results from the 1958, 1964, and 1970 presidential elections; results from the 1964 by-election in Curicó; results from the 18 July 1971 by-election in Valparaíso; and results from the March 1973 parliamentary elections.] Santiago: Servicio Electoral.

UNITED STATES

Central Intelligence Agency. Cable transmissions on coup plotting. 18 October 1970. National Security Archives. Online: <http://www.gwu.edu/~nsarchiv/NSAEBB/NSAEBB8/ch27-01.htm>.

———. Memo on the genesis of Project FUBELT. 16 September 1970. National Security Archives. Online: <http://www.gwu.edu/~nsarchiv/NSAEBB/NSAEBB8/ch03-01.htm>.

Helms, Richard. Briefing for the National Security Council. 6 November 1970. National Security Archives. Online: <http://www.gwu.edu/~nsarchiv/NSAEBB/NSAEBB8/ch08-01.htm.

Karamessines, Thomas. Operating guidance cable on coup plotting. 16 October 1970. National Security Archives. Online: <http://www.gwu.edu/~nsarchiv/NSAEBB/NSAEBB8/ch05-01.htm>.

Korry, Edward. Cables to the Department of State on the election of Salvador Allende and efforts to block his assumption of the presidency. 4 September 1970. National Security Archives. Online: <http://www.seas.gwu.edu/nsarchive>.

National Security Council. "Options Paper on Chile (NSSM 97)." 3 November 1970. National Security Archives. Online: <http://www.gwu.edu/~nsarchiv/NSAEBB/NSAEBB8/ch24-01.htm>.

Rubottom, Roy R., Jr. Department of State Bulletin 6601. 3 February 1958.

U.S. Congress. House. Committee on Foreign Affairs. *United States-Chilean Relations.* 93rd Cong., 1st sess. 6 March 1973.

U.S. Congress. House. Committee on Foreign Affairs. Subcommittee on Inter-American Affairs. *United States and Chile During the Allende Years, 1970–1973.* [Hearings held between July 1971 and September 1974 before the Subcommittee on Inter-American Affairs of the Committee on Foreign Affairs.] Washington, D.C.: Government Printing Office, 1975.

U.S. Congress. Senate. Select Committee to Study Governmental Operations with Respect to Intelligence Activities. *Covert Action.* Hearings before the Select Committee to Study Governmental Operations with Respect to Intelligence Activities. 94th Cong., 1st sess., 4–5 December 1975.

U.S. Congress. Senate. Select Committee to Study Governmental Operations with Respect to Intelligence Activities. *Covert Action in Chile, 1963–1973: Staff Report of the Select Committee to Study Governmental Operations with Respect to Intelligence Activities.* 94th Cong., 1st sess., 18 December 1975. Washington, D.C.: Government Printing Office.

Newspapers and Magazines

CHILEAN

Aurora (Santiago)

Chile Hoy (Santiago)

El Clarín (Santiago)

Diario Oficial de la República de Chile (Santiago)

La Epoca (Santiago)

Ercilla (Santiago)

Eva (Santiago)

Fiducia (Santiago)

El Mercurio (Santiago)

La Nación (Santiago)

La Patria (Santiago)

La Prensa (Santiago)

Punto Final (Santiago)

Puro Chile (Santiago)

¿Qué Pasa? (Santiago)

Ramona (Santiago)

El Rancagüiño (Rancagua)

Santiago Times

La Segunda (Santiago)

El Siglo (Santiago)

La Tercera de la Hora (Santiago)

La Tribuna (Santiago)

Las Ultimas Notícias (Santiago)

U.S. AND BRITISH

Chicago Tribune

Christian Science Monitor

Liberation

New York Times

The Times (London)

Wall Street Journal

Washington Post

Interviews

Aguayo, Carmen Gloria. Interview by author. Tape recording. Santiago, 7 June 1994.

Alessandri, Silvia. Interview by author. Tape recording. Santiago, 23 March 1994.

Alvarez, Rubi. Interview by author. Tape recording. Santiago, 11 November 1994.

Armanet, Victoria. Interview by author. Tape recording. Santiago, 17 March 1994.

Arraya, Cristina. Interview by author. Tape recording. Cerro Navia, 29 November 1993.

Aymans, Fresia. Interview by author. Tape recording. Cerro Navia, 29 November 1993.

Baltra, Mireya. Interview by author. Tape recording. Santiago, 31 January 1994.

Barrientos, Juanita. Interview by author. Tape recording. La Florida, 4 October 1993.

Basaez, Gabriela. Interview by author. Tape recording. Santiago, 3 March 1994.

Becerra, Soñia. Interview by author. Tape recording. Lo Prado, 11 June 1994.

Bitar, Sergio. Interview by author. Tape recording. Santiago, 10 December 1998.

Blas, Nora. Interview by author. Tape recording. Las Condes, 11 April 1994.

Boetsch, Eduardo. Interview by author. Tape recording. Providencia, 20 June 1994.

Bran, Olga. Interview by author. Tape recording. Las Condes, 11 April 1994.

Cademartori, José. Interview by author. Tape recording. Chicago, 19 March 1999.

Campos, Beatrice [pseud.]. Interview by author. Tape recording. Puente Alto, 3 February 1994.

Campos Menendez, Enrique. Interview by author. Tape recording. Las Condes, 5 April 1994.

Chonchol, Jacques. Interview by author. Tape recording. Santiago, 13 December 1998.

Cofré, Victoria. Interview by author. Tape recording. Santiago, 2 February 1994.

Cornejo, Inés. Interview by author. Tape recording. Santiago, 21 June 1994.

Correa Morandé, María. Interview by author. Tape recording. Santiago, 4 January 1994.

Correo, Consuelo. Interview by author. Tape recording. Vitacura, 23 November 1994.

Cousiño, Marta. Interview by author. Tape recording. Providencia, 11 March 1994.

Cox, Alejandrina. Interview by author. Tape recording. Vitacura, 24 June 1994.

Cox Balmaceda, Virginia. Interview by author. Tape recording. Vitacura, 17 May 1999.

Daniel [last name withheld]. Interview by author. Tape recording. Puente Alto, 16 December 1998.

Díaz, María Eugenia. Interview by author. Tape recording. Pedro A. Cerda, 16 March 1994.

Dubost, Mirta. Interview by author. Tape recording. Iquique, 5 May 1994.

Durán, Rosa Elvira. Interview by author. Tape recording. Renca, 26 November 1993.

Errázuriz de Guzmán, Carmen. Interview by author. Tape recording. Las Condes, 9 December 1993.

Eva [last name withheld]. Interview by author. Tape recording. Pedro A. Cerda, 13 December 1993.

Felíu, Olga. Interview by author. Tape recording. Santiago, 30 November 1993.

Fernández, Raquel. Interview by author. Tape recording. Santiago, 18 May 1994.

Flores, Juanita. Interview by author. Tape recording. La Florida, 31 March 1994.

Frei, Carmen. Interview by author. Tape recording. Santiago, 4 May 1994.

Fuentes, Fidelina. Interview by author. Tape recording. Talca, 13 February 1994.

Gallo, Nellie. Interview by María de los Angeles Crummett. Notes. Santiago, 19 July 1974.

Gazmuri, María Olivia. Interview by author. Tape recording. La Reina, 19 April 1994.

Geraldo, Sara. Interview by author. Notes. Valparaíso, 2 December 1993.

de Gregorio Aroca, José. Interview by author. Tape recording. Santiago, 4 August 1999.

Grez, Carmen. Interview by author. Tape recording. Providencia, 4 June 1994.

Guzmán, María Pía. Interview by author. Tape recording. Providencia, 4 November 1993.

Henriquez, Myrna. Interview by author. Tape recording. Ñuñoa, 5 October 1993.

Hernández, Hilda. Interview by author. Tape recording. Santiago, 5 October 1993.

Huerta, Magaly. Interview by author. Tape recording. Providencia, 18 October 1993.

Infante, María Teresa. Interview by author. Tape recording. Las Condes, 15 December 1993.

Jara, Silvia. Interview by author. Tape recording. Santiago, 18 May 1994.

LaPorte, Tom. Telephone interview by author. Chapel Hill, N.C., 28 October 1994.

Larraín, Elena. Interviews by author. Tape recording. Providencia, 16 March and 8 July 1994.

———. Interview by María de los Angeles Crummett. Notes. Santiago, 18 July 1974.

Leon, Laura. Interview by author. Tape recording. Santiago, 6 June 1994.

Lombardi, Bianca. Interview by author. Tape recording. Valparaíso, 7 February 1994.

Lydia [last name withheld]. Interview by author. Tape recording. Pedro A. Cerda, 13 December 1993.

Mahn, Liliana. Interview by author. Tape recording. Santiago, 16 January 1994.

Maillet de la Maza, Teresa. Interview by author. Tape recording. Valparaíso, 14 June 1994.

Marcuello, Ana Eugenia. Interview by author. Tape recording. Rancagua, 8 June 1994.

Markmann de González Videla, Rosa. Interview by author. Tape recording. Santiago, 5 January 1994.

Matthei, Evelyn. Interview by author. Tape recording. Las Condes, 30 April 1994.

Maturana, Lucía. Interviews by author. Tape recording. Santiago, 26 October 1993, and Las Condes, 11 April 1994.

Medina Loes, General. Interview by author. Tape recording. Santiago, 24 December 1998.

Meyer, Antonia. Interview by author. Tape recording. Providencia, 26 May 1994.

Miranda, Carmen. Interview by author. Tape recording. Rancagua, 8 June 1994.

Muñoz, María. Interview by author. Tape recording. Conchalí, 2 April 1994.

Navarro, Maruja. Interview by author. Tape recording. Las Condes, 15 December 1998.

Navas, Sara. Interview by author. Tape recording. Vitacura, 5 November 1993.

Olivares, Pamela. Interview by author. Tape recording. Las Condes, 15 January 2000.

Onofre Jarpa, Sergio. Interview by author. Tape recording. Providencia, 4 August 1999.

Otero, Fernanda. Interview by author. Tape recording. Las Condes, 15 October 1993.

Otey, Nydia. Interview by author. Tape recording. Valparaíso, 7 December 1994.

Oyarzún, María Eugenia. Interview by author. Tape recording. Providencia, 22 March 1994.

Peinenao, Blanca. Interview by author. Notes. Ñancul, 19 February 1994.

Pérez, Lily. Interview by author. Tape recording. Las Condes, 3 December 1994.

Pérez de Arce, Hermógenes. Interview by author. Tape recording. Providencia, 9 June 1994.

Pilquinao, Irene. Interview by author. Tape recording. La Florida, 8 October 1993.

Poblete Corfo, Anabela. Interview by author. Tape recording. Iquique, 5 May 1994.

Poduje, Miguel Angel. Interview by author. Tape recording. Santiago, 5 April 1994.

Porras, Hilda. Interview by author. Tape recording. Maipú, 15 June 1994.

Posada, Aurora. Personal communication. Chicago, 24 February 2001.

Prat, Francisco. Interview by author. Tape recording. Valparaíso, 12 April 1994.

Pulido, Nora. Interview by author. Tape recording. Santiago, 29 November 1993.

Ripamonte, Silvia. Interview by María de los Angeles Crummett. Notes. Santiago, 7 June 1974.

Rodríguez, Paloma [pseud.]. Interview by author. Tape recording. Santiago, 7 June 1994.

Romo, Alicia. Interview by author. Tape recording. Las Condes, 14 December 1993.

Rubio, Ximena. Interview by author. Tape recording. Rancagua, 8 June 1994.

Saenz, Carmen. Interviews by author. Tape recording. La Reina, 4 December and 27 December 1993.

San Martín, Beatrice. Interview by author. Tape recording. Santiago, 15 March 1994.

Sazo, Olga. Interview by author. Tape recording. Cerro Navia, 12 June 1994.

Senler-Berz, Edith. Interview by author. Notes. Santiago, 22 June 1994.

Soto, Graciela. Interview by author. Tape recording. La Florida, 25 October 1994.

Telep Quezada, Carlos. Interview by author. Tape recording. Teno, 23 December 1993.

Torres, Ernesto. Interviews by author. Tape recording. Santiago, 6 August 1999 and 29 December 1998.

Torres, María. Interview by author. Notes. Chicago, 9 March 1998.

Vargas, Ruperto. Interview by author. Tape recording. Villarrica, 16 February 1994.

Vicuña, María. Interview by author. Tape recording. Las Condes, 22 December 1998.

Vidal, Virginia. Interview by author. Tape recording. Santiago, 14 April 1994.

Webster, Jack. Telephone interview by author. Southern Pines, N.C., 8 November 1994.

Zelaya Leiva, Ana. Interview by author. Tape recording. Los Andes, 28 January 1994.

Secondary Sources

Agee, Philip. *Inside the Company: CIA Diary.* New York: Stonehill, 1975.

Aguayo, Carmen Gloria. *Des Chiliennes: Des femmes en luttes au Chile et Carmen Gloria Aguayo de Sota.* Paris: Des Femmes, 1982.

Allende, Isabel. *Paula.* New York: Harper Collins, 1994.

Allende, Salvador. *La via chilena hacia al socialismo.* Santiago: Ediciones Palabra Escrita, 1989.

Andreas, Carol. "The Chilean Woman: Reform, Reaction, and Resistance." *Latin American Perspectives*, no. 15 (September 1977).

Antezana-Pernet, Corinne. "MEMCh en provincia." In *Disciplina y desacato: Construcción de identidad en Chile Siglos XIX y XX*, edited by Lorena Godoy, Elizabeth Hutchinson, Karin Rosemblatt, and M. Soledad Zárate. Santiago: Sur/CEDEM, 1995.

———. "Mobilizing Women in the Popular Front Era: Feminism, Class, and Politics in the Movimiento Pro-Emancipación de la Mujer Chilena (MEMCh), 1935–1950." Ph.D. diss., University of California, 1996.

Arrate, Jorge. *La fuerza democrática de la idea socialista.* Santiago: Las Ediciones del Ornitorrinco, 1985.

Arrate, Jorge, and Paulo Hidalgo. *Pasión y razón del socialismo chileno.* Santiago: Las Ediciones del Ornitorrinco, 1989.

Aylwin, Mariana, Sofía Correa, and Magdalena Piñera. *Percepción del rol político de la mujer: Una aproximación histórica.* Santiago: Instituto Chileno de Estudios Humanísticos, 1986.

Bacchetta, Paola. *Gendered Nationalisms: The RSS, the Samiti, and Their Different Projects for a Hindu Nation.* New Delhi: Kali for Women, 2001.

Baldez, Lisa. *Why Women Protest: Women's Movements in Chile.* New York: Cambridge University Press, 2002.

Bambirra, Vania. "Liberación de la mujer y lucha de clases." *Punto Final*, no. 151, 15 February 1972.

Berger Gluck, Sherna, and Daphne Patai, eds. *Women's Words: The Feminist Practice of Oral History.* New York: Routledge, 1991.

Biehl del Río, J., and Gonzalo Fernández. "The Political Pre-requisites for a Chilean Way." In *Allende's Chile*, edited by Kenneth Medhurst. London: Hart-David, MacGibbon, 1972.

Bitar, Sergio, and Crisóstomo Pizarro. *La caída de Allende y la huelga de El Teniente: Lecciones de la historia.* Santiago: Las Ediciones del Ornitorrinco, 1986.

Blee, Kathleen M. "Evidence, Empathy, and Ethics: Lessons from Oral Histories of the Klan." *Journal of American History* (September 1993).

———. *Women of the Klan: Racism and Gender in the 1920s.* Berkeley and Los Angeles: University of California Press, 1991.

Bodenheimer, Susanne. "Stagnation in Liberty—The Frei Experiment in Chile, Part II." *NACLA Newsletter* 3, no. 1 (March 1969).

Boetsch, Eduardo. *Memoirs.* Santiago: n.p., n.d.

Bouvier, Virginia Maria. *Alliance or Compliance: Implications of the Chilean Experience for the Catholic Church in Latin America.* Syracuse: Syracuse University Press, 1983.

Bridenthal, Renate, Atina Grossman, and Marion Kaplan, eds. *When Biology Became Destiny.* New York: Monthly Review, 1984.

Bunster, Ximena. "Surviving Beyond Fear: Women and Torture in Latin America." In *Women and Change in Latin America,* edited by June Nash and Helen Safa. South Hadley, Mass.: Bergin & Garvey, 1986.

Burnett, Ben G. *Political Groups in Chile: The Dialogue Between Order and Change.* Austin: University of Texas Press, 1970.

Campbell, Beatrix. *The Iron Ladies: Why Do Women Vote Tory?* London: Virago, 1987.

Castañeda, Jorge G. *Utopia Unarmed: The Latin American Left After the Cold War.* New York: Vintage, 1994.

Centro de Estudios de la Mujer. *Mundo de mujer: Continuidad y cambio.* Santiago: Centro de Estudios de la Mujer, 1988.

Chaney, Elsa M. "Old and New Feminists in Latin America." *Journal of Marriage and Family* 35, no. 2 (May 1973).

———. *Supermadre: Women in Politics in Latin America.* Austin: Institute of Latin American Studies/University of Texas Press, 1979.

Chavkin, Samuel. *The Murder of Chile: Eyewitness Accounts of the Coup, the Terror, and the Resistance Today.* New York: Everest House, 1982.

———. *Storm Over Chile: The Junta Under Siege.* Chicago: Lawrence Hill, 1989.

Chinchilla, Norma Stoltz. "Mobilizing Women: Revolution in the Revolution." *Latin American Perspectives* 4, no. 15 (Fall 1977).

Chuchryk, Patricia. "Protest, Politics, and Personal Life: The Emergence of Feminism in a Military Dictatorship, Chile 1973–1983." Ph.D. diss., York University, 1984.

Collier, Bernard. "Eduardo Frei Is Trying 'A Revolution Without the Execution Wall.'" *New York Times Magazine*, 19 February 1967.

Collier, Simon, and William F. Sater. *A History of Chile, 1808–1994*. Cambridge: Cambridge University Press, 1996.

Collins Weitz, Margaret. *Sisters in the Resistance: How Women Fought to Free France, 1940–1945*. New York: John Wiley & Sons, 1995.

Conde, Yvonne M. *Operation Pedro Pan: The Untold Exodus of 14,048 Cuban Children*. New York: Routledge, 1999.

Constable, Pamela, and Arturo Valenzuela. *A Nation of Enemies: Chile Under Pinochet*. New York: W. W. Norton, 1991.

Cooper, Marc. "Chile and the End of Pinochet." *The Nation*, 26 February 2001.

Correa, Sofía S. "La derecha en Chile contemporáneo: La perdida del control estatal." *Revista de Ciencia Política* 11, no. 1 (1989).

Correa Morandé, María. *La guerra de las mujeres*. Santiago: Editorial Universidad Técnica del Estado, 1974.

Covarrubias, Paz. "El movimiento feminista chileno." In *Chile: Mujer y sociedad*. Santiago: UNICEF, 1978.

Cristi, Renato, and Carlos Ruiz. "Conservative Thought in Twentieth-Century Chile." *Canadian Journal of Latin American and Caribbean Studies*, no. 30 (1990).

Crummett, María de los Angeles. "El Poder Femenino: The Mobilization of Women Against Socialism in Chile." *Latin American Perspectives* 4, no. 15 (Fall 1977).

Cusack, David F. *Revolution and Reaction: The Internal and International Dynamics of Conflict and Confrontation in Chile*. Denver: University of Denver, Graduate School of International Studies, 1977.

Davis, Nathaniel. *The Last Two Years of Salvador Allende*. Ithaca: Cornell University Press, 1985.

de Deus Simoes, Solange. *Deus, Pátria e Familia: As mulheres no golpe de 1964*. Petrópolis, Brazil: Vozes, 1985.

Delsing, Riet. "Sovereign and Disciplinary Power: A Foucauldian Analysis of the Chilean Women's Movement." In *The Gender of Power*, edited by Kathy Davis, Monique Leijenaar, and Jantine Oldersma. London: Sage, 1991.

Dinges, John, and Saul Landau. *Assassination on Embassy Row*. New York: Pantheon, 1980.

Donoso Loero, Teresa. *La epopeya de las ollas vacías*. Santiago: Editora Nacional Gabriela Mistral, 1974.

———. *Historia de los cristianos por el socialismo en Chile*. Santiago: Editorial Vaitea, 1975.

Drake, Paul. *Socialism and Populism in Chile, 1932–1952*. Urbana: University of Illinois Press, 1978.

Dulles, John F. W. *Unrest in Brazil: Political-Military Crisis 1955–1964*. Austin: University of Texas Press, 1970.

Dunkerly, James. "The United States and Latin America in the Long Run (1800–1945)." In *The United States and Latin America: The New Agenda*, edited by Victor Bulmer-Thomas and James Dunkerly. Cambridge: Harvard University Press, 1999.

Durham, Martin. *Women and Fascism*. London: Routledge, 1998.

Dworkin, Andrea. *Right-Wing Women*. New York: Wideview/Perigee, 1983.

Eckstein, Susan, ed. *Power and Popular Protest: Latin American Social Movements*. Berkeley and Los Angeles: University of California Press, 1989.

Escobar, Arturo, and Sonia E. Alvarez. *The Making of Social Movements in Latin America: Identity, Strategy, and Democracy*. Boulder: Westview, 1992.

Evans, Les. *Disaster in Chile: Allende's Strategy and Why It Failed*. New York: Pathfinder, 1974.

Evans, Sara. *Personal Politics: The Roots of Women's Liberation in the Civil Rights Movement and the New Left*. New York: Knopf, 1979.

Falcoff, Mark. *Modern Chile 1970–1989: A Critical History*. New Brunswick, N.J.: Transaction, 1989.

Fernández, Elisa. "Beyond Partisan Politics in Chile: The Carlos Ibáñez Period and the Politics of Ultranationalism Between 1952–1958." Ph.D. diss., University of Miami, 1996.

Fischer, Kathleen B. *Political Ideology and Educational Reform in Chile, 1964–1976*. Los Angeles: UCLA Latin American Center, 1979.

Fisher, Jo. *Mothers of the Disappeared*. London: Zed, 1989.

———. *Out of the Shadows: Women, Resistance, and Politics in South America*. London: Latin America Bureau, 1993.

Fleet, Michael. *The Rise and Fall of Chilean Christian Democracy*. Princeton: Princeton University Press, 1985.

Foxley, Alejandro. *Para una democracía estable*. Santiago: CIEPLAN, 1985.

Francis, Michael, and Patricia A. Kyle. "Chile: The Power of Women at the Polls." In *Integrating the Neglected Majority: Government Response to Demands for New Sex-Roles*, edited by Patricia A. Kyle. Brunswick, Ohio: King's Court Communications, [1976].

Frazier, Lessie Jo. "Memory and State Violence in Chile: A Historical Ethnography of Tarapaca, 1890–1995." Ph.D. diss, University of Michigan, 1998.

Fuerzas Armadas de Chile. *Libro blanco del cambio de gobierno en Chile.* Santiago: Editorial Lord Cochrane, 1973.

Furci, Carmelo. *The Chilean Communist Party and the Road to Socialism.* London: Zed, 1984.

Garreton, Manuel A., and Tomás Moulian. *Análisis coyuntural y proceso político: Las fases del conflicto en Chile, 1970–1973.* San José, Costa Rica: Editorial Universitaria Centroamericana Educa, 1978.

Garrett-Schesch, Pat. "The Mobilization of Women During the Popular Unity Government." *Latin American Perspectives* 2 (Spring 1975).

Gaviola, Edda, Lorella Lopresti, and Claudia Rojas. *Segundo informe de avance: La participación política de la mujer en Chile 1964–1973.* Santiago: n.p., n.d.

Gaviola, Edda, Lorella Lopresti, and Claudia Rojas. "Chile Centro de Madres: ¿La mujer popular en movimiento?" In *Nuestra memoria, nuestro futuro: Mujeres e historia, América Latina y el Caribe.* Santiago: Isis Internacional, n.d.

Gaviola Artigas, Edda, Ximena Jiles Moreno, Lorella Lopresti Martínez, and Claudia Rojas Mira. *"Queremos votar en las próximas elecciones": Historia del movimiento femenino chileno 1913–1952.* Santiago: Centro de Análisis y Difusión de la Condición de la Mujer, 1986.

Geiger, Susan. "What's So Feminist About Doing Women's Oral History?" *Journal of Women's History* 2, no. 1 (Spring 1990).

Gerassi, John. *The Great Fear in Latin America.* New York: Collier, 1967.

Gil, Federico G., and Charles J. Parrish. *The Chilean Presidential Election of September 4, 1964: An Analysis.* Washington, D.C.: Institute for the Comparative Study of Political Systems, 1965.

Gil, Federico G., Ricardo Lagos, and Henry A. Landsberger. *Chile 1970–1973: Lecciones de una experiencia.* Madrid: Editorial Tecnos, 1977.

González, Victoria, and Karen Kampwirth. *Radical Women in Latin America: Left and Right.* University Park: The Pennsylvania State University Press, 2001.

Gordon, Linda. "Nazi Feminists?" *Feminist Review,* no. 27 (September 1987).

de Grazia, Victoria. *How Fascism Ruled Women: Italy, 1922–1945.* Berkeley and Los Angeles: University of California Press, 1992.

Guzmán, Jaime. *Escritos personales.* Santiago: Editorial Universitaria, 1992.

Halperin, Morton H., and Jerry J. Berman. *The Lawless State: The Crimes of the U.S. Intelligence Agencies.* New York: Penguin, 1976.

Hartmann, Heidi. "The Unhappy Marriage of Marxism and Feminism: Towards a More Progressive Union." In *Women and Revolution,* edited by Lydia Sargent. Boston: South End Press, 1981.

Hiriart de Pinochet, Lucía. *La mujer chilena y su compromiso histórico*. Santiago: Editorial Renacimiento, n.d.

Hutchinson, Elizabeth Quay. "'*El fruto envenenado del arbol capitalista*': Women Workers and the Prostitution of Labor in Urban Chile, 1896–1925." *Journal of Women's History* 9 (Winter 1998).

Jaquette, Jane S., ed. *The Women's Movement in Latin America: Feminism and the Transition to Democracy*. Boston: Unwin Hyman, 1989.

Jara, Joan. *An Unfinished Song: The Life of Victor Jara*. New York: Ticknor & Fields, 1984.

Jeansonne, Glen. *Women of the Far Right: The Mother's Movement and World War II*. Chicago: University of Chicago Press, 1997.

Jetter, Alexis, Annelise Orleck, and Diana Taylor, eds. *The Politics of Motherhood: Activist Voices from Left to Right*. Hanover: University Press of New England, 1997.

Jiles Moreno, Ximena, and Claudia Rojas Mira. *De la miel a los implantes*. Santiago: Corporación de Salud y Políticas Sociales, 1992.

Jones, Mark P., and Patricio Navia. "Assessing the Effectiveness of Gender Quotas in Open-List Proportional Representation Electoral Systems." *Social Science Quarterly* 80 (June 1989).

Kaplan, Temma. "Female Consciousness and Collective Action: The Case of Barcelona, 1910–1918." *Signs* (Spring 1982).

———. "Rethinking Identity in Latin America." Paper presented at the Latin American Studies Seminar on Rethinking Identity in Latin America, Yale University, 1994.

———. *Taking Back the Streets: Women, Popular Democracy, and Collective Memory*. Berkeley and Los Angeles: University of California Press, forthcoming.

Kaufman, Edy. *Crisis in Allende's Chile: New Perspectives*. New York: Praeger, 1988.

Kay, Diana. *Chileans in Exile: Private Struggles, Public Lives*. London: Macmillan, 1987.

Kersten, Katherine. "What Do Women Want? A Conservative Feminist Manifesto." *Policy Review* (March 1991).

Kirkwood, Julieta. *Ser política en Chile: Los nudos de la sabiduria feminista*. Santiago: Editorial Cuarto Propio, 1990.

Kissinger, Henry. *White House Years*. Boston: Little, Brown, 1979.

Klatch, Rebecca E. *Women of the New Right*. Philadelphia: Temple University Press, 1987.

Klimpel, Felicitas. *La mujer chilena: El aporte femenino al progreso de Chile, 1910–1960*. Santiago: Editorial Andrés Bello, 1962.

Klubock, Thomas Miller. *Contested Communities: Class, Gender, and Politics in Chile's El Teniente Copper Mine, 1904–1951*. Durham: Duke University Press, 1998.

Knight, Alan. "Subalterns, Signifiers, and Statistics: Perspectives on Latin American Historiography." Paper presented at the Latin American Studies Association meeting, Miami, March 2000.

Knudson, Jerry W. *The Chilean Press During the Allende Years*. Buffalo: State University of New York, 1986.

———. "Late to the Feast: Newspapers as Historical Sources." *Perspectives* (October 1993).

Koonz, Claudia. *Mothers in the Fatherland: Women, the Family, and Nazi Politics*. New York: St. Martin's, 1987.

Labarca Goddard, Eduardo. *Chile invadido: Reportaje a la intromisión extranjera en Chile*. Santiago: Empresa Editora Austral, 1968.

Landis, Fred. "Psychological Warfare and Media Operations in Chile, 1970–1973." Ph.D. diss., University of Illinois, 1975.

Langguth, A. J. *Hidden Terrors*. New York: Pantheon, 1978.

Larguia, Isabel, and John Dumoulin. "Toward a Science of Women's Liberation." *NACLA's Latin America and Empire Report* 5, no. 10 (December 1972).

Lavrin, Asunción. *Women, Feminism, and Social Change in Argentina, Chile, and Uruguay, 1890–1940*. Lincoln: University of Nebraska Press, 1995.

Leacock, Ruth. *Requiem for Revolution: The United States and Brazil 1961–1969*. Kent: Kent State University Press, 1990.

Lechner, Norbert. *El sistema de partidos en Chile*. Santiago: FLACSO, 1985.

Lernoux, Penny. *Cry of the People*. New York: Penguin, 1982.

Levine, Daniel H. *Religion and Politics in Latin America: The Catholic Church in Venezuela and Colombia*. Princeton: Princeton University Press, 1986.

Levinson, Jerome, and Juan de Onis. *The Alliance That Lost Its Way: A Critical Report on the Alliance for Progress*. Chicago: Quadrangle, 1970.

Loveman, Brian. *Chile: The Legacy of Hispanic Capitalism*. New York: Oxford University Press, 1988.

———. *Struggle in the Countryside: Politics and Rural Labor in Chile, 1919–1973*. Bloomington: Indiana University Press, 1976.

MacEoin, Gary. *No Peaceful Way: Chile's Struggle for Dignity*. New York: Sheed and Ward, 1974.

Maldonado, Carlos. *Grupos paramilitares de derecha en Chile, 1900–1950*. Santiago: n.p., 1992.

Marchetti, Victor, and John D. Marks. *The CIA and the Cult of Intelligence*. New York: Knopf, 1974.

Mattelart, Armand, and Michèle Mattelart. *La mujer chilena en una nueva sociedad: Un estudio exploratorio acerca de la situación e imagen de la mujer en Chile.* Santiago: Editorial del Pacífico, 1968.

Mattelart, Michèle. "Chile: The Feminine Side of the Coup, or When Bourgeois Women Take to the Streets." *NACLA's Latin America and Empire Report* 9, no. 6 (September 1975).

———. "La mujer y la linea de masa de la burguesía: El caso de Chile." In *La mujer en América Latina,* edited by María del Carmen Elu de Leñero. Mexico City: Secretaría de Educación Pública, 1975.

May, Elaine Tyler. *Homeward Bound: American Families in the Cold War Era.* New York: Basic Books, 1999.

McGee Deutsch, Sandra. *Counterrevolution in Argentina, 1900–1932: The Argentine Patriotic League.* Lincoln: The University of Nebraska Press, 1986.

———. *Las Derechas: The Extreme Right in Argentina, Brazil, and Chile, 1890–1939.* Stanford: Stanford University Press, 1999.

———. "Gender and Sociopolitical Change in Twentieth-Century Latin America." *Hispanic American Historical Review* 71, no. 2 (1991).

McIntosh, Elizabeth P. *Sisterhood of Spies: The Women of the OSS.* Annapolis: Naval Institute Press, 1998.

Miller, Francesca. *Latin American Women and the Search for Social Justice.* Hanover: University Press of New England, 1991.

MIR. *What Is the MIR? Notes on the History of the MIR.* Oakland, Calif.: Resistance, 1977.

Molyneux, Maxine. "Mobilization Without Emancipation? Women's Interests, the State, and Revolution in Nicaragua." *Feminist Studies* 11 (June 1985).

Moreno de Valenzuela, Aída. "History of the Household Workers' Movement in Chile, 1926–1983." In *Muchachas No More: Household Workers in Latin America and the Caribbean,* edited by Elsa M. Chaney and Mary García Castro. Philadelphia: Temple University Press, 1989.

Moss, Robert. *Chile's Marxist Experiment.* New York: John Wiley & Sons, 1974.

Moulian, Tomás. "Desarrollo político y estado de compromiso. Desajustes y crisis estatal en Chile." *Estudios CIEPLAN* 8 (July 1982).

———. *La forja de ilusiones: El sistema de partidos 1932–1973.* Santiago: FLACSO, 1993.

Moulian, Tomás, and Isabel Torres Dujisin. *Discusiones entre honorables: Las candidaturas presidenciales de la derecha entre 1938 y 1946.* Santiago: FLACSO, n.d.

Munizaga, Giselle. *El discurso público de Pinochet: Un análisis semiológico.* Buenos Aires: CLACSO, 1983.

NACLA. "The Blockade Takes Effect." *North American Congress on Latin America* 7, no. 1 (January 1973).

———. "Chile: The Story Behind the Coup." *North American Congress on Latin America* 7, no. 8 (October 1973).

———. *New Chile*. New York: NACLA, 1973.

The National Education Department of the Socialist Workers Party. *Fidel Castro on Chile*. New York: Pathfinder, 1982.

Navarro, Marysa. "The Personal Is Political: Las Madres de Plaza de Mayo." In *Power and Popular Protest: Latin American Social Movements*, edited by Susan Eckstein. Berkeley and Los Angeles: University of California Press, 1989.

Neuse, Steven M. "Voting in Chile: The Feminine Response." In *Political Participation in Latin America*, edited by John A. Booth. New York: Holmes and Meier, 1978.

O'Brien, Phil, and Jackie Roddick. *Chile: The Pinochet Decade*. London: Latin American Bureau, 1983.

Operations and Policy Research. *Chile Election Handbook*. Washington, D.C.: Operations and Policy Research, 1963.

Otero, Fernanda. "Tras los pasos de la identidad femenina." *Veintiuno* 2, no. 6 (June 1992).

Oxman, Veronica. *La participación de la mujer campesina en organizaciones: Los centros de madres rurales*. Santiago: Academia de Humanismo Cristiano, 1983.

Pardo Vásquez, Lucía. *Una interpretación de la evidencia en la participación de las mujeres en la fuerza de trabajo: Gran Santiago 1957–1987*. Santiago: Universidad de Chile, 1989.

Parker, Dick. *La nueva cara del fascismo*. Santiago: Empresa Editora Nacional Quimantú, 1972.

Passerini, Luisa. *Fascism in Popular Memory: The Cultural Experience of the Turin Working Class*. Cambridge: Cambridge University Press, 1987.

Pérez, Cristián. "Guerrilla rural en Chile: La batalla del Fundo San Miguel (1968)." *Estudios públicos* 78 (Fall 2000).

Peteet, Julie. "Icons and Militants: Mothering in the Danger Zone." *Signs* 23, no. 11 (1997).

Petras, James F. *Chilean Christian Democracy: Politics and Social Forces*. Berkeley: Institute of International Studies, 1967.

———. "Nationalization, Socioeconomic Change, and Popular Participation." In *Chile: Politics and Society*, edited by Arturo Valenzuela and J. Samuel Valenzuela. New Brunswick, N.J.: Transaction, 1976.

————. *Political and Social Forces in Chilean Development.* Berkeley and Los Angeles: University of California Press, 1969.

Petras, James F., and Robert LaPorte Jr. *Cultivating Revolution: The United States and Agrarian Reform in Latin America.* New York: Random House, 1971.

Phillips, David Atlee. *The Night Watch.* New York: Ballantine, 1977.

Pinochet, Augusto. "Un año de construcción." *Mensaje presidencial 11 septiembre 1973–11 septiembre 1974* (Santiago: n.p., 1974).

————. "La Junta de Gobierno se dirige a las mujeres de Chile." In *Las mujeres y la dictadura militar en Chile,* by Teresa Valdés. Appendix I. Santiago: FLACSO, 1987.

Pollack, Benny, and Hernan Rosenkranz. *Revolutionary Social Democracy: The Chilean Socialist Party.* London: Frances Pinter, 1986.

Power, Margaret. "Defending Dictatorship: Conservative Women in Pinochet's Chile and the 1988 Plebiscite." In *Radical Women in Latin America: Left and Right,* edited by Victoria González and Karen Kampwirth. University Park: The Pennsylvania State University Press, 2001.

Powers, Thomas. *The Man Who Kept the Secrets: Richard Helms and the CIA.* New York: Knopf, 1979.

del Pozo, José. *Rebeldes, reformistas y revolucionarios.* Santiago: Ediciones Documentas, 1992.

Prado, Danda. "Mujer y política." *Punto Final,* no. 176, 30 January 1973.

Prats González, Carlos. *Memorias: Testimonio de un soldado.* Santiago: Pehuén Editores, 1985.

Rabe, Stephen G. *The Most Dangerous Area in the World: John F. Kennedy Confronts Communist Revolution in Latin America.* Chapel Hill: University of North Carolina Press, 1999.

Robinson, William I. *A Faustian Bargain: U.S. Intervention in the Nicaraguan Elections and American Foreign Policy in the Post–Cold War Era.* Boulder: Westview, 1992.

Roberts, Kenneth. *Deepening Democracy: The Modern Left and Social Movements in Chile and Peru.* Stanford: Stanford University Press, 1998.

Rosemblatt, Karin. *Gendered Compromises: Political Cultures and the State in Chile, 1920–1950.* Durham: University of North Carolina Press, 2000.

Roxborough, Ian, Philip O'Brien, and Jackie Roddick. *Chile: The State and Revolution.* New York: Holmes and Meier, 1977.

Rupp, Leila J. "Mothers of the *Volk:* The Image of Women in Nazi Ideology." *Signs* 2, no. 21 (1977).

Sánchez Díaz, Gerardo. *Archivo Salvador Allende: Los trabajadores y el gobierno popular.* Puebla: Universidad Nacional Autónoma de México, 1986.

Sanders, Thomas G. "Military Government in Chile." *The Politics of Anti-Politics,* edited by Brian Loveman and Thomas M. Davies. Lincoln: University of Nebraska Press, 1978.

Santa Cruz, Lucía, Teresa Pereira, Isabel Zegers, and Valeria Maino. *Tres ensayos sobre la mujer chilena: Siglos XVIII–XIX–XX.* Santiago: Editorial Universitaria, 1978.

Sater, William F. *Chile and the United States: Empires in Conflict.* Athens: University of Georgia Press, 1990.

Schesch, Adam, and Patricia Garrett. "The Case of Chile." In *Uncloaking the CIA,* edited by Howard Frazier. New York: Free Press, 1975.

Schirmer, Jennifer. "The Seeking of Truth and the Gendering of Consciousness: The Co-Madres of El Salvador and the CONAVIGUA Widows of Guatemala." In *VIVA: Women and Popular Protest in Latin America,* edited by Sarah A. Radcliffe and Sallie Westwood. London: Routledge, 1993.

Schneider, Cathy. "Radical Opposition Parties and Squatters Movements in Pinochet's Chile." In *The Making of Social Movement in Latin America: Identity, Strategy, and Democracy,* edited by Arturo Escobar and Sonia E. Alvarez. Boulder: Westview, 1992.

Scott, James C. *Weapons of the Weak: Everyday Forms of Peasant Resistance.* New Haven: Yale University Press, 1985.

Scott, Joan Wallach. *Gender and the Politics of History.* New York: Columbia University Press, 1988.

Scully, Timothy R. *Rethinking the Center: Party Politics in Nineteenth- and Twentieth-Century Chile.* Stanford: Stanford University Press, 1992.

Sigmund, Paul E. *The Overthrow of Allende and the Politics of Chile, 1964–1976.* Pittsburgh: University of Pittsburgh Press, 1977.

———. *The United States and Democracy in Chile.* Baltimore: The Johns Hopkins University Press, 1993.

Skidmore, Thomas E. *Politics in Brazil 1930–1964: An Experiment in Democracy.* London: Oxford University Press, 1967.

Smith, Brian H. *The Church and Politics in Chile: Challenges to Modern Catholicism.* Princeton: Princeton University Press, 1982.

Spooner, Mary Helen. *Soldiers in a Narrow Land: The Pinochet Regime in Chile.* Berkeley and Los Angeles: University of California Press, 1994.

Stallings, Barbara, and Andy Zimbalist. "The Political Economy of the Unidad Popular." *Latin American Perspectives* 2, no. 1 (Spring 1975).

Stevens, Evelyn P. "Marianismo: The Other Face of Machismo." In *Female and Male in Latin America*, edited by Ann Pescatello. Pittsburgh: University of Pittsburgh Press, 1973.

Strobel, Margaret. "Consciousness and Action: Historical Agency in the Chicago Women's Liberation Union." In *Provoking Agents: Gender and Agency in Theory and Practice*, edited by Judith Kegan Gardiner. Urbana: University of Illinois Press, 1995.

Supplee, Joan. "Women and the Counterrevolution in Chile." In *Women and Revolution in Africa, Asia, and the New World*, edited by Mary Ann Tétreault. Columbia: University of South Carolina Press, 1994.

Swerdlow, Amy. *Women Strike for Peace: Traditional Motherhood and Radical Politics in the 1960s*. Chicago: University of Chicago Press, 1993.

Tilly, Louis A., and Joan W. Scott. *Women, Work, and Family*. New York: Routledge, 1989.

Townsend, Camilla. "Refusing to Travel *La Via Chilena:* Working-Class Women in Allende's Chile." *Journal of Women's History* 4, no. 3 (Winter 1993).

Treacy, Gerald C., S.J. *Five Great Encyclicals*. New York: Paulist Press, 1939.

Unidad Popular. *Programa basico de la UP*. Santiago: Impresora Horizonte, n.d.

Urzúa, Germán. *Historia política electoral de Chile 1931–1973*. Santiago: Tamarcos-Van, 1986.

Waters, Vernon A. *Silent Missions*. Garden City, N.Y.: Doubleday, 1978.

Valdés, Teresa, and Enrique Gomariz. *Mujeres latinoamericanas en cifras*. Santiago: FLACSO, 1992.

Valdés, Teresa, and Marisa Weinstein. *Mujeres que sueñan: Las organizaciones de pobladoras en Chile, 1973–1989*. Santiago: FLACSO, 1993.

Valdés, Teresa, Marisa Weinstein, María Isabel Toledo, and Lilian Letelier. *Centros de Madres 1973–1989: ¿Solo disciplinamiento?* Santiago: FLACSO, n.d.

Valenzuela, Arturo. *The Breakdown of Democratic Regimes: Chile*. Baltimore: The Johns Hopkins University Press, 1978.

Valenzuela, Erika Maza. "Catholicism, Anticlericism, and the Quest for Women's Suffrage in Chile." Working Paper 214. The Helen Kellogg Institute for International Studies, University of Notre Dame, 1995.

Valenzuela, María Elena. *La mujer en el Chile militar: Todas ibamos a ser reinas*. Santiago: CESOC-ACHIP, 1987.

Vandecasteele-Schweitzer, Sylvie, and Daniele Voldman. "The Oral Sources for Women's History." In *Writing Women's History*, edited by Michelle Perrot. Oxford: Blackwell, 1984.

Vekemans, Roger. *Marginalidad, incorporación e integración*. Santiago: DESAL, 1968.

Verba, Ericka Kim. "The Círculo de Lectura de Señoras [Ladies' Reading Circle] and the Club de Señoras [Ladies' Club] of Santiago, Chile." *Journal of Women's History* 7, no. 3 (September 1995).

Vidal, Virginia. *La emancipación de la mujer*. Santiago: Editora Nacional Quimantú, 1972.

Winn, Peter. *Weavers of Revolution: The Yarur Workers and Chile's Road to Socialism*. New York: Oxford University Press, 1986.

Index